#44-92 BK Bud Aug 92

**NORTH CAROLINA
STATE BOARD OF COMMUNITY COLLEGES
LIBRARIES
SOUTHEASTERN COMMUNITY COLLEGE**

SOUTHEASTERN COMMUNITY
COLLEGE
WHITEVILLE, NC

Textiles and Politics
The Life of B. Everett Jordan

B. Everett Jordan in 1972. (*Jordan family albums*)

Textiles and Politics:
The Life of B. Everett Jordan

From Saxapahaw to the United States Senate

Ben F. Bulla

Carolina Academic Press
Durham, North Carolina

Copyright © 1992 Ben F. Bulla
All rights reserved
ISBN 0-89089-486-8
LCCN 91-76747
Manufactured in the United States of America

Carolina Academic Press
700 Kent Street
Durham, North Carolina 27701
919-489-7486

To my mother:
Margaret ("Maggie") Shoffner Bulla

"More is thy due than more than all can pay."
—*Shakespeare*

Contents

Foreword	ix
Preface	xi
Acknowledgments	xv
Introduction	xvii
1. Appointment of the "Seat-Warmer" *or* "Everett Who?"	3
2. And Henry Harrison Jordan Begat...	37
3. Warp and Weft *or* Strings of Sellars	69
4. "You Will Never Make a Mill Man!"	81
5. Putting Saxapahaw on the Map	111
6. The "Pied Piper"	127
7. "The Whole Ball of String"	149
8. Transplanted Hollies—The Gruber Connection	167
9. Mill Head and Mill Hands	181
10. A Mill Man Goes to Washington	209
11. Loaves and Fishes	237
12. "The Protector"	261
13. "Everett, Have You Lost Your Mind?"	285
14. "And I Bequeath..."	297
Notes	317
Bibliography	357
Index	365

Foreword

On these pages, Ben Bulla, a longtime colleague of B. Everett Jordan, recounts Jordan's rise from a floor-sweeper in a textile mill to the executive ranks in the industry—and ultimately to the halls of the United States Senate representing his state of North Carolina.

The author has interviewed an array of people: mill workers, leaders of industry and government, merchants, friends, family members, and countless others. From these interviews and other sources, he has drawn a sharp and objective personality portrait. It describes a life that is sometimes authoritarian, frequently benevolent, always pragmatic, and occasionally disturbing to his more conservative business associates. Yet he never ceased to be a committed servant of the people.

The emergence of Senator Jordan as a man of his own mind and convictions is an interesting account of personal growth and deeply held convictions that had originally been molded by his circuit-riding preacher-father. He voted for Alaska as well as Hawaii statehood and opposed the Vietnam war—to the dismay of his fellow Southern conservatives. He backed all legislation to aid education. As a conservationist and environmentalist, he aggressively advocated the Wilkesboro Reservoir, the Falls of the Neuse project, and the lake that was later to be named after him. He supported the Peace Corps and voted for the constitutional amendment that abolished the poll tax as a condition for voting.

Jordan's position as chair of the Senate Rules Committee made him a center of power; yet, his record clearly indicates he never used it ruthlessly.

There emerges here, then, the life of a dedicated servant of the people who cared deeply for those with whom life had dealt harshly and unfairly. He believed that the proper function of governmental power was to preserve our natural as well as historical heritage and to maintain the forward motion of our democratic society. These characteristics were always evident during the years that I worked with him on educational and various other matters.

This volume is a candid and highly readable account of the life of a distinguished son of North Carolina.

William Friday

Preface

In 1981, when the family of the late B. Everett Jordan asked me to be the biographer of their father and husband, I was somewhat surprised and expressed several reservations. Various people believed that this writer could not and should not assume the biographer's role for his employer and longtime associate. Their reasons were logical enough.

Everett Jordan initially employed me in July 1940. I had been working for him and his Sellers Manufacturing Company for more than a third of a century at the time of the senator's death in March 1974 and have continued to be employed by the company to the present. The question of biographical objectivity was obvious: How could a trusted employee and close associate write without prejudice or bias? Wouldn't the ensuing product merely be a "bought biography," a rose-colored portrait, a hagiography—the life of a saint?

Another criticism of my proposed authorship was that the biography of a major public figure such as a United States senator, who served during one of the most turbulent periods in our nation's history, should be researched and written only by professional historians or biographers—not by a person like myself who has spent his entire working life in the office of a textile company, dealing mainly with figures, not with words.

On the other hand, there were major, if not compelling, reasons why I *should* write Jordan's biography. Indeed, for this purpose, I had several excellent advantages that were not available to other biographers. For more than three decades, as Jordan's financial officer and confidant, I had worked closely with him on a day-to-day basis. This gave me firsthand knowledge about his temperament and attitudes, his professional and other associates, his economic and political activities, and his personal and family life. Beyond these factors, I also possessed a good understanding of the textile industry, his all-consuming interest. In addition, as his comptroller, I was also highly familiar with the fairly intricate records of the companies he directed. Other biographers would be denied these formidable advantages.

Yet the objectivity problem was real. How best to deal with it would be a constant and vexing challenge that would not go away. I will confess then that though I—like everyone else—may sometimes see through rose-tinted lenses, I would prefer to think that I am mostly free of self-serving bias. But can this really be? If, therefore, there is such a thing as "honest bias," then I must plead guilty. Do not our cherished friends usually see us in a more favorable light than our avowed enemies? Consequently, I feel that the reader should be alerted to these difficulties from the beginning and know that I have conscientiously sought to achieve maximum biographical and historical objectivity.

Probably the strongest demonstration of my success in this regard is the fact that, because only relatively few documents were available for a biography of Jordan, it was essentially based on a large group of interviews with many of the people in various walks of life who knew him well. The reader will note that the interviewees, who were encouraged to be objective in their remarks, are frequently critical of Jordan.

This was even true of his own family members, who were always candid and honest in their observations and sometimes provided firsthand and intimate knowledge that was otherwise unavailable. A tremendous amount of courage is required for any family to allow an outsider to delve into all recesses of their lives and write the unvarnished truth that is so crucial for any credible biographical endeavor. Many, probably most, families would never consent to this sort of prolonged and probing investigation; a prominent and justifiably proud family whose "star" is about to have his life potentially laid bare for everyone to scrutinize is certainly in a delicate position.

Indicating its objectivity, this biography thus represents a multifaceted, diverse, and sustained "we" view of many observers of Jordan as they saw and remembered him—warts and all—rather than the localized and lone "I" view of the author, though often my personal knowledge affirmed the viewpoints of others.

Senator Jordan had been dead nearly a decade before I began to research the biographical materials. Because he could no longer speak directly for himself, what would be my sources? Inasmuch as no diaries or other personal writings of any consequence had survived, the key to the inquiry into "Who was Jordan?" would have to be found elsewhere. As I saw it, the main source of revelation would need to be extensive interviews with surviving family members, friends, political contemporaries, former employees, and longtime business associates. Of necessity, my effort became a major venture into oral history.

Over a period of eight years, I interviewed a wide range of persons, some of whom had known the senator from early childhood to his final years. Because they were scattered far and wide, I traveled from the tiny riverside community of Saxapahaw to cities and byways throughout the length and breadth of North Carolina; as distant as Wellington, Kans., Pottstown, Pa., and Naples, Fla.; or as exciting as the hallowed halls of Congress.

Ben F. Bulla

Acknowledgments

I am deeply indebted to a host of people for their contributions to this book. First of all, it would not even have been possible without the sorely needed assistance of the oral interviewees. Too numerous to list here, they are all individually credited in the Bibliography.

It is, however, appropriate to single out one key interviewee: William ("Bill") M. Cochrane, labeled by some people as North Carolina's "third senator." Because he had served as the administrative aide of B. Everett Jordan during his entire tenure as a senator, had worked in a like capacity for Senator W. Kerr Scott, and is still on the scene as senior adviser to the Senate Committee on Rules and Administration, his knowledge was invaluable to me—though my persistence during several interviews must have taxed his patience.

I also extend my gratitude to all the members of the B. Everett Jordan family: his late widow, Katherine, Ben E., Jr., John M., and Rose Ann Jordan Gant. They provided unfailing as well as unstinting assistance and encouragement during all phases of preparation and publication of this book; in addition, they were completely honest and straightforward during interviews in response to my queries concerning their husband and father.

Deserving of special recognition is my highly efficient office aide, Mary C. Love, who rendered crucial assistance by transcribing all my tape-recorded interviews; deciphering my inscrutable penmanship; typing the manuscript; and, equally important perhaps, constantly prodding me to finish my task. Also, because she worked in an adjacent office, she provided a keenly perceptive albeit captive sounding board.

Two professors particularly at the University of North Carolina in Chapel Hill assisted me in the classroom as I prepared to write this biography: Dr. Peter F. Walker, professor of history; and Dr. Jacquelyn Dowd Hall, associate professor of history, director of the Southern Oral History Department, and co-author of *Like a Family*, which was judged by her peers to be a classic in oral history.

I also thank all those people who provided photographs, which were sometimes rare family copies.

For preliminary editorial assistance, I am grateful to Dr. Roland W. Tapp, of Swarthmore, Pa., a publishers' consultant and former associate editor at Westminster Press; and Doris M. Kendrick, of Winston-Salem, N.C. They critiqued the entire manuscript and made numerous invaluable editorial suggestions.

My senior editor, Robert G. Ferris, of Durham, N.C., accomplished the final editing, aided me in performing the surgery that was required to reduce the manuscript to publishable form, guided the manuscript through the publication phase, and prepared the index.

I also appreciate all the services provided by Carolina Academic Press, especially its director, Keith Sipe, and Mayapriya Long, who designed this volume. Juanita Brown Ferris proofed it.

Other sources, in whatever capacity, are credited in the Notes and Bibliography.

Introduction

"I looked over Jordan"—B. Everett Jordan—"and [whom] did I see":* a preacher's son who had both the skill and audacity to hit with his rifle the wooden cross standing high on his father's church steeple; the "smartest kid that ever walked this earth," in the estimation of his well-to-do uncle; a "smart-aleck" and a "wild boy" in the eyes of a lovely lass from Wellington, Kans., who could not understand why he never said "I'm sorry" to her; a man who seemed to think "he could do anything," or, so at least, his admiring wife believed; "the best damn yarn salesman I ever knew," as judged by a loyal customer and prominent civic leader; a shrewd, hard-working, and eminently successful textile executive and mill owner, as appraised by his business associates.

Other evaluations of B. Everett Jordan by those who knew him well include: a strong-willed leader who had few, if any, self-doubts; a pragmatist who staunchly believed that "God helps those who help themselves"; a powerful United States senator, who had an uncommon awareness of the needs of the common man and who, according to his political peers, strove for nearly fifteen years to fulfill those needs among his constituents; and a man who took care of his own, particularly his family and friends—including, according to some people, the president of the United States.

---

*Quotation from the first verse of the spiritual "Swing Low, Sweet Chariot."

Textiles and Politics:
The Life of B. Everett Jordan

1

Appointment of the "Seat-Warmer"
or
"Everett Who?"

At eight-thirty Saturday morning, April 19, 1958, the telephone rang in businessman-politician Harold Makepeace's Asheville, N.C., hotel room. Picking up the receiver, he heard a familiar voice with its usual crisp, businesslike tones: "Harold, this is Luther. I haven't slept a wink all night. In business and in politics I have never been under such pressure. At three o'clock today, I'm announcing that I am appointing B. Everett Jordan,[1] of Saxapahaw, to fill the unexpired term of [U.S.] Senator Scott."[2]

Luther Hartwell Hodges, governor of North Carolina (1954–61), felt an obligation to confide in his campaign manager and personal secretary concerning the most important appointment that he would make as the state's chief executive. After the call, Makepeace, who had driven from his Sanford, N.C., home to the western part of the state on a political mission for Hodges, quietly reflected upon his longtime friend's choice—a choice that Hodges claimed to have made from a list of thirty-three potential appointees. Although Makepeace knew and liked textile executive and mill owner Everett Jordan, he was not his first choice. His own selection would have been Ben Trotter, an attorney from Leaksville (now Eden), who was Hodges's close personal friend, hometown neighbor, and legal counselor in business matters.[3]

Makepeace's logic for favoring Trotter's appointment was simple. The governor, he thought, should appoint his trusted friend for the remaining two years of Senator Kerr Scott's term. By so doing, the seat would later be readily available for the governor himself. As Makepeace later put it: "Why didn't he appoint someone that was a close friend and attorney like Ben Trotter to keep the seat warm until his term expired as governor? Then he [Hodges] could run. But he was not interested. I wasn't the only one that tried to get him to do it."[4]

Everett Jordan was certainly not the first U.S. senator from North Carolina to be appointed by a governor to serve out the term of a deceased predecessor. In the decade immediately prior to Senator Scott's death, three other U.S. senators from the state had died in office: Joseph Melville Broughton on March 6, 1949; Willis Smith on June 26, 1953; and Clyde R. Hoey on May 12, 1954. Appointments of their successors had prompted Jordan himself to respond earlier, when asked about his going to the nation's capital as a senator: "No, that's not for me. I don't want to come home in a box."[5]

According to Howard White, editor of the Burlington (N.C.) *Daily Times-News*, Jordan had indeed been offered an appointment to the U.S. Senate at least once before. After Hodges's announcement, the former pointed out:

> Mr. Jordan never has told us, but we know that this is the second opportunity he has had to go to Washington. Upon the death of Senator Willis Smith, Governor William B. Umstead offered the senate vacancy to Mr. Jordan, who declined it. The appointment then went to Alton Lennon. This was one reason many people in the area, who knew about the previous offer and were hearing some speculation on Mr. Jordan being offered the seat, would not believe that he would be the man this time. He had been offered it before and turned it down, and there was no reason to believe that he would accept it this time if Governor Hodges offered it to him.[6]

There is good reason to believe that Everett Jordan was not surprised "a'tall"[7] on the day of the appointment, for, according to one well-placed source,[8] he had been aware of the governor's intentions at least two days earlier. On Wednesday, April 16, W. Kerr Scott, North Carolina's junior United States senator, had died suddenly at Alamance General Hospital, in Burlington. Stricken a few days earlier by a heart attack, he was nevertheless thought to be improving, and his death only one day before his sixty-second birthday was unexpected.[9]

The following day, April 17, Harold Minges, veteran highway patrolman and chauffeur for Governor Hodges, picked up the chief executive in Raleigh and drove him to the Alamance County farm home of W. Kerr Scott. There, Minges's solemn passenger found that "Miss Mary," Scott's widow of one day, and who was Everett Jordan's first cousin,[10] had gone to the cemetery of nearby Hawfields Presbyterian Church to choose a burial plot for her husband. When the limousine pulled up at the cemetery, Mrs. Scott immediately recognized the governor and also Minges, who had been her husband's driver when he, too, had served as governor (1949–53). Hodges expressed his condolences, inquired about the funeral service to be held the next day (Friday), and then departed. His destination was Saxapahaw, barely a dozen rolling miles from Scott's Hawfields farm.[11]

Hodges had visited Everett Jordan there before on numerous occasions. For many years, both business and political interests had kept the two men in close contact inasmuch as both came from textile backgrounds and had known each other through their association in the Rotary Club.[12] In a series of business ventures, the two friends had also invested as partners in a number of Howard Johnson restaurants in Virginia and North Carolina.[13]

Their political ties were even closer. Jordan had formerly chaired the state Democratic committee and had been instrumental in many successful fund-raising efforts for the party and its candidates. Currently, he was serving as a national Democratic committeeman. Through all these activities, he had maintained a close affiliation with Hodges, also a Democrat.[14]

As a matter of fact, Jordan, as he had so often before with other businessmen whom he encouraged to run for public office, had urged Hodges to become a candidate for lieutenant governor of North Carolina in 1952, his first elective office. In a phone call to Hodges, who was at his Leaksville home, in Rockingham County, attending to personal business matters, Jordan achieved his goal by stressing to Hodges that the latter had always advocated in his speeches the need for businessmen to become more involved in politics.[15]

Everett Jordan had been successfully maneuvering handpicked candidates into office long before he singled out his good friend from Leaksville for lieutenant governor in 1952. Because Jordan was well aware of Hodges's proven leadership ability as a top executive

Governor Luther H. Hodges. (*Jordan family scrapbooks*)

with Fieldcrest Mills and also because his association with him in Howard Johnson restaurant ventures evidenced Jordan's faith in the former's integrity, Hodges's entry into the political arena is but another specific example of Jordan's influence on political candidates who shared his views and were deemed worthy of election.[16]

Six months after Hodges was elected as lieutenant governor, he and Jordan traveled to Europe together to attend the Rotary International Conference in Paris. There, Jordan maneuvered successfully to elect his friend to a directorship of Rotary International.[17] Jordan, in Hodges's eyes, was not only a trusted business associate but also a savvy politician who knew how to see that his chosen candidate was elected. Hodges may well have been reflecting thoughtfully upon these experiences as Minges drove from Kerr Scott's farm home to the cotton-mill community on that somber day in April.

Appointment of the "Seat-Warmer"

Luther H. Hodges and Everett Jordan ca. 1958.
(*Jordan family albums*)

Hodges and Jordan met behind closed doors in Saxapahaw. The precise details of their conversation is not known, but subsequent events clearly indicate its general content and overall purpose. Minges later confided to a highly placed state politician[18] that Hodges told Jordan that he was his choice to serve out the remaining two years of Senator Scott's unexpired term. But Hodges attached a condition: He wanted to select a new chair for the state Democratic party and would appoint Jordan on condition of his support for the current chair's ouster.[19] At that time, the position was held by John D. Larkins, Jr., who later on (in 1961), supported by both Senators Jordan and Ervin, was appointed to serve as federal judge for the Eastern North Carolina District.[20]

Hodges was first and foremost a businessman; Larkins, on the other hand, was a career politician and party loyalist. Hodges, although a successful industrialist, had a limited background in politics and was not, in the traditional sense, "married" to the party machinery. Hodges sought efficiency in government just as he did in business: His appointments reflected that over-arching goal as he appointed to office those he considered the best qualified, regardless of party.[21]

To John D. Larkins, Jr., who had spent his entire adult life working in and devotedly serving the Democratic party, this lack of party loyalty was next to treason. Such political flexibility was all but unthinkable to ranking loyalists like himself, who at age twenty-six [1936] had become the youngest member of the North Carolina senate. He served eight more sessions, chaired many influential committees, was well known to be a power to reckon with in the Democratic party, and in 1960 ran unsuccessfully in the Democratic primary for governor.[22]

Predictably then, Larkins was among the first to voice his strong disapproval of Hodges's failure to reward "the troops in the trenches" with fat political plums—especially coveted appointments. As early as the fall of 1956, rumors had abounded that the governor and his party chairman were having serious differences. Speculation persisted that Larkins would be summarily removed from office because numerous county chairmen in the party were volubly unhappy with the governor's political practices, and Larkins had noticeably not defended the governor. Until 1958, however, Hodges had not been presented with a ready opportunity to remove Larkins. Thus, after his surprise appointment of Jordan to the U.S. Senate, he quickly "promoted" Larkins to national committeeman to succeed Jordan.[23]

In his published memoirs, Larkins writes: "... there came a time when the state chairman of the Democratic Executive Committee was to be named. Governor Hodges recommended to the committee that I be named national committeeman instead of [state] chairman and that Woodrow Jones, who is now chief judge of the United States District Court of the Western District of North Carolina, be elected as state chairman. So Woodrow succeeded me in the fall of 1958."[24]

On Saturday afternoon, April 19, at three o'clock, exactly twenty-four hours after Scott's funeral service, Governor Luther Hodges of-

Appointment of the "Seat-Warmer"

The Saxapahaw community, gearing up for Jordan's election the following year, honors the new senator in 1959 on his sixty-third birthday (*left to right*): Robert ("Rob") Collins, a veteran Jordan mill employee, Jordan, Governor Luther H. Hodges, Jim Douglas, Lawrence Paris, local boys. (*Jordan family scrapbooks*)

ficially announced that, after carefully considering a list of thirty-three possible candidates, he was appointing sixty-one-year-old B. Everett Jordan, of Saxapahaw, as United States senator to replace Senator Scott.[25]

Most political observers across the state were surprised by the selection. Certain newspapers had been bubbling with conjecture by the political analysts, but the consensus was that Hodges himself had his eye on the Senate seat and would make a bid for it in the general election in 1960. According to the press, Hodges, it was generally believed, had made only a "seat-warming" appointment. One newspaper cartoon was titled "I Looked Over Jordan and What'd I See—?" It shows a knowing Hodges crouched behind a beaming mannequin of Jordan, as "Timothy T. Tarheel" looks on in amazement. A sign saying "1960" is attached to Hodges's coat, indicating that he fully expected to assume the seat at that time.[26]

Other editorials and cartoons presented similar views, and in the minds of many political observers there was good reason to believe that the Jordan appointment had indeed been made by Hodges to carefully preserve the office for himself. A Greensboro editorialist, three days after the Jordan appointment, opined: "He [Hodges] does the unpredictable; he generally saws off the limb onto which the 'expert' prognosticators have crawled; he makes his own decisions. There is such an obviousness about the latest turn of events that conclusions based on it may be altogether wrong. Trying to foretell what Luther Hodges will say or do is a mighty ticklish undertaking."[27]

One of the few editors who differed from prevailing opinion was Holt McPherson, in the *High Point* (N.C.) *Enterprise*:

> Time will tell, of course, [the] wisdom of the nomination. Our good wishes for his health and success in that difficult assignment are with Senator Jordan. His is, as pointed out editorially here right after the appointment, a warm seat. But the man has had a lot of experience in handling difficult situations in emerging from a parsonage to one of the foremost figures in business and political life of our state.
>
> But what we started out to do was recount that column we did a number of years ago when our thesis was that the Jordans had become the most influential family in the state when judged by impact and usefulness.
>
> This development merely underscores that premise. Everett at that time was chairman of the State Democratic Executive Committee, president of the North Carolina Citizens Association, which has been largely the voice of business in the state, head of the big Sellers Manufacturing Company, the man who had contributed heavily to Kerr Scott's successful political venture that won the governorship, and a generous supporter of worthy causes in the state.[28]

Nevertheless, most observers confidently concluded that Jordan was merely a "seat-warmer" for Hodges, who, at the 1960 general election only two years away, would take over the "saved" chair from his accommodating friend. As a matter of fact, Jordan told his friend Willie Mull, whom he and Mrs. Jordan met on their way to the train heading for Washington, that "he was just taking over until the next election came...[that he was] 'just going to stay about

This cartoon, by Hugh Haynie in the *Greensboro* (N.C.) *Daily News* ca. April 20, 1958, intimates that Hodges had designs on Jordan's senate seat in the forthcoming 1960 general election. (*Ben E. Jordan, Jr.*)

this one appointment and [he would] be right back here.'" As Mull pointed out, however: "But he was just like the rest of them that go up there; there's not many of them that want to leave!"[29]

Depiction of Governor Luther H. Hodges in hot water following his appointment of Everett Jordan as a "seat-warmer" in 1958. Cartoon by Hugh Haynie, *Greensboro* (N.C.) *Daily News,* ca. April 20, 1958. (*Ben E. Jordan, Jr.*)

To all appearances, the public's skepticism of Hodges's motives was fully justified. Jordan had never run for an elective office. Because he was a successful textile industrialist, he was mostly known in business, not political, circles, where he had been affiliated with various organizations on both the state and national levels.

Probably the most important of these was the North Carolina Citizens Association (later the North Carolina Citizens for Business and Industry and known as "The Voice of Business"), one of the most influential business-oriented organizations ever created in the state.[30] Established in Raleigh on December 11, 1942, by a group of industrialists, bankers, and public leaders, it launched a statewide move to curb non-essential government spending and foster balanced budgets. Other goals included trying to encourage and help the North Carolina legislature and the U.S. Congress to provide the types of laws and their administration that would be best for the business people of the state.

The principals were persons who had already distinguished themselves in business and industry. Of the forty citizens gathered at the Sir Walter Hotel in Raleigh to make plans for the newly chartered association, the two principal spokesmen were bankers R. G. Stockton, of Winston-Salem, and R. L. Pope, of Thomasville, both prominent figures statewide. Also there to give full support to the group was U.S. Representative Robert L. Doughton (Dem.-N.C.), chairman of the powerful House Ways and Means Committee.

The mere assembly of these well-known leaders was enough to make the news. But they had a specific task to accomplish. Back in the early 1930s, North Carolina's state and local governments had been in fiscal distress; and it was even questionable whether basic services such as public education could continue to be financed.

There were other issues that developed and needed attention, many of which these leaders thought were not being properly addressed. Under President Roosevelt's New Deal, the growth of the national government had mushroomed, along with budget deficits. Then World War II came upon the nation, and government spending roared into high gear as the guns boomed in Europe, Africa, and the Far East. The Citizens Association thought that someone in addition to the state and federal government should be concerned and active in the future of both the country and the state of North Carolina. For example, what would be the tax policies for postwar economic growth and diversification for the state, one of the heirs of the Confederacy still trying to catch up with the states of the North and East?

In 1942 the Citizens Association was looking ahead, beyond the conclusion of the war and the economic "normalization" that would follow. Guidance and input were sorely needed; and these citizens, successful in their own positions in business, banking, manufacturing, and the professions, felt that they could offer help. The association was chartered as a non-profit organization supported by its members; and it sought to be, officially at least, identified as non-partisan in its work with governors, congressmen, and state legislators.

Everett Jordan had been involved in the work of the association from the beginning and had served two terms as its chairman (1948–51). The only other person to serve two such terms was Richard G. Stockton (1951–53). The roster of Jordan's contemporaries also chosen to serve as chairmen reads like a "Who's Who" in North Carolina business and finance:

R. L. Pope, Thomasville banker, 1943–44
J. S. Ficklin, Greenville tobacconist, 1944–45
Don S. Elias, Asheville publisher, 1945–46
Julius C. Smith, Greensboro insurance executive, 1946–47
H. M. Wade, Charlotte businessman, 1947–48
Richard G. Stockton, Winston-Salem banker, 1951–53
R. S. Dickson, Charlotte business executive, 1953–54
Allen H. Sims, Gastonia banker, 1954–55
Sam N. Clark, Tarboro business executive, 1955–56
Leo Harvey, Kinston diversified businessman, 1956–57
R. Grady Rankin, Gastonia textile manufacturer, 1957–58
Edwin Pate, Laurinburg diversified businessman, 1958–59
Holt McPherson, High Point editor, 1959–60
G. Harold Myrick, Lincolnton banker, 1960–61
W. Herbert Weatherspoon, Raleigh utility executive, 1961–62
William B. McGuire, Charlotte utility executive, 1962–63
Howard Holderness, Greensboro insurance executive, 1963–64
William H. Ruffin, Durham textile manufacturer, 1964–65
R. Dave Hall, Belmont textile manufacturer, 1965–66
John F. Watlington, Jr., Winston-Salem banker, 1966–67
Halbert M. Jones, Laurinburg textile manufacturer, 1967–68
J. C. Cowan, Jr., Greensboro textile manufacturer, 1968–69
Wm. E. Stevens, Jr., Lenoir furniture manufacturer, 1969–70
Shearon Harris, Raleigh utility executive, 1970–71
Thomas I. Storrs, Charlotte banker, 1971–72
H. Dail Holderness, Tarboro utility executive, 1972–73
Thomas M. Belk, Charlotte merchandising executive, 1973–74

Appointment of the "Seat-Warmer" 15

According to the later recollections of Lloyd E. Griffin, who as executive vice-president directed the North Carolina Citizens Association for twenty-five years,[31] Jordan, despite his conservatism in fiscal matters, was anxious to "see things happen" and favored "things that were good for the economy of the state." Jordan, even when he later served in the U.S. Senate, worked closely with Griffin over the years to advance the goals of the association. As Griffin later recalled:

> Everett was an influential fellow among certain groups; he had more of a churchman's viewpoint if you understand what I mean by that. He had a viewpoint that if you could get something done by doing good, then O.K., let's go. Well now, that should be everybody's viewpoint, but unfortunately it's not. Most of the fellows have this question: "What do I get out of this?" Well now, Everett and Henry [Everett's younger brother], I found, were a little different. Apparently, their parents were of the same viewpoint; I don't know about that, I may be wrong completely about it, but Everett, I do know, was anxious to work in and throughout wherever he could for what seemed to be good.

In 1958 most people in North Carolina were largely unaware of Jordan, despite his prominence in the business world. He was practically unknown, in fact, outside of Saxapahaw, a tiny cotton-mill community perched on the banks of the Haw River in the southeastern edge of mostly rural Alamance County. There, however, he was known to all because he reigned supreme as mill owner, manager, and patriarch.[32]

Jordan was also equally unknown to the general public for his role in local and state politics, where he was a force to be reckoned with. Until 1940, grim economic necessity required that he devote nearly every waking hour to manufacturing and selling yarns. The mill's operation was literally his life. But the economy, as well as the mill's fortune, was on the upswing just prior to World War II; and he began to be more interested in state-level politics. Until then, behind-the-scene involvement in local county elections had required all the time he could spare.[33]

The vast majority of the electorate did not even know his name, much less his political stance. Yet he, Clyde Gordon, Reid Maynard, M. B. Smith, Mayor Earl Horner, and Judge Leo Carr of Burlington, Cameron Tew of Haw River, furniture manufacturer L. P. Best of Mebane, Ralph Holt, Sr., Kerr and Ralph Scott, Boman Sanders, Will and Ben May, John Shoffner, the Glen Raven Gants, Dolph Long, Dr. Willard Goley, the McEwens, and a handful of others operated behind the local political scene to make things happen and to elect their people. Members of this relatively small group quietly made contacts with key people in each community within the county. The group included a smattering of professionals, but consisted mainly of businessmen and upper-level manufacturers who largely financed their chosen candidates. On the county level, most of these men were members of the Burlington Rotary Club; and, before and after club meetings at the Alamance Hotel, they would plan their strategy. As Gordon put it, they would "talk and pretty well pick—handpick—[candidates for each office], and we could elect most anybody we picked in the county."[34]

At that time, approximately the 1930s through the 1950s, to elect a candidate or candidates did not involve much money, literally a pittance compared to elections a couple of decades later. The candidates were financed almost totally by the manufacturers along with some other business firms. After the party planners had selected their slate of candidates, they would pass the word along, and, as Gordon explained, "You gave them some money...but, again we didn't go back and ask for any special favors for ourselves. It was just a matter of putting good people in office. The whole system has changed so much now [1981] that it makes it very difficult [to elect good people]."[35]

In a 1986 interview, Best recounted the names of numerous prominent men and families from Alamance County who had been associated with Everett Jordan in political affairs. Best and also Clyde Gordon, Jordan's intimate friend and a prominent civic and business leader from Burlington—among others—give much credit to the Saxapahaw political planner for selecting and encouraging good people to run for public office.[36]

In this context, Best said: "He [Jordan] was interested in his community, he was interested in his county, he was interested in his state, and he was interested in the United States as a whole, and even foreign countries. His mind was unlimited as to scope in his interests and seeing that humanity was served in the proper way—whether it was the Boy Scouts in Saxapahaw or whether it was some project the president of the United States was undertaking."[37]

Best stressed the importance, especially in those earlier days—as well as now—of choosing the most qualified candidates for the offices of sheriff and the county commissioners. For these offices and those on a higher level on up to the governor's position, Best lauded Everett Jordan for singling out and supporting the most talented individuals: "I remember that every governor that Senator Jordan supported was elected."[38]

In all this wheeling and dealing, Everett Jordan played a leading role and in doing so earned the reputation of being one of the most effective fund-raisers within his party. It was this reputation that won him appointment as chairman of the state Democratic party, where again he excelled in raising money.[39]

While Jordan was chairman of the state Democratic party and Clifton ("Cliff") Blue was the party secretary, Elizabeth ("Lib") (Mrs. W. T.) Johnston performed the secretarial work at the party's headquarters in Raleigh. In this capacity, she had a privileged close-up look at the party chairman and the way he operated:

> I don't know how he did it; he knew *just exactly* how to get something accomplished that he wanted! It's a gift, I suppose, and he didn't make people mad doing it—maybe a few. He, definitely, was a good student of human nature and a great diplomat. I think he had a lot of wisdom, a lot of understanding. I never thought about Everett as being somebody really important, real big. To me he was down-to-earth. I could go to him about any problem, no matter how little, even when he was in Washington in the Senate. I could call him up about something personal or something that was so absolutely unimportant, and he would take time with me like it was the most important thing in the world. I just never saw anybody like him in my life. He could come into a room and put everybody at ease. You would think, oh, here comes the senator, or here comes this millionaire, or this and that and the other. He would come in and sit down, and he would joke and talk to people; look over those [eye] glasses, and be just as down-to-earth as anybody walking on the streets in overalls and didn't have a dime in their pocket. He

knew how to talk to the...average person. He was just as much at home in the White House as he would be in a tiny little mountain shack here in Montreat.[40]

Daniel Joshua Walker, better known as "D. J.," a highly respected Burlington attorney as well as a Democratic party member and a veteran of Alamance County politics, also commented on Jordan's role in state politics: "After Kerr Scott was elected governor, he got the state Democratic executive committee to appoint Everett Jordan as chairman of the party for the state. He made a real good chairman and carried the elections again in 1950. I was very active in Democratic politics in the county and also in some of the state races from then on up until around 1970, when I became less active, but I got to know Everett Jordan during all that time. While Everett was state Democratic party chairman...I'm sure we didn't have any statewide Republican victories during Everett's term."[41]

Dr. William C. Friday, prominent North Carolina educator and close observer of the political scene, recognized that Jordan had a hand in the election of Governors J. Melville Broughton (1940), R. Gregg Cherry (1944), W. Kerr Scott (1948), William B. Umstead (1952), and Luther H. Hodges (lieutenant governor in 1952 and governor in 1956). Friday stated: "Everett Jordan's role became more important as those names moved down the line...[They] were all good governors. And they weren't all business-oriented people either. I think that what this says is that Mr. Jordan, like so many other people in public life in North Carolina, understood the importance of having good government—clean government—and always looked for people who didn't have about them any suggestion of manipulation or any question about their character or integrity. That was important to Everett Jordan, and that's why you have such quality people in that [governor's] list."[42]

Friday was also commendatory about the ethics of Jordan's fundraising:

> You hear all kinds of allegations about [the undue influence of] the different blocs, like the textile organization or the power companies or the merchants' association...But it's the way people survive in politics; it's the only way they can. They contribute the money that puts on the campaign. Senator Jordan was very conversant with all those people because he was one of them. He knew what he was

doing; he knew who he could trust. He knew where the money was; he knew who would make the contributions. And he always kept it on a high plane, not sinister politics and mean politics, the way you see it played in other states. His pitch was always "What's in the [best] interest of the state?" This man, in my view, would make a good whatever-he-was-running-for because he put the state's interests first, not his own ambition. B. Everett Jordan lived a life like that, and I'm sure that would be what he would look for in dealing with people in the corporate community who financed these campaigns. He wouldn't take money from anybody and everybody. That's the kind of man he was.[43]

Admittedly, Jordan had been active in the state Democratic party as a fund-raiser and as its chairman. No one denied that he was well versed in practical matters, but he had had no real experience or training in the direct day-to-day administration of government affairs. Because he never sought publicity, his name was unfamiliar to the man on the street. The top leadership of the Democratic party, however, knew about his influence and were not quite so astounded as the popular press.[44]

Hodges, in contrast to Jordan, was a businessman-turned-politician who eminently qualified for political service. Like Jordan, he had been an outstanding industrial leader, having served as vice-president of the Marshall Field Company before taking early retirement in 1950. But here the similarity between the two men ended. In November 1952 Hodges was elected as lieutenant governor, along with William B. Umstead as governor, on the Democratic ticket; and Hodges quickly proved himself to be an able leader in his role as Speaker of the North Carolina senate. His record was impressive: As lieutenant governor, he streamlined the operations of the senate, eliminating eight of that body's thirty-six overlapping committees. During this time, Governor Umstead, who had suffered a heart attack two days after his inauguration, was in rapidly declining health; and Hodges quickly became responsible for administering state government to a much greater extent than most of his predecessors.[45]

After Umstead's death early in his term—November 7, 1954—Hodges succeeded him as the state's chief executive. In the minds of many—especially those in the business community—Hodges earned his reputation as one of the state's most respected and ef-

Jordan (*right*) with three prominent North Carolina Democrats around 1950 (*left to right*): State Senator John D. Larkins, Jr., U.S. Senator and ex-Governor Clyde R. Hoey, U.S. Representative (Chapel Hill area) Carl Durham. (*Jordan family scrapbooks*)

fective governors. During his tenure (1954–61), a greatly expanded industrialization program attracted numerous large corporations into the state. His administration initiated and began development of the highly regarded Research Triangle Park. North Carolina became known as the "Dixie Dynamo," and Governor Hodges was lauded as the chief engineer. Many political seers envisioned a national-level career for this vigorous statesman when he left the governor's mansion.[46]

But it must be emphasized that, if the Jordan appointment was a political expedient contrived by Hodges to further his own senatorial ambitions, no evidence of such a plan has ever been uncovered. Neither Hodges nor Jordan even hinted at such a scheme. In any case, the outcry in the press over Jordan's appointment and later his own acquired affinity for the office precluded any "payoff" of covert political debt in the elections of 1960.

Interviews of those closest to Everett Jordan for this volume shed no further light on Hodges's possible intentions or secret aspirations. If he and Everett Jordan had an "understanding," no one today is willing to come forth to confirm this possibility. On the other hand, neither is anyone absolutely sure that the two men did not privately entertain this eventuality. "There is many a slip twixt the cup and the lip," and much political "brew" intended for the gullet often spills into the gutter for naught.

Katherine Jordan, later discussing her husband's appointment, pointed out that he had asked her: " 'Would you be willing to go to Washington and let me finish the term of Kerr Scott in the Senate?' And I said, 'How long would that be?' and he replied, 'Two years,' and with a little hesitation I answered, 'Well, that isn't long, and I'm always interested in seeing new things and new people. Our children are grown and away, and there's no particular reason for our staying here on account of our family. I think it would be a good experience, and I'd be glad to go.' "[47]

Katherine Jordan further related that her husband seemed to be both surprised and pleased that Hodges chose him because "Luther had many friends who were capable and who would have been pleased with such an appointment." Hodges, she thought, understood her husband's political philosophy and interest in the state and was aware that he had helped elect several governors. She also knew the prominent role Jordan played in Kerr Scott's election to the governorship.[48]

Governor Scott's younger brother, a veteran state senator from Alamance County, Ralph Scott, confirms the significant and, perhaps, deciding role that Everett Jordan played in electing his brother to the state's highest office: "Kerr was one of these candidates that did not have any money, and Everett supported him very heavily financially... They didn't raise money back then like they do now. He had a hard time getting money, but Everett backed him up in every way he could, not only with his own money but he got his friends to contribute... I doubt that Kerr would ever have been governor if it hadn't been for Everett and folks like him that backed him up. Everett knew people, industrial leaders and political leaders, all over the state, and Kerr wasn't so well known. I don't think Kerr could have won without Everett's help."[49]

Later on, however, the relationship between Jordan and Kerr Scott soured. Cliff Blue in his newspaper column "Comments on People & Issues" made this observation:

> When he (Jordan) was appointed to the United States Senate in 1958 by Governor Luther Hodges, Terry Sanford, then a candidate for governor, blasted the appointment, saying that Hodges could not pawn him off as a Scott [meaning Kerr Scott] man, for Jordan was reported to have been a supporter of Alton Lennon instead of Scott in the 1954 Democratic primary when Scott won over Lennon in a tough and close primary battle.
>
> However, in the intervening years Sanford and Jordan have become close political allies. Sanford refused to consider opposing Jordan for the Senate in 1966 and in 1968 Jordan was Sanford's biggest booster for vice president on the Democratic ticket, and again for chairman of the Democratic National Committee in 1969. Months ago, before he was tapped for the Duke [University] presidency, Sanford let it be known that he would not consider running for the U.S. Senate against his good friend Everett Jordan in 1972.[50]

Blue had been secretary of the state Democratic party when Everett Jordan was the state party chairman. Both men originally received their appointments through Kerr Scott, who had enjoyed their considerable support in his election to the governorship in 1948.[51]

In a 1983 interview for this volume, Blue contended that the reason that a rift occurred between Jordan and Kerr Scott, Alamance County's two most powerful politicians, who were back-door neighbors and related by marriage, was their differing philosophies of statecraft: Scott was a liberal and Jordan a conservative.[52]

North Carolina's present junior U.S. senator, Terry Sanford, was, at that time, a rising star on the state political scene and quite familiar both with the maneuvering within the party and the philosophy of the principals involved. He said: "Well, I first knew about Everett Jordan when he emerged along with Kerr Scott in my consciousness. I suppose I had known that Kerr Scott was commissioner of agriculture; I suppose I, at the Institute of Government, had corresponded with him a couple of times, but I really didn't know Kerr Scott. Then he ran for governor and Everett...was one of his close associates—and Scott made him chairman of the party. At a time shortly thereafter, I [was elected as] president of the Young Democrats...when [Jordan] was chairman of the party, and I knew him in that relationship."[53]

Sanford said that, during that period of time, Jordan had a tiff with Kerr Scott when Jordan rejected a list of delegates, including Sanford, that Scott proposed to attend the Democratic party's national convention at Chicago in 1952.[54]

However, Sanford stated: "Now, I don't remember anything but pleasant feelings with Everett Jordan during that period of time. Whatever problems he had with Scott, there was no reason for him to have any problems with me. In the first place, I couldn't have crossed him if I had wanted to. But I was a fairly active president of the Young Democrats...Everett always came to [the] meetings [when prominent speakers were scheduled]. We didn't really have a structure where the Young Democrats were dependent on the senior party...Everett Jordan was kind and gracious to me."[55]

As for Hodges singling out Jordan to replace Scott in the U.S. Senate, Sanford remarked: "I didn't especially care who Hodges named to the Senate. I wasn't a candidate, though several people my age were." Sanford favored Voit Gilmore, his erstwhile classmate at the University of North Carolina.[56]

Not only did Gilmore enjoy a close personal relationship with Hodges, but he was also eminently qualified for consideration. He had an A.B. in journalism and political science as well as M.A. and

Ph.D. degrees in geography from the University of North Carolina at Chapel Hill; had served as an officer in the Naval Air Transport Service in World War II; had been mayor of Southern Pines (1953–57); had operated a successful lumber business; and was active in travel-industry affairs.[57]

Gilmore later stated that he believed the reason Hodges chose Jordan was because he was enormously indebted to him not only because of his hard work and effectiveness in harnessing the Democratic party in the state, but also because he was a very effective party national committeeman. Gilmore also believed that, as fellow businessmen of the same age, they "could share confidences and really trust each other." Also, Gilmore believed that Hodges could count on Jordan's loyalty and straightforwardness while he was in Washington.[58]

Gilmore added: "I talked [on the phone] with Governor Hodges [as well as having a personal visit] on two or three occasions, but one time he called me and said, 'Voit, I'm seriously considering you for the Senate appointment.' And he said also, 'I've got various considerations—I've got some serious obligations out there'... He made the point that he had a very high regard for me, and he thought I had a background of educational, political, and perhaps social and also physical [capabilities]... that would, 'prompt me to make you a serious consideration [for the Senate appointment].' "[59]

Gilmore said that Hodges claimed that he had other obligations concerning the appointment, but wanted to know if Gilmore would be able to handle the position if offered because of his business activities or other commitments. Gilmore said he could, but stated "that I thoroughly understand the commitments that you have—I think I brought up Everett Jordan's name or else Governor Hodges did—and I said, 'There's a man that's got wide respect across the state. He would immediately have widespread approval, and I don't think you would be in a position to have to defend anything.' I said, 'I'm proud of my own reputation and record, and I appreciate your thinking of me in connection with our age difference that would give me a long-term run at the Senate position. But, as a real friend, I want to put you at ease about any sense of obligation.' "[60]

Gilmore received a call back from the governor about the time that Harold Makepeace did, informing Gilmore that Jordan was being appointed. However, Gilmore responded as follows: "I have nothing but pleasure and happiness with what you're telling me, and I'm even delighted that someone that's as good a friend as Everett could possibly be your choice."[61]

As for Jordan being a seat-warmer, Gilmore averred: "Hodges disavowed that to me. He said, 'I don't plan to do it.'"[62] Nevertheless, Gilmore, like many others, was certainly not ignorant of the allegations about Hodges's intentions and his potential for public service at the highest national levels. As Gilmore said, "Hodges always indicated interest in the national level of politics, and I thought myself, with all of his energy and all of his zeal, and the profound distinction of having been the longest serving governor in the history of North Carolina [up to that time]...that he would have made an outstanding senator. He would have packed about as much experience as anybody we had ever had from North Carolina and hence springboard on into Washington. Of course, his political successes in his races in North Carolina were phenomenal, so there was little question that he could go as far as he wanted to go."[63]

Sanford also indicated that friends of Joseph ("Joe") C. Eagles, Jr., thought he should have the Senate seat vacated by Kerr Scott's death. Unquestionably, Eagles caused Luther Hodges some difficult moments before he struck him from the top of his list of possible appointees. It is easy to see why Eagles may well have been one of the reasons Hodges failed to sleep a wink the night before he made his choice known. The forty-seven-year-old, four-term state senator from Wilson had been a wheelhorse for the Hodges administration, and he possessed all the qualifications for ably filling the vacant seat. In the legislature, Eagles was known as a "doer" rather than a "talker."[64] And, according to the press, no one played harder for the Hodges team in the 1957 legislature than he did. The news media called him the Hodges administration's "Ace in the clutch" as he maneuvered to get Hodges's program enacted.[65]

Eagles served on the Advisory Budget Commission in 1955, and as recently as January 1958 Hodges had named his stalwart ally—a 1931 Phi Beta Kappa graduate of the University of North Carolina who earned a law degree from the institution with honors in 1934—as chair of the important State Tax Study Commission. In addition, Eagles, a conservative and successful businessman in Wilson, where he was a tobacco warehouseman and farmer, shared similar views with businessman Hodges.[66]

At his news conference for Eagles's appointment as head of the Tax Study Group, Hodges said: "He's [Eagles] a very strong man. He knows pretty well the State's problems...is a good student...and a fearless person. I believe he will do an outstanding job as chairman." Others also thought highly of Eagles, and some speculated that he might have his eye on the statehouse in some future race.[67]

In any event, Hodges telephoned Eagles to keep him informed before he announced his decision to appoint Jordan. Although Hodges did not tell Eagles in this call that his name was under consideration, the fact that Hodges called Eagles—and also Gilmore—before making a public announcement is proof enough that he gave serious thought to both men and that he owed each of them the courtesy of letting them know his intentions in advance.[68]

Terry Sanford later explained his own public reaction to Everett Jordan's appointment:[69] "There were two or three things that I could have done. I could have applauded it and been overlooked; it wouldn't have made any difference [because] I didn't have any particular standing. I decided that I wouldn't applaud it for two or three reasons. One of them was a mundane political reason. In the first place, Ben Roney, who was the administrative assistant to Scott, and some other [Scott] staff members left [after Senator Scott's death]. However, Bill Whitley did stay on with him [Jordan]; and, of course, Bill Cochrane became his [number-one] aide."[70]

Sanford continued:

> I thought we needed to keep Scott's organization, which I had put together as much as anybody else. I certainly, at that time, intended to run for governor...probably right away. But that was the way I could assert that I now have the right to speak for the Scott organization. So, I said, in effect, that if he [Hodges] wants to name his own business partner[71] to the U.S. Senate, let him do it...forthrightly...[Don't] let him come palming this off as his having named a "close associate and friend of Kerr Scott to carry on the Kerr Scott

Appointment of the "Seat-Warmer" 27

Senator Jordan presents senatorial service awards to "Bill" Cochrane (*left*) and "Bill" Whitley (*right*). (*Jordan family scrapbooks*)

program," when everybody knew that for whatever else went on between them, they certainly weren't headed in the same direction politically and philosophically. That's not to criticize either one. It turned out that Jordan was a whole lot more like Scott than Hodges probably thought he was.[72]

Sanford believed that, by failing to applaud the Jordan appointment, he would be recognized in many places as the "young inheritor" of the Scott group, a role that no one else was occupying. North Carolina was then a one-party state where organizations were formed around personalities. Therefore, Sanford put himself "in the leading role as deliberately and as consciously" as he knew how.[73]

Yet, Sanford said he did not have all that much against Everett Jordan:

> I didn't really want to be a foe, and I had my very close friend Bill Cochrane staying with Jordan, so he [Cochrane] asked me to come to the little luncheon that they had when Jordan was sworn in...Everything in the air was cleared [for me] at that time. And I think, though I don't know for sure, that the air was cleared as far as Everett was concerned. I think he understood politics well enough to know that Scott's people didn't like his being put in that position. My connections with him from that point on were much more constructive, not that anything hadn't been constructive—I'd say much more amiable.[74]

Political highways, however, are seldom free of bumps, dips, and unexpected turns. Sanford's experience at the 1960 Democratic convention in Los Angeles attests to this fact, when he found himself on the "wrong side," or so thought North Carolina's Big Three: Everett Jordan, Sam Ervin, and Luther Hodges.[75] Sanford supported John Kennedy, whereas the other three backed Lyndon Baines Johnson (LBJ). Sanford contended, however, that "Hodges was not really for LBJ," but really just "wanted to stop Kennedy so the convention—as it likely would have—would turn to Adlai Stevenson. And Stevenson could find no better qualified person to run for vice-president than Luther Hodges."[76]

Sanford added:

> There were seventy-six delegates as I recall...At least sixty-five of them had been active in my [primary] campaigns [for governor]; a great many of them were old Scott people. They were just about all my people. Now, Luther asked me if—said it would mean a great deal to him—if I would name him chairman of the delegation...So, I said, "Of course." Well, he used that chairmanship to embarrass me. I didn't expect to carry the majority of North Carolinians with me [in support of Kennedy]. I knew this was shocking, but I also knew it ought to have been done. And I'm glad I did it—always have been. But I had a hard time there, and they sent Bill Cochrane out to Los Angeles to bring me "back to my senses"—for God's sake—before I threw over my chances to be governor and destroyed the party in North Carolina.[77]

Sanford felt he "was pretty badly treated considering [that] I was the Democratic nominee for governor, and I had to lead the ticket." However, Jordan invited Sanford to dinner with him, Katherine, and some friends with whom they were visiting. Sanford said, "He was just very gracious, very kind. I suspect he saw I had been abused. Well, I was very grateful for that little kindness, and it didn't seem very significant, but I told him that we'd be running together, and I wanted him to know something: That, though people were saying the opposite, that I would never run against him; that I'd always support him. And I did."[78]

Concerning Jordan's selection by Hodges, few if any politicians are totally immune to the allure of prestige and power. Almost any state-level politician would be pleased if not delighted—as Katherine Jordan remembered that Everett was—to join the U.S. Senate for two years or any term, however brief. But to say that in the spring of 1958 he was "surprised" by his appointment to the free world's most powerful and prestigious deliberative body is highly questionable, for he certainly expected to be rewarded—eventually—for his massive endeavors on the party's behalf.

Alluding to the unpublicized political expectations of the Saxapahaw yarn-spinner, Harold Makepeace in an interview for this volume recounted the immediate circumstances relating to Jordan's appointment by Hodges. But first he refers to Hodges's election as lieutenant governor of North Carolina in 1952:[79] "I was Luther's so-called campaign manager; he knew hardly anyone in political life in North Carolina. He was active in Rotary International, and that was our base in getting him elected as lieutenant governor...Meeting with Everett [and Hodges] in the business of the restaurants, we discussed a lot of politics. Everett, back then, I think, wanted to be governor of North Carolina...because he would say something to me about Luther progressing so fast. He would say that Luther hasn't come up through the ranks like they did back then: Cherry, Umstead, Broughton, and Gardner. You knew a number of years ahead of time who the next governor was going to be."[80]

Makepeace was well versed in the history and customs of North Carolina politics and referred to the fact that his own brother served three terms in the state senate and two terms in the house; therefore he was privy to much "insider information": "Everett would talk to me knowing I was going to tell Luther, and Luther would do the same thing, knowing that I was going to tell Everett. I was the go-between a lot of times on what each one was thinking. As I said, Everett said, 'Luther is just going too fast; he ought to come up through the ranks.' "[81]

In 1987 Margaret Jordan Sprinkle, Everett Jordan's younger sister, made this insightful comment about her brother's appointment to the U.S. Senate: "Everett was chairman of the state Democratic party, and he had gotten Scott elected governor. When Senator Willis Smith died, Scott appointed Frank Porter Graham, who was president of the University of North Carolina, to take his place. Everett thought that Scott owed him and was very disappointed that he didn't get the job. Graham was very liberal, and Everett couldn't agree with that. He got over that, but at one time Everett was very bitter toward Kerr. Later on when Graham came up for election, a lot of Everett's friends who had wanted him appointed instead of Graham voted against him, and Graham was defeated."[82]

So on that April Saturday of his appointment, one may imagine that B. Everett Jordan's beaming face revealed much pleasure, anticipation, and triumph—but little surprise, especially because of his earlier role in local and state politics. Every Democratic governor after Broughton had eagerly sought his support, and Jordan always seemed to be on the winning side. By the time of his appointment to the U.S. Senate, the politically wise party leader knew as much as anyone about what was really going on in state politics.[83]

To say that Everett Jordan was an eminently successful industrialist and a power in the Democratic party does not fully depict the man himself.[84] A person did not soon forget an encounter with this bold entrepreneur and master manipulator, a forceful individual who made things happen. One could not escape the piercing scrutiny of his wide-set, steel-gray eyes, as they probed his subject for weaknesses and strengths—eyes that looked straight at you from underneath firm brows—eyes that seldom flickered with uncertainty. Whether he was a mill hand, overseer, plant superintendent, office worker, salesman, or a U.S. senator, one was acutely aware of his unwavering analytical gaze.

Each spoken word received his intense attention. Every assertion was evaluated and retained for future reference by this astute listener. In Jordan's presence, a discreet person knew the truth ought to be handled with care, for what he said would be verified eventually and compared with the vast storehouse of knowledge and experience cataloged in his listener's keen memory. His strategy was to let others speak first, so that he could analyze their positions before he revealed his own. He was far too shrewd to tell all he knew about his own plans and designs, but what he did say left little room for equivocation. If he did choose to expose his own position, he enunciated his thoughts with a lucid firmness. It was the language of a forthright man: "No. Yes. Do. Don't. I will. You can."

As the chief executive of his company, he was accustomed to making quick judgments and having his orders followed explicitly. Consequently, the subordinate knew exactly what was expected of him. If, on the other hand, Jordan was not ready to commit himself, his reply would be: "I'll think about it." He would not forget his promise, but he would give the reply in *his* own good time.

Nearly six feet tall, Everett Jordan was built on a powerful, somewhat stocky, frame. Through moderation in food and drink, even on into his last years, he maintained his ideal weight at about 200 pounds. Whether sitting behind his desk or standing in a room with others—regardless of their stature or status—one had the distinct impression that this dominating man was just as big, if not a little bigger, than anyone present. He always seemed to be the one totally in charge. Invariably clad in a full business suit of subdued shades—usually dark gray—his outward appearance changed little over the four seasons. Regardless of the weather, he apparently felt no need to add or subtract clothing to stay perfectly comfortable. His health, to all appearances, was robust most of his life; and, except for his final illness, there was scant evidence of physical change, other than the signs of normal aging.

His chin and jaw showed strength equal to the rest of his strong profile. His firmly chiseled, intense face featured a Roman nose that seemed to steer him forward on a relentless course. There was sternness in his slightly pressed lips, yet also hints of an easy smile. He did not get shoved around, nor did he shove others, but he did press hard. Early on, his successful wooing and winning of the lovely Katherine McLean to be his life-mate, over established and somewhat preferred suitors, is proof enough of his determination and persistence. Then, later in the business world, he challenged entrenched, better equipped, and superior yarn producers who were suppliers to the knitting and weaving trades. Almost invariably he ended up with more than his share of the market.

His bearing was indicative of his self-confidence and firm determination, traits inherited from his father, perhaps, and acquired in part from his experience as the eldest of four sons. A born optimist with a booming voice—so often the mark of a salesman—he was never moody; rather, he sought release in action when under stress or faced with a difficult problem.

As the son of a Methodist minister, Everett Jordan heard the value of ethics and morals incessantly exhorted upon him from the day he was born. Strict honesty must have been one of these prized traits, one evidently imparted by both parents. Time after time, customers, business associates, and family friends affirmed that "his word was his bond."

Everett Jordan was not a timid person. He had definite ideas about what he wanted, and he was not hesitant in relentlessly pursuing his goals. A paramount example was his acquisition of control and ownership of Sellers Manufacturing Company, an endeavor that he started from scratch, aided by the guardianship of his uncle Charlie Sellers. His resounding success in achieving this goal is typical of how he operated because, when he chose a course of action, he spared neither himself or others as he focused all his energies to see it through to completion.

Appointment of the "Seat-Warmer"

Rose Ann Jordan Gant shed light on this aspect of her father's personality in telling about his total dedication to the mills: "The only thing he knew to talk about was the mill; and he would talk about it to anybody that came in there [their home], and I was just not able to talk about the mill—there was just no communication. Sometimes I would ride the whole trip to town [Burlington—fifteen miles away] without saying a word because I couldn't think of anything to say, nor could he."[85]

This attitude was revealed by the topics that Rose Ann said were discussed around the Sunday afternoon dinner table: "Well, when he was home we usually came down here [to Saxapahaw] for Sunday dinner, and what they talked about was Sellers Manufacturing Company *ad infinitum, ad nauseam* forever and forever; and daddy and Roger [Gant, Jr.] and John [Jordan] and Ben [Jordan, Jr.], or whoever he could gather up, would go look at the mill."[86]

As a result of such all-consuming dedication, Everett Jordan seldom if ever came up empty-handed in his undertakings.

Everett Jordan was rising high on the tide of fortune when Luther Hodges, governor of North Carolina, singled out his trusted friend for the United States Senate. Now Jordan would ride his own tide even higher.

On May 5, 1958, at 12:13 p.m. EDT, the former youthful floor-sweeper in a textile mill, held up his right hand and answered "I do" to the oath from Senator Carl Hayden, president pro tem of the Senate. From the gallery, more than 400 people looked on and applauded North Carolina's new junior senator. Many of those people were family members and close friends from back home.[87]

Despite the questions raised at the time about the propriety of his having been thrust so suddenly into the United States Senate, B. Everett Jordan quickly dispelled these doubts and won over his public as indicated in this press account: "While former President Johnson was [Senate] majority leader," Hodges recalled years later, "he told me that Everett Jordan, more than any other freshman [congressman] he had seen, made himself at home and knew how

In this cartoon, Jordan supports himself for re-election in the 1960 general election, disputing the contention that he was a "seat-warmer" for Governor Luther H. Hodges. Bill Saunders, *Greensboro* (N.C.) *Daily News*, July 29, 1959. (*Ben E. Jordan, Jr.*)

Appointment of the "Seat-Warmer" 35

to handle himself in the Senate. This was simply because he knew how to work with people."[88]

A newspaper cartoon in July 1959 pictured a confident-looking Senator B. Everett Jordan and a reporter representing the North Carolina press. Jordan was holding the body of another man—himself—in his arms, and the caption reads, "Yes, as a matter of fact, I am supporting somebody next year"—referring, of course, to the upcoming election (1960).[89]

The state's new junior senator did "keep the seat warm" for nearly fifteen years—but for himself alone, only leaving office on January 3, 1973.

2

And Henry Harrison Jordan Begat...

The name Jordan can be traced back to the Middle Ages. In the records of that era, it is spelled variously: Jourdain, Jorden, Jordon, Jourdon, and Jurdan.[1]

The first Jordan to reach the shores of the present United States was Samuel (Se'l Jourdan), who arrived at the Jamestown colony in Virginia in 1609. Other Jordans followed him, and the name is found among the earliest census reports and legal documents in the Virginia colony and in other locations. Many people bearing the name found their way into North Carolina, South Carolina, Georgia, Tennessee, and eventually regions farther west.[2]

One of these was Milas Chauncey Jordan, Sr., Everett Jordan's great-grandfather. Everett's grandfather was Milas (Miles) Chauncey Jordan, Jr., a farmer and deputy sheriff who resided in northern Iredell County, N.C., in the Olin community—"where people know each other by name and trust each other by nature."[3] Olin was first known (1855) as "New Institute" for the Methodist Academy there. Two years later, it was named Olin. Located almost due north of Statesville, twelve miles away, it is skirted today by Interstate 77, one mile to the west.[4]

Everett's father, Henry Harrison Jordan, was born in Olin; and, because his parents were staunchly affiliated with the Baptist church, Olin's Methodist Academy may have provided young Henry his first opportunity to associate with persons of other religious beliefs. At any rate, the Methodist church was destined to play a paramount role in his career.[5]

Milas Chauncey Jordan, Jr. (1837–1920), B. Everett Jordan's grandfather. (*Mary Jordan Hintz*)

Lucy Ann Edwards Jordan (1840–1926), B. Everett Jordan's grandmother. (*Mary Jordan Hintz*)

Everett's grandfather Milas[6] married Lucy Ann Edwards in 1860 or 1861, and this Iredell County farm couple had eight children, seven of whom lived to maturity. Watt Jordan died at age twelve or thirteen, and the other five sons were Henry Harrison, Thomas Chauncey, William Alvis, Robert Alexander, and Claude Alvin. The two daughters were Margaret Missourri Ann (called "Maggie"), who never married; and Mary Esther, who was engaged to be wed, but died of tuberculosis on July 10, 1901.[7]

Iredell County, like much of the rest of North Carolina after the Civil War (1861–65), was not an easy place to make a living, both for the small farmer as well as for those on the usually larger farms in the eastern section of the state. The South was prostrate in defeat; its agricultural lands were ravaged, run-down, and unproductive. Reconstruction was slow and painful. The industrious and frugal farmers of the so-called "one-horse dirt farms" survived—but only barely. Some of the more fortunate ones gained income from other sources than the soil.[8]

Milas Chauncey Jordan, Jr., born on January 7, 1837, was one of those who enhanced his meager livelihood by becoming a county deputy sheriff. The wages were modest, but steady, and not subject to the perils of weather, depressed prices, undeveloped markets, insects, and poor production from fields farmed season after season. The hillsides, as is characteristic of that part of the country, were especially subject to erosion and loss of vital nutrients.[9]

The Civil War broke out in 1861; and Milas, Jr., twenty-four years old, soon joined up. Richard ("Dick") Edwards, one of the brothers of Lucy Ann (Edwards) Jordan, the wife of Milas, served with him in the same Confederate regiment. Milas took care of Dick when he suffered from smallpox during the war. Milas, himself, came home with a scar on his arm caused by a Yankee Minie ball.[10]

Being a deputy sheriff was serious business—pursuing criminals and serving as executioner. Milas's other duties were usually less demanding and dangerous; some of them were reported by the *Statesville* (N.C.) *Record and Landmark* newspaper:

> From Sweet Home news: M. C. Jordan came very near being killed one day last week. He was out sulky riding when his mule took fright and ran away and altogether demolished the sulky. Mr. Jordan suffers from internal injuries. As usual the mule was unhurt. [October 1, 1880]

> The first of last week Deputy Sheriff M. C. Jordan carried to the penitentiary three negroes convicted in the late term of the Iredell Superior Court. [January 7, 1881]

> Miles [Milas] Jordan was in town the fore part of the week and reported if the buds had been ten minutes later than they were, stock in Sharpesburg would have perished to death. The people were plumb out of food; and it was a question whether the buds should burst or the cattle die. [May 6, 1881][11]

It is not clear just when Milas Jordan moved to Lenoir, N.C., but the family attended Lower Creek Baptist Church there.[12] Three of Milas's and Lucy's sons, Henry Harrison, Thomas Chauncey, and Robert Alexander, became ministers. The last of these remained true to his father's Baptist faith, but health problems cut short his ministry. Henry, like Tom an apostate from his Baptist upbringing, became a Methodist Episcopal minister.[13]

Henry Harrison Jordan was inclined to be noticeably more scholarly and formal than the average Baptist minister in rural North Carolina of his day; and the more formal structure and organization of the Methodist Episcopal church was possibly a factor in his joining. In addition, a Mooresville merchant and good friend, W. L. Sherrill, who had preceded him into the ministry, was a Methodist; and the two men remained close throughout their lives.[14]

After farming, operating a meat market, and serving as jailers, Milas and Lucy Ann moved from Lenoir, N.C., to the tiny village of Rutherford College, in Burke County, where there was a Methodist academy—a high school and junior college—named for the settlement. In 1912–14 Everett and Henry Jordan, their grandsons, lived with them while the boys attended Rutherford College high school. Milas was not impressed with Everett. As Mary Jordan Hintz later explained: "I think Everett had fooled around in school—I'm not sure—and Everett didn't graduate; and Aunt Annie [Everett's mother] was so disgusted and angry that he hadn't made the grade, and that might have been the reason he was [sent] here two years. Grandpa just thought that Everett wasn't paying any attention to anything serious, and grandfather—I heard him say this: 'Aaa Lord, he'll never amount to anything!' I just wish grandpa could know the successes he later achieved."[15]

While Milas and Lucy lived in Rutherford College, their son William ("Bill") Alvis Jordan, a farmer, married a young widow with three children. When their daughter, Mary Jordan (later Hintz), was twelve, Bill's wife died; and Mary, who had lived with or near her grandparents all her life, came along with her father to live permanently with them.[16]

Because the Jordans had lived in Lenoir, when their friends from Caldwell County came to Rutherford College for commencement, Milas would generously invite them to dinner. And they all knew that Lucy was a good cook. For a while, the couple had run the jail in Lenoir; and somebody said that the people in jail did not want to get out because they were so well fed—quite a compliment to Lucy's cooking.[17]

Henry Harrison Jordan (1862–1931) as a young man. He was Milas and Lucy Jordan's first son and Everett Jordan's father. (*Mary Jordan Hintz*)

William ("Bill") Alvis Jordan (1869–1931), Everett Jordan's uncle. (*Mary Jordan Hintz*)

Sisters and brother of Henry Harrison Jordan, aunts and uncle of Everett Jordan (*left to right*): Margaret ("Maggie"), Robert ("Bob"), Esther. (*Mary Jordan Hintz*)

Reverend Thomas ("Tom") Chauncey Jordan (1868–1939), Everett Jordan's uncle. (*Esther Jordan Arledge*)

Reverend Henry Harrison Jordan (1862–1931), Everett Jordan's father, late in his ministerial career. (*Ben E. Jordan, Jr.*)

All these grateful dinner guests were certainly not Baptists or Baptist ministers. One notable exception was Professor Melvin Hinshaw, president of Rutherford College at the time that Milas's son Henry Harrison chaired the school's board of trustees. Professor Hinshaw and his wife were seated at the Jordan's table about every two weeks for Sunday dinner immediately after church. As Mary Jordan Hintz recalled: "Now they were Methodists, and grandpa and grandma were Baptists, but that didn't make a bit of difference when the chicken was that good!"[18]

Living in the home of her grandparents for so many years, Mary Jordan (Hintz) had an opportunity to become well acquainted with her father's brothers. In addition to uncle Bob, who had lived there, there was uncle Henry Harrison Jordan, the father of Everett; Thomas ("Tom") Chauncey Jordan; and Claude Alvin Jordan, the youngest son.[19]

Claude married Mary Alice ("Mayce") Blackwelder from Hickory, N.C. In his early working life, he was employed by a lumber company and was later a partner in a funeral home in Hickory.[20]

Tom Jordan was ordained as a minister of the Methodist Episcopal Church (South) in 1899 or 1900, approximately ten years after the ordination in the same denomination of his older brother, Henry. Tom was admitted as a minister by a church conference held in Washington, D.C.; his first pastorate was at Manassas, Va.[21]

Tom Jordan married Henrietta Engle Warfield, a first cousin of Wallis Warfield Simpson, renowned for her marriage to the Duke of Windsor who, as King Edward VIII, abdicated the English throne in 1936 for "the woman I love." Henrietta was from Howard County, Va., and her wedding to Tom Jordan took place on June 12, 1901, in Manassas. She and Tom had two children: Esther Mae Jordan (later Arledge), born July 20, 1904, in Andrews, N.C.; and Thomas Carlyle Jordan, born July 13, 1909, in Spray, N.C. The latter died December 26, 1976, in North Hollywood, Calif. In 1986 Esther Mae Jordan Arledge resided in Richmond, Va.[22]

The Reverend Tom Jordan, after serving a couple of years at Manassas, transferred to the North Carolina Conference and served Methodist churches in Spray, Lilesville, Reidsville, Summerville, Davidson College, Rutherfordton, and Asheville, where he retired until his death on January 18, 1939.[23]

Mary Jordan Hintz had several recollections concerning her uncle Henry, Everett Jordan's father. She especially appreciated his providing the home in Rutherford College for her grandparents, herself, and other members of the Milas Jordan family, including her father, Bill, who was not too well. In addition, she believed her uncle Henry helped her receive a high school education.[24]

Henry, Mary thought, was somewhat formal and did not have much "foolishness" about him. Yet he was essentially a kind person behind the facade of a tall, straight minister in a swallow-tailed coat and high-wing collar, the attire worn by the clergy of his time. She was proud of this handsome uncle because he looked very much the part of a preacher with his well-groomed hair, dark mustache, and elegant ways. His speech was somewhat formal and had the tone of a serious-minded servant of the Lord, in Mary's opinion. She added, "He was kind, rather businesslike though; and I never saw him laugh and carry on like some people would. Even so, uncle Henry was compassionate."[25]

Henry H. Jordan, like most fathers, wanted his children to have more opportunity to succeed than he had been provided by his parents, Milas and Lucy Ann, who struggled on their small Iredell County farm to endure the rigors and deprivations of the Civil War and Reconstruction. Henry Harrison Jordan's formal education was, perhaps, through the fourth-grade level—he was fortunate to receive even that. But he learned to read, and he never stopped. He did so voraciously until he became a public schoolteacher; and, while he taught, he read law under Major Harvey Bingham in his Statesville, N.C., office.[26]

The *Statesville Record and Landmark* recorded several of his activities as a teacher and educational administrator:

Fairview Academy, Shiloh Township, is now in a flourishing condition. On April 5th next, H. H. Jordan of Statesville will be connected with the school as assistant principal. [April 2, 1886]

From Amity News: H. H. Jordan commenced our free school last Monday and has a large attendance, there being about 60 pupils already enrolled. [February 2, 1888]

Amity Hill News: The public school taught by our efficient teacher, H. H. Jordan, closed with appropriate ceremonies. A nice New Testament was presented by the teacher to the scholar having the most headmarks. [March 29, 1888][27]

On September 24, 1888, the North Carolina Supreme Court issued licenses to practice law to twenty-six applicants. Henry H. Jordan, of Iredell County, was on the list, certified to practice in the "113th year of American Independence."[28] A partner in the firm of Bingham and Caldwell, he practiced in Mooresville, N.C., and operated in the state courts for the counties of Iredell, Mecklenburg, Rowan, Cabarrus, and Catawba.[29]

Many of Jordan's legal, as well as political, activities were chronicled in the *Statesville Record and Landmark*:

> The mayor stated the object of the meeting was to consider the objections urged by J. F. McLean to the location of the cottonseed warehouse and whether the board would reconsider their action of their last meeting. H. H. Jordan was heard in behalf of Mr. McLean, after which the board declined to reconsider their action. [June 20, 1889]
>
> H. H. Jordan, our lawyer, is quite sick at the Johnston House. [June 29, 1889]
>
> H. H. Jordan is again occupying his office after an absence of about six months. He still looks worse for his struggle with typhoid fever, but is coming around all right. [October 21, 1889]
>
> Sam Woods was arraigned before Esq. A. M. Walker yesterday morning to answer the charge of beating his sister. The litigants were all colored. Woods was defended by our lawyer, H. H. Jordan. [March 20, 1890]
>
> The Mooresville convention proceeded to nominate for mayor, S. C. Rankin. Yesterday when the polls were opened a somewhat different ticket was put out with H. H. Jordan at the head. He, however, told them not to vote for him as he did not want the office. Nevertheless, the Radical Methodist ticket, made up almost entirely of Presbyterians, was elected, with H. H. Jordan as mayor. [May 8, 1890]
>
> Mr. Jordan told his friends early in the morning not to vote for him, for he did not want the office and would not serve if elected, and then went and remained in all day. He had been quite ill for several days before and was still too weak to be on the street all day. [May 15, 1890]
>
> The Democratic voters of Coddle Creek township met at the academy at Mooresville and organized a campaign club with H. H. Jordan as secretary. The following delegates were elected to the state con-

vention of Democratic clubs: H. H. Jordan, A. Leazar and R. H. Tomlinson. [September 25, 1890][30]

H. H. Jordan, Esq., is absent this week at court in Salisbury. [May 7, 1891]

In 1891 Henry Harrison Jordan switched vocations once again: this time to the ministry. He was apparently strongly influenced to do so by his close friend and Mooresville merchant W. L. Sherrill, who preceded him by a year in the clergy.[31]

Not long before he entered the ministry, in February 1891, Jordan took another pivotal step in his life, marriage: "H. H. Jordan made a pleasant trip last week to Burlington (N.C.), where he and Miss Annie E. Sellars, daughter of Dr. and Mrs. B. A. Sellars, were married Tuesday evening by Rev. R. Ricks, pastor of the Christian Church. Mr. and Mrs. Jordan arrived here [Mooresville] on Thursday evening and are at the Johnston House. They will reside at the Sherrill house on 1st Street south."[32]

Four news items in the *Statesville Record and Landmark* cover Jordan's religious activities just before and just after he joined the clergy:

Rev. F. H. Wood, H. H. Jordan and M. W. White left this morning to attend the District Conference at Lenoir. [July 16, 1891]

Sunday evening at the Methodist Church there was an entertainment in interest of the Sunday Schools. The superintendent, H. H. Jordan, made some timely and appropriate remarks. [July 30, 1891]

H. H. Jordan, who for the past year has been superintendent of the M. E. Sunday School here, recently obtained a license to preach and will apply for admission into the conference at its present session at Asheville. [November 12, 1891]

At the Methodist Church Sunday night, Rev. H. H. Jordan preached from Ecclesiastes 11:9, portraying the solemnities of the general judgment. Those who heard him speak well of this, his first effort, in his new calling. He has been assigned to work on the Lenoir Circuit in Caldwell County. [November 19, 1891][33]

There were, no doubt, those who questioned the wisdom of giving up a new but thriving law practice for a profession that, in comparison, would offer meager financial compensation. But H. H. Jordan was a man with firm convictions who was committed to

Mary Jordan Hintz, Everett Jordan's first cousin. She grew up in the home of their grandparents, Milas and Lucy Jordan. (*Mary Jordan Hintz*)

make his "full contribution" to the "good of humankind."[34] In his eyes, this was the opportunity to do just that.

One of those with misgivings about Henry's decision was his own father, Milas. Mary Jordan Hintz recalls that her grandfather Milas later said of his son, "I just chuckled when they told me Henry had gone into the ministry. I thought it was a joke!" Mary allowed, "He just couldn't imagine his boy being a preacher." Mary thought that Milas may not have believed that his oldest son was that serious, though she herself always thought her uncle Henry was very serious. She said, "I never thought of him as a person having fun. He had more serious things on his mind."[35]

Milas, a "very narrow Baptist,"[36] may also have been concerned about his son's switch to another denomination. The Baptist tenet

"Once a Baptist, always a Baptist" had been breached unabashedly by his independent-thinking son. Could his non-conforming Henry ever reach heaven?

In spite of his father's misgivings, H. H. Jordan, in clerical cloak and with horse and buggy, faithfully traversed the Lenoir Circuit of the Methodist Episcopal church on a salary of $250 a year. He was given this appointment by the Methodist Episcopal Church South Conference at its November 11–16, 1891, session, held in Asheville, N.C.[37]

His salary was not always in cash. Struggling parishioners, themselves short of currency, often would give preachers their next best: produce from the soil, including potatoes, meat, molasses, and the like. Margaret Jordan Sprinkle, the minister's youngest daughter, recalls this story about her oldest brother, Everett, and her father's compensation: "I remember one time papa married a couple and they asked, 'How much do I owe you?' and papa said, 'Oh, anything you would like to give.' And the man didn't give him anything, but he said, 'When I come to town again with some potatoes I'll give you some.' Well, he *didn't* come with those potatoes; and one day Everett came rushing in with a bag of potatoes and said, 'I met the man you married downtown with his load of potatoes, and I just collected your wedding fee!' "[38]

Margaret surmised: "Henry [Everett's younger brother] wouldn't have done that—Henry was a student. He read a lot; he was the quiet one, and Everett was always in mischief."[39] Conceded—but Everett invariably got results—one way or the other. This incident was a portent of things to come when Everett Jordan would be his own man.

Margaret also said, "I enjoyed grandpa and grandma Jordan more than grandma Sellars. Grandma Sellars was rigid, a disciplinarian. She had money and she was generous [to us]. Grandma Jordan and grandpa Jordan were hearty, and he was a great storyteller. He used to sit with us and tell us stories. They lived at Rutherford College and their front porch looked out on Brown Mountain."[40]

Margaret Jordan Sprinkle continued her recollections: "Preachers move around so much you don't get to see your family. Mother would take us to her parents' home [the B. A. Sellarses in Burlington] every summer, and I didn't get to visit grandma and grandpa

Everett Jordan (*left*), his older sister Lucy (*center*), and younger brother Henry (*right*). (*Mary Jordan Hintz*)

Annie Sellars Jordan with her first son, Everett, and daughter Lucy. (*Mary Jordan Hintz*)

Jordan until I was big enough to go. Frank and Charlie and I went up and spent a good bit of time in Rutherford College—just the three of us."[41]

Margaret Jordan Sprinkle in a 1982 interview recalled that B. Everett Jordan "was sort of 'the roughneck' in the family!" And the evidence is ample that the preacher's non-conformist son asserted his personality even as a small child. This bold incident occurred at the Mocksville Methodist Church when Everett was only four years old. Margaret's version of this story is as follows: "Papa was preaching a very serious sermon one time, and he noticed that people were all smiling and kind of giggling and he felt something behind him. Papa wore a Prince Albert coat—all preachers did then—and Everett had gotten behind him and was pulling that coattail apart and peeping between papa's legs, grinning at the people. [One version has it that Everett was not only grinning at the congregation, but also making 'funny faces.'] He was always doing things like that."[42]

Mary Jordan Hintz heard one of Everett's brothers say that he was "the bane of papa's existence," and she remarked: "It was embarrassing to a minister to have his son always getting into something."[43]

For example, Charles ("Charlie") H. Ross, of Morganton, Everett's schoolmate and boyhood friend, tells why he was taken out of the high school in Morganton and sent to his grandparents to attend high school at Rutherford College:

> We were in school together, and Everett was always "full of himself" as you can imagine, very outgoing and full of pranks. In school here, he got into some kind of difficulty over some prank or something, and that sent him down to Mr. Hairfield's office. He was the principal—at one time he was a lawyer. Anyhow, at that time, if a boy got out of line it usually meant the hickory switch. So Mr. Hairfield started to proceed with the punishment, but Everett took the hickory switch away from him and gave Mr. Hairfield a going over.
>
> The result was [that] Everett's father sent him down to Rutherford College, which was pretty much a high school—a church-oriented thing...
>
> Everett was probably fifteen or sixteen; anyhow, that was the last time I was with him as far as school goes because in 1913 I went to State A & M [in Raleigh], which is now State College. I think Everett went to Trinity. [Everett attended Trinity College, now Duke University, for one year, 1914–15.][44]

The Reverend H. H. Jordan was zealous in projecting the proper image of a preacher. Margaret pointed out that "he didn't want his children to do anything to reflect on him." She recalls that, when her father was serving the Methodist Church in Marion, "there was a big empty lot next to us where the circus came every year. That's another thing we weren't allowed to attend. We could look from our yard down to the circus, but we couldn't go. One day a little girl took me to ride on the merry-go-round, and I looked up and there was papa! I was just riding around having the best of time and I thought, 'Oh, he'll scold me for this.' He took me by the hand and said, 'Well, I don't believe I'd do that; people frown on a preacher's child doing that,' but he didn't scold me."[45]

Lucy Jordan Taylor (later Way) with her son Oscar and daughter Elizabeth. Lucy was Everett Jordan's older sister. (*Mary Jordan Hintz*)

But "that Everett" was something else—the bane of his father's existence, for sure. One may imagine his chagrin if he had known the truth about some of Everett's "doings." Some of the more innocent capers were told in later years by Everett Jordan himself. In his pre-school years, he swung on the shutters of the two-story parsonage in Mocksville, and Everett delighted in telling how the shutters sagged thereafter from the weight of the parsonage kids.[46]

North Carolina's Senator Sam Ervin told this story about the teenaged Everett when he lived in Morganton, where his father was pas-

A 1981 view of the erstwhile Methodist parsonage at 728 N. Main Street in Mocksville, N.C., where Everett Jordan once lived with his family. (Photo by author)

tor of the Methodist Church: "Everett was more inclined to have fun than he was to study. He was sometimes a little mischievous. We had a YMCA, and—whoever was running it—one day he caught Everett and some more boys shooting craps, which wasn't supposed to be the customary occupation of a preacher's son. I don't think his pa ever learned about it though."[47]

Perhaps, up to this point, Everett's gravest injury to his father's self-imposed image of puritanical conduct was the occasion when Reverend Jordan was still pastor in Morganton. Everett took his rifle and told his friend: "I can hit that cross!" which was high on top of his father's church steeple. Everett pointed his .22 rifle, carefully aimed, pulled the trigger, and a resounding "plunk" was heard. Years later, when the church was torn down to build a new one, there was indeed a bullet hole in the old wooden cross. Margaret concluded, "He *had* hit it! No other preacher's son would have done that"[48]—quite a contrast, indeed, between Margaret's riding the merry-go-round and Everett's practicing marksmanship on the church cross.

Charles H. Ross, recalled those early years in a 1982 interview: "Living that close to the Jordans, naturally Everett and I ran together. There was a grocery store nearby, and Everett worked in there. It was my understanding that his father, H. H. Jordan, had an interest in that grocery store. Everett, I think, delivered groceries, but he also helped himself to the cookies and that sort of thing."[49]

Ross, who played on the neighborhood baseball and football teams with Ervin and Jordan, continued: "I played center because I used to be the fat boy in town... It was more or less 'pick-up football' but we did play Hickory [N.C.]. We would go down there and play those guys... They had coaches and everything—it was just murder! We didn't have headgear or anything else. I used to kid Everett—he played right guard beside me—I'd tell him he played guard and never even got his hat knocked off! Then he'd turn around and tell somebody else that *I* never got *my* hat knocked off."[50]

Reverend Jordan, on Sunday afternoons, required his children to stay in the house, where they could read, sing, and listen to the Victrola, but could not play hopscotch or jump rope in the yard, where folks could see them. Dance floors, of course, were off limits at all times for the children of this Methodist preacher. Margaret Sprinkle: "I got fed up with parsonage life. I wasn't allowed to dance; I couldn't even go *look* at dances, and Everett wasn't supposed to, but, when we lived in Gastonia, he went out to the country club and someone came and told papa, 'I saw your son out there dancing.' And Everett said [later to his betrayer], 'Did you tell about your daughter leaving the dance floor and going out on the golf course during the dance? Tell him about that!' "[51] Dancing was sin, pure and simple, and H. H. Jordan was not about to let his children practice sin—certainly not in front of his parishioners!

Of her four brothers, Margaret thought that possibly Charlie was more like her father in that "Charlie was very dignified, very proper—they always called him 'the preacher.' He would come to me and say, 'Margaret, do you need a new dress?' and he would give me money to get one. He wanted to keep up appearances. He was very proper, and he married a very proper wife."[52]

Henry, Everett's younger brother, shared his father's love for books. According to Margaret, "You know, as he lay dying on his bed in Cedar Falls, he would quote Shakespeare—he had a wonderful memory of poetry. Yes, he was a student—always bookish, more than anybody else in the family."[53]

The Reverend H. H. Jordan was scholarly and well-read, and many of the books he loved best were from his own huge home library. As Margaret said, "As a district superintendent, he carried a big briefcase of books with him—you know the latest books on preaching—for his preachers. He said, 'Now you need to be studying; here's some books; I'll lend them to you.' That was one of his great theses: 'Get an education.' "[54]

Each year, H. H. Jordan would go down to Trinity College (now Duke University) and teach a course in the pastor's school. He felt that preachers ought not ever to quit learning, and he set the example. But the minister's example—books and reading—never "took" with Everett Jordan. He let others do his reading for him, usually his staff but, most of all, his wife, Katherine.[55]

H. H. Jordan's entrepreneur side was evidenced, however, in the career of his oldest son. Tracing her father's activities and revealing his business inclinations, Margaret said, "Papa said if you try to save a man's soul, you ought to also save his body." And he backed up his words with action: "Mama's father [B. A. Sellars] died and left her some money; and she and papa and a Mr. Jake Hanes built a chair factory here [in Mocksville]. There was unemployment in Mocksville, and he started the factory to give work to his parishioners...I have two of the chairs upstairs; and the granddaughter of that Mr. Hanes has a lot of them because I sat in one of them last night at her house. The plant was right down here by the railroad, and they said sparks from an engine set it on fire and it burned. By that time, we were in Walkertown, and papa started another one—another chair factory."[56]

At his death in 1931, H. H. Jordan left an estate of $50,000, which Margaret said "was good for a preacher whose salary was, I doubt, ever more than $3,600. They opened the H. H. Jordan Lending Library at Duke Divinity School with that money."[57]

Speaking of the early years, Margaret said, "Of course money was tight then. When papa married and went to the Lenoir Circuit, his salary was $250 a year—most of that was molasses and sausage and what not. Then, many years later, when we got up to Morganton, his salary was $1,000 a year; and he preached every Sunday afternoon at the State Hospital for the Insane [now Broughton Hospital]. He got $200 a year for that, so we had $1,200 a year to educate three children. [Charlie, Margaret, and Frank were enrolled at Trinity in Durham at the same time—actually there were four children in school because Lucy was in New York studying, too.] Then in 1915 papa went to Gastonia—$3,000 a year! We were in the money and then, in 1920, when he went on the district it was $3,600 a year."[58]

"Now mama always had a little money. Her father was wealthy—all the Sellarses had money." Annie Sellars Jordan acquired from her father, B. A. Sellars, a one-sixth interest in the Burlington department store bearing his name. In lieu of dividends, Annie usually received dry goods, mostly clothes and dress goods, materials to make dresses and other apparel for her two girls and herself. Reverend Jordan's children were "turned out" as well if not better than any of his ministerial peers' offspring. Annie saw to that.[59]

As Margaret remembers, "Mama liked pretty things because she had grown up in a family where there was a store, and every year she would go spend two weeks at grandma's (Sellars); and, when I came along, Lucy, my sister, was big enough to stay at home, and mama took Frank and me with her. She had a little trunk, and mama would fill it with cloth, ribbons, and laces to bring back home with her and have a dressmaker to come in and make us pretty clothes."[60]

Regardless of how meager his salary or how great the demands of family, H. H. Jordan never spent beyond his means. Rather, as Margaret stated, "No matter what our salary was, he bought a little building and loan stock every week. He always had building and loan." When Reverend Jordan lived in Gastonia, the South's new and upcoming textile center, he bought stock in some of the cotton mills: "He [papa] was frugal and mama was, too. You know those Sellarses are frugal...Papa would start those factories [furniture and chairs] and when he sold he got a good settlement—he was a pretty solid businessman."[61] Amen! Son Everett learned at his father's knee. He, too, practiced frugality and made discreet investments that yielded handsome dividends.

Margaret described her father in this way: "Well, he was a sentimental man—warm and emotional. In the winter we would sit by the stove, and he would take me in his lap and read to me. Sometimes I remember the stories were sad, and I'd stick my head under his coat so he wouldn't know I was crying. Of course, he knew it. He could feel it, but he was a very loving sort of person—showed his love and his emotion."[62]

"Wherever he went, he was a very popular preacher and minister. People loved him. When he went to Gastonia and his four years were up, Mr. Joe Separk, who was the wealthiest man in our church—he was a big textile man—told him 'You aren't leaving!' And papa said he had to, that preachers moved every four years. Mr. Separk said that he would get him back, so at the end of one year we came back to the district and stayed six more years as district superintendent (presiding elder) in Gastonia. Wherever Papa went he had a lot of friends. He got around and he knew people; he had a wonderful memory for names."[63]

As a disciplinarian, Margaret judged, "He wasn't severe; he just did what he thought was his duty."[64]

Concerning her father's preaching emphasis, Margaret felt that he dwelt more on love and compassion than law and justice: "I never heard him preach 'hell-fire' sermons. He was very gentle, and people loved him so. Now, if papa had been a hell-fire preacher, they would have been afraid of him...People loved him and he was always surrounded by people. His sermons were the 'gentle, loving God' instead of a fierce and angry God."[65]

Sam Ervin knew Everett Jordan's father when he was a minister in Morganton and he and Everett were teenagers: "[Reverend Jordan] was a very fine preacher...had a good deal of eloquence and a good deal of emotion in his preaching. He was not to any great degree a 'fire and brimstone' preacher. He had a tendency to preach on the kinder aspects of religion, like love and service to others and things like that, instead of trying to 'scare the devil' out of people."[66]

This sort of theology must have seemed pretty watered down to that branch of the Baptist faith in which Milas Jordan had grown up. If Milas ever had occasion to hear son Henry preach on God's love and mercy, it probably reaffirmed his suspicion that Henry was "not serious enough" to be in the pulpit.

Ervin continued: "Reverend Jordan preached here in Morganton for four years, like most Methodist ministers, then moved on. That was the First Methodist Church, of Morganton, which is still in existence up here."[67]

Charlie H. Ross, of Morganton, in a 1982 interview gave his impressions of Reverend Jordan:

> My first recollection is when Everett's father came here as a minister...[in] 1910...That would make us fourteen years old at the time. [Everett Jordan, Sam Ervin, and Charlie Ross were the same age.] The Jordans lived in the parsonage, which was right next door to the church...and we lived...just around the corner from the Jordans. We could sit in our house and hear [Reverend Jordan] preaching. They did a lot of hollering back then. Even Mr. Jordan would get into "high gear" sometimes. You wouldn't be doing justice to the Lord unless you did a lot of hollering and bearing down pretty heavy. Yeah, he'd bear down on them—those old-timers did—and he was an old-timer.[68]

Everett Jordan, as a fifteen-year-old youth, knew even then how to take good care of himself, and it was a skill that he mastered and practiced all his life. Ross revealed another side of his young friend: Everett, the entrepreneur. Ross remembered when Everett "got into the junk business when he was a boy. He would gather up old iron and that sort of stuff and sell it."[69]

Roger Gant, Jr., Everett Jordan's son-in-law (husband of Rose Ann), tells the story he heard about the time Everett, as a youth in his scavenging business, one day brought home a wagonload of empty whiskey bottles from the local barroom. He intended to sell them, too, but, when his father saw them, that was the end of his son's bottle business.[70]

In comparing Everett to his minister-father, Ross felt they were physically much alike: "Mr. Jordan was a big, muscular man—and a very aggressive man—and Everett was also aggressive. I think they were very much alike. Reverend Jordan was more of a student-type than Everett. He was a public-spirited man—like I said—he would go in the court...know what was going on. Everett and Reverend Jordan were interested in politics."[71]

Ross was aware that H. H. Jordan was a lawyer before he became a minister: "He was a lawyer and he loved to go down there in court and help plead the case if assigned to him or if he was against somebody, he'd probably take over. He made a lot of enemies—I mean the wrong kind of folks—but he did spend a lot of time down there in the court...that was his diversion; instead of playing golf, he was in court. There was a lot of bootlegging and that sort of thing. [Reverend Jordan would] bear down on those folks. That was part of his ability in court. They'd let him do some talking against those fellows."[72]

However, Ross observed, "Some of the members of Reverend Jordan's congregation thought he spent too much time in the courtroom—I don't mean it as disrespect—but I mean they felt that he should be seeing about how the widows and orphans were getting along rather than being up there and trying to regulate how people should live on the outside. He was very much against the barrooms and that sort of thing."[73]

Margaret Sprinkle gives further insight to her father's strong antidrinking stand: "I remember as a child, papa was fighting for prohibition and there was a little song, 'North Carolina Will Go Dry'...Papa's father, Milas Jordan, drank and he [H. H. Jordan] was always opposed to drinking. Grandpa Jordan wasn't a drunk, but he did drink and papa objected to it very much and [therefore] fought whiskey all his life."[74]

At least one son, Everett, was not inclined that way, being a moderate imbiber. The story is told that his younger son, John, as a young boy in disapproval once poured his father's whiskey in the kitchen sink.[75] But Everett Jordan's moderate drinking never interfered with his work.

Reverend Jordan believed in and practiced taking care of his family; and, in this respect, few could surpass Everett Jordan. One of the best examples of this trait in Henry Harrison's life can be seen in his personal sacrifice and dedication in educating his children. Five of the six (a seventh died in infancy) were college graduates and did graduate work. The one exception was—easy to guess—Everett. He was far too busy for an education to "take" on him. As

Charles H. Ross in 1982. (Photo by author)

his sister Margaret contended: "Everett was never a student—he went to Trinity College at Durham, and he didn't do *any* good there!"[76]

D. K. Muse, an Alamance County politician, tells it this way: "The president of Trinity College, where Everett was enrolled, called Reverend Jordan and told him to take Everett home—that he just wasn't suited for college."[77] This dropout later became a United States senator and one of the most distinguished citizens in North Carolina. He served on the board of trustees of three institutions of higher learning: Elon College, Duke University, and American University. Many of his larger monetary gifts were directed to the cause of education.[78]

Margaret Jordan (Sprinkle), Everett Jordan's younger sister, at the age of twenty-one. (*Mary Jordan Hintz*)

Contrary to his minister-father's example of "Do as I do," according to Margaret Sprinkle, Everett once said to his own son John: "I wish you would study your reading more. What are you going to do when you get grown?" John replied, "I'll do like you do: I'll let mama read to me!"[79]

H. H. Jordan planted good seed—some of it was just late in coming up.

Charles ("Charlie") Jordan served as executor of his father's estate. According to him, "In papa's papers I found a large number of notes—all in small amounts of, say $20, $47, and the like—he had signed in order to help youngsters get to college. They used to say that papa helped more young people get an education than any other minister in the Western North Carolina Conference [of the Methodist Church]."[80]

Starting in 1925, Charlie Jordan spent his entire working life with Duke University. From 1925 to 1941 he was assistant secretary, from 1941 to 1958 secretary and vice-president, then director of the Division of Public Relations and vice-president emeritus. While at Duke—like his father—he earned the reputation of befriending students who were struggling financially to matriculate. According to his nephew Reverend Mike Jordan, a Methodist minister in the Western North Carolina Conference, many alumni said that without Charlie Jordan's help they never would have gotten through Duke.[81]

Regardless of his lackluster performance in the classroom at Trinity College (present Duke University), Everett Jordan was one of its most ardent supporters and boosters. He bought season tickets to his alma mater's football games and rejoiced immensely in victories as he entertained his customers and friends. After the games, he would take them to his Saxapahaw home for cocktails and dinner. His guests would break up with laughter at his hilarious tales. He retained a copious mental file of rustic and other tales to be recounted whenever the occasion arose. After a hearty meal and an evening peppered with his homespun humor, he usually ended up with some additional orders from his guests for yarn from his spinning mills.[82]

Further proof of his special fondness for Duke University is shown in his choice of schools for his three children: Ben, Rose Ann, and John. All three are Duke graduates.[83] Because Everett Jordan, during this stage of his life, was so immersed in textiles, one might have thought he would have encouraged one if not both sons to attend North Carolina State University, at Raleigh, which then, as now, was noted for its textile school. Further evidence of his high regard for Duke is shown by his long tenure on its board of trust-

Duke Chapel, Duke University. The Jordan family has long been closely associated with Duke University. Everett Jordan served on his alma mater's board of trustees for thirty years. (*Duke University*)

ees, actively serving from 1943 to 1971, and as trustee emeritus during the years 1972–74. On March 1, 1974, the university awarded him an honorary LL.D. degree.[84]

Chester Davis wrote a full-page feature story on October 29, 1961, in the *Winston-Salem Journal and Sentinel* entitled "The Jordan Brothers: Remarkable Quartet." He lauds the feats of Reverend Henry Harrison Jordan's four sons—Everett, Henry, Charles, and Frank—but is quick to give credit to their father. At that time, Everett was in the U.S. Senate; Henry was being touted as a gubernatorial candidate for the 1964 race; Charles was vice-president of Duke University; and Frank was superintendent of the Winston-Salem District of the Methodist Church.

Davis, after identifying some of the four's most notable achievements and impact on North Carolina public life, gave credit where it was due: "You end up just about where you started—with a man named Henry Harrison Jordan, a man who lived so well that he has continued to live as a vital force in this state through his four sons. Reverend Jordan did not raise his youngsters on a 'Do as I say, not as I do' basis...he set the example by his own conduct."

Two of the four sons of H. H. Jordan—Everett and Henry, his two oldest—shared some major personal characteristics: both were shrewd politicians, they demonstrated remarkable adaptability to new positions and situations, they were usually effective in obtaining sought-after results, and both were excellent storytellers. In addition, both of their careers embraced politics and the textile industry. Nevertheless, Henry always stood in the shadow of Everett, never reached similar heights, and did not achieve his fullest potential in a political sense. Still, his career was noteworthy.

Henry, or Dr. Henry, as he was familiarly known throughout North Carolina, practiced dentistry for more than two decades in Belmont, N.C. Becoming afflicted with back trouble, he made a major and smooth career switch. He became associated with brother Everett as an officer and director of Sellers Manufacturing Company and its corporate affiliates. Moving to Cedar Falls, N.C., he also served as manager of the newly acquired Jordan Spinning Company (Sellers Manufacturing Company No. 2).[85]

Henry's eldest son recalled in 1986 that his father, despite his bad back, "had the nerve to think that he could run a cotton mill sitting down, which is exactly what he did. I [Henry II] remember him reading books at night early in the war [World War II] on the mechanical side of spinning. Sometime later in my life, we were walking through that cotton mill, and he said that after a while he learned to tell when it was running good. He could sense it."[86]

A Democratic party leader, Dr. Henry was first appointed to the state Highway Commission by Governor Gregg Cherry in the years 1945–49. Then, as only one of the ten commissioners who supported W. Kerr Scott's candidacy for governor, he served as chairman of the commission in the period 1949–53 during Scott's administration, when an epochal road-building program was conducted. It consisted mainly of farm-to-market roads and principally the paving of secondary roads.[87]

Highly instrumental in the success of this program, Henry traveled to every county in the state to convince people to vote for the necessary $200 million bond issue, which was to be financed by a one-cent-a-gallon sales tax on gas. North Carolina's secondary roads are—quite literally—concrete proof of Dr. Henry Jordan's successful handling of Scott's road-improvement program, which is considered to be one of the most—if not the most—notable accomplishments of Scott's unusually distinguished administration.[88]

Henry Jordan was also state senator from Randolph County in the years 1956–58, and was a top potential Democratic candidate for governor on three occasions, the last time in the 1964 gubernatorial race.[89] By that time, he had developed severe health problems; and, if he had entered and won the campaign, he would not have been able to serve out the term inasmuch as he died on February 29, 1968, a victim of cancer, as was his father.[90]

On all three occasions, for some reason or other, Henry—though in his prime—ultimately chose not to run for the office. For example, in the 1956 race, when Luther Hodges was re-elected to a full term as governor, Henry Jordan's candidacy had seriously been contemplated by party leaders, but he finally demurred. Earlier, Terry Sanford, who knew many people all over the state and had just successfully managed Kerr Scott's statewide campaign for U.S. senator, had met with Everett and Henry Jordan as well as Kerr Scott and agreed to support Henry's candidacy. Sanford pursued this course, though it brought a protest from Hodges, whom Sanford said did not forgive him for a long time.[91]

As to the reasons for Henry Jordan's change of heart and decision not to run, Sanford felt that Hodges had probably persuaded Everett Jordan to convince Dr. Henry not to run. Sanford did not believe, as some people did, that Hodges's appointment of Everett to the U.S. Senate in 1958 was a payoff for his influence on Henry not to run for governor in 1956.[92]

Knowledgeable sources contend that Everett Jordan exerted a major influence on his younger brother's decisions. As Bill Coch-

Reverend Henry Harrison Jordan's four sons in 1960 (*left to right*): Everett, Henry, Charles, Frank. (*Jordan family albums*)

rane later recalled: "Henry [Jordan] had actually stepped aside and [did] not run for governor when Luther [Hodges] ran because Senator Jordan was committed to support his business partner Luther Hodges [Howard Johnson restaurants]. I don't think Senator Jordan pressed Henry on it, but Henry was [contemplating] running for governor and would have had an excellent chance of being elected, but he stepped aside."[93]

Henry Jordan's political influence extended to the national level. He was a good friend of President Harry Truman. When W. Averell Harriman sought to become the Democratic party's nominee for president in 1956, Truman called Dr. Jordan and asked him to support Harriman in North Carolina. Harriman visited Jordan at his Cedar Falls home to obtain his advice. Jordan supported Harriman for the nomination, but the latter lost out to Adlai Stevenson.[94]

Later on, when John F. Kennedy ran for president, party leaders sought to persuade Dr. Henry Jordan to run Kennedy's campaign in North Carolina because they felt he was "the only man that can bring the factions together," according to his son Henry II. The latter continued: "My father didn't know Kennedy; he had never really gotten anybody elected that he didn't know, and what he stood for. But [father] believed in the Democratic party, and he said that he would." Kennedy carried North Carolina in his successful campaign for the presidency.[95]

Pictured here at Senator Jordan's Raleigh headquarters during the 1960 election campaign, when Henry served as chairman for his brother's successful re-election, are (*left to right*): Katherine Jordan, Mary (Mrs. W. Kerr) Scott, Senator Jordan, Henry Jordan and wife, Mary Ruth Rankin Jordan. (*Jordan family albums*)

And Reverend Henry Harrison Jordan also begat a son named Benjamin Everett. This non-conformist son did not fit into the pious mold of either his circuit-riding father or that of John Wesley, the founder of Methodism. Nor was this first son of Henry Harrison a total renegade. Rather, he was a pragmatic individualist, who, once committed, worked with all his might to achieve his goals. Everett Jordan's life may have been shaped by an unspoken vow to himself to refute his grandfather's prediction: "Aaa Lord, he'll never amount to anything!"[96]

3

Warp and Weft
or
Strings of Sellars

"We have our Jordan family reunion right around Christmas; we always eat well, have a good time and tell stories about each other, and pick on each other. This last year [1985] it was in Winston-Salem, the Henry H. Jordan II family hosted it, and I did something for which some of them probably would liked to have shot me on the spot. I did a tongue-in-cheek version of the game Trivial Pursuit—Jordan style—and asked some questions to see if they would come up with the answers.

"The first question was, 'What was the name of our grandmother's mother, Mrs. B. A. Sellars [B. Everett Jordan's grandmother]? What was her first name, and why has nobody in the family named their child after her?' Her name, of course, was 'Frusannah.' That was reason enough why no one named their child after her!" Thus concluded the Reverend Mike Jordan when interviewed in 1986 by the author of this book.[1]

The family of Anne ("Annie") Sellars, Everett Jordan's mother, dates back to colonial times. Two brothers, Thomas and Willis Sellars, emigrated from England to America and settled in Pennsylvania.[2]

Thomas Sellars, Sr., the immigrant and B. Everett Jordan's great-great-grandfather, was born some time between 1740 and 1745, probably in England. The date he moved from Pennsylvania to Orange County, N.C. (that is, the part that is now Alamance County), is unknown. However, colonial records of North Carolina show his signature on two petitions, dated 1765 and 1768. These were sent from Orange County to Royal Governor William Tryon of North

Carolina: one opposed taxes and the other the discharging of magistrates.[3]

Sellars was known as a "Regulator," a label that gained distinction in Piedmont North Carolina at the Battle of Alamance (May 16, 1771), when a small, nondescript "army" of farmers and backwoodsmen fought and were defeated by Governor Tryon's Loyalist forces, which were recruited from eastern North Carolina.[4]

Thomas Sellars, Sr., married sometime before 1782, but his wife's name is obscure. Some think she was a Nellie Holt because this name was found in an old family Bible belonging to Thomas Sellars, Jr. The birth date of Nellie is given as February 18, 1756, which would be about right for the wife of Thomas, Sr.[5]

Thomas, Sr., and his wife had two sons: Thomas, Jr. (1782–1865); and Willis (1788–1843), who apparently was named after his father's immigrant brother. It is also believed that Thomas, Sr., had two daughters: Eliza, who married John Harden, and Polly, who wed Martin Loy.[6]

On August 20, 1783, Thomas Sellars, Sr., received from the state of North Carolina 10 pounds and 2 shillings, plus 1 shilling and 2 pence in interest, presumably for military service rendered in the Revolutionary War. He apparently used this money to acquire land from the state. In August 1785 he bought 400 acres of land on the south side of the Haw River in Orange County in what is now the Hopedale community in Alamance County.[7]

According to tradition, Thomas, Sr., was married before the Revolutionary War; was captured at some point during the conflict in the South and held prisoner in Charleston, S.C., until the close of the war; and his wife, not hearing from him for a long time, believed him to be dead until he walked into their home after the end of the war.[8]

Thomas Sellars, Jr., the great-grandfather of B. Everett Jordan, married Nancy Rainey (1795–1881) on December 31, 1812 or 1813 (both dates are recorded in family records). Nancy Rainey Sellars was the daughter of Benjamin Rainey (1758–1811) and his wife, Nancy Sullinger Rainey (1758–1826).[9] Benjamin's will, dated April 17, 1811, reveals that he was a wealthy and prominent planter and slave owner[10] in Orange County, N.C., and also in Tennessee, where his property was located "on the waters of Tronbull Creek."[11]

Thomas Sellars, Jr., and Nancy Rainey Sellars had eleven children, ten of whom lived to adulthood.[12] The third child, a son (born 1816) named Benjamin Abel Sellars,[13] was B. Everett Jordan's grandfather.

Benjamin Abel Sellars, or "B. A.," was educated at the University of Pennsylvania, where he graduated from medical school with honors in 1844. In the summer of 1850, the country doctor married Miss Frusannah Elizabeth Kime. On his wedding day, Dr. Sellars, lacking a few months, was twice the age of his bride, who had not quite turned seventeen.[14]

He was the typical rural "horse and buggy doctor," serving patients within traveling distance of his home on the northeastern edge of Randolph County. Their early home was still standing in 1987 on S.R. 2417 between Kimesville and Liberty. The house was just barely inside Randolph County and sat on a knoll a short distance off the right side of the road as one approached from Kimesville. Sometime later, the B. A. Sellars family moved to Alamance County at a site on the Haw River near Hopedale, which was also the home place of Dr. Sellars's father, Thomas Sellars, Jr.[15]

Dr. Sellars's eleven children rode on a horse-drawn wagon to school at Company Shops, now the town of Burlington. On the back of the wagon a "tongue" projected—a sturdy, wooden, squared-off timber—that the seven Sellars boys clung to as they bounced and lurched over the rutted dirt roads. The four girls were more properly and safely seated inside the swaying wagon. All the children attended the Union School, which was located on Union Avenue in Burlington. The structure—now long gone—at one time served a dual purpose: as a non-denominational sanctuary on Sunday and as school classrooms on weekdays.[16]

Dr. Sellars, like Reverend Henry Harrison Jordan, believed in education and sent most of his children to college. Three of his daughters, including Everett Jordan's mother, Anne ("Annie") Elizabeth Sellars, attended Greensborough Female College, later the Methodist-affiliated Greensboro College. Her older sister, Eliza Sellars White, the mother of Mary White, who became North Carolina Governor W. Kerr Scott's wife, was already enrolled at Greensborough Female College when Annie started as a freshman in 1880. She attended from 1880 to 1883, and came home a year before her

Frusannah Kime Sellars and her husband, Dr. Benjamin Abel (B. A.) Sellars, Everett Jordan's maternal grandparents. (*Dorothy Sellars Brawley*)

class graduated to help care for her mother, who was in poor health.[17]

During Annie's three years at Greensborough Female College, or "GFC" as she referred to it in her letters, she corresponded regularly with her parents and other family members, particularly her sister Eliza. These letters reveal much about the life of a young college girl in the latter part of the nineteenth century—a simple way of living in sharp contrast to the fast pace of the following century.[18]

Yet, many of the topics Annie discussed in her letters were almost exactly like those covered by her twentieth-century counter-

Everett Jordan's maternal grandmother and her eleven children. *Top row, left to right*: Mary Sellars Walker, Frusannah Elizabeth Kime (Mrs. B. A.) Sellars, Benjamin Rainey Sellars; *middle row*: Thomas Leonidas Sellars, Eliza Sellars White, Annie Sellars Jordan, David Ernest Sellers; *bottom row*: Charles Victor Sellers, Flora Sellars Brooks, Fred W. Sellers, John E. Sellars, Walter Raleigh Sellars. (*Dorothy Sellars Brawley*)

parts: courses and grades; plans upon returning home during school vacations; school "epidemics"; and, though the costs differed greatly between the centuries, *clothes*.

This last subject was the major emphasis in Annie's letters. She discussed the latest styles as well as the clothes she was wearing and planned to wear, and she prodded her mother to complete the sewing of various outfits and send them to her. Although the spinning of yarn to provide fabric for clothes was, of course, destined to preoccupy the mind and energy of her first-born son, Everett, the young Greensborough Female College student could not then have realized that clothes and textiles would be so vital to her future offspring.

Another likely similarity in the letters of both nineteenth- and twentieth-century women students is the emphasis given to boy-girl relations (at least those aspects they wish to discuss with their parents). Annie recounted a couple of episodes:

> There is three or four girls up here that do not get out of one trouble before they get into another.
>
> There was three or four drinking boys up here all yesterday eve. They called for three of about the fastest girls in college, Alice Garret, Lina Mallory and Judie Steel. Dr. Jones would not let them go down so they took it upon themselves to go on the third floor and talk out of the window to them and Dr. Jones slipped up there on tip toe and caught them nicely, and if he and Mrs. Jones dident give it to them I'll give up. They promised they would not do it anymore, but that night a crowd of boys from downtown brought the Italian band from Raleigh up serenading and the very same girls fixt up a bouquet put their names on it and threw it out of the window to them and after the band had gone Dr. Jones said he thought he heard talking out there and went and found a crowd of boys, ask them what they were doing and their reply was that "They were picking up bouquets, notes and so on that ladies threw down there," and oh how mad Dr. Jones was. He had to give them another lecture Friday night... Well just one week from tonight and the grand calisthenic entertainment comes off. We heard the boys down the street called it the leg show. I am certainly glad I am not in it. I think I will enjoy looking on much better.[19]

Annie's letters also reveal that her mother, Frusannah, was not the only frugal member of the Sellars family.[20] As the young student once said after she had been away from home for several months: "I haven't spent but ten cts. and that was for apples."[21]

Annie was a hard-working student—a scholarly trait she failed to bestow on her first son, Everett. As his nephew was to say in a 1986 interview: "We used to laugh about how fast he [Everett] had gone through Duke University. He learned everything he needed to know in a year!"[22]

Annie also demonstrated obedience to parental authority when she wrote her mother for permission to come home to attend a conference—presumably a church conference—and at the same time agreed to abide by her mother's wishes. Later, as a mother herself, she expected and received a similar response from her own

Frusannah Kime Sellars, Everett Jordan's grandmother, spins yarn on her eighty-fourth birthday. (*Dorothy Sellars Brawley*)

six children. This was to be humorously revealed by a story later related by Reverend Mike Jordan, her grandson. In her day, instead of the modern practice for parishioners to provide an occasional meal for the pastor, frequently the procedure was reversed. In anticipation of this situation, Annie, who was married to Reverend H. H. Jordan, always tried to have enough food on hand for any unexpected guests as well as for her own family. However, the supply was low one Sunday, when some visitors arrived to eat dinner with them:

> Grandma didn't have enough food so she took all six of the children back in the kitchen—that was Everett, Henry, Lucy, Charlie, Margaret, and Frank—and said, "Now listen here; there's not enough food to go around, and when that chicken passes in front of you, you just politely say, 'no thank you, I don't believe I care for any,' and pass it on, and if you don't you know what you'll get." Well, everyone knew what they would get, so as hard as it was for those

young'uns when that platter passed, they would not take any and they'd pass it on. Each of them thinking they would get their reward when dessert time came along and they would be able to make up for the chicken they didn't get to eat by having [more] dessert. What they didn't know, grandma didn't have enough dessert either, and at the end of the meal she stood up and looked at them—and probably kind of glared at them around the table so none of them would say anything—she said, "All right, all of you who wouldn't eat any of my chicken can't have any dessert!"[23]

Like her son Everett, Annie, as a college student, showed consideration for those on a lower social stratum. In one of her letters, she sent greetings to two of the family's servants, who apparently were black.[24]

Serious student though she was, Annie engaged in her share of minor pranks. On one occasion, her grade was lowered because she made funny faces in class.[25] As some people would later say, when four-year-old Everett made faces from his father's pulpit: "He got it natural!"—from his mother, to be sure.

No one then could have predicted that this lively schoolgirl would grow up to be the mother of a United States senator and benefactor of her alma mater. But in 1986 Greensboro College named its theatre, what had once been a dining hall and later the recreation hall on the first floor of the main building, the "Annie Sellars Jordan Parlor Theatre." Shortly before his death, Everett Jordan, in honor of his mother, made gifts to the school totaling more than $18,000 for the new theatre facilities, making them much more suited for their present role.[26]

Annie Elizabeth Sellars (1862–1937), like her husband, Henry Harrison Jordan (1862–1931), was nearing her twenty-ninth birthday on her wedding day in the late winter of 1891. The ceremony was held on February 17 at the Christian Church in Burlington, N.C., Annie's hometown, which her father had helped re-name from Company Shops by serving on the committee that made the decision. Annie had once vowed, "I will never marry a preacher—definitely not a *Methodist* preacher!"[27] Her husband was a lawyer on

Home of Benjamin Abel and Frusannah Kime Sellars at the corner of Church and Front streets, Burlington, N.C., sometime before 1900. Everett Jordan accompanied his mother and father here when they visited his maternal grandparents. (*Dorothy Sellars Brawley*)

her wedding day, but before the year was out he would become, of all things, a circuit-riding Methodist preacher.

Both the newlyweds had been born in 1862 while muskets were blazing and cannons roaring as the Civil War raged. It did not end until three years later—after the lives of many of the finest men on both sides had been extinguished.

The South, which served as the battlefield, in defeat was left devastated and groveling under the heels of the so-called Reconstruction government. For those south of the Mason-Dixon line, President Abraham Lincoln represented their principal hope for compassion—but John Wilkes Booth assassinated both of them. In the postwar years, the South found few sympathizers in the North.

Annie's circumstances while growing up in Alamance County were not as austere as her husband's were on the Iredell County farm. Her father, Dr. B. A. Sellars, had become relatively prosperous from his medical earnings and also as a merchant. In 1849 he witnessed Alamance County's partition from Orange County; Graham replaced Hillsborough as the county seat for the newly formed Alamance. In 1871 Dr. Sellars established a drug and dry goods store in a two-story frame building on Front Street in Burlington, which was later occupied by Pollard's Insurance Company. Sellars also continued his medical practice.[28]

As adults, three of Dr. Sellars's sons decided to change the spelling of their name. As his granddaughter Dorothy Sellars Brawley explained: "Mother told me that uncle Charlie, uncle Fred and uncle Ernest decided to change it [Sellars] to Sellers because it was easier to write an 'e' than it was an 'a.' In looking through some of the old family records, there were a few 'e's, but more 'a's. There was even one that came over from Germany and they spelled it Sellozs or something—a German spelling."[29]

The Sellars business was known as "B. A. Sellars and Sons," as various sons joined Dr. Sellars in the store's operation. The original store housed general merchandise in a large central room. Smaller rooms were located on either side, one containing a drug store and prescription room and the other serving as a storage room for horse and cow feed. Near the turn of the century, Dr. Sellars's oldest son, Benjamin Rainey Sellars (1855–1916), moved the store to Main Street. Two other brothers, Thomas L. (1857–1940) and Walter R. Sellars (1873–1954), entered the business upon their return from school and remained active until well into the 1900s.[30]

Originally, the Main Street building occupied half of the depth of the block. The open lot fronting onto Spring Street was a tethering place for customers' horses and buggies. The building was expanded and re-modeled in the 1930s and greatly enlarged and renovated in 1977.[31]

The store became an Alamance County landmark and an anchor for Burlington's downtown shopping center. It also made a meaningful contribution to the sons and daughters of its founder. Sometime after 1986, the store moved to a new location on South Church Street.[32]

Everett Jordan's first cousin Dorothy Sellars Brawley, like other relatives the author of this volume interviewed, was refreshingly candid in her comments about family members: "I am told that grandmother [Frusannah Sellars] never threw string away, and she had a big ball of string." And about Charlie Sellers, Everett's benefactor: "And after uncle Charlie Sellers married Annie Morrow, I remember—things stand out in a child's mind—I remember that they would go on these trips while they were in the mountains [at Montreat, N.C.], and Annie Morrow always wanted peaches and grapes. Uncle Charlie would say, 'Don't need them.' And that would finish that. Occasionally he would break over and buy a basket of peaches or grapes but that was so seldom... he did *not* throw money away."[33]

After Charlie Sellers and Annie Morrow were married, they lived with Charlie's mother, Frusannah. Frusannah considered Annie's daily baths to be wasteful of water and soap. Her critical comment was: "I hope I don't ever get that dirty!"[34]

The B. A. Sellars family has another notable and persistent trait: honesty. In 1981 this was affirmed by Reid A. Maynard, longtime business and civic leader in Burlington and Alamance County and also a yarn customer and old friend of Everett Jordan: "As for Everett, there wasn't a more likable guy in the world than he was. All you had to do was to know him. He was honorable and honest in everything. He might not tell you all he knew, but whatever he told you was just like his uncles, old man Charlie and Ernest and Mr. Walter. I'd just as soon have their word for anything as to have their signature. Those Sellarses would not lie to you. I never knew one that would. You could just count on them, and Everett was the same way. He didn't care much about signing his name but he would tell you he would do something and he would do it. You didn't have to worry about that."[35]

In textile parlance, oftentimes more than one name applies to the same item or object. For example, yarn salesmen are referred to by some people, usually by old-timers, as string peddlers. Woven fabrics have yarns or threads going lengthwise and crosswise, and are referred to as the "warp and filling," or "warp and weft," and also as "warp and woof" (favored by the British).

As one examines Everett Jordan's "life fabric," two distinct family threads can be seen in the warp and weft. Characteristics of both Henry Harrison Jordan and Annie Elizabeth Sellars are easily distinguishable; and, as in any fabric, each thread contributes an equal share to the strength and quality of the finished product. If Frusannah Sellars, the frugal preserver of string and bath water, could have seen the finished fabric in the life of her grandson Everett, she would have been more than pleased with the Sellars strings she saw in the warp and weft.

4

"You Will Never Make a Mill Man!"

"Everett is headed for hell—right straight!"[1] In the mind of the Reverend H. H. Jordan, his oldest son—then under the tutelage of his uncle Fred Sellers—was well on his way to that most dreaded destination of sinners. Fred, a Wellington, Kans., jewelry store owner, did not even attend church on Sunday; he fished and hunted. He would, moreover, rather tell raucous stories any day than listen to a pious sermon. "No, that wild west Kansas was no place for his son"[2]—of that fact, the Methodist preacher had no doubt.

In 1921 twenty-five-year-old Everett Jordan liked his uncle Fred and his carefree style of living, and he reveled in this distant place where he was free from the rigid scrutiny of his father in Gastonia, N.C. There, Reverend Jordan, the former pastor of the Main Street Methodist Church, was now the presiding elder for the district. This was Everett's second stint of living in the home of his uncle Fred and aunt "Lula" (Louisa) Sellers and working as a clerk in his uncle's jewelry store. He liked selling watches and rings as well as fitting eyeglasses, and he thought his uncle Fred could tell "the funniest stories."[3]

In later life, Everett Jordan had a vast reservoir of stories that had originated with his uncle. On the appropriate occasion, he often selected one of them to illustrate a point. His audience might be a yarn customer, his mill or office staff, or close friends he was entertaining. Also, in Washington in the presence of other congressmen, he told his homespun stories, well flavored with uncle Fred's "wild West" and Saxapahaw's cotton-mill world.[4]

Katherine Jordan recalled this story, which she heard her husband tell many times: "Uncle Fred tells about the old maid that had not been well a'tall and someone said, 'Sally, you should try beer.

That will increase your appetite and be good for you. It's good medicine.' So several weeks after that uncle Fred saw Sally and asked her how she got along with the beer and Sally said, 'You know, I've taken a tablespoonful every day, and I can't see a bit of change!' "[5] For thirty years, Everett Jordan taught an adult Sunday school class at the Saxapahaw Methodist Church, and this is the kind of story he might have used to illustrate a lesson on moderation or temperance.

The first time Jordan clerked in his uncle's jewelry store was after attending Trinity College (now Duke University) in 1914–15, but he did so poorly that he dropped out. The fact is that he was not a scholar then or ever. As a youngster, he was intrigued by doing things with his hands, making furniture, building a so-called car, and tackling whatever handyman project that came along. Books were not his forte—a disappointment to his father, who read and treasured them as long as he lived and encouraged his family, fellow preachers, and everyone else to do likewise. But the preacher's earnest exhortations fell on the deaf ears of his eldest son, a pragmatist, always too busy doing something else to take time to read and reflect.[6]

In 1921 Everett made his second sojourn in the "wild West." His first stay had begun in 1915 and lasted until 1918. This came about when his formal schooling had ended after one brief year in college; and, at the invitation of Fred Sellers, his uncle, Everett headed west to Wellington, Kans., nearly halfway across the continent. There, amid the jewelry and eyeglasses, he cajoled would-be customers to buy (when the impatient Sellers himself had failed to make a sale) and forgot all about behaving like a preacher's son. This casual Midwestern life-style appealed to Jordan, who had long chafed under the disciplinarian—"look proper"—mode in which he had grown up. Reverend H. H. Jordan thought differently: "They were heathen Westerners—didn't even go to church."[7]

On the Sabbath, Fred Sellers did not have to worry about piety or parishioner perception: He and his nephew might go hunting or fishing or simply listen to tall tales told by their fellow townsmen as they lounged about in their favorite gathering places—and that was not in church pews. Lula Sellers, though, was a devout member of the Wellington Congregational Church, which she attended regularly with her daughter, Marie.[8]

"You Will Never Make a Mill Man!" 83

A 1982 view of the building (*left center*) in Wellington, Kans., where Fred Sellers and his nephew Everett Jordan sold jewelry and fitted eyeglasses. (Photo by author)

The Wellington, Kans., that Everett Jordan knew was a country town, then as now, in the flatlands of the Wheat Belt. Endless miles of grain land stretch out in every direction. Wellington, founded in 1871, lies almost due south of Wichita and is not more than a half-hour's drive from the Oklahoma border. The Chisholm Trail, over which more than 3 million cattle moved north to Abilene on their way to the Chicago and New York markets, originally ran just a few miles west of the town site.[9] The wide-open country bespeaks of freedom and independence.

One of the eight founders of Wellington was A. A. Jordan, but no close kinship, if any, is known to exist with the Reverend H. H. Jordan clan in North Carolina. A. A. Jordan may have been involved in the ploy whereby Wellington was chosen as county seat over its competitor, Sumner City, which was on the Chisholm Trail: A furrow was cut in the trail routing it through Wellington.[10] Thus, if Everett was not a blood relation of A. A., he certainly had a kinship in spirit, for the former was also proficient in the use of ploys. He learned the following one from his tutor, Fred Sellers, as later recalled by Everett's first cousin, Dorothy Sellars Brawley. If he had known, the Reverend H. H. Jordan would have been aghast:

Everett and uncle Fred both told about Everett's method of fitting glasses and, with each telling, the two roared with laughter. When the customer came into the store, Everett would stand behind the counter that held the glasses. He would turn his head, lick his finger, and smear the lens before putting the glasses on the customer. "How are these?" "Well, not so good." Everett would select another pair, same lens, but smear it less this time and ask, "How about these? They cost more but they are stronger." "Well, they're better, but still kind of blurred." Everett said, "O.K., I can take care of that. Try these. They're stronger and cost a little more, but you get what you pay for." This time he again handed the customer identical glasses, but less smeared. After about the third "stronger" and more costly selection—the one with no smear—the customer would say, "Oh, these are fine. I'll take them!" The "taken" customer left thinking: "My, that young fellow sure knows how to fit glasses!"[11]

Whether he knew it or not, Everett Jordan's first arrival in Wellington, in 1915, was an event—at least for the younger set. A newcomer in a small town always evokes a certain amount of curiosity—if not excitement—for the opposite sex. In 1916 Jessie Wiley (later Voils) was a lovely girl in her late teens. She had come from her hometown in Hunnewell up to Wellington to attend high school. Immediately, she and Marie Sellers became good friends and participated in the limited social life of the city, which centered around the activities of the Congregational Church, where Lula Sellers was a prime mover.[12]

In 1982 Jessie Wiley Voils recalled her memories of Jordan: "I think we were...a little disappointed. He wasn't what I'd call a handsome boy, but he was vivacious—you've heard the expression 'cutting a swath'? And I would say he was very good in that store ...I thought he was an awful smart-aleck...[and] he was kind of a wild boy...I can't say that I was too impressed really, and I don't think he was with me. Now he may say that he was, but I don't really think that he was." According to Jessie, Everett was tall and thin and not particularly good-looking.[13]

In his senior years, Everett Jordan talked enough about Jessie Wiley to convey the notion that she was his Kansas girlfriend. Jessie's most unforgettable encounter with him, which was at Park House, the local recreational center, occurred not long before he left Wellington for military service in World War I. At a party he

Jessie Wiley Voils in 1969. (*Bradley's Redwood Studio*)

jokingly approached her with a sharp butcher knife that was to be used to cut the watermelon for party refreshments and threatened to cut off one of her curls. In warding him off with her arm, the knife severed a major artery in her arm and she passed out. She never heard from him then about the episode, and she did not see him again until many years later.

Although she recovered without any complications, having only a large scar as visible proof, Everett's attitude toward the incident remained an enigma to Jessie: "Good gosh! He didn't even come to see me. I thought that at least Everett could have sent me some flowers or called up to see about me. He didn't do anything of the kind. I never heard from him a'tall. And I was at home because they had to call the doctor."[14]

Jessie's experience was not unique in this respect. Everett's wife, Katherine, and also his daughter, Rose Ann, confirm that he never learned how to say "I'm sorry" in so many words. He might give a conciliatory gift or do something special to make amends for a domestic misunderstanding, but he was never known to express a verbal apology. Rose Ann, for example, vividly recalled her father's

Park House, Wellington, Kans., in 1982; in B. Everett Jordan's day, it was a social center. (Photo by author)

taking the family to Gastonia to compensate for some behavior of his that had been upsetting to her mother: "Daddy knew mama loved to go to Gastonia and visit my grandfather, and it was his way of making atonement, but he would not apologize."[15] No one in or outside the family could recall ever hearing Everett Jordan say, "I made a mistake, I'm sorry." But he was known to change course and attempt to make amends.[16]

Everett Jordan was grown up and conceivably still unaware of his future and its direction as he approached his twenty-second birthday and prepared to leave for basic military training. He left the States on his way to France as World War I wound down in 1918 and the armistice was signed on November 11. The impatient youth had not chosen or embarked on any set course or formed any known goals for his future, but for the next year or so the U.S. Army would direct his comings and goings.

When he learned that he was being drafted, Everett told his father he would like to come home to North Carolina before going into service and asked him to "do something" so that he could make a brief visit. Reverend Jordan promptly notified his eldest son that there was "no legitimate reason" to delay his departure in order to come home, and that he was not about to lie to accomplish the wishes of his son. The youth went into military service on schedule.[17]

Because the November 1918 armistice was officially declared only twenty days after his scheduled sailing to France, the young draftee probably never heard a hostile shot, and his tenure was confined to serving in an army of occupation in the land of a defeated enemy. For this reason, his tour of duty was uneventful; and he never reached a higher rank than private.[18]

Most of his hitch was apparently served in Germany. Because of the long hours of duty, diversions were few to escape the boredom—though he did enjoy a swim in the Rhine River. In the service, as elsewhere in his career, he always believed in self-preservation. His biggest challenge was to improve his daily rations, as he maneuvered both with and against his buddies in that field of battle: surreptitious forays to neighboring farms to supplement their austere army rations.[19]

When Jordan went overseas, he was assigned to Casual Company A, Tank Corps, A.E.F. (American Expeditionary Force). To amuse themselves, the tank crews would startle the farmers as they drove through the countryside by popping their heads up out of the top of the tank just as they passed by.[20] After Jordan returned home, he delighted in recounting these mundane incidents, as he embellished the most everyday happenings with his own zesty humor.[21] Subsequent to his tank service, he and others from that service—their combat skills no longer needed because of the war's end—were reassigned to the 819th M.T.C. (Motor Transport Company), Third Army. There, their experience with tanks was helpful in repairing and operating motor vehicles.

Everett's letters—like those of soldiers in most wars—were filled with griping about army life in general and the food as well as his officers in particular; acknowledgment of receipts of letters and packages and requests for more of them; pleas for and announcements of arrivals of money; descriptions of the country and his army activities; discussion of his plans for the future; cautioning his

Pvt. Everett Jordan, during World War I service. (*Mary Jordan Hintz*)

parents not to worry about him; expressing hope for his safe return and reunion with his loved ones; and demonstrating impatience to return home and resume civilian life. He felt his unit's role in Europe was a waste and chafed as he restlessly bided his time for the day when he would return to the States, rejoin his uncle Fred, and resume the life that had been intruded upon by the war.

As Jordan had done just before he entered the military service, in June 1919 he made another special appeal to his father—this time to do everything possible to get him out of the army. What Everett thought the Reverend H. H. Jordan could do—he may have shared the notion of young people in all generations that parents can do anything—is not known. The U.S. military is a huge and powerful organization, infinitely larger and far less inclined to respond to the minister's exhortations than his Monroe, N.C., flock, recalcitrant though they might have been. The youthful tank driver's impatience with his low status was succinctly summed up with: "I am tired wasting my life and strength over here for nothing!"[22] And that, if anything, ought to stimulate a response from the minister-father who wasted nothing, certainly not his talents and time.

And Everett's peremptory last request is almost a command to his father: "Answer soon!" Everett Jordan was never noted for his patience: He did not theorize, rather he sought action, a trait evident early in his growing-up and persistent throughout his long life. His impatience is vividly demonstrated in two events recounted later in this volume: one in which he first drove a car at the age of nine; and the other on his wedding day, when he made a disruptive outburst during the ceremony.

The exact date of Everett Jordan's return to the States is not known, but, when he did come home, he went back to Wellington, Kans., and his uncle Fred's jewelry store to resume his former job. If left to his own devices, he might never have returned to his native state, but the Reverend H. H. Jordan was well versed in the biblical story of the prodigal son, and he certainly would not fail to seek out his own eventually.[23]

In late 1921 or early 1922, Everett was still employed by his uncle Fred, who was considering making his nephew a full partner and possibly his successor because he had no sons.[24] Inasmuch as Everett had never relished living under the reproachful eye of his father, he was thoroughly enjoying his uncle's permissiveness. Therefore, in 1921–22 the young man felt no compelling need to return home and be once again under his father's jurisdiction.[25]

The Reverend Jordan, increasingly distraught, was convinced that something had to be done to get his son into a better environment: Everett *must* come home. But what could he do to persuade his son to leave that distant, evil place? Reverend Jordan sought help from one of his former parishioners, Joseph H. Separk.[26]

Separk taught the men's Bible class at Main Street Methodist Church, in Gastonia, and was one of its most supportive members. He held his former pastor in high regard as evidenced by the fact that, when Reverend Jordan had completed the normal four-year assignment of Methodist ministers, Separk earnestly requested that he stay on, as recounted earlier. And Separk, the one-time principal of Gastonia's first high school, had influence in Gastonia—and beyond—far greater than that of a Bible-class teacher.[27]

In 1900 Separk had married May Gray, the daughter of George A. Gray (1851–1912), one of Gastonia's most successful pioneer cotton-textile manufacturers. In 1887 Gray was one of the organizers of Gastonia Cotton Manufacturing Company, the town's first cotton mill. He also played a major role in establishing the textile industry in Gaston County and in changing the local economy from an agricultural to a manufacturing base.[28]

The mill had an authorized capital of $150,000 and carried authority to increase it to $500,000, which was done in 1892 and then to $800,000 in 1920. In 1923 the mill's owners were James Lee Love, Cornelia S. Love, and J. Spencer Love. The last of these later moved to Burlington, N.C., and formed Burlington Industries (originally Burlington Mills), considered to be one of the country's largest textile manufacturers.[29]

The construction of the Gastonia Cotton Manufacturing Company plant in 1887 was credited with being the catalyst for the rapid increase in Gastonia's population, for a large number of mills were built soon thereafter. The city became known as a place of employment for struggling farmers in the Piedmont as well as mountain people from western North Carolina, some of whose meager income was boosted by the illegal production and sale of "moonshine" liquor.[30] Although the hours were long and the wages were low, the pay was a vast improvement over what they had had before, and they were grateful merely to have a job. Especially after the Loray Mill strike ended in 1929, the mill owners sent their trucks as far as the westernmost counties in the state recruiting prospective mill workers and then would teach them how to work in the mills.[31]

The hum of spindles was welcome music not only to the ears of Gaston County's farmers, moonshiners, and sawmill laborers, but also to their counterparts throughout Piedmont North Carolina and the entire Southeast, where textile mills were being built everywhere by the turn of the twentieth century. Most of the mills sought locations along falling streams where waterpower could be cheaply produced, but, in the case of Gastonia, the mills chose steam power and access to a railroad.[32]

Gray, his son, J. Lander Gray, and his son-in-law, Joe Separk, were officials in a number of other Gastonia area textile mills. Their names became synonymous with the successful manufacture of cotton textiles, primarily combed yarns, and their companies were referred to as the Gray-Separk Mills. Two of those mills were the Gray Manufacturing Company, organized in 1904, and Myrtle Mill, Inc., organized in 1918. Separk usually held the office of secretary-treasurer and Gray that of president.[33]

When Reverend Jordan approached Separk, the latter listened attentively to his former pastor's anguished plea for help. And, yes, Separk thought he could do something. He promised to give Everett a job in one of his mills, if he would come to Gastonia. Reverend Jordan wasted no time in communicating this job offer to his eldest son in Kansas.[34]

Besides Separk's influence, the Reverend H. H. Jordan had another weighty factor on his side as he awaited his son's reply. He lived in a time when the husband and father was the undisputed head of the house and, as such, he commanded respect and obedience. Too, it was biblical—"Children, obey your parents in all things: for this is well pleasing unto the Lord,"[35]—and, especially to this father, obedience was the epitome of Methodism.[36]

Every rule and precept preached and practiced by the preacher-father may not have been fully absorbed by the independent-thinking eldest son, but he was not totally impervious. Too, by then he was older and more mature. So, for whatever reason, Everett Jordan acquiesced. Separk kept his promise and gave Everett his first mill job, as floor-sweeper at Myrtle Mill, Inc., in Gastonia.[37]

Separk called Everett an "engineer" so he could be promoted more rapidly; and it is doubtful that he actually swept mill floors more than a few days—a week or so at the most.[38] But, as the years

The Gray Mill, Gastonia, N.C., viewed from the south, in the 1980s. This was the second mill Everett Jordan ever worked in, and he was superintendent before he left. (Photo by author)

passed and Jordan recounted his textile experiences, he was quick to point out that he had started out as a sweeper, the least-skilled job in a cotton mill—and the lowest paid.[39]

After these humble beginnings, Separk gave his new ward every possible advantage; and, in time, Everett became mill superintendent, first at the Myrtle Mill and next at the Gray Manufacturing Company. During his five to six years in these mills, Jordan, the apprentice, had ample opportunity to observe and study the dynamics of a cotton mill, to learn the ways and thinking of mill hands, and how best to handle difficult employees. He also had a chance to work with both labor and management and to become intimately acquainted with the factors involved in running a mill.[40]

In the 1920s Gastonia was the ideal place to be for people who wanted to gain experience in the textile industry because the Gaston County town was fast becoming the recognized leader in the manufacture of fine-combed yarns, the product that Everett Jordan would make in Saxapahaw. Throughout his life, he frequently referred to his mill work in Gastonia, its people, and the lessons he learned there in the Myrtle and Gray mills—particularly in the Gray Mill, where he was superintendent at the time he left for Saxapahaw in 1927.[41]

Many of the employees who worked at Gastonia later followed their former co-worker and supervisor to Saxapahaw. These, in turn, influenced their friends and other family members to come work in Everett Jordan's mills. Jordan's understanding of and empathy with the mill workers would serve him well, not only in the Myrtle and Gray mills, but for his entire life, whether it was in a textile setting or in the United States Senate. This trait was his forte: he understood people—people who *did* things, and those who worked for a living with their hands merited a special, respectful niche in his thinking. Gastonia, however, offered Everett Jordan more than just a job and training. There he met the one person who would wield more influence on his adult life than anyone else. This auspicious event occurred shortly after his arrival in Gastonia from Kansas.[42]

A young bookkeeper named Homer Culbreath was employed in the Gray-Separk office. He was engaged to Mary McLean; and, having met and been impressed by Everett, he asked him to be one of his groomsmen for his wedding in November 1922. Mary had asked her cousin Katherine Augusta McLean, the daughter of Robert and Rose May McLean, to be a bridesmaid. Katherine was a pretty, twenty-four-year-old Gastonia schoolteacher who was very popular with both her male and female peers.[43]

Following is Katherine McLean Jordan's later account of her first meeting and ensuing date with the man whom she would marry almost exactly two years later:

> ... after that wedding rehearsal, I'd had a few dates with Chuck Adams, who was one of the superintendents of the Gray-Separk chain of mills; and he and I were good friends, and we made a date after the rehearsal. After the wedding the next night, Everett asked Chuck if he could have a date with me. I suppose Chuck wasn't particularly interested in me anyway, so he said, "Sure." He was a good friend of Everett's. So that was really the first date I ever had with Everett. That was November, and for Christmas he sent me—I don't know if it was a dozen or two dozen beautiful red roses. He would remember Christmases, but as for birthdays—for many years I would have

my feelings hurt because he did not remember—I'd have to say, "Well, this is my birthday!" But he was not one of these people that was always bringing presents.[44]

More dates followed, but Everett quickly learned that he had more serious competition than just his accommodating friend Chuck Adams. One of Katherine's suitors was a young Gastonia doctor named Bahnson Weathers. When Everett came to court Katherine at her home on New Hope Road, he found that Dr. Weathers was the "top contender," being rated first by both Katherine and her mother.[45]

"Dr. Weathers was also very thoughtful," Katherine remembered, "and would bring me candy. Everett would laugh and say, 'I'm so glad "Doc" gave you this box of [good] candy. You tell him to give you some more!' But I learned, after a number of years, not to have my feelings hurt because of his thoughtless disposition. I would tell him what I wanted, and he would say, 'Well, you get it—that'll be fine.'"[46]

Katherine added; "Now he was very fond of jewelry: I don't know whether he acquired a taste for it working in his uncle Fred's jewelry store or not, but he loved jewelry; and if I had shown any interest in [it] he would have just *lavished* [it] on me... He felt like he was the one that knew about jewelry but as far as candy and flowers—he didn't think about it. If I would say, 'Everett, I want some candy,' well, he would go get the biggest box you've ever seen and was just tickled to death to do it, but it was just not his initial thought."[47]

Everett Jordan had many compensating traits even if he frequently seemed lacking in the social graces—or perhaps he only appeared insensitive in this area. Young Katherine McLean was impressed with his strong qualities. As she later put it: "Everett was a go-getter. He and Dr. Weathers were entirely different. If Dr. Weathers had been as aggressive, I probably would have married *him* because he was just the sweetest kind of person."[48]

Continuing, the woman who was Everett Jordan's loving wife for fifty years made a telling and significant statement: "Everett thought he could do anything, and *I'm* sure he could!" Katherine Jordan always had absolute faith in his ability.[49] She was fittingly described in her funeral eulogy as a "balcony person"—one who happily

"You Will Never Make a Mill Man!" 95

Katherine McLean Jordan (1898–1987), wife of Everett Jordan. (*Jordan family albums*)

cheered and faithfully encouraged the man whom she truly believed could do anything.⁵⁰

Although Mrs. McLean preferred Dr. Weathers, Everett made a big hit with Katherine's father. When Everett came to see Robert McLean's favorite daughter, whom he fondly called "Kitten," Mr. McLean would come and sit in the parlor and talk to his future son-in-law. Usually they discussed business affairs; and the pretty daughter, ignored, would doze until her father left the room.⁵¹

Their wedding date was November 29, 1924, a red-letter day for B. Everett Jordan. He was twenty-eight and his bride was twenty-six. On this joyous occasion, the First Presbyterian Church of Gastonia, where the McLeans were members and Katherine taught a children's Sunday school class, was completely filled. Many of the town's most prominent citizens, including Joe Separk, were present. Among Katherine's neighbors in attendance were a young mother, Connie Baber Williams, and her only son, Jim Baber Williams, a family that would become and remain lifelong friends of the Everett Jordans.[52]

Dr. J. H. Hinderlite, the Presbyterian pastor, and the Reverend Henry H. Jordan, the groom's father, officiated. It was quite an affair; everyone was dressed in their finest. The wedding liturgy proceeded flawlessly, but, near the end, Reverend Jordan paused briefly. To his consternation, he heard his son say in a loud whisper that could be heard by the entire congregation: "You through?" This unexpected interruption brought a wave of suppressed titters from the amused assemblage. Reverend Jordan's aplomb was no doubt somewhat shaken by his son's rash outburst. But Everett remained nonchalant and eager for the ceremony to end, for he had wasted enough time while he was standing around with the army of occupation in Germany.[53]

From this day forward, although Katherine McLean Jordan always modestly disclaimed it, she exerted more direct influence on B. Everett Jordan than anyone else. The two worked together as an inseparable team, each giving unstinting loyalty to the other. Although he did not necessarily involve her in his decision-making on mill problems, political issues, or any other responsibility he shouldered, probably far more than even he himself realized, his reasoning and actions were tempered—and oftentimes determined—by an awareness of his wife's preferences and beliefs.[54]

Joseph M. Neel, one of Everett Jordan's most trusted employees and a friend and confidant, once remarked to his superior: "Mr. Jordan, you get a lot of your information from the bedroom, don't you?" The sly reference to Katherine Jordan's contribution to her husband's work and career was so obviously on target that Jordan smiled and indicated that his partner was indeed very knowledgeable and helpful.[55]

Following Katherine Jordan's death on August 15, 1987, the board of directors of the Sellers Manufacturing Company adopted a me-

"You Will Never Make a Mill Man!" 97

Everett Jordan at about twenty-four years of age. (*Jordan family albums*)

morial resolution in honor of the widow of its founder. The resolution read, in part:

> ...her family, friends and the community at large suffered an incalculable loss [but] no one could have realized her inestimable value any more than her husband, whom she adored.
>
> The achievements of Sellers Manufacturing Company's founder, B. Everett Jordan, were many and impressive, but his greatest feat was not made in industry or in government. His paramount success was achieved when he wooed and won Katherine Augusta McLean to be his wife on November 29, 1924. We cannot measure her worth in dollars or with any other material yardstick. Yet, she contributed more to her husband's [total] success than anyone else.
>
> Katherine Jordan was the epitome of the supportive wife. She did not shirk—[instead] she sought out every opportunity to promote

Katherine and Everett Jordan on 1955 trip to Egypt. (*Jordan family albums*)

Everett Jordan in all areas of his life and activities. Always she stood at his side and where Everett went, Katherine went. In Katherine Jordan, Biblical Ruth had her peer.[56]

These qualities were recognized by most of those people who knew Katherine Jordan. For example, former North Carolina Congressman Richardson Preyer said in 1981: "[She] was one of the most beloved people in Washington...loved for her graciousness, her charm, and her compassion. She was an enormous asset to the senator. I don't know if she had any influence on him concerning legislation or not, but I think her part on the whole image of the senator as an honorable and decent man...made a tremendous contribution. I don't know any wife in Washington that was any more highly regarded than Mrs. Jordan. I would think that she and Lady Bird Johnson would rank in the top."[57]

Edward Gruber, a business associate of Everett Jordan, praised Katherine for her "work on behalf of the church and the people of Saxapahaw...[especially] the mill hands...[and] the sick." Continuing, Gruber stated: "[She] was a great partner; she contributed to

"You Will Never Make a Mill Man!" 99

Everett Jordan (*seated second from left*) and Katherine Jordan (*seated far right*) pose in Japan during their trip to the Far East in 1957, the year before he was appointed to the U.S. Senate. (*Jordan family scrapbooks*)

many of Everett's attributes... I think that the two of them worked this way all of their life... there wasn't any semblance of phoniness that you could attribute to either Katherine or Everett in their relationship with the... mill hands."[58]

Before Everett Jordan came to Gastonia, he had earned only modest wages clerking for his uncle Fred Sellers. By 1927, although he had become a mill superintendent, his income had not permitted him to do much more than to barely support his wife and one-year-old son, Benjamin Everett Jordan, Jr., born on July 18, 1926. The young couple did own a few household furnishings and a well-used, secondhand T-Model Ford.[59]

Even though Jordan was not earning a lot of money, he relished his responsible position as mill superintendent. He had excellent rapport with the mill hands, and they appreciated his willingness

Benjamin ("Ben") E. Jordan, Jr., Everett and Katherine Jordan's first son, at about the age of thirty. (*Jordan family albums*)

to come to them for advice and information about the daily, inner workings of the mill. Regardless of his supervisory position, he always seemed to be one of them because he quickly learned to speak their shop-floor language. If a machine did not perform as it should, he was always on the scene, inquiring, observing, and learning.[60]

Basically, he was ever an optimist. When most men complain, their wives are the first to be burdened. According to Katherine Jordan, her husband was never a complainer; not once could she recall his bemoaning a setback or expressing any doubt that he would accomplish any task or achieve his objectives. He had no time for such foolish luxury—he was too busy doing what had to be done. She said, "I never knew him to be pessimistic. If he was, I couldn't tell it. I certainly think his optimism went all the way through his life."[61]

Rose Ann Jordan Gant, Everett and Katherine Jordan's only daughter, at about the age of thirty-one. (*Jordan family albums*)

Nevertheless, Everett Jordan knew that he had not yet "arrived" in 1927 even if he did bear the title of superintendent, was the father of a healthy namesake, and enjoyed the steadfast support of an admiring wife and constant companion. He had, to all appearances, settled down; now his minister-father must have felt that finally his "problem son" was on the right road. At this juncture, another uncle, Charlie Sellers, abruptly intervened.[62] This unexpected intervention would shape and direct the remainder of B. Everett Jordan's life. And just who was uncle Charlie, other than being one of his mother's six brothers?

None of the eleven children of Benjamin Abel and Frusannah Sellars was known to be extravagant or wasteful—certainly not Charlie, who cut his own hair, carefully saved his money, and invested it discreetly. He was best known for his C. V. Sellers Art Store, in

John McLean Jordan, Everett and Katherine Jordan's younger son, at about the age of twenty-five. (*Jordan family albums*)

Burlington, where he developed photographs and sold such items as picture frames, shotgun shells, guns, wallpaper, and sporting goods.[63]

In a 1981 interview for this volume, Reid A. Maynard, a business and civic leader in Burlington and Alamance County who knew all the Sellers/Sellars in Burlington, described Charlie in this way: "Uncle Charlie Sellers was a great guy...you know he bought that mill down there and gave it to Everett to run...Old man Charlie liked Everett; he was his favorite nephew. Charlie Sellers was supposed to be a very wealthy man at that time, had a hundred or two hundred thousand dollars around here in the banks...he bought that Saxapahaw plant and mill village and gave it to Everett to get him down here."[64]

Even so, Charlie was known to be extremely frugal.[65] For example, one fall or early winter day four-year-old Rose Ann, the only

"You Will Never Make a Mill Man!" 103

Roger Gant, Jr., husband of Rose Ann
Jordan Gant. (*Rose Ann Jordan Gant*)

daughter of Everett and Katherine Jordan, decided to walk home from Burlington, where she had been visiting her grandmother Mrs. H. H. Jordan, to Saxapahaw—a distance of fifteen miles. As Paul Morrow, Jr., a nephew of Charlie Sellers, later recollected: "Katherine was all upset, and old Mrs. Jordan, she called down—old man Sellers never did have a telephone in his store, so if you wanted to call him you had to call Foster Shoe Store, which was below him on the first floor, and they would holler up the stairs—so Mrs. Jordan called for them to get Charlie to the phone. She said, 'Charlie, you go find Rose Ann!'" The frantic searchers found the four-year-old girl at the edge of Graham, a good two-mile trek, and right on course.[66] Business needs—forget personal convenience—could not induce Charlie Sellers to squander his money on a telephone.

Paul Morrow did not fully know the source of Charlie Sellers's wealth, but did say: "He must have just *saved* it because he didn't *spend* any money at all. He wore his shoes—you could see his

Ellen McMasters Jordan, wife of Ben E. Jordan, Jr. (*Ben E. Jordan, Jr.*)

Margaret Carter Jordan, wife of John M. Jordan. (*Jordan family albums*)

socks through the toes. He'd have a pair for Sundays and one for everyday. When they just got so he could not wear them any more, he'd buy a new pair. He'd wear them for years and years... Changed the 'a' in Sellars to 'e,' said it didn't take as much ink to write 'e' as it did to write an 'a' and he was real serious about that, too. He believed in saving everything. He wouldn't throw a thing away. That shop looked just like a junk shop all over."[67]

Charlie Sellers married Annie Morrow, part owner of Morrow and Bason, a Burlington ladies millinery store, on July 31, 1919. After courting her for twenty-five years, he married her suddenly at the age of fifty-four; she was about five years younger. At the spur-of-the-moment marriage ceremony, one of the participants later said, Charlie's pants had a big patch in the back.[68]

The taciturn Charlie Sellers conducted business the same way he did his marriage. According to Dorothy Sellars Brawley: "Uncle Charlie was on the board of directors at Sellers Manufacturing Company.[69] When they would have a directors' meeting—and Everett would tell this—uncle Charlie, uncle Ernest, and uncle Walter would march in, sit down, and Everett would go over the minutes. Everett said that if they said 'Unh' it passed; if they sat silent, it didn't pass. That was the way they carried on their business meeting!"[70]

Annie Morrow Sellers's nephew, Paul Morrow, Jr., was a longtime employee of the C. V. Sellers Art Store and had lasting impressions of his uncle by marriage, as he recalled in 1987 memories of working in an upstairs location on the opposite side of Main Street from the present Sellars Department Store building.[71]

After the Sellers Manufacturing Company was organized, the board of directors held its meetings in the art store. Paul said: "I would bring out those old gun shell boxes for them to sit on and the old rickety wicker photo studio furniture—then, if they would have a meeting during the Christmas season, [uncle Charlie] would have me stand out there to keep the customers out during the meeting."[72]

Paul continued: "He was a pretty shrewd businessman, too—he could make a *little* deal—he didn't try to get it all at one time. He just made a little now and then, and I guess he might have inherited some from his father; I don't know how much. He had the first Ford agency here—I think Atwater's got it after he gave it up." This was during the time Ford was just getting established, and Sellers told Paul that he dealt directly with Henry Ford.[73]

Paul Morrow, Jr., and Everett Jordan had at least one thing in common: their uncle Charlie took an early interest in each of them when they were only boys; and, after they were adults, provided each with a job.

Everett's nephew the Reverend Mike Jordan provided candid insight into the relationship between Everett and his uncle Charlie: "Uncle Everett was often described as a self-made man. And I remember there was a newspaper article that used that phrase, and aunt Margaret chuckled when she saw it and said, 'Yes, self-made by uncle Charlie Sellers!' "[74]

Everett had struck the fancy of his miserly but well-to-do uncle when he was only nine years old. Charlie took the boy for a ride one morning in his new car, the first in Burlington. He promised Everett another ride in the afternoon. According to Margaret Jordan Sprinkle, at the appointed time, Charlie "looked out his store window and there was the nine-year-old Everett in his car yelling that he was ready to 'go ride'! [He] had driven the car out of the garage,

On a 1939 trip to Florida, Everett Jordan and his family pose with his uncle Charlie Sellers and his wife, Annie Morrow Sellers. Charlie's 1939 Chrysler is in the background. *Left to right*: Everett, Charlie, Ben, Jr., Annie, Rose Ann, and Katherine. (*Paul E. Morrow, Jr.*)

driven it up Front Street, down Main Street, all alone. Uncle Charlie thought Everett was just the smartest person ever to come along. Not many adults could drive a car. So he was a great favorite of uncle Charlie's...I said Everett made his first money the day he drove that car—nine years old!"[75]

Charlie's brother Fred was also impressed by their headstrong nephew. Margaret Jordan Sprinkle believed that Everett had many traits that were characteristic of the Sellars family: "All of mama's people liked him [Everett]—he was more like their family—they *did* things and they were adventurers."[76]

Charlie Sellers was not so much an adventurer like his brother Fred, who left the home nest to go west, but he was a shrewd businessman and investor. The frugal investor learned that White-Williamson and Company, which owned an idle cotton mill in the village of Saxapahaw, in the southern part of Alamance County, was in receivership, and that the mill property and village would be sold at the courthouse in Graham, N.C., the county seat. Charlie Sellers thought, in 1927, that this would be a good investment for him if the price was right. And it was.[77]

Furthermore, Sellers thought his favorite nephew, in Gastonia, would be just the man to manage and operate the mill. That nephew was not only one more smart fellow, but he had also always been attentive to his eccentric uncle. And Sellers was genuinely appreciative of this, for few people, including his own kin, were inclined to devote much personal attention to the brusque businessman.[78]

Charlie Sellers knew where the money was in the Sellars family. He also knew through his business dealings who had disposable capital in Burlington and the immediate vicinity. This particular individual might not win any popularity contests, but his family, customers, and associates all liked to make a good return on their investments, and they were happy to put their trust—and money—into Charlie's cotton mill. It was perched on the banks of the Haw River at Saxapahaw in one of the most isolated rural sections of Alamance County, twelve miles south of Graham and fifteen miles from Burlington.[79]

Charlie Sellers found Everett Jordan very receptive to his plans and proposition. The latter especially liked the top role that he would play. Sellers not only appreciated his nephew's expressions of concern and affection, but he was convinced that, if Everett could drive a car at the age of nine, he certainly could run a cotton mill at the age of thirty-one. And Katherine Jordan knew Everett Jordan "could do anything."[80]

The opinions of these two persons, who meant the most to Everett Jordan and who had the most at stake in him at this stage, must have been reassuring to the newly designated mill manager as he made ready to take over an aging, run-down, and, in many respects, obsolete spinning mill and an equally decrepit mill village. But this vote of confidence was not unanimous. One key figure in Jordan's life at this time, an experienced and able textile mill man, no less, thought differently.

Jim Williams knew the identity of this doubter; Jim may have been the only one who did except for Everett Jordan. Katherine Jordan and Charlie Sellers, if they had known, would have thought such a doubter to be an absolute atheist. Jim knew only because Jordan had confided in him.[81] Because this was not the kind of knowledge that Everett was apt to share with just anyone, it is interesting that he would tell his general-store operator. Traditionally, employees and people in the community referred to the store as the "company store," which it was in effect.

Jim Williams had been a ten-year-old member of the congregation who had cause to snicker at the "You through?" remark of Everett Jordan during his wedding ceremony. Seven years later, he was approaching his seventeenth birthday when his widowed mother, Connie B. Williams, and his grandfather J. R. ("Dad") Baber moved to Saxapahaw in late March 1931. The family had come from Gastonia at the invitation of Jordan. He wanted Dad Baber and his daughter Connie to run the general store.[82]

Jim soon became his grandfather's right-hand man as he uncrated and shelved groceries and merchandise, became a meat-cutter, waited on customers, and delivered groceries. His mother did most of the book-work and operated the cash register. Baber helped out and oversaw the total business.[83]

Everett Jordan was impressed by the integrity and efficiency of the store operators. Although he was not prone to confide his innermost feelings and thoughts to everyone, as the years went by, he was inclined to be more open with Jim and his family. After an arduous workweek that included a multitude of demanding duties in every phase of the mill's activities—sales, administration, manufacturing—the budding entrepreneur would stop by the store and chat for a while with his younger friend. In this period of his life, Jordan smoked cigarettes; and, as he replenished his supply on a late Saturday afternoon, he would have a casual conversation upon whatever topic came to mind—most times the mill and its people.[84]

On one occasion, after several years of manning the textile operation and when red ink was running more sparsely in the books of his mill, Everett Jordan, for whatever reason, revealed to Jim the assessment of Joe Separk of himself, Separk's own former mill superintendent: "Jim, Mr. Separk told me, 'You [Jordan] will never make a mill man!' "[85]

No one can say for sure what effect Separk's appraisal had upon the thinking and motivation of the young textile industrialist, but it is safe to assume that Jordan determined then, if not earlier, to disprove Separk's prediction.

The fact that Jordan remembered and confided Separk's evaluation to a friend is indication enough that he did not shrug off lightly

J. R. ("Dad") Baber in front of the Everett Jordan residence sometime during the 1940s. Baber left his Gastonia home to come and operate the general store in Saxapahaw for Jordan. (*Jim B. Williams*)

Connie Baber Williams in the early 1930s. About that time, as a widow, she came to Saxapahaw to work in the general store with her son, Jim Baber Williams, and her father, J. R. Baber. (*Jim B. Williams*)

Jim Baber Williams, in 1935, the year he married Ann George. (*Jim B. Williams*)

Ann George Williams in 1935. Three years earlier she had come to Saxapahaw to teach in the first grade, where one of her pupils was Ben E. Jordan, Jr., as he was also later in the third grade. She and the rest of the Williams family were close friends of the Everett Jordan family. (*Ann George Williams*)

the prediction as of no consequence. Jordan may have thought back to an earlier time when he had written to his father: "You shan't lose anything on me."[86]

One's success formula is seldom confined to one factor. In Everett Jordan's case, personal attributes such as hard work, perseverance, determination, an abundant amount of native intelligence, and a deep understanding of people certainly played the major roles.

All these, and more too, would be needed by Jordan to transform Saxapahaw's pioneer—but failed—mill and dilapidated village into an integrated, viable enterprise. It would be an uphill battle, as his friend and business colleague David F. Swain later explained: "He was trying to put back together...[a] 'pile of junk'...that he and his family were able to buy. It needed so much that it was always a problem to just keep the seams together, and the quality did leave a lot to be desired. But there was where he had to do some pretty fancy talking."[87]

5

Putting Saxapahaw on the Map

In 1927 Highway 93 ran in a southeasterly direction from Graham, the county seat, through the southern part of Alamance County, on its way south to Chatham County—just missing the village of Saxapahaw, a mile or so to the east and dotted across both sides of the Haw River.[1] About five miles of the road were paved from Graham down to John Holt's store. Beyond there, however, it was a "machine-widened," dirt roadway; and more horse-drawn vehicles than automobiles traversed its dusty, rutted, winding surface. It would be many years, not until the late 1930s, before the road would be straightened and paved to become Highway 87.[2]

On this warm September day, Everett Jordan, likely preoccupied with the rush of recent events involved in his departure from Gastonia and concentrating on steering his laboring T-Model Ford over the unaccommodating road, probably failed to appreciate what a much earlier traveler had seen and described.

John Lawson, an English explorer and historian, in his overland trek through Alamance County around 1700, visited among the Sissipahaw (later changed to Saxapahaw) Indians on the Haw River. He described the area as being the "Flower of Carolina." The land, he wrote, was extraordinarily fertile. Most of it was covered with heavy timber such as oaks and scaly-bark hickories and was, in his estimation, capable of supporting thousands of immigrant families. Even then, he foresaw the potential waterpower of the swiftly flowing Haw and surrounding streams. As for the Indians, he found them very friendly and well fed on dried venison and bear meat.

Although he encountered no trouble with the Indians there, a decade later, while exploring the Neuse River, he was murdered by those of a different tribe.³

White people first came in sizable numbers to inhabit the village of Saxapahaw and its environs sometime between 1740 and 1750. The exact date the village came into being is apparently unknown. Many of the early settlers came to Alamance County down the Great Wagon Road from Pennsylvania and were locally known as the Pennsylvania Dutch ("Deutsch," or German).⁴

In addition to the Dutch, Quakers from Pennsylvania and Scotch-Irish Presbyterians from Ulster migrated simultaneously into the county. Methodists and Baptists were also particularly well represented. The Saxapahaw community was in between the Presbyterians, who settled largely in the Hawfields community to the east, and the Quakers, or "Friends," who settled to the southwest along Cane Creek in the Snow Camp community.⁵

These people were freeholders—farmers not planters—and they lived a simple agricultural life. Working from dawn until dusk, the men built houses, barns, and fences, cleared land, and plowed; the women sewed, cooked, made clothes, and performed other household duties. The crops were corn, wheat, and flax, which were cultivated with elemental bull-tongued plows; orchards consisted of apple, peach, cherry, and pear trees; the kitchen gardens provided vegetables of all kinds as well as plants for medicine and various food flavors. The livestock included cows, horses, sheep, hogs, chickens, turkeys, and geese. Farm implements were crude, and threshing methods were primitive. Because of the long hours of work, social activities were minimal: visiting and helping neighbors, going to church as well as associated affairs, and attending weddings.⁶

As time went on, this way of life was replaced by a new era. During the first quarter of the twentieth century, Alamance County felt the onslaught of industrialization by the textile industry, as the former superintendent of Gastonia's Gray Mill arrived on the local scene along with fast-approaching autumn.

The well-worn Ford chugged laboriously over the rutted dirt road. At last, just ahead, Everett Jordan saw a small sign at an unpaved intersection on Highway 93 that pointed to "Saxapahaw." He turned to his left and drove the final mile to his fateful destination.

In later years, many of Everett Jordan's suppliers, customers, and other visitors often had difficulty finding the tiny, isolated mill-village and discreetly kidded the mill manager about the fact that "Saxapahaw was not on the map!" After enduring for many years this slight of the mapmakers, Jordan finally complained to the North Carolina highway department as well as to the various oil companies that distributed maps and persuaded them to show the village's name.[7]

In a 1981 interview, Senator Sam Ervin, Jr., recounted this story about Senator Jordan explaining Saxapahaw's location. Jordan's peers in Washington would ask him where he lived, and—with tongue in cheek—the yarn spinner-turned-lawmaker's reply went like this:

"My home is in Saxapahaw."

"Senator, where is Saxapahaw?"

"Saxapahaw is near Swepsonville."

"And, senator, where is Swepsonville?"

"Swepsonville is on the river below Ossippee."

"But, senator, where in the world is Ossippee?"

Then Jordan, with a look of total disbelief on his face—incredulous that anyone did not know about Ossippee—after an emphatic pause, would smile broadly and say: "Why, Ossippee is just below Altamahaw."

And that would provoke a hearty guffaw among all present. By that time, Jordan would confidently and facetiously assume that the inquirer must know exactly where Saxapahaw was located: on the Haw River in the string of textile-mill communities that lined the river's banks throughout the entire length of Alamance County.[8]

Then and now, the Haw River divides the village of Saxapahaw into two parts. The village churches and school are on the south side; and the mill, company-store building, and mill offices are on the north side. In 1927 a single lane, steel-girder bridge spanned the river, which, at this point, has a low, sandy island that divides the water flow. The mid-section of the 900-foot bridge widened out over the island to permit vehicles to pass at this point, thus serving as the only passing lane after one came over either span of the bridge. Also, on the north side of the river bank, a short wooden bridge spanned the tailrace that accommodated the flow of water all the way from the wooden dam upstream down to the west end of the mill to the water turbine located there. Underneath the bridge, corn often grew from one end of the island to the other—that is, when floods from heavy rains did not wash the crop away.[9]

Looking straight ahead from the narrow bridge approach, Everett Jordan could have seen the mill offices and company store, housed in a two-story red-brick building on the hillside rising sharply up from the river. To the left, a few feet from this imposing structure, stood a two-story white frame house that would be his home for the rest of his life. Just to the right, on the river bank, he saw the mill, the reason for his journey.

This was the spinning and weaving mill, idle for the past four years, that John Newlin, the Quaker pioneer mill owner, had established in 1844. If Jordan ever had reason to question his wisdom in coming to this place, he must have experienced it on that September day. The unkempt, destitute, uninviting mill and village were enough to make him wonder if he should have stayed in Gastonia. Broken window panes, sagging doors, missing porch steps, weeds and uncontrolled growth, buildings bereft of paint—the whole scene a picture of neglect and virtual abandonment. The only visible inhabitants were a few poorly clothed idlers, dirty children playing in the dusty streets, and mangy cats and dogs roaming everywhere.[10]

The mill and its people had, however, seen better times under John Newlin's management and also with his successors. But the depression of 1920, following World War I, caused the collapse of the market for cheap cotton gingham and tubing. Additionally, most of the machinery was old and too obsolete for modern competition. The most recent previous owners, White-Williamson and Company, had been forced into receivership.[11]

In selecting a site for their mill, John Newlin and two of his sons, James and Jonathan, were forced to locate on the north side of the

Haw River. If the choice were being made today, in all probability, the plant would be placed on the south side, where the terrain is more level and spacious. The north side is not only quite hilly, but the soil is red clay; on the south side, by a quirk of nature, the soil is sandy, which was a major factor in the days when there were no paved roads and, in winter, the sticky red clay becomes almost impassable. However, the south bank of the river is stony, and it was impossible with the technology of the time to cut a race from the dam down to the mill site on that side. Another factor weighing against the north side was that it was not until many years later that a bridge was built to span the river; and John Newlin, the boss himself, had to reach his mill on horseback, crossing each day by the rough, rocky, and treacherous ford.[12]

The mill building was constructed of brick made from the red clay along Motes Creek, less than a mile from the mill, and the sand for the mortar was obtained from the opposite side of the river. This structure was a red-brick two-story built over a basement. Heating was provided by fireplaces and lighting by candles and oil lamps. The building measured ninety-six feet long by forty-two feet wide and stood where the latter-day mercerizing department once operated. There was an arched opening underneath the floor where the water from the race ran across the over-shot waterwheel that turned all of the moving machinery by means of a line shaft. Because of this shaft arrangement, it was impossible to stop one machine without halting the operation of the entire plant.[13]

Using slave labor, the Newlins dug a millrace to channel the water from a three-foot-high rock dam across the Haw River, the first dam ever erected on this site, down the north bank of the river and all the way to their cotton mill nearly a mile away. There is some question as to who actually built this first dam. Some people contend that it was the Thompson family, which operated the original gristmill, the first mill of any kind at Saxapahaw; the reasoning was that they must have had a dam upstream to furnish waterpower for the wheel that turned the machinery. Others, however, maintain that John Newlin was the first to harness the full power of the river.[14]

Oral tradition provides a number of interesting but varying stories pertaining to the slave help used by Newlin in establishing his plant. The following account seems to be the most plausible. Because the Newlins were Quakers, their religion and their own convictions would not allow them to own slaves. A certain Foust woman, who lived below Bethel Church near Snow Camp, was settling her estate along about this time and planned to set her slaves free; and some people believe that, because Newlin was a man of considerable learning, she consulted him for assistance in the matter. Needing the slaves primarily for digging his race, he made the stipulation with her that, if she would let him have them, he personally would carry them to free territory north of the Mason-Dixon line after his project was completed. There are many conflicting stories as to what actually took place thereafter, but it is generally conceded that one of John's sons, Oliver, did take them north, possibly to the state of Ohio, and set them free.[15]

Although Newlin's firm was organized in 1844, it was not until four years later that the physical plant was completed and ready to begin production. At first the mill did nothing but spin yarn. The number of active spindles is not known, but Newlin's nearby competitor over at the village of Alamance, Edwin M. Holt, started out with 528 spindles in 1837 and by 1861 had 1,200. Therefore, it is reasonable to surmise that the Newlins had an approximately equal number.[16]

Sometime later, the building was enlarged, and looms were installed in 1854. In addition to producing small twenty-four-pound bales of coarse cotton yarn, which was sold largely to owners of household looms throughout the country, the Newlins began to turn out woven cotton cloth, which they dyed with their own equipment.[17]

The mills of Holt and Newlin and the mill at Cane Creek (known as Holman's Mill) were not only the first cotton mills in Alamance County, but were also among the first in the state and in the South as well.[18] The mammoth plants of today dwarf these pioneer mills, but in their day they were of major social and economic importance in their areas.

In 1863, during the Civil War, North Carolina's Governor Zebulon B. Vance ordered that a large quantity of baled cotton then stored at Graham be delivered to "Messers. John Newland [sic] & Sons at Saxapahaw Factory" to be manufactured into cloth and yarn. This

In this turn-of-the-century scene, the old gristmill is at left, and the race runs under the mill building to generate waterpower. (*Bruce G. Hackney*)

cloth was to be delivered to the quartermaster department of the Confederate army, and the yarn was to be sent to Virginia to be exchanged for leather to be made into shoes for the soldiers. Some North Carolinians still boast that their soldiers were the best-dressed troops in the rebel army, and "Saxapahaw Factory" played a conspicuous part in earning that distinction.[19]

In 1867, two years after the end of the Civil War, John Newlin died. His sons James and Jonathan and George Guthrie, a minor stockholder, continued to labor under the difficulties of the postwar Reconstruction Era and the so-called "carpetbagger" administration. Finally, in 1873, they decided to sell out to the eminently successful Edwin M. Holt, by then the owner of a number of cotton mills throughout the county. And so the Newlins, after twenty-five years of continuous operation, relinquished their hold on Saxapahaw industry—including the old gristmill they had operated in conjunction with the cotton factory as well as a tannery and a boarding house.[20]

Holt took his two sons-in-law, Dr. John L. Williamson and Capt. James W. White, into partnership and operated the mill under the name of Holt, White, and Williamson until 1884, the date of Holt's death. His heirs, Ben, George, and Edwin Williamson, Mrs. John Williamson, and Mrs. James White, as well as the surviving partners, then went under the name of White-Williamson and Company, incorporated in 1906.[21]

The reconstituted company expanded the mill throughout and installed knitting machines that enabled them to produce tubing.[22] The rolls of tubing were called "ades." Mr. and Mrs. George Williamson named two of their ades in honor of their little girls, calling them Ethel Ades and Bonner Ades, and on the label of each roll appeared a small picture of the two girls. The output now consisted of ginghams, tubing, and some flannel and outing goods.[23]

The entire production was sold to commission houses in Philadelphia and New York for the manufacture of aprons, bonnets, pants, and other wearing apparel. Some of the goods were ultimately shipped to South America and the West Indies.[24]

In addition to expanding the production facilities, White-Williamson and Company built a new turbine and generator power plant, a vast improvement over the old water system. This was done in 1917 after the death of George Williamson, at which time the mill again changed hands. This time, the controlling interest was sold to Finley Williamson and his brothers, Lawrence, Walter, and Banks Williamson.[25]

The economic status of Alamance County (Orange County until 1849) was no different from that of its sister counties or the rest of North Carolina and the South in general as the last wave of the industrial revolution spread southward from its primary American base in New England. In the course of time, the South became in-

Employees of White-Williamson and Company in front of the Saxapahaw mill about 1890. The young girls in the forefront are (*left to right*): Sallie Dodson (Guthrie) (1), Molly Crutchfield (Morrow) (2), unidentified (3), Mattie Cheek (4), Ella McVey (Pickard) (5), Leona Dodson (Lashley) (6), "Vonie" Johnson (Crutchfield) (7). On the far left, three men have been identified: Peter Johnson (9), Elwood Cheek (10), James Cheek (11). This view was taken from the east end of the mill. None of this structure is outwardly visible in the present-day mill building, but portions of the interior show evidence of this early edifice. (*Sellers Manufacturing Company, Inc.*)

dustrialized and changed from an economy dominated by plantation agriculture and one-horse dirt farms into a textile-manufacturing economy.[26]

Two of these pioneers, Holt and Newlin, had started spindles turning to make cotton yarn and cloth and had become front runners in moving the South to its new economic status. But neither they nor their successors wrought a quick panacea for their employees and fellow men. Many and diverse were the problems confronting the people of the South, and solutions did not come easily in their generation nor in those that followed, though some progress was made. Cotton mill "hands" did manage to survive on their meager fare.[27]

After the Civil War, the South was impoverished and its primary need was for an opportunity to work—work that would sustain a people who had been slave owners but now were themselves slaves in an impotent agricultural economy. Most of the small farms had been tilled to death; commercial fertilizer was not in wide use; and depleted nutrients were not being replaced. A tiny minority, plantation owners and businessmen, did enjoy limited luxuries, but the vast majority of the people were on the bottom spectrum, eking out their existence on a hand-to-mouth basis and having little prospect of improvement—until the advent of the textile mills.[28]

The South lacked the financial resources to establish manufacturing enterprises, and the North was in no mood to reconstruct its defeated foe. As a matter of fact, industrialists and businessmen there insisted that the South could not succeed in its textile venture—though they recognized the excellent supply of waterpower. They claimed that Southern labor was too unskilled, the region was too remote from markets, its streams were not sufficiently clear for bleaching and dyeing, and capitalization was inadequate.[29]

But why should the South, possessing a strong waterpower resource, send its major staple, cotton, to New England, for a pittance compared to the profits that would accrue from textile manufacturing. Southern emissaries fanned out into the North to obtain financial aid. Commission merchants there, usually in return for serving as agents for a mill's output, lent capital; and textile-machinery manufacturers agreed to take stock in payment for their machines.[30]

Slowly and persistently the South overcame its problems. The skills of labor advanced, artificial humidifiers expedited the smooth run of cotton, the regional market was exploited, and large profits went back to the plants. But numerous problems were created.[31]

Some of the troublesome obstacles to social well-being and progress were partially overcome, but it took time, generations in fact, to eradicate the abuses of children and women labor; long hours; subsistence wages; the extreme paternalism of the company-owned mill village; the reluctance of Southern legislatures to enact restrictive regulations; and the ignorance of poor whites, who provided most of the labor for the industrial conversion from farm to textile mill.[32]

Restricted capital meant slow urban growth and a population that was poor, thinly settled, often clannish, unwilling or unable to migrate, and shackled by lack of education. In South Carolina, for example, two-thirds of the poor whites could neither read nor write; the slaves were denied this opportunity by law; and even the children of wealthy families lacked good facilities for home-study.[33]

The mill owners had to build houses, stores, churches, recreation facilities—usually a baseball field and later community or recreation buildings and gyms—for the workers, who themselves were hardly able to earn the bare necessities. Generations would come and go before Southern textile workers would enjoy a better way of life.[34]

An old White-Williamson and Company time book, salvaged by John Steele, shows employee names, rates, and wages paid in 1910.[35] Many of the family names shown are still prevalent in the area. Most of the rates were $1 per day, except for weavers, who were paid a piece-rate and their earnings were therefore slightly higher. The mill's total payroll for a full sixty-hour workweek was approximately $800. Total rents withheld for all employees averaged $15 per week and total weekly deductions for "merchandise" around $60.

As the nineteenth century ended and the twentieth began, the flow of cotton manufacture to the South had accelerated because more and more New England and Northeastern capitalists, cost-conscious in a highly competitive industry, were attracted by cheap labor in the home states of King Cotton. It was a good move for both capital and labor. Poor whites moved quickly from mountain farms and tenant holdings. It was a new day, a chance to earn a steady wage.[36]

According to Broadus and George Mitchell, "the enterprises were phenomenally successful. Dire predictions of the North were promptly disappointed. Production was standardized on cheap, coarse goods; the raw hands learned rapidly, glad of the chance for bread. Nobody grumbled about the long hours, the low wages and the work of children; surplus profits went back into the ventures to render them larger and more autonomous."[37]

The Mitchells also stated: "North Carolina replaced Massachusetts as the leading cotton manufacturing state and by 1927 the cotton-growing states had 61.9 percent of the establishments in the country and 60.2 percent of the number of wage-earners and in 1926 had 57 percent of the active spindles."[38]

Hourly rates for the four leading states in 1926 were—according to samples collected by the federal government—in North Carolina $.28, South Carolina $.25, Georgia $.25, and Alabama $.24. Northern earnings in 1926 were 55 percent higher than those in the South despite a shorter working week.[39] In 1927 the average earnings of the Southern operator were $637.17 a year, or $12.94 a week.[40]

The legal workweek limit in North Carolina and Georgia was sixty hours per week, South Carolina fifty-five hours, and Alabama had no limit. No Southern state prohibited night work for women, and eleven-hour days and twelve-hour nights were common. Many of the mills in the region also worked five hours on Saturday. Massachusetts, which was affected most by the textile industry's exodus to the South, had limits of forty-eight hours a week and no night work for women.[41]

In terms of cost in 1926, in a typical Southern mill running fifty-five hours per week, the cost of manufacture was 16.8 percent less than in a Massachusetts mill running forty-eight hours; or, put another way, $6.73 per spindle, of which $4.53 was attributable to a savings in labor. The Southern mill saved 33 percent in taxes, the same in power, and 25 percent in maintenance.[42]

T-Model Ford in the 1920s parked in front of the Saxapahaw building that housed the offices of the Sellers Manufacturing Company. (Photo by Walter O. Hackney; *Bruce G. Hackney*)

Sellers Manufacturing Company mill building in the early 1940s. (Photo by Walter O. Hackney; *Bruce G. Hackney*)

Thus, the stage was set: Everett Jordan in 1927 would deal with conditions and forces already in place. His task would be to fit in and to cope with them as best he could. As for the Saxapahaw factory and village, he would be starting almost from scratch. But he *could* scratch—hard.

Ready and anxious, the thirty-one-year-old Jordan had finally reached his destination. He parked his car and, instead of going to the office, headed straight for the mill to take a "look-see." He undoubtedly hoped the inside was in better shape than what he saw on the exterior.

John Steele, a retired employee of Sellers Manufacturing Company and the son of Robah Steele, who was White-Williamson's watchman on duty, later related this account of what happened on that first day:

Alson T. Davis and his employer Everett Jordan examine the watch presented by Jordan on the occasion of Davis's retirement after many years of loyal service as master mechanic and electrician. (Photo by Pat Bailey)

He came down and wanted to go in the mill and my daddy told him he couldn't go in. Mr. Jordan said, "Yes, I can. I bought it." And he started to come on in the door. My daddy pulled out a .38 pistol and said, "This says you ain't a'coming-in! You'll have to go back up there to Graham and see Scott[43] at the bank and get a note." So he went back up there and brought Scott back with him and [Jordan] said, "I reckon I can come in now."

So he let him come in, and after he looked over the mill he told my daddy to just carry on like he was doing and he would be working for him from then on. Then he wanted to know if there was someone who knew about the pipes and water-wheel and things [mill equipment]. Daddy told him to see Alson Davis, who lived up there where Ceton Quakenbush lives [now]. So Mr. Jordan went up there and hired him to look after the pipes in the mill and everything while it was standing until they got it running.[44]

Thus, Robah Steele became Everett Jordan's first employee. And Alson Davis, the second person to go on his payroll, was recognized as one of Jordan's most faithful and key employees in his role of master mechanic and self-made electrician.[45]

From that startling encounter with Steele and until his death nearly forty-seven years later, no one ever stood in Everett Jordan's way or told him what he could or could not do in the mill. He was in charge—absolutely.

Difficult years were ahead. But Saxapahaw's spindles started turning again in 1927, and Everett Jordan's mill doors remained open through thick and thin—even during the Great Depression, which began in 1929 and lasted through most of the thirties. He kept bread on the table—and the gravy became a little more palatable and nourishing.

The "Pied Piper"

Margaret Jordan Sprinkle, Everett Jordan's sister, recalled in 1982: "I remember uncle Charlie [Sellers] said, 'Everett, if you are going to run a mill, you've got to own controlling stock. If you don't, you better not put your life into it.' All of the [Sellers] family bought some stock, but Everett didn't have a lot of money to put into it then, so uncle Charlie put at least 51 percent in [his] name."[1]

The records show, however, that this did not happen immediately when the mill properties, which included 7,944 spinning spindles and 316 looms as well as 500 acres of land encompassing the village consisting of approximately 40 tenements,[2] were purchased in September 1927 for $140,000 by Charlie Sellers and his wife, Annie M. Sellers, at the receiver's sale of White-Williamson and Company. Nonetheless, Charlie saw to it that his favorite nephew eventually did acquire control.[3]

At the first stockholders meeting, on September 15, 1927, the ten subscribers to stock were listed:

C. V. Sellers	T. L. Sellars
R. H. Whitehead	D. E. Sellers
J. H. Brooks	W. R. Sellars
R. O. Sellers	H. W. Jordan
W. W. Sellers	B. E. Jordan

The three incorporators named in the certificate of incorporation were: R. O. Sellers, J. H. Brooks, and B. E. Jordan. The minutes of the first annual meeting, held on January 10, 1928, show the number of shares of stock represented in person and by proxy. The stock was issued and sold at its par value of $100 per share. Stockholders present and the shares they owned at the time of the first annual meeting were:

Dr. J. H. Brooks	100	W. R. Sellars	100
D. E. Sellers	60	R. O. Sellers	100
C. V. Sellers	750	B. E. Jordan	300
T. L. Sellars	50	W. W. Sellers	40

Total shares represented in person: 1,500.

The following shares were represented by proxy:

Miss Bessie Sellers	10	R. H. Whitehead	50
Mrs. W. R. Burke	50	Dr. O. L. Miller	150
C. C. Cornwell	25	L. K. Thompson	25
W. H. May	50	Dr. H. W. Jordan	50

Total shares represented by proxy: 410.

A total of 1,910 shares were voted, which, according to the minutes, constituted a majority of the stock outstanding. The total number of outstanding shares was not given. However, a recapitulation of the shares of stock outstanding as of June 2, 1931, shows a total of 2,952 shares and ownership as follows:

C. V. Sellers	825	L. K. Thompson	30
B. E. Jordan	430	Walter M. Williams	30
Dr. Oscar L. Miller	250	C. C. Cornwell	25
J. M. Coble	120	George H. Fowler	25
Dr. J. H. Brooks	110	Dr. R. G. McPherson	24
W. R. Sellars	110	Marie Sellers	11
R. O. Sellers	110	Mrs. F. W. Sellers	11
Dr. H. W. Jordan	50	Bessie Lea Sellers	11
W. H. May	85	Mary A. Walker	11
T. L. Sellars	77	Joe M. Neel	50
F. W. Sellers	75	Mrs. H. H. Jordan	10
D. E. Sellers	72	John Brooks	10
R. H. Whitehead	55	Fannie C. Sellers	10
Mrs. W. R. Burke	55	Edith Walker	6
J. T. Black	55	James Bracey	5
John Shoffner	55	Mrs. E. A. White	5
C. E. Fogleman	55	Mrs. W. Kerr Scott	3
W. W. Sellers	44	Osborne White	1
J. E. Sellers	40	Mary Kerr Scott	1

Total shares: 2,952

Four days later, on June 6, some 750 shares were transferred from C. V. Sellers to B. E. Jordan. At this point, the two men's combined stock ownership was only 42½ percent of the outstanding stock, but gradually they became the majority stockholders.

Seven years later, at the stockholders meeting on June 6, 1938, C. V. Sellers voted only 125 shares in his name, and B. E. Jordan voted the 2,073 shares that he owned. (An additional 30 shares were voted in his wife's name.) This gave Everett control of 52.3 percent of the 4,015 shares issued and outstanding.

Charlie Sellers died in 1941, naming his nephew B. Everett Jordan as his executor and chief heir. Now no one could challenge Everett's absolute control of the company. Uncle Charlie had promised Everett that he would put him in charge of the mill if he would leave his job as superintendent of the Gray Mill in Gastonia and come to Saxapahaw. As expected, Sellers kept his word to the letter. At the first directors meeting on September 15, 1927, C. V. Sellers was elected as president and B. E. Jordan was elected as secretary-treasurer; the secretary-treasurer was also designated in the bylaws as "General Manager" of the company.[4]

Once in the driver's seat, Everett Jordan never relinquished his title or authority. He was soon in complete charge and, during Charlie Sellers's lifetime, enjoyed his uncle's blessing and support. Even so, the frugal Sellers kept careful surveillance on his young mill manager, who was always fully aware of his benefactor's scrutiny.

Paul Morrow, Jr., Charlie Sellers's nephew and longtime employee, gave an example in a 1983 interview: "I went in [a restaurant] one day for lunch, and Everett was sitting up at the counter eating, and I went up and sat down beside him and said, 'Lawww, Everett! Uncle Charlie sure would be proud of you being a senator now.' Old Everett said, 'The hell he would—he'd say I ought to be out selling yarn!' And that's about right," Paul concluded.[5]

During Charlie Sellers's tenure as president, Jordan stayed in constant and close contact with him. Almost every Sunday afternoon, Everett and his family would visit the Sellers's Burlington home after entertaining them for dinner in Saxapahaw. While there, they would make a tour of the mill. On Monday nights, Everett attended the Rotary meeting in Burlington, after which he would call on Charlie before returning home.[6]

After the death of Sellers there was no one to look over Jordan's shoulder: he was beholden to no one and the board of directors—consisting entirely of kinsmen and loyal friends—found little to object or recommend to the aggressive, independent-thinking entrepreneur. Everett Jordan, nevertheless, respected his board as well as its authority and took great pains to win the approval of its members.[7]

If Jordan had a proposal or resolution requiring board action, and he was not sure of a member's acceptance, he would "pre-sell" that member by a visit or telephone call. Then, at the meeting, he knew in advance exactly where he stood, so that seldom, if ever, did his recommendations fail to pass.[8]

Archie K. Davis, a former chairman of Winston-Salem's Wachovia Bank and Trust Company's board, also served on Jordan's board of directors for more than a quarter of a century and had a banking relationship with him for many years before. Davis later recalled that Everett made his own decisions, offered positive recommendations, and the board supported them. As Davis said, "That's not to say that we were just a sounding board and nothing else, but there just weren't many things, as long as Everett was at the helm, that a good board would find to question."[9]

Davis continued: "He believed in efficiency of operations and... would come in with requests to approve certain expenditures to improve plant efficiency and the like. All you had to do was look at his accounts receivable to see how carefully they were handled. You never saw a bunch of past dues... He did not believe in long-term debt; and, if he borrowed any money on a long-term basis, he paid it off in a year if he could."[10]

One of the reasons Jordan was a "first-class mill man," according to Davis, was that he delegated the plant and business management to well-qualified people, but, "when it came to marketing, he was out front selling all the time."[11]

Perhaps even more important to Jordan's success, both in the mill and the U.S. Senate, was how effectively he attracted, trained, and retained good people, including both plant and office personnel. As his brother-in-law Dr. Henry C. Sprinkle recollected: "I never saw any man who could so universally win the deep devotion of his associates as Everett did, and, even the people that he sold to, they were his lifelong friends."[12]

The "Pied Piper" 131

Eugene Gordon, of Greensboro, federal judge for the Middle District of North Carolina and a longtime friend of Jordan's, put it this way in a 1981 interview: "Everett was somewhat like the Pied Piper. After you got to know him you would follow him. He had leadership qualities that were unusual, not in the sense of being eloquent in speech or that sort of thing. [He had] a quiet sort of personality...but it didn't take you long to realize that here was someone you could trust."[13]

Roger Gant, Jr., retrospectively appraised his father-in-law's ability to attract and keep employees at all levels: "I think Everett just liked people...and he never met anybody that stayed a stranger very long. He just liked them for what they were, whether they were business-related or not. He...understood them and...their [human] frailties. He never belittled anybody because of [their] frailties...He was very big, generous, and understanding of the way people are put together and the way they acted and what they needed."[14]

Roger continued: "He had very close associations with people of all levels in his mill; he didn't value the friendship of the mill superintendent any higher than he did the floor-sweeper. Went to church with all of them. He was not impressed by class or clothes or material ownership of the people he knew. As far as I could tell, he equated them all, which, I think, is unusual."[15]

Perhaps Gant's analysis helps explain how the "Pied Piper" of "Gastony" attracted his devotees there and then led them away with him to Saxapahaw, and also why the ex-White-Williamson and Company employees got on and stayed on Jordan's payroll, along with a host of others, from such faraway places as Thomasville, Ga., Greenville, S.C., Chattanooga, Tenn., Charlotte, and the mountains of North Carolina.

Concerning Jordan, Roger Gant also said:

> I think he was able to attract employees at a lower wage than we [Glen Raven Mills] could. That may have been his personality, too. People liked him and liked to work for him. If they had problems, why, he helped them solve them. He had a much closer personal relationship with the employees than we have had in many years. Back when my grandfather or even my father and his brother were running the company, the relationship with the employees was very close. My father would walk through the mill and, like Everett, he

knew everybody by their first name and knew their children, knew what church they went to, and knew what illnesses they suffered from. It was a much closer personal relationship than now, principally because today there are so many more employees [Glen Raven Mills had about 3,000 in about a dozen plants spread from Georgia to the Virginia line] and it's just hard to know them... I guess the real reason, though, is the style of management. I tend to manage from my office by paper more than by getting out in the mill and talking to the employees.[16]

One of Jordan's early recruits was Joe Neel, from Thomasville, Ga., who had attended Emory University and whose urban upbringing and his activities in his family's clothing store made him an unlikely candidate to live and work in the isolated cotton-mill village of Saxapahaw—an environment he never dreamed of. Yet, he was employed by Jordan and his mills for forty-six years, coming in January 1928, only four months after Jordan, and staying with Sellers Manufacturing Company until he retired in 1974. He became one of the mill man's most trusted lieutenants, so much so that eventually Jordan put Neel in complete charge of day-to-day yarn manufacturing as plant superintendent and later as a vice-president.[17]

Neel met Jordan while the former was in Gastonia visiting his cousin Rose and her husband, Dr. Oscar Miller, who was the biggest stockholder in the Saxapahaw mill after Everett Jordan and Charlie Sellers. When Jordan came by the Miller home, the discussion turned to his starting the cotton mill. Oscar Miller bet Neel $100 that he could not work two weeks in the mill. Neel won the bet, but he had to start by wiping the grease off newly received machinery.[18]

Neel felt that he was an "outsider" because most of Jordan's mill employees came from two sources: the local folks and his former workers as well as friends in Gastonia's cotton mills.[19] Much, if not most, of his supervisory staff also came from Gastonia, especially in the early years. When the shrewd mill manager recruited a supervisor, he knew that he would bring with him—then or later—the trained employees that Jordan needed. A good many of the old-time residents in the Saxapahaw community today arrived by way of Gastonia and Belmont.[20]

However, many of White-Williamson and Company's former employees were still around in 1927 and soon sought work with Jor-

Everett and Katherine Jordan with "Joe" Neel in 1933. (*Jim B. Williams*)

Joseph ("Joe") M. Neel in the 1970s. During his lifelong service, he was one of Jordan's most dependable and trusted employees. (Photo by author)

dan at Sellers Manufacturing Company. Once the mill began operating, people from all around the southern end of Alamance County began knocking at his door seeking employment.[21]

In his train of followers, Saxapahaw's "Pied Piper" did not have a more devoted employee than Alson T. Davis, whom Jordan fondly called "A. T.," who in turn called his boss "Mr. Jerden."[22] As Joe Neel said, Davis was paid $20 a week—that was "working sixty or seventy hours a week just like the rest of us, doing everything. Davis, I tell you, he was some gem! That guy loved that place down there, and he would have worked himself to death...[He] could do anything with machinery that you could do. And loyal—my goodness! I've seen him [work] thirty-six hours without stopping. Mr. Jordan would get Doc Williamson to open the store, and he would get four or five cans of 'pok-n-beans' and things and take them down, and Old Davis would eat and keep a-working. Just a bear for work."[23]

Robert Hunter, a black man who worked on the machinery with Alson Davis, Joe Neel, and numerous others under the sway of the Pied Piper were tremendously impressed by his personal example: No job was too menial for him and his clock had no hands. In every project, large or small, that concerned the mill, Everett Jordan was on hand, not just visible, but supervising, always the man in charge, and—as the role model—pitching in and helping regardless of blue-collar or white-collar label.[24]

Hunter later recalled: "Sometimes Mr. Jordan would be there. You see, he wasn't a man that would stand back. If you was in a ditch in a rough spot, repairing a pipe, he'd jump down in that ditch with his Florsheim shoes and help you. You don't catch many men like that. I've been in a strain a many a time; be down in a ditch with pipe caulking and lead, and he'd see me down there and he'd tell them boys to get in there, and he'd dive in there and help us, too."[25]

Leon Madden, a third-generation employee of the Saxapahaw plant and still working on-site until his retirement from Dixie Yarns, the successor company to Sellers Manufacturing Company, added to Hunter's perception of how Everett Jordan operated: "You might be there working by yourself on something and all of a sudden he [Jordan] would speak to you. He'd be right over your shoulder... [Once a man was working on the plumbing] right up under the mill... to get to this place you have to go to the back side of the mill, get underneath the floor, and crawl all the way over here at the street side. Mr. Jordan [who suddenly greeted the man] was dressed up—just came from church—didn't seem to bother him a bit! He just knew—in the business and everything—he knew what was going on, and he found it out for himself."[26]

Madden's admiration for the mill owner and manager knew no bounds: "Regardless of what level anyone was on, he [Jordan] could talk to them. He could talk on their level; he could talk to a wino; he could manage with him, or he could mix it with the mighty, the high officials in the government and so forth. [Also] if you worked for him, he held you responsible for what you knew; and what you didn't know he didn't hold you responsible for. If you didn't know it and went to him, he would give you the answer, and if he didn't know himself he would find somebody that had the answer for you."[27]

The "Pied Piper"

Four Sellers Manufacturing Company old-timers (*left to right*): E. Leon Madden, Robert A. Hunter, Kent W. Miller, John H. Smith. (*Jim B. Williams*)

Tasks in and around a cotton mill are not considered easy work. Some jobs are just harder than others. This was definitely true when Everett Jordan was struggling to establish his mill and attain profitability. Air conditioning had not yet arrived, and the prejudicial label "lint head," applied somewhat disparagingly to cotton-mill hands, was significant in that it more aptly described the working conditions of lint-filled mills. Workers would joke about carrying home the mill's profit in cotton that clung to their clothes and hair.[28]

Everett Jordan worked hard, and he worked his people equally hard. One time Joe Neel convinced Jordan that he could not continue to stand working 100 hours, but the former commented: "Mr. Jordan didn't care how many hours you worked. You could work 200 hours a week if you wanted to, but if you ever asked to be off, he would let you off. If you didn't ask off, that was your business. Just work yourself to death; that's all right—he didn't do it—but if you wanted off a week or so, just ask for it."[29]

Holidays never interfered with Jordan's own work schedule, and he expected his people to follow his example. If the job required that they stay on duty, he insisted they did so—even on holidays, including Christmas.[30]

Old Saxapahaw wooden dam (*left*) and construction of concrete dam (*center*) in October 1938. (*Paul E. Morrow, Jr.*)

Because Jordan genuinely enjoyed being with his business associates and customers, practically every social event and outing revolved around people involved in his business life. At a dinner party in his home or a football game at his cherished alma mater—Duke—one would always find Clines and Garrous from the Hickory area or Gordons and Maynards from Burlington, as well as a host of others who contributed to his mill's success. When his auditors from A. M. Pullen and Company's Greensboro office came to Saxapahaw and there was not a suitable restaurant in the village, he fed them in his home and shrewdly used the time to discuss the mill's operations and finances.[31]

Because Jordan had no hobbies or particular recreational interests, the mills gave him ample opportunity to enjoy himself. He was immersed in unending work that demanded his attention and energies for every waking hour of the day. One of those ever-present opportunities for work was the dam, more appropriately called that "damn dam" in those trying early years.[32]

In 1927 and until 1938, the ancient wooden structure across the Haw, located just above the present thirty-foot-high concrete dam, was damaged frequently and major portions were washed away by spring freshets and other flood waters in between. Without the power generated by the flow of the Haw River, Jordan could not operate the Saxapahaw mill; and, years later after the Great Depres-

The "Pied Piper"

The Saxapahaw dam at flood stage in 1939. (*Paul E. Morrow, Jr.*)

sion of the 1930s, he could boast: "The only time we curtailed operations or sent our people home was because of lack of power." The shortage of power was due to two causes: no rain or the dam had washed out.[33]

In 1938 Jordan permanently corrected that problem when he built the present concrete dam, a tremendous undertaking at that time for the exasperated entrepreneur. The thirty-foot-high structure, including the powerhouse and abutments, spans nearly 1,000 feet and originally impounded the largest body of water in Alamance County. Finally, Everett Jordan had ample power, both literally and figuratively, inasmuch as power was an element he appreciated, relished, and used in all of his endeavors relating to family, business, and politics—indeed, in all aspects of his life.[34]

In Saxapahaw, every employee—mill hand, plant supervisor, office administrator, whoever—knew who was in control. No one questioned Jordan's authority, and each was aware that, if his or her condition or future could ever hope to be improved, ultimately advancement must come through him. Those who failed to accept or recognize the mill owner's position did not linger very long on his payroll. He tolerated only a limited amount of freedom and authority on the part of any employee—including supervisors and executives. One learned to do things Jordan's way if he or she planned to stay on his payroll.[35]

Robert B. ("Rack") Robinson and his wife, Hazel, worked at the Gray Mill (in Gastonia) for Everett Jordan before he came to Sax-

The 1945 flood inundated the Saxapahaw bridge over the Haw River. A portion of the mill is visible in the background. (Photo by Walter O. Hackney; *Bruce G. Hackney*)

West end (Mercerizing Department) of Sellers Manufacturing Company plant, which was inundated in 1945 by the Haw River, in background at the right. (Photo by Walter O. Hackney; *Bruce G. Hackney*)

Saxapahaw Methodist Church, where the Jordan family worships, during the 1945 flood. At the flood's peak, the waters were two feet higher than pictured here. (Photo by Walter O. Hackney; *Bruce G. Hackney*)

apahaw and, at his request, came to work for him again at Saxapahaw, moving to the mill village on December 31, 1928. "Rack" later explained why they heeded Jordan's call. After the latter hired Frank Norman, of Gastonia, to be his new spinning-room overseer, Jordan sent Norman to Gastonia, where "Rack" was then working for Parkdale, just across the street from the Gray Mill, to hire some of Jordan's former employees, including "Rack" and Hazel. The two agreed to come, and Jordan moved them and all their furniture on the mill truck.[36]

The couple were appalled: "The houses were awful; the roofs leaked—back then Jordan didn't have money, but he worked to remodel these houses so people could live in them. And the mill was just as bad." "Rack" and Hazel also found that many of the residents were mean and did a lot of heavy drinking and fighting—especially on Saturday nights. However, the two pointed out that Jordan did not tolerate much of this, and they said that he had encountered the same problems earlier in Gastonia.[37]

In a 1986 interview, Arthur ("Ott") Barrett also commented about Jordan's limited tolerance of drinking behavior. Many times the mill hands, including Barrett, would sprawl around on the post office floor to sober up on weekends. When Jordan arrived to pick up his mail, he would step over the bodies and never disturb them, but he expected each one to be on his job fully sober and ready to work come Monday morning.[38]

Because "Rack" Robinson had worked in a number of Gastonia's cotton mills as well as those in Spartanburg, S.C., Dallas, N.C., and other widely scattered locations and because of Saxapahaw's unattractive appearance—dilapidated village and mill[39]—it is interesting that the Robinsons would come and spend the remainder of their lives working for Everett Jordan. That they did further verifies Judge Gordon's "Pied Piper" description of the mill owner and reveals how the mill hands interacted with him. As "Rack" Robinson said: "The first time I ever met him [Jordan, in Gastonia] I thinks 'Well I don't know about you whether you are good or bad.' I figured they [Gray Mill] would probably run him off for being mean to people, but he wasn't. He made them people learn that he loved them, and he's trying to help them. You had to *learn* to like him; it would take a month or two, but you learn to like him. You had to be around him a while to find out what a good fellow he was."[40]

"Rack" Robinson's wife, Hazel, commented about employees taking complaints to their overseers: "Sometimes they would and sometimes they wouldn't. They'd just go where they *knowed* they'd get some help."[41] And there was no question in Hazel's mind just *where* that help was.

Concerning Jordan's management style at the Gray Mill, in Gastonia, "Rack" commented: "He got that mill to running, and it was running splendid when he left... He's just one of the nicest guys you ever met in your life. Now, he could run a mill. There wan't no doubt about that. I worked for him longer than anybody, I guess." In all, Robinson worked nearly a half century for Everett Jordan.[42]

Robinson explained why so many of the employees on Jordan's mill payroll made the trek from the Gastonia and Belmont areas. When the Loray Mill strike of 1929 took place, both Everett Jordan and "Rack" Robinson were working in Saxapahaw.[43] This strike, however, had a tremendous impact on the textile industry far beyond the boundaries of Gaston County; and scholars, historians, and others give this confrontation between labor and management much credit for Southern textile mills never being successfully organized by labor unions to any great extent until the late 1970s—

and even then with much controversy.⁴⁴ Many people came to Saxapahaw seeking work after losing their jobs due to the Loray strike.⁴⁵

During these times of labor unrest, rumors reached Everett Jordan that a so-called "Flying Squadron" was on its way to Saxapahaw. Robinson recalled: "They were mean, that bunch was... They would just ride up to a mill and tell you to get the hell out of there. They'd stop it off. I think Mr. Jordan got a hint that they were on their way down here, so he got in the National Guard.⁴⁶ Had them at every door [of the mill] and at the bridge down there, and they'd search every car that came across there. They never did get here. But Mr. Jordan had soldiers [National Guardsmen] up here at the store and on top of the mill, and on the hill down there... with machine guns and with live ammunition, too."⁴⁷ Just as Everett Jordan did not go into a board meeting unprepared, neither did he go empty-handed into any other affray.

"Rack" Robinson praised his long-admired boss and old friend: "He was an unusual man. Most people that have businesses, they have to be rough to get it going—but he didn't. He wasn't rough to nobody. He could get more out of you than anybody you've ever seen. You'd do things for him that you wouldn't do for nobody else. I don't know [why]. He could ask you to do something that you wouldn't have done for nobody else in the world and you'd go ahead and do it. He just had that way of approaching you. If he wanted something done, he got it done just because people liked him, you know."⁴⁸ This charisma was probably the most pronounced characteristic of his personality.

Another characteristic was his willingness to come to the aid of employees who were sick or were facing other difficulties.⁴⁹ These included both black and white employees, and a goodly number of the actions involved loans, usually unsecured, to make down payments on homes. He usually responded favorably to the petitions that he felt were deserving. For example, a longtime black employee of Jordan's, Kent Miller, made the following comment: "So far as I know, I haven't heard anybody [among the black employees] say anything bad or nothing unkind about him. One thing about him, he would do you a favor if he knew you really *needed* a favor. He did me several like that. He helped me when I built my house

Hazel A. Robinson, wife of "Rack" Robinson and longtime employee of Everett Jordan's mill. (*Ruth Robinson Marley*)

Robert B. ("Rack") Robinson, one of Everett Jordan's "Pied Piper" followers from Gaston County. (*Ruth Robinson Marley*)

...He told me not to tell nobody else about it because he knew other people would want him to do the same thing for them. He helped George Thompson [another black employee], too, when he built his house."[50]

Kent continued: "I think he got most of the black votes in the Saxapahaw area because a lot of the people around here that knew him, knew if he could do them a favor he would do it. Just like when the roads were being built. You say something to Mr. Jordan about it—if there were enough houses to do so—he would help them get a road in. I don't mean get them paved; I mean get them pulled up and graded...We talked to him [about these problems] and he got on the phone several times, and then in another day or two the people [the road crews] were down there."[51]

Jordan also made donations of $500 each to two of the black churches.[52] Although he was a member of the Saxapahaw United

Methodist Church, he did not confine his financial support to his own denomination, but gave generous assistance to Baptists, Friends, and other churches in the area, particularly for building projects.[53]

Everett Jordan had learned the mill business by working side-by-side in the mill with the people who operated the machines. He kept an open-door policy and welcomed information from whatever source, but especially from the machine operators. After all, he said more than once: "They're the folks who produce the yarn."[54]

As Joe Neel stated: "If you had any problem you would tell Mr. Jordan if you wanted to. It wasn't any secret. For instance, John Wright [a mill employee] used to tell Mr. Jordan everything that happened [in the mill] over at the church every Sunday."[55] There were a number of "John Wrights" whom Jordan relied upon for information.

One mill superintendent, Wilson Aultman, attempted to change the practice of employees bypassing their immediate supervisor and going directly to the mill owner by establishing a chain of command. As Neel said, "What we had always been used to was to take it to Mr. Jordan." Other factors were involved, but the new system contributed to Aultman's early termination of employment at Jordan's mills.[56]

"Rack" Robinson understood Jordan's mill policies. As the former stated, "Mr. Jordan told me, and Joe Neel did too, that if you wanted to find out what was what [going on] in the mill, you ask a "hand," not the overseer. Said they worked on machines and they knew what was going on. Overseers didn't run the machines. That's the way Jordan found out a lot of things—just walking through, and people would stop and tell him something, and he'd talk to everybody. He'd stop and say 'How's everything going?' They'd just haul off and tell him. They didn't know, but he was writing all of it down in his mind."[57]

Jordan's policy was to fill the mills with machines, and to keep personnel in the office to a bare minimum. He considered those in the office merely a necessary evil because they did not directly produce yarn. On the other hand, spinners, doffers, twister-tenders, machine operators—all these were vital to converting raw cotton into yarn for him to sell. Jordan, on occasion, verbally expressed his disdain for "white collar overhead." His approach was simple: have no more desks in an office than were absolutely necessary because they meant non-production salaries. Although for years he insisted on having a monthly audit by outside auditors, he never cared at all for detailed reports. His concern was for "the bottom line." From time to time, he would merely ask the bookkeeper: "How much money do we have in the bank?"[58]

As treasurer, for years he signed all checks; and, when he did entrust this responsibility to others, he required co-signatures. Even then, he examined invoices paid in his absence, especially those relating to reimbursement of expenses to people who traveled for sales or administrative purposes. He kept a particularly close watch over other categories, too, such as machinery repairs and mill supplies. His perpetual contention was that most of the cost of repairs and supplies were due to neglect, abuse, and poor management by supervisors. In management meetings, he seldom failed to reprove his superintendents for what he considered excessive costly machinery repairs.[59]

The mill office was kept under equally close scrutiny and tight control. On one occasion, after Jordan had been in the U.S. Senate for some time, he came through his company offices and saw a handful of stamped envelopes that had been spoiled with incorrect addresses. Although the office manager explained that some spoilage was inevitable, and that the post office would redeem all the stamps, the senator delivered a five-minute lecture about the evils of wasting office supplies and how the office staff should exercise more care in its work.[60]

On another occasion, the office had just acquired a new NCR400 accounting machine. The senator looked it over and inquired about the price. When told, his reply was: "Harrumphh! We could have bought a new Cadillac for what that thing cost!"[61]

Weekends, particularly Saturdays, were his favorite time for staff meetings with both mill and office personnel. The senator personally assisted in the listing of county property taxes, usually on Saturday afternoons at his office. Regardless of whether or not a specific need existed, he expected his salaried people to be in their offices on Saturday mornings. He never accepted the idea that the headquarters in Saxapahaw could close on Saturdays, even though

The "Pied Piper" 145

his staff in Washington very seldom kept office hours then. It was as if he had two standards of conduct, an observation that could be applied to other activities and situations, even with his own family.[62]

Ben Jordan, his son, retrospectively provided an example of this double standard: His father told Ellen, Ben's wife, that he stayed in Hot Springs, Ark., three weeks every year. Only six months before that, Ben had to obtain a special dispensation to spend ten days on a cruise with Ellen and her dad. A week at a time off was all that he received. Two weeks vacation was just unheard of for anybody else except Everett Jordan.[63]

Ben explained: "He had a standard for himself and a standard for everybody else. I guess we all do. I don't know that I criticize that, except that he was so adamant about what one does as being head of the company: 'You don't leave because you have to be an example to the people working with you and for you.' He said that didn't really apply to him because he had customers with him."[64]

In Everett's defense, however, one can surmise that the hardworking "do-it-all" mill man probably realized that he had to obtain occasional relief from the constant pressure of his job in order to survive. Although no one ever can recall hearing him complain about his work or his health, his daughter, Rose Ann, later recalled that, when she was a child, her father suffered from terrible headaches, though she never remembered his being sick in any other way.[65]

Jordan's chief retreat was his summer home in the mountains at Montreat, N.C. The family usually stayed there for a month or longer during the summer. He would generally travel there on the train Thursday nights and arrive at the Black Mountain, N.C., railroad station the next morning and be met by Mrs. Jordan. He returned by train late Sunday afternoon. Weekend guests were usually customer- or family-related. Other, extended, vacations were often with customers.[66]

Everett Jordan never let anyone who worked for him forget that the mill was—or should be—top priority for himself and them, too. John, the younger son, in an interview for this volume stated: "He was always trying to program [me]—he wanted me to grow up just like him, I guess—work in the mill and think nothing except mill—

textiles. I didn't mind at all, but I had other interests." John's interests, among other things, included cattle and politics. His father approved of neither for his son, even though he himself owned a farm and was a politician. John quoted his father: "You're not going to make a living with cows, don't fool with them!"[67]

Shortly before the senator's death in 1974, he confided to his old friend Clyde Gordon that he did not fully approve of John's running for political office—at that time a seat in the North Carolina house of representatives—but, because he was going to run anyway, would Gordon support him. Gordon agreed to do so.[68]

Although the two were alike in many respects, this father and son disagreed on numerous occasions and on various issues. Yet, John always held his father in high esteem, if not awe: "He was the best [as a mill man]—especially I think in this organization [Sellers Manufacturing Company]. I'm the closest thing to daddy because he worked all the time, and he loved his work. He enjoyed his work; he was a motivator and a mover of people. He communicated; he was firm but fair. So if you don't mind work in a textile business—any business for that matter—you succeed. You just don't get ahead eight to five."[69]

Everett Jordan did get ahead. But he had a lot of help. When the board of directors hired him in 1927, they set his salary at $500 a month, an annual salary of $6,000, an excellent sum at that time. Mill hands were making 20 cents an hour, or $12 for a sixty-hour week.[70] In the early 1930s, typical annual incomes and salaries were: lawyer $4,218, congressman $8,663, doctor $3,382, railroad executive $5,064, and engineer $2,520.[71]

During those first years, Jordan had to resolve two questions: What would his product be? Who would help him produce it? There was no question about who would do the selling, that is, until his mill outgrew the capability of one man.

Roger Gant, Jr., Everett Jordan's son-in-law and president of Glen Raven Mills, stated in 1987:

> [Everett Jordan] was very smart about not only management, but about the technology of running the spinning mill...[and] recognizing his limitations, too. When he took the mill over in 1927, it was a spinning and weaving mill, and the warps were still on the looms. The assumption was that he could continue to operate as an

integrated weaving mill. But Everett said, "I don't know anything about those looms, and I *do* know something about spinning frames. So let's crank up those spinning frames. We're not going to run those looms, at least not for the time being." He never did run the looms, and he eventually replaced looms with spinning frames when he could afford it. So he recognized that there were possibilities—opportunities—available to him in the spinning business without having to take on a new technology about which he knew nothing.[72]

During the late twenties into the forties, Piedmont North Carolina—with Alamance County in the forefront—was becoming the men's and ladies' hosiery manufacturing center. This boom created a terrific demand for fine-combed yarns and, a little later, for mercerized cotton yarns—the two products that Jordan decided his mills should concentrate on producing. His timing was nearly perfect.[73]

Roger Gant paid tribute to the achievements of the transplanted Pied Piper of Gastonia: "Everett created that mill from when it was [re-] started in 1927 until his death. It was his handiwork. He had hired all the key people; he had lived in the village with most of the employees and their families. And his relationship with that business was almost a perfect illustration of entrepreneurship at its best."[74]

Everett Jordan, however, did not achieve success overnight, and some had misgivings from the beginning. As his sister Margaret Jordan Sprinkle commented: "Everything around there [Saxapahaw] was just run-down... We just felt like he was undertaking a hopeless situation, really, but it wasn't long before he had it straightened out."[75]

Sales increased substantially from the very first year of operation. But, to make the business outlook even more difficult, the mill was barely going again when the Great Depression set in. Countless cotton mills, plants, and businesses of all descriptions—even banks—failed during the terrible thirties when the depression was at its worst.[76]

Nevertheless, Everett Jordan and Sellers Manufacturing Company were survivors and in 1936—for the first time—the mill's net earnings account showed a positive balance. That year, in appreciation for his leadership and accomplishments, the board of directors voted Everett Jordan his first raise in salary, from $6,000 to $7,500 per year, and in 1937 Sellers Manufacturing Company paid the first dividend to its exceedingly patient stockholders.[77]

In 1938–39 B. Everett Jordan, secretary-treasurer and general manager of Sellers Manufacturing Company, could take a quick look at his economic situation and relax, ever so slightly. His mill hands were at work, the waters of the Haw were being impounded by the new dam, the turbines were turning spindles at full capacity, and it was no longer necessary to sell more company stock to meet his payroll.[78]

"The Whole Ball of String"

When the Reverend H. H. Jordan was pastor of the Methodist church in Morganton, N.C. (1911–14), he baptized Willie C. Mull, whose parents and siblings were also members of the church. Willie's father, an attorney and judge, taught the men's Sunday school class, and the minister and his family were frequent Sunday dinner guests in the Mull home. Willie was the same age as Reverend Jordan's third son, Charlie; and his oldest sister was the same age as Everett, the preacher's first son.[1]

According to Mull, the Reverend Jordan was so popular that the congregation tried in vain to have his tour extended beyond the normal four years. Mull explained the minister's techniques: "Back in those days they had the parsonage right beside the church so the preacher would be handy to fight the devil...[Everett's] daddy was a good old-fashioned small-town preacher. He could whip the devil up and down the aisles...At that stage in my life, I was more interested in getting out [of church] and going down to the river than I was in listening to the sermon. I wouldn't know whether he was a good preacher or not. He'd shout enough to wake you up if you went to sleep."[2]

Mull grew up in Morganton and for a while attended the same school as Sam Ervin, who, like Everett Jordan, was several years Mull's senior. Ervin, later a fellow senator of Jordan, at one time practiced law with Mull's father. According to Mull, Sam Ervin's father was also an "old-fashioned" Baptist preacher.[3]

Mull's first business association with Everett Jordan was when he started a silk-throwing plant at Saxapahaw in 1930. Mull at the time was working for John Shoffner at Standard Hosiery Mills, in the village of Alamance: "That was the first time I ever really knew Everett except when he was in school. In those days, they didn't know much about silk around here—it was just coming down South—had been up in the East, and ladies' hosiery was made up there, too. When they [Sellers Manufacturing Company] had problems with the yarn—and they had plenty of them in those days—Everett was his own troubleshooter."[4]

Furthermore, Mull explained, "He was his own technician, his own salesman, his own boss—as a matter of fact he did the whole job!" That "whole job" entailed every facet of the operation and management of his yarn-manufacturing enterprise. Yet, despite this multitude of responsibilities, Jordan seemed to take everything in stride. As Mull put it: "He always seemed to be—regardless of how much trouble he had—able to take it. At least, he didn't show any [exasperation] around the customer."[5]

Just as he was unperturbed by his miscue in his own wedding, his aplomb was not shaken by customers' complaints about bad yarn nor by political opponents who attacked his position and record. Those who worked closely with him had difficulty recalling an occasion when he lost his composure.[6] For example, he kept his equanimity in replying to caustic and derogatory appraisals of his conduct at the hearings in the controversial Bobby Baker case, perhaps the most vexing issue he ever had to deal with as a senator.[7]

Often he defused his critics with a story. As Willie Mull said, "Everett was a *good* story-teller. He *always* had a good story to tell! A lot of them were based on—he had adapted the stories to—the people of Saxapahaw."[8] Frank Longcrier, one of Jordan's executives, put it this way: "Everett Jordan always had the wit, the story, the humor, the personality to attract—just like a magnet. He was so charming in this that no one ever felt otherwise than to like him—to respond to him."[9]

Alton Smith, a friend and associate of Jordan, said: "[Jordan] was really amusing and interesting to be around... He was a very cordial person, a great raconteur, and he would entertain you for hours with stories and observations about people and their nature. In conversation, he would finish his series of stories and he'd then turn to you and say, 'Well, now it's your turn.'"[10]

Clyde Gordon was, perhaps, Everett Jordan's most trusted friend; when Jordan had occasion to go to Burlington and his schedule permitted, he would find time to stop by Gordon and Mull's office.

Before and after Jordan went to Washington, Gordon—as much as anyone—was Jordan's political confidant. Through this association, Willie Mull, too, was further exposed to Jordan's personality and practices. Another business relationship was fostered through Century Hosiery Mill, owned and operated by Gordon, Mull, and Chester H. Roth. Century did not actually own any knitting machines, but bought yarn from Sellers, Dixie, and other suppliers, and had it shipped to contract knitters. According to Mull: "To start with, Sellers's yarn didn't compare a'tall, but over a period of time it got to where we thought it was as good as Dixie's, which we thought was probably number one."[11]

Although Roger Gant, Jr., correctly stated that Everett Jordan declined to go into weaving because it was something that he knew nothing about,[12] he was never timid when it came to trying out new processes in the spinning and processing of yarns (see also chapter 8). Many times he tried—what were for him—difficult and innovative processes, just as he did when he became first a silk throwster and later on a mercerizer, using a chemical process that strengthens and improves the quality and appearance of cotton yarns.[13]

More than that, Everett Jordan was always an experimenter. In the development of one new yarn-manufacturing process for Sellers, Willie Mull played a major role: "I got the patent for Elasticot[14] yarn in my name and signed it over to Sellers Manufacturing Company. Joe Neel and I went over to the patent attorneys in Charlotte [N.C.], but I had previously made the yarn at Standard Hosiery in Alamance. I had charge of their texturing mill—the old-fashioned way with up twisters—and put the plant in the old Rufus Wilson building at Alamance. Kayser-Roth still has a knitting plant there."[15]

Eventually, on the assumption that Standard Hosiery held a prior patent, Roth's company entered claims for royalties on the Elasticot yarn made and sold by the Sellers Manufacturing Company, but, as Mull said, "by making Elasticot the way our patent called for, our patent was just as good as theirs. They couldn't make the yarn our way, and we couldn't make it their way without royalties. Since I had made both yarns, I knew the differences."[16]

Everett Jordan promptly sought legal counsel and, with Mull's knowledge and help, saw to it that Sellers never paid any royalties to Roth. Yet, in the process, he did not allow the proceedings to create ill will between the management of the two contending companies. As Mull said, "[Jordan] would have made a good preacher, if he had been so inclined. And he made a good politician ... But his best years were over before he got up to Washington. He told me he didn't plan to stay, but, I think when most of them get up there, the most important thing in the world is [for them] to get reelected!"[17]

Mull continued: "Everett was strictly a back-room operator. He didn't ever want to be out in the limelight until the last job he got—running for senator. Then, of course, he wanted publicity, but prior to that Everett *didn't* want publicity. He wanted to make a deal in the back room and let somebody else get the front of it. He just wanted the reins. They accused him of being rather ruthless when it came to trading-off."[18]

Mull outlined other attributes of Jordan:

> Everett was good at patching things up and smoothing things over. You could be mad as the devil at him about something [yarn or politics], and he could come in and smile, shaking hands and talking with that big mouth of his, and when he left it was all honey. He could have been a "big shot" in Washington if he had gone into it earlier. He was the kind of guy that people would vote for. Whatever [difficulty] he got into, somehow or other he would squirm around and get out of it.
>
> He worked hard; there's no question about that. And he was smart. He didn't know anything about cotton yarns when he got into that Sellers thing down there. He had to learn, but he learned fast, and he was able to get good people to work for him. Of course, the most important thing for any successful business is having good people to help you. Ain't nobody smart enough to do it all themselves.[19]

Jordan was quite aware of his own capabilities and limitations. His son John remembers him saying, on one occasion, that someone had criticized his poor grammar and he had responded: "True, I may not know or use perfect English, but I have the money to hire folks that can."[20]

On innumerable occasions, employees and associates were amazed by Everett Jordan's vast memory and penchant for practical details, particularly those relating to the mill's operation. For example, he called Kenneth W. Tisdale, one of his mill superintendents, on a cold night and directed him to go down to the plant and check the fire pump to see that it was protected from freezing; if it were not, water would not be available in case of a fire.[21]

According to Tisdale: "He was always thinking; from past experience he knew everything. He could remember more than anybody I have ever seen. He knew every motor that had ever been taken out in the past. If you happened to need, say, a fifty-horsepower motor, he'd say, 'Well, wait a minute. What happened to the one that was taken out of the pump room five years ago, or ten years ago?' You might have junked it, but you better not tell him you [did so]! You'd better find it."[22]

As Tisdale said, "Mr. Jordan remembered. He remembered all the electrical circuits; he knew where everything was in the mill. One day Joe Neel was telling him that we had to dig a well over at Cedar Falls [N.C.] because they had to have more water. Mr. Jordan said, 'Joe, right up there on the hill is a well, and it's got about fifteen gallons a minute that they quit using a long time ago.' Joe said he didn't know anything about it, but he went over there, and it *was* there. And you know, it was tied into the water system!"[23]

Tisdale continued: "Mr. Jordan was down-to-earth. He had a common down-to-earth explanation—sensible explanation—for everything that happened. He always kept in mind saving money, whether it was in manufacturing, in his personal life, or anything." Late one evening when Tisdale was managing the Royal Cotton Mill plant, at Wake Forest, Jordan arrived and apologized for being late. He said that, because he was nearing seventy, he had been seeking a copy of his birth certificate at the Bureau of Vital Statistics in Raleigh. He stated that " 'when you get to be seventy, you can earn all the money that you can and still draw your Social Security check...You know, I need that Social Security! I've paid into it and I deserve it, and you know the best thing about it, it's tax free.' "[24]

As Tisdale pointed out: "[Jordan] never let up. He worked every single day like he had to earn his living; this is what he knew. All he knew was work. No hobbies. Not long after I came here, he was telling me about having been to Florida. Well, not knowing him very well, I asked him if he had done any fishing. He said, 'Mr. Tisdale, all the fish I ever catch are customers. I just fish for customers.' "[25]

When Everett Jordan's estate was probated by his executor, Wachovia Bank and Trust Company, the bank officers were astounded to find essentially none of the personal possessions usually left by men of comparable wealth and position. There was, for example, no sports equipment, such as golf clubs or fishing tackle, no guns or expensive rings, indeed, no jewelry of any type except for his wristwatch, a Timex, which had cost him less than $20.[26]

Practically all Jordan's acquaintances and colleagues knew that he was a workaholic. This trait shaped and directed his personal, business, and social life.[27] In this respect, Katherine Jordan said Everett resembled his father: "[Everett] was the happiest when he was working. He never enjoyed playing golf or fishing and hunting or any of the recreational things that a man usually enjoys."[28]

Staley Gordon, one of Clyde Gordon's younger brothers and a Burlington hosiery manufacturing executive, as a young man had worked for Jordan in 1931–32. He said that, though the workweek ranged from sixty to eighty-five hours, "no one worked any harder than Everett did."[29] Staley pointed out that Jordan "had a lot of energy, and he had a lot of friends. He wanted other people to work, but he set a good example... Everett really hustled; he was a good fellow."[30] Staley gave an example: "I remember one time the mercerizing machine broke down, and he put on some old clothes and came down there, and it took twenty-four hours to get it going; that's how long he stayed down there. I did, too. I got so tired and sleepy that if I leaned on a post I would go to sleep, but he was still going strong." Staley explained that Jordan was then doing all the selling. But he would schedule his trips tightly so that he could be back in Saxapahaw as soon as possible—though his schedules were exhausting.[31] Dave Swain, a close professional colleague of Jordan, believed that the latter was "indefatigable."[32] Katherine Jordan thought her husband's "hobby" was work—unending work.[33] To his employees, he was a tireless role model, and no one ever called him an idler.

Tisdale gave another clue as to how his boss's mind worked where the plant was involved: "He would spend thousands of dollars to increase production, or to improve quality, but he'd fight you down the road for a sheet of paper if you used it and you didn't need to use it."[34]

"The Whole Ball of String" 155

Kenneth W. Tisdale in 1967 at the Royal Cotton Mill Company in Wake Forest (N.C.), where he served as Jordan's plant manager. (*Kenneth W. Tisdale*)

By starting out with a run-down mill and not having the capital to replace the outdated machinery with new, Everett Jordan had to patch, repair, and improvise as best he could. That was not always good enough. Because of the second-rate equipment that took many years to replace or to modernize and because of Jordan's conservative policy of pay-as-you-go, yarn quality was a constant problem. When problems with quality arose—W. C. Mull and others said he had plenty of them—Jordan had to resort to the one skill that he used most adeptly: salesmanship. Washington circles might call it diplomacy.[35]

To avoid the need for this type of salesmanship, Jordan trained Joseph Neel to help him in troubleshooting. One problem was the quality of the mercerized yarn. Mull, who worked for Standard Hosiery Mills, a purchaser of the yarn from Sellers Manufacturing Company, contended that the "mercerized yarn was terrible. You just couldn't dye it uniformly ... it wasn't uniformly stretched and shrunk with caustic. It had streaks in it; it knit all right, but it wouldn't dye in the lighter shades where the streaks showed up.

It took Sellers a good while to work it out. I don't believe [this occurred] until they hired a fellow from ... Chattanooga, Tennessee."[36]

Jordan experienced even more difficulties with silk-throwing. As a matter of fact, according to Reid Maynard, his friend and a fellow textile executive, Jordan never did solve them, and the yarn remained of poor quality. The problem became moot, however, when World War II cut off the supply of silk from Japan; and, after the war, nylon gained the ascendancy over silk.[37]

Frank Longcrier worked for Southern Franklin Processing Company in Greenville, S.C., before coming to Saxapahaw to work for Sellers Manufacturing Company in May 1944. Jordan hired him to be his sales manager and to assist in administrative duties. By that time, Sellers had made tremendous improvements, but quality still "had a ways to go." As Longcrier explained: "The yarns we made were competitive in price ... Everett Jordan never had the reputation of making the highest-quality yarn in the world, and he didn't. But he made an acceptable yarn at a price that he could sell it and make some money. We, no doubt, could have bought a better-quality yarn [yarns bought for further processing], but we would have paid several cents more per pound for it."[38]

Frank Longcrier, like Neel, Davis, the Millers, and many others, stuck with Everett Jordan until he retired. As sales manager, Longcrier was a key man in directing the company through the trying times of World War II and the ongoing expansion of operations that eventually comprised three spinning plants, along with dyeing and mercerizing plants, and a peak employment of nearly 1,000 employees by the time of Jordan's death in 1974.[39]

Jordan possessed the capability, regardless of the setting, to elicit a favorable response. Longcrier contended that Jordan had a tremendous capacity for names and faces, and that he would tend to dominate any arena he was in because he gained a quick understanding of people and situations. Longcrier provided the following example: One night the two of them were returning from the Royal Cotton Mill at Wake Forest to Saxapahaw when a young policeman stopped them for speeding. As the policeman was about to give them a ticket, Jordan asked: "Aren't you Jim Whitaker's boy?" and identified himself as Everett Jordan. The policeman recognized him, and the motorists were given only a warning instead of a ticket.[40]

In regard to what motivated Everett Jordan, Longcrier said:

> I think his motivating force goes back to when he was a kid. He was the son of a Methodist minister, moving from place to place every three or four years... every time they moved, they had to re-establish themselves, [and gain the] respect and admiration of their peers... [this would mean] all of the boys in the community... Everett was the oldest. He was the toughest; he was the fighter. He had to "whup" everybody in town everywhere he moved; or he had to whup enough of 'em to let 'em know that he could... Now, later on, there was a more genteel manner or methods. I think you have to go back to that starting-point as a fighter. If he had been a softie, he could have been pushed around just any old way, but Everett Jordan was *never* pushed around. He was never pushed around as a kid and that comes on in later life... There's no question that Everett Jordan wanted to succeed.
>
> In his family life, he was very devoted and loyal—to his brothers and sisters, his children, and to his wife... His church was more important to Everett Jordan than to most people... In order for him to contribute what he wanted to in these areas of his life—family, church, and social services—he knew he had to succeed in business. Now I think that area is the driving force of Everett Jordan... I understand his father might have been a rather shrewd businessman, but he didn't have many resources to work with. They had to scratch. That all has to be tied together to come to the bottom line ... of what made Everett Jordan tick.[41]

Longcrier pointed out that Jordan did not socialize the same way other people did: he usually incorporated his social life with his work. His guests, mostly customers or suppliers, were very important to him and he considered them as friends. Longcrier added: "Everett Jordan had a zest for life and accomplishment."[42]

In their heyday (the 1940s and 1950s), it would have been difficult to find three men who exerted more influence in local civic, political, and business matters than Everett Jordan, Clyde Gordon, and Reid Maynard. Maynard organized Grace Hosiery Mill in Burlington in 1925, two years before Jordan came to Alamance County. Shortly afterward, he organized the Tower Hosiery Mill and from 1943 to 1945 was chairman of the National Association of Hosiery Manufacturers.[43]

Maynard was one of Jordan's early mercerized-yarn customers.

W. Franklin ("Frank") Longcrier, Jr. He came from Greenville, S.C., in 1944 to become sales manager and vice-president of Sellers Manufacturing Company at its Saxapahaw office. He retired after Jordan's death.
(*W. Franklin Longcrier, Jr.*)

He later recalled an incident during a cold spell when his superintendent, Red Scott, discovered some mercerized cones that were virtually solid ice. Mercerized yarn standards permitted a limited percentage of moisture, but, because yarn was sold by the pound, yarn processors tried to provide maximum moisture in their product. Water—in this case from the Haw River—was far cheaper than long-staple cotton shipped in from the Western states.[44]

Scott called Jordan to examine the frozen cones. Maynard observed: "You know Everett would run around like a guy who was making $25 a month to look after all those little problems." At least in this case, he was rewarded. As Maynard stated, "Well, Everett would convince [Scott] that this, that, and another was the reason for it, you know; and, before he left, he had everybody happy! Everett was a politician and the best salesman you ever saw."[45]

As the years went by, Jordan, the mill man, improved his spinning plants at all three locations—Saxapahaw, Cedar Falls, and Wake Forest—but it was a long, uphill struggle.[46] As Frank Longcrier contended, Sellers's yarns were "acceptable" in the trade—but they were not "tops."[47]

In 1949 Jordan hired W. Louis Jackson, who had grown up in the school of hard knocks in Clover, S.C. He was a flint-nosed mill man who knew cotton-mill machinery from long practical experience; he was, in many respects, very much like his new boss. Jordan started him as superintendent at the Wake Forest Royal Cotton Mill plant, which Jackson said he found to be "in bad shape."[48]

Jackson managed to increase production substantially, but, while he was doing so, the Saxapahaw office continually prodded him. In the 1950s he left his position temporarily because of a "pretty rough" strike he attributed to low wages—though he had managed to raise wages a little by putting the employees on piecework instead of an hourly basis. He thought that poor machinery and maintenance were responsible for many of Royal's problems.[49]

Later, Jordan brought Jackson to Saxapahaw and directed him to work with job assignments, production, quality, and cost-control in all of Jordan's four manufacturing plants. Jackson made numerous improvements in the machinery and improved quality as well as production. As a result, Jordan told him: "I [Jackson] don't know how many times in the presence of I don't know how many people, [he stated] that I'd made him more money than any man that had ever worked for him!"[50]

Rarely could anyone remember Everett Jordan's having openly given credit or recognition for a job well done to anyone within his business organization.[51] The complimentary statement attributed to Jordan by Louis Jackson is, therefore, exceptional. Jordan felt, perhaps, that to praise his employees' work performance openly might prompt demands that he would be reluctant to deal with. Or it may have been, as John Jordan later said of his father, "I would say that probably his greatest weakness would be wanting [too much] credit [for himself]."[52] Certainly, when it came to the mills, he was not inclined to share with others any praise due. This disposition may have stemmed, partly at least, from his efforts to prove to uncle Charlie Sellers that he—and he alone—could and did do the job that had to be done. In short, he had to justify his uncle's investment of both faith and money in Everett Jordan.[53]

No question about it, Jordan had an uphill battle that men of lesser fortitude and talent would not even have attempted—much less won. Boman Sanders, of Burlington, N.C., his longtime customer and friend in both business and politics, verified retrospectively what many others have said: "Everett pitched in, with not the best of equipment; he just kept working, and he gradually improved the mill. When he first started selling yarn, I wouldn't say it was the best yarn in the world, but I'd call him up sometimes when I had a complaint about it, and he'd come up to the office. I think he was the best salesman I ever knew, and [eventually] I'd be sorry I'd called him! You know, he went on and developed that plant into one of the best in the state, and he became very successful."[54]

Sanders continued: "...and all the time he was engaged in his own business, he took time off to take a vital interest in the welfare of Alamance County; and he certainly improved his property at Saxapahaw. Later on, because of his interest in the county, he became interested in politics, and he was appointed to the Senate by Luther Hodges. Howard White, of the Burlington paper [editor of the *Times-News*], asked me what kind of senator I thought he would make. I told him I didn't know about that, but that he would be the best damn salesman in Washington! It proved out that he was very successful [there]."[55]

Sam Rankin, president of Ramseur Interlock Knitting Company, Ramseur, N.C., who is related to the Jordan family by marriage and was a customer of Jordan's, also thought that he was an outstanding salesman for the following reason: "Everett was always the same... [He] was the same [the day of his swearing-in ceremony for the Senate]... when a whole bunch of us went out to dinner—as he was in the early 1950s when I knew him in New York, and he and I and Harry Stelter would go out together. It made no difference [where he was]. He was always the same. He was an honest man— a hard bargainer, hard driver, worked hard, but he was honest—had integrity. If he told someone he would do something, he did it; and that's the main part of anyone's success in business: living up to his word."[56]

David Swain accounted for the latter's salesmanship in this manner: "Everett Jordan would sit opposite a customer...look him in the eye...and tell the customer, 'I want to help you. If you give me a chance, I will make it profitable for you, and me, too.' He looked so sincere and convincing that the customer believed him."[57]

Another effective sales technique of Jordan was to tie an additional order onto the previous one, as Willie C. Mull pointed out: "Well, he'd agree to give you a deal if you would take out another contract on mercerized yarn—mercerized yarn and silk, too. You bought on a contract of so many pounds to be shipped over a period of months [usually]. If there was a problem with the yarn, he'd agree to make it up to you on the next contract. He was smooth enough to tie another order along with the previous one. He wouldn't just settle it. He was good at that."[58]

The success of Everett Jordan with the mills he headed was recognized throughout textile circles, especially in the areas where he operated and was best known, but he also surrounded himself with well-qualified sales people who had excellent reputations: Harry Stelter, in New York; Frank Shannonhouse, in Charlotte, N.C.; Joseph Klumpp, in Philadelphia; David Swain, in Chicago;[59] Robert H. Griffith, in Chattanooga; Bill Fawcett, in Boston; and Bill Wetzell, in Gastonia, who first worked with Shannonhouse and then, after Shannonhouse's retirement, was joined by J. W. ("Jake") Miller, Jr. But the foremost salesman of all, of course, was Everett Jordan. In the pursuit of business, he would drive his shiny, black Cadillac from Saxapahaw to pay calls on key textile customers and sales offices in Boston, Chicago, Philadelphia, New York, Charlotte, Chattanooga, and points in between.[60]

In addition to his excellent sales, manufacturing, and administrative staff, Jordan enjoyed the good fortune to have other successful businessmen who were good friends of his and who stood by him and vice versa: Carl Cline (J. A. Cline and Son, Hildebran, N.C.); Al Garrou (Waldensian Hosiery Mills, Valdese, N.C.); and Ed Gruber[61] (Spring City Knitting Company, in Pennsylvania).[62]

Yes, Saxapahaw's number-one entrepreneur had help, but he also helped himself. As Sam Rankin said: "But what the man put together in his life has to speak [for itself]. Everett Jordan started with a broken-down old weave mill in Saxapahaw, and you can see

Frank M. Shannonhouse, Jr. (1899–1970). He sold more of Sellers Manufacturing Company's production than anyone else for many years, and was a major factor in Jordan's early success. Later on, he and W. L. ("Bill") Wetzell formed the partnership of Shannonhouse and Wetzell, yarn brokers for Sellers and others. (*Ann Shannonhouse Glover*)

what he built out of that! I doubt if 30 percent of the machinery in that mill in 1927 was modern enough to operate, even during the depression, but he ran it, and the same was true at Cedar Falls. I remember going in [that] plant, and it certainly didn't have modern machinery, but they ran it until they could replace it and put something better in there."[63]

David F. Swain represented Everett Jordan's yarn mills in the Midwest from 1937 until his retirement in 1969. His association with and loyalty to Jordan clearly demonstrates what Sam Rankin was talking about. First, Jordan was a friend to Swain and encouraged him to go into business for himself. After that, he worked tirelessly to assist Swain in selling yarns. In the process, he earned his undying appreciation.[64]

Swain met Jordan when the former was employed as a yarn salesman in the Midwest by the Klumpp-Glynn department of Bliss Fabyan Company, New York City, which had been employed by Everett Jordan to sell the mercerized yarns of Sellers Manufacturing Company. Jordan offered to journey to the Midwest to help Swain to get started because Bliss Fabyan had no yarn business in the region, and Swain was starting from scratch.[65]

Jordan encouraged Swain to go out on his own because he wanted the latter to be his direct representative. This was not an easy decision for Swain, but Jordan assured him that he could do it—and that he, Jordan, would help in every way possible.[66]

On occasion, Jordan would join Swain in the Midwest and travel with him on his sales calls. When Swain set up his Chicago office, the Midwest was not using a large volume of the type of yarns produced by Sellers Manufacturing Company; the mills there already had their sources of supply. Everett Jordan did not spin all the yarns that he mercerized for Swain's accounts; he also purchased yarns from a number of other spinners. However, those yarns that he did spin were produced at the lowest cost possible in order to compete successfully with the entrenched yarn producers, who usually could offer superior quality. His continued success proves that he did compete by having lower prices and also was adept in the producing and selling of yarn counts to his advantage.[67]

According to Swain, personality played a key role in Jordan's success: "Everett had a very warm, outgoing personality with evidence of a sincere wish to be of service." The Reverend Henry H. Jordan's son probably did not absorb all of his father's exhortations—but the concept of rendering service and making his time available to others was evidently indelibly imprinted on the mind of young Everett. Swain merely confirmed what a host of other observers had seen as well.[68]

For example, in a 1987 interview for this volume, Dr. William C. Friday, ex-president of the University of North Carolina system, stated: "But the thing I remember so vividly about him [Jordan], he was such a warm and generous man. And with his time. When you

Clyde W. Gordon (1902–86). This Burlington, N.C., industrialist and civic leader, who was closely associated with Everett Jordan in business, political, and civic affairs, was considered to be his most trusted confidant. (*Eugene A. Gordon*)

Reid A. Maynard (1896–1983), Burlington, N.C., hosiery manufacturer, civic leader, friend, and customer of Everett Jordan. The two worked closely together in various political and civic endeavors. (*James W. Maynard*)

knew him and he knew you, then you did have a friend. Mrs. Jordan, too. They made a great team."[69]

Of all of Everett Jordan's many friends, few, if any, enjoyed a more intimate relationship with him than did Clyde Gordon. In the early 1920s, John Shoffner[70] was becoming established in the hosiery business at the Standard Hosiery Mills in the village of Alamance; and, like Everett Jordan later on, was surrounding himself with competent people. One of his top executives then was young Clyde Gordon. The Standard Hosiery Mills, one of Everett's first customers for silk, also purchased a lot of mercerized cotton yarns from him. Later, in the 1940s, after Gordon joined Chester Roth and Willie C.

Mull in acquiring the Century Hosiery Corporation, the firm split its business between Dixie Mercerizing Company and Sellers. Sellers received the major part, but Century had two sources of supply in case of emergency.[71]

Willie Mull's contention that Everett Jordan did the whole job—"the whole ball of string"—goes unchallenged. And he was always in command. According to Saxapahaw's former postmaster Edgar Cashwell, "Bigfoot" was one of the nicknames covertly used by villagers and employees for the mill owner: "Bigfoot Jordan. When he put his foot down, that was it."[72]

The finished product inescapably bore its maker's likeness. The ball may have had some uneven threads; it did not boast a perfect circumference, but it would roll, and Jordan rolled, too. Holding his ball of string, he had no doubts "a'tall" that he would reach his destination.

8

Transplanted Hollies—The Gruber Connection

In the southeastern corner of Alamance County—as in many other places in North Carolina—holly trees grow luxuriantly in the wild. Some of these same trees, long ago transplanted, still grace the estate of the Edward Gruber family in Pottstown, Pa., and thereby hangs a tale.[1]

Spring City Knitting Company, Spring City, Pa., was by far Everett Jordan's biggest and most profitable yarn customer. Edward ("Ed") Gruber operated the company after he took over from his father, Ira Gruber, with whom Everett Jordan had established the initial business relationship.

The history of Spring City Knitting Company began with Ira, an immigrant, whose own father had settled on a thirty-eight-acre farm in Berks County, Pa., and who, in order to make a living, "farmed out" his fourteen children to neighbors.

After one harvest, however, Ira visited his married sister in Spring City. For a while, he worked for his brother-in-law, who was a pattern-maker in a foundry. But Ira soon took up carpentry, making wooden cases for shipments from an underwear mill next to the foundry. He was paid $4 a week, but the owner retained $3 as savings for the youth. Within two or three years, the latter was superintendent of the plant. Irritated because he could never obtain the full amount of the "savings" still owed him, which probably amounted to $8,000–10,000, he quit and went into the underwear business with $256 and never borrowed a penny. To begin operations, he purchased two used sewing machines and a knitting machine; and, for purposes of economy, made only one small size of underwear.

Like the Reverend H. H. Jordan, the senior Gruber saw the value of education and sent his son, Edward, to preparatory school at Mercersburg, Pa., and later the Wharton School of Business,[2] in Philadelphia. Unlike B. Everett Jordan, who attended Trinity College (present Duke University) for only one lackluster year, Edward graduated.

He then came to work for the Spring City Knitting Company. His father trained him for the job and served as a role model—not unlike the approach of Everett Jordan with his employees and two sons. By finding out what was wrong on the floor and moving quickly to solve it and expedite the shipment of orders, even if night work were involved, Edward Gruber quickly gained a knowledge of the business.

This was the same management technique that Jordan used. He endlessly troubleshot in his own plants and was apt to appear on the scene at any time of his choosing, day or night. And, like Edward Gruber, he learned the mill business from personal observation and action rather than from studying a textbook or obtaining second-hand assistance or advice.

The two men were similar in another way. To get the job done, Gruber spared neither himself nor his employees. The same can be said of his friend from Saxapahaw, and stories abound to support the comparison. Whatever deadline, obstacle, or challenge, Everett Jordan did not back down but sallied forth like a conquering knight. He, too, had to deal with the Great Depression, a time that demanded superb salesmanship merely for survival. Nevertheless, like Gruber, he kept selling his mill's production. Nature—the flood waters of the Haw River and the accompanying interruptions of his plant's operation due to lack of waterpower—afforded Jordan numerous opportunities to demonstrate his ability to lead his troops. When portions of the wooden dam washed away, the waterwheel stopped, and spindles quit turning, Everett Jordan would grab a hammer, put on his boots, and work by the side of his black and white mud-spattered laborers until production was resumed.[3]

The similarities of the Grubers, both father and son, and Everett Jordan do not end at this point. In 1985 Edward Gruber provided this striking example: "There were two people that ran the place for my father. They were Bill Council—his man Friday in the of-

Transplanted Hollies—The Gruber Connection

Edward ("Ed") L. Gruber. As head of the Spring City (Pa.) Knitting Company, he was not only Everett Jordan's biggest customer but was also an admirer. (*Edward L. Gruber*)

fice—and my uncle, who was sort of the plant superintendent. Nevertheless, it was a one-man show. My dad wouldn't let them buy a broom to sweep the floor without his permission. Nobody did anything without his permission. He bought the yarn and put the prices on everything and did the selling."

In 1982 John Jordan pointed out that his father had the same approach: "As I matured, like all men, I did want to make *some* decisions—even little decisions."[4] To further illustrate his exasperation with his father's insistence on doing everything his way, John recounted an argument they had about whether to buy wooden or paper bobbins: "Daddy...wanted to buy new spindles to fit old wooden bobbins. My reasoning was: We're going to buy new spindles anyhow, and, yes, we would have to buy new paper bobbins and throw away the old wooden bobbins, but we could get faster speeds, better yarn—no one was keeping wooden bobbins; they were just obsolete. I had talked to a number of manufacturers, and they would sell us either one; it didn't make any difference to them. But they thought we would be crazy to buy wooden bobbins. We would be the only mill around that still had [them]."[5]

This occurred rather late in the senator's career, when his older son, Ben, was serving as president and running the company on a day-to-day basis, and John was superintendent of one of the spinning mills. As John later said:

> I would have thought that, as a father, he would liked to have seen his son make a decision and say, "Yes, let's try those; that's a good idea," instead of, "No, you're wrong and we're not going to buy paper bobbins; we're going to stick with wooden bobbins." Then, apparently after he had checked around and found that I was right, he didn't call another meeting and say, "Yes, after investigating this matter I found that John is correct, and, yes, I think we should buy paper bobbins." This was also true when Daddy was dealing with Joe Neel [vice-president in charge of manufacturing] or anybody else. I don't recall a single time in my life when *I* was right. To my knowledge, he never said, "John, that's a good idea; let's do that." If we did it, it was his idea.[6]

In other words, every idea, every plan, every purchase or decision—except the most inconsequential concerning the mills—was Everett Jordan's. John elaborated: "As you recall, when daddy was in the Senate he would come home maybe once or twice a month on weekends. Even though Ben [Jordan] was supposed to be running the company, daddy was still running it. And did until he died. If we were going to buy some equipment, even a copy machine, he had to make the final decision."[7]

John continued: "Daddy would be having a meeting in his office [Saxapahaw] discussing with Ben and me, Louis Jackson, Joe Neel, and Frank Longcrier about whether to buy a million dollars worth of machinery, and [because some constituent would call up with some relatively trivial problem] he would stop the meeting and have our top management just sit there and wait" until he finished talking. This was particularly frustrating to John and the others when two or three such interruptions would occur on a Saturday morning—particularly because they felt they did not need his decision on some of the matters.[8]

In Everett Jordan's situation, by the time his two sons were old enough to take an active part in the business, he had been the chief executive officer and manager for long and trying years, had achieved notable success, was justifiably proud, and had supreme confidence in his own ability. He was not about to let sons Ben and John—or anyone else—make a mess out of his hard-won handiwork. Consequently, he retained command to the end. In all likelihood, this same scenario would have been carried out by Ira Gruber if the decision had been left in his hands.

This did not occur, however, because, within a matter of months after Edward Gruber started working for his father, one of the two key executives left for health reasons, the other died, and Ira Gruber was hospitalized on and off for more than a year. Edward was forced to gain management experience quickly. His father continued on the board of directors until his death, but participated only intermittently in management—living on and off in Canada and Florida.

Yet the roots of the Gruber-Jordan relationship had been established years earlier by Ira and Everett. As Edward Gruber later recalled:

> The last year I was in college, the summer of 1930, Everett came to visit my father; and my father took him over to his farm called Bellewood in Pottstown [Pennsylvania], where I live now. My father was rebuilding the house and doing a lot of landscaping. When Everett got back home, he went out and dug up a bunch of holly trees and sent them up to my father [as a gift] to plant around the house. Some of those trees are out there now. They were native North Carolina hollies, but they never have any red berries. I have a lot of English hollies that I got some time ago; when I bought them, I got male and female. You have to have both male and female or they won't pollinate. I guess that may be the reason we never got any berries on the holly trees that Everett sent up to my dad. I could see Everett Jordan [with my dad] riding around the farm looking at the holly trees.

Everett Jordan, in those days, did not know anything at all about the pollination of holly trees, but he knew a lot about people and how to motivate them. His insight and understanding paid off handsomely, especially with the Grubers. Eventually, Edward Gruber and his knitting mills bought so much yarn from Jordan's spinning mills that Jordan first had to determine Gruber's requirements before he could set up production schedules.

The close business interdependence of Edward Gruber and Everett Jordan originated in 1932, when the former took advantage of an opportunity to manufacture women's panties at high profits. To produce them, he needed some pink 60/2 mercerized yarn. The only mercerizer he knew was Everett Jordan, who was just beginning to use the process with cotton yarns. The mercerized underwear sales boomed so fast that Jordan's mills could not take care of all of Gruber's yarn requirements. Accordingly, he procured another supplier, Ewing-Thomas, owned by Cannon Mills, which wanted about ten cents more a pound than Jordan. Jordan pointed out that this was the fixed price of the Durene Association of America.[9] To help Gruber, Jordan, in confidence, sold him the mercerized yarn at five cents a pound less than he had been charging and said to Gruber: "If you buy two pounds from me and one from them [Ewing-Thomas], then you're ahead of the game."

Jordan, fighting the price-fixing, continued to advise Gruber on how much he could buy from him, how much to buy from somebody else, and who to buy it from. However, the Durene Association of America blamed, not Jordan, but Ewing-Thomas for submitting price information to the Spring City Knitting Company. But for years Jordan actually set the price of mercerized yarn; there was the Durene Association price and the Spring City price. Complaints from the association continued for a few years, but it finally reached the point where other members of the association met Jordan's price.

The ladies' cotton underwear program lasted for only a few years because practically all underwear producers had started to utilize Durene, which meant price-cutting, and everyone started making lingerie out of rayon and other manmade fibers. Therefore, Gruber began to manufacture men's underwear, first with carded yarn and later with combed yarn. He and Jordan also continued their joint product improvement program. The latter blended silk with cotton as well as linen with cotton, and tried some other fibers. Out of all these blends, Spring City Knitting Company made sample garments, which were always on the desks of buyers for Penney's and Sears when they were looking for something new.

In another innovation, Jordan introduced Pima cotton to Gruber; convinced him that it would make a beautiful yarn; and evolved the correct mixture of Pima cotton, of high quality and price (double that of white cotton because so little was grown). The ratio decided on was 60/2 Pima in shorts, 50/2 in briefs, and 22/1 for T-shirts because it was found that plied mercerized Pima was too heavy and the cost was high. For years, the Sellers mills produced 22/1 Pima for Gruber under the "Pima Prince" program. Numerous other Southern mills also produced this type of yarn for Gruber.

About this time, Gruber made some underwear out of a blend of polyester and cotton yarn, but DuPont would not allow the use of polyester on a knitting machine. Their representatives said it would pill[10] and could only be used as a weaving yarn. So Jordan dyed some yarn using a dye that only affected the polyester, leaving the cotton undyed. Making up some underwear, Gruber, who found out that it was the cotton that was pilling and not the polyester, showed them to DuPont, which authorized Spring City Knitting Company to sell to them but no one else. This offered little advantage because polyester cost $4.50 a pound. When DuPont cut the price to $1.00 per pound, Penney's started to buy Gruber's garments in a week's time. Accordingly, as usual, the Sellers mills started to make polyester and cotton blends, which Jordan had devised for Gruber.

As Gruber later recalled: "Anytime I needed something new, I went to Everett, and he made it." As a matter of fact, Gruber said he "never made a move without talking to Everett." Gruber continued: "This evolution of the underwear business all starts with Everett Jordan. That's the reason I'm telling you all this in detail. Everett was not only innovative and creative, but he knew the spinning. We'd go to other people to try to get them to make the same thing, and they couldn't make it. When we got to the place that we used the yarn faster than Everett could make it, then he would tell somebody else what to do. He would tell them how to make it."

After a while, Gruber's arrangement with Penney's worked so well that he was practically running his whole plant for that company. He had been using carded and combed cotton yarns, but he needed to upgrade his product to obtain a better price. Again, he turned to his resourceful friend, Jordan, and asked what kind of yarn to use. Jordan's advice was two-ply mercerized cotton yarn, counts 50/2 and 60/2, which was Durene yarn made by Sellers Manufacturing Company. Penney's at this time wanted something for a big sale, an anniversary, or similar event. Gruber decided to try a new twist: He packaged the garments three to a package to sell for one dollar. Also, he heeded Jordan's advice and put the Durene label on the underwear. To the elation of the two of them as well as Penney's, the three-pack was a highly successful program.

Therefore, the mutual trust between the two mill owners waxed ever stronger. As Gruber later explained: "Everett and I were sitting over in Spring City one day, and I told him that the Swiss-ribbed shirts made of mercerized yarn lost their elasticity when they are bleached. He said, 'Why don't you make them out of bleached yarn?' So we made the Swiss-ribbed shirts out of the bleached yarn. At some place along about then, Everett put in a bleaching kier." As Jordan did on so many other occasions, he adapted his plants to serve the needs of his customers.

After the polyester program ended, Gruber and Jordan agreed they needed to have a product that would sell for a higher price. Gruber had been reading about DuPont's program on qiana,[11] which was to replace silk. In the meantime, Jordan had been experimenting with nylon, but it turned yellow. Next, the two tried orlon, the wool counterpart. That would not bleach. So Jordan procured some qiana staple and made 80's (yarn count size) out of the qiana blend.

Gruber developed the qiana program for Penney's, but any new program for that company created a demand from Sears for a new product for them, too. Once again, Gruber made a telephone call to Saxapahaw and explained the situation to his dauntless innovator. Egyptian cotton had the longest staple (fiber length) of any cotton on the market, and was also the costliest. Jordan obtained some Egyptian cotton and called the new yarn spun for Gruber's Sears program "Royal Egyptian." The name "Egyptian," of course, came from the cotton; and "Royal" came from the name of one of Jordan's spinning mills, Royal Cotton Mill Company, where the yarn was spun. As Gruber explained: "Everett even labeled the stickers in the cones 'Royal Egyptian'! You see, all things originated down at Sellers." This Sears program represented another triumph for Gruber and Jordan.

Another yarn that Sellers developed and produced for Spring City was called "Nylile," made of nylon and cotton. According to Gruber, Jordan himself coined the name "Nylile." This yarn had a tight twist and gave the cloth a more "sculptured" look, that is, it was not fuzzy.

There were other programs that Gruber created for the major department-store chains, programs whose origin started with Everett Jordan in this manner. According to Gruber: "We used to just sit around and talk... We would talk and talk. I didn't know what you could or could not do. I just kept asking Everett questions." And Jordan knew or found the answers.

In 1968 Gruber, after becoming the largest men's underwear manufacturer in the United States, sold his company to Cluett, Peabody, and Company, Inc. But he, like Everett Jordan, had become too work-oriented to retire fully and subsequently served as a consultant for Penney's.

Although eminently successful and rightfully proud of his own achievements, in his interview for this volume, Gruber emphasized the contribution Everett Jordan had made to Gruber's own company as well as to the entire textile industry. Gruber also not only praised Jordan's integrity, friendliness, geniality, honesty, and generosity but also rated him as "one of the true friends he could number on one hand."[12]

As Gruber explained: "I used to call Everett on the phone and say, 'Hey, I'm in trouble!' He had a saying: 'It's all right to get into trouble, as long as you don't draw any blood.' Or he would say, 'You're going to have to go get a surgeon's license,' or something like that. He had so many homey statements."

In the 1985 interview, Gruber submitted proof of why he considered Jordan to be one of his two or three authentic friends when he said again: "Hey, I'm in trouble." This time, his request for help from Jordan was not about yarns but concerned Edward Gruber, personally. He had come to an impasse in his private life, one that he could not handle: an acrimonious dispute with his father. But Everett Jordan had never learned to say "I can't," nor, "I won't" to a friend.

Because of Penney's expansion in the Western United States and recognition of the fact that much of this business, as well as that of Sears, would be lost should someone else build a plant in that region and thereby lower transportation costs and improve service for customers, Edward Gruber and his board of directors decided to build a plant there. They finally chose Scottsdale, Ariz. In sharp contrast to California, that state had a right-to-work law, practically no unions, and a low tax rate.

As Gruber started to build the plant, his father, Ira, who owned 83 percent of the company's stock and who had been participating in almost no decisions, said he had never agreed to build a factory in Arizona, accused two of the board members of falsifying the minutes of the meeting when the board agreed to build such a factory, fired the two on the spot, and gave his son one year in which to either buy him out or vice versa.

To determine what sum to offer his father, Edward hurried down to talk to Jordan. The two arrived at a figure of $2,500,000. Unable to obtain a loan for that amount from the Philadelphia bank he had done business with, Gruber again turned to Jordan, who, working with Archie K. Davis, chairman of the board of Wachovia Bank and Trust Company, Winston-Salem, helped Gruber obtain a loan for about $1,900,000 from Wachovia. Jordan also loaned Gruber $200,000–300,000. According to Gruber, nobody in the industry ever knew that Jordan had any money in the Spring City Knitting Company. Gruber paid off the Wachovia loan in four years and three days.

When Gruber, accompanied by Jordan and Davis, made his unsuccessful attempt to secure the loan from the Philadelphia bank, somehow the subject of fox hunting came up. One of the sedate bankers asked Jordan: "Did you ever go fox hunting?" Jordan, who did not have the slightest notion of how these urbane sportsmen conducted a fox hunt, quickly replied, "Oh, yes!" and proceeded to tell how he—the preoccupied Saxapahaw entrepreneur, with no time for sports and hobbies—ran his fox hunt back home. Jordan explained that he would stand in a fence corner, wait for the dogs to show up, and then go along a creek bank and chase the fox out. He said, "All a fox is good for is shooting." The stodgy Philadelphia bankers, who had been fox hunting all their lives wearing fancy red riding coats, were appalled.

Transplanted Hollies—The Gruber Connection

When Gruber started negotiations to sell Spring City Knitting Company to Cluett, Peabody, and Company, Inc., it became necessary to retrieve his stock, which Gruber had endorsed and was being held in Jordan's office as security for the loans he had made to Gruber to buy out his father. In the transaction, for Spring City to obtain possession of the stock, Gruber had agreed to pay a fixed rate of return that would accumulate year to year and become due and payable whenever the principal was paid. As Gruber later explained: "I know when I went in to see Everett, I had a worksheet where I had it all worked out showing how much interest was due year by year with a grand total, and I rounded out the figure. I had a check for the total and I said, 'Everett, now if this isn't agreeable to you, let me know.' He looked at it, took the check, and said, 'That's fine.' It was done just that quick. That's the kind of guy Everett was. He could have put a gun to my back and said, 'I need another half-million' or something like that—or more, God only knows—but not Everett."

Credit has been defined as "Man's trust in man." Jordan's relationship with Gruber is one—but only one among many—examples of how the Methodist minister's son practiced faith in his fellow man—when he thought that trust was warranted.

According to Gruber, one of Jordan's favorite statements was as follows: "You're never wrong, but you're not always right." And Everett Jordan was never known to admit to a mistake—at least not publicly. He never even told Edward Gruber that he had given Gruber's father hollies that would not produce berries.

Gruber, who had worked closely with Jordan over the years, admired him. "[He was] the most honest man that I ever met in my life...Everett was not only a man of integrity, a man with a nice friendly smile; he was not only genial, but he was a very generous man. Everett would go out of his way to be helpful. He did this so often, it became a part of his life. I know, in walking around through the plants, if he ran into somebody, whether they be black or white, especially black, if he knew someone was having trouble

178   The Life of B. Everett Jordan

The "Old-Timers Club," consisting of Sellers Manufacturing Company employees with twenty or more years of service, meets in the early 1950s at the Saxapahaw United Methodist Church. *Front row, left to right*: Hugh Allen, Nell Hardin, Johnnie Ellington, Hazel A. Robinson, John Shaw, Jessie Johnson, Lillie Roberson. *Second row*: J. R. ("Dad") Baber, Floyd Petty, William H. Bloxsom, Sr., Roosevelt ("Rosie") Hardin, Troy Knighten, George G. Phillips, unidentified, Grady Quakenbush, Aretta Hall. *Third row*: Clarence Mann, Lannie Petty Wright, Ola Smith Phillips, Clarabel L. Cates, Thelma ("Red") McAdams, unidentified, Bettie Neal. *Fourth row*: Robert B. ("Rack") Robinson, John Wright, Pride C. Overman. *Fifth row*: Arthur Thacker, Randa D. Haithcock, John J. Madden, Glenn H. Cates, unidentified, W. Grover Neal, Jim Crutchfield, Joe Thomas, Alson T. Davis, Charlie Hunter, Grover Crisson, Kent W. Miller, R. C. Crutchfield, Robert Neal Smith, Joseph M. Neel, W. Adrian Jobe, Calvin C. Saunders, B. Everett Jordan, Cephus Knighten. (*Margaret Alice McLean*)

at home, or something like that, he would go out of his way to see how he or his company could do something to be helpful."

Gruber continued:

> Jordan had a personality all his own. He was like a magnet, a magnet that attracted substance. Also, Everett was always in complete command of himself and of the situation. To go one step further, he was usually in complete command of the people with whom he associated and surrounded himself. He was in command because of his personality, his integrity, his friendliness, and his understanding. Everett had the unusual knack of understanding the other man's prob-

lems. This is one of the greatest attributes anyone can have, and those who have it are unusual. That person attracts confidence and trust. Everett Jordan was dedicated to the real fine principles of life. I had no way to know, but, if I were asked, I would have to say that I believe that Everett was a very religious person, because of his dedication to his family, his employees, his company, to any project in which he was interested.

All this adds up to his being a very religiously disciplined gentleman. I'm using the word "gentleman" advisedly because Everett was at times and always a gentleman. He had the respect of all those people that I mentioned. And in turn, which is probably more important, Everett Jordan respected them, each and every one of them. I know this from walking with him into the store in Saxapahaw and by accompanying him through the plants. Whomever he saw—whether it be some woman or man that worked in the store, a mill maintenance man, boiler room employee, a supervisor, a quilling machine operator, and so on throughout the whole plant—he never walked past anybody without a greeting, and in turn he was greeted in the most friendly way.

The offices of Sellers Manufacturing Company and its affiliated companies are housed today in a two-story, red-brick building whose uncertain nineteenth-century history pre-dates Everett Jordan's occupancy. The structure, clinging to the side of a hill rising sharply up from the north side of the Haw River, faces south, affording a view of the bridge spanning the river. Near the top of the steep bank fronting the edifice, a flagpole topped by the American flag rises above the slope and is gracefully flanked on either side by two dogwood trees.

More conspicuous than the dogwoods, however, are two large holly trees, carefully spaced on opposite sides of the flagpole. These commercially grown trees were also gifts—gifts from the Old-Timers Club, the twenty-year veteran employees of Sellers Manufacturing Company—proudly given to their boss, B. Everett Jordan. These hollies are adorned with red berries and represent an enduring and sustaining relationship between employee and employer. The mutually profitable relationship wrought between Jordan and the two Grubers was instigated by Jordan's knowledge of human nature and his gift of hollies—hollies sans berries. He took the resources at hand—a run-down cotton mill, holly trees, his native talents—and produced yarns, sales, profits, and friendships.

9

Mill Head and Mill Hands

"The colored employees thought he was a wonderful man—thought a lot of him," observed Robert Hunter, one of Everett Jordan's first black employees, while he was being interviewed for this volume in 1981. He was a pleasant and still powerfully built man, even at the age of three score and ten. As he stood erect, his six-feet-four-inch, lean, muscular frame just slightly stooped from many years of manual labor, one easily visualized the strength of his earlier days when he wielded sledgehammer, shovel, or crowbar as he accompanied Alson Davis, Jordan's all-purpose electrician, plumber, and master mechanic, on his rounds in the Saxapahaw mill and village. Davis, also a physical giant in his day, would not tolerate anyone who failed to put his shoulder to the wheel or pull his own weight. Neither did Hunter spare himself. Consequently, the two men understood each other, were compatible, and made a great team for their chief, Everett Jordan.[1]

During the early years when Everett Jordan was striving to mold the mill into better shape and to make the village more livable, Hunter's wages were twelve cents an hour and the other fifteen or so black yard hands were paid at the same rate. According to Hunter: "Back then we had to handle all that cotton by hand [500 pounds per compressed bale], weighing it and stacking it up to the top of the cotton shed. All that was done by hand. And all these ditches around here [water lines and drainage pipes], we had to dig 'em by hand."[2]

Hunter's excellent performance did not escape the watchful eye of the mill manager, who increased his hourly wages by five cents. Whoever had a complaint could go straight to the man at the top, and in a few days some of the yard help complained to Jordan about their wages being less than Hunter's. They received a quick and pointed reply: "Robert's worth more than you all are!" That ended the negotiations, and the men went back to work.[3]

In 1938 construction of the concrete dam across the Haw River at Saxapahaw was a notable event. At one point, when enough sand was not being pumped above the dam down to the construction site, Jordan appeared on the scene and directed the foreman to release Hunter to work on the sand pumps. Then, stated Hunter, "[the foreman] told him he'd rather he would take any man there except me, said I kept the job going...Mr. Jordan said, 'Well, you can't build no dam if you ain't got no sand, can you?' So he sent me up to run the sand pumps...I'd say it took us about two years to build that concrete dam. And I worked at Cedar Falls and Wake Forest, too. Never heard Mr. Jordan speak a cross word to none of the help ...had some wonderful years here."[4]

After Everett Jordan, Alson Davis was probably Hunter's most admired co-worker: "Worked with Alson Davis; he was a workin' man! I've seen him knocked down a many a time down there in that powerhouse. He would grab them switches [without protective gloves because 'he didn't have time to mess with them']. One time I thought he was dead. I went and picked him up." On another occasion, Hunter said, Davis was "knocked off a stack of yarn; [a] 220 hit him on the top of his head...Another time [when we were] splaying them big ropes [in the diesel room]...one of them... struck him right in the [groin]."[5]

Alice Abernathy, Alson Davis's youngest daughter, recalled the job hazards her father encountered and his long work hours: "I remember he fell from the top story [of the mill building, three stories high] one time and broke his shoulder...[After] they put a cast on him, he went right on back to work [as he did at other times] ...often spending night after night working on that engine, not getting any sleep...It [all] looked so dangerous to me, and I just knew, as a child, that my dad would be killed there."[6] But Alson Davis was a survivor and worked for Jordan's company until he retired.

Everett Jordan and Alson Davis, both robust men, had similarities other than physical. Each reveled in his work and was more concerned with getting the job done than in finesse or workmanship. Therefore, neither was opposed to shortcuts—a policy fraught with risk but one that produced results. Commenting on the admiration

Robert A. Hunter, one of Everett Jordan's early veteran black employees, in 1989. (Photo by author)

George D. Thompson. One of Everett Jordan's most loyal and versatile black employees, he served the family as gardener, chauffeur, butler, chef, and handyman. (*Dorothy Thompson*)

Margaret Alice McLean in the 1960s. She was Everett Jordan's sister-in-law, personal secretary, and longtime receptionist for Sellers Manufacturing Company. (*Margaret Alice McLean*)

John W. ("Jake") Miller, Jr. (1921–70), in 1958. He came to Saxapahaw from Chattanooga, Tenn., as a teenager and worked all his adult life for Everett Jordan's companies as a clerk, order expediter, and salesman. (*Alice Davis Abernathy*)

Senator Jordan and mill employee-political supporters from Saxapahaw in 1960 (*left to right*): George Phillips, Aretta Barrett, W. Adrian Jobe, Jordan, Alson T. Davis, Allene T. Foust. (*Jordan family scrapbooks*)

that the two men had for each other, Alice Abernathy made this observation: "I think it was because Mr. Jordan was so down to earth. He would come down and work with daddy a lot of times, when he first came to Saxapahaw. You know in starting out, he would get down and help do the dirty work. They did a lot of work together in the beginning, and I think that Mr. Jordan tried to speak to daddy on his own level; he didn't try to act like a big boss, or anything over him. I think daddy had a lot of respect for him for that reason."[7]

Charlie Page, another retired employee of Sellers Manufacturing Company, gave his evaluation of the mill owner and patriarch. Like many employees of Jordan, Page started to work for him as a teenager and spent most of his working life in the Saxapahaw plant. Page commented: "I thought the world of him! I didn't think there was anybody like him—him and his wife both. I mean there weren't no better people in Saxapahaw than them. They have always been good to me. Every time I see them they speak; I don't care where I was at. They could see me walking on the road between here and town, and they'd stop and pick me up—him or her. They're wonderful people! Now a lot of people thought he was stuck-up 'cause he had plenty of money, but, now, they wasn't stuck-up. I don't know how much money he had, but they were the friendliest people I ever seen in your life."[8]

Although Page never heard any other employees comment about Jordan, the former knew a lot of them did not like him. He attributed this to Jordan's wealth. However, Page contended that "there wasn't no finer person—no finer person. They acted just like me and you. They might have had plenty of money, but they'd talk and all. I thought the world of them. If things didn't go right down there in the mill, I'd come to him and he'd get them right. I know that."[9]

Charlie Page observed: "One thing about it, when Mr. Jordan run it [the mill], he knew things had to be carried out right. I heard him say one time—he had a meeting down there in the mill after a boss man had fired a hand, and they had gone to him about it—he said, 'I'm gonna tell you right now, don't fire my help!' He said, 'A hand means a lot. I can get a boss man anywhere, but it's hard to pick up a good hand!' And I thought he had a point there—you could get a boss anywhere quicker than he could get a hand."[10]

The mill owner's basic policy was to keep the spindles turning. Section hands—overseers—did not operate machines, a fact that Jordan never forgot. And he expected—even encouraged—mill hands to come to him. Usually, they got more attention and credibility from the mill owner than their own supervisors and managers. That, at least, is the opinion of many, including his son Ben, who said, "He took far more time to listen to the draw-frame tender than to the overseer of the card room. Joe Neel picked up on that—that was daddy's way of learning what was going on. Unfortunately, in some instances, you would get only one version, whereas someone else might have a completely different idea about what was happening. In which case, you might come up with a conclusion that might be erroneous."[11]

Ernest Cagle, another ex-employee, later stated: "[Jordan] was a real mill man, and he was real good to work for... He run full all the time and he made good stuff, good yarn... They never was no seconds or thirds [at the mill] when the machinery was not speeded up like it is now. And he didn't have hands double-loaded. You run thirty sides [spinning frames, two sides per frame]... now. Or you pretend to run thirty sides spinning. When the end comes down in the spinning room and it's goin' in the waste bin, you ain't makin' no money! It's goin' to waste. He was a real good mill man."[12]

Ernest Cagle (1913–90) (*left*) and Jack Paris (*right*). Cagle worked at various jobs for many years in Jordan's Saxapahaw plant; and Paris, a local storekeeper and politician, was one of Jordan's loyal informants and supporters. (*John M. ("Mac") Jordan, Jr.*)

Everett Jordan earned respect from his loyal mill hands in many ways. One of them, Greef Smith, later recalled: "Mr. Jordan was a second daddy to me. We had so many hospital bills and sickness; he came to my rescue. He loaned me money. I [only had to] ask him...I worked for him here all those years, and I'd pay it back regular...I remember right after we bought this home from him, it seemed like everything hit me all at once. I...said, 'Mr. Jordan, it looks like I'm going to have to let you have the house back. I don't see how I'm going to make it the way things are going.' He said, 'Do you want it?' I said, 'Sure I do!' He said, 'Well, let me worry about that.' That's a second daddy what is a second daddy."[13]

Mattie Smith, also once an employee of Sellers Manufacturing Company, shared her husband's sentiments: "You could go to [Jordan] and ask for help and he was willing to help you. He helped those who would help themselves. Greef nor I ever asked a favor of him that we didn't get...and they [Mr. and Mrs. Jordan] did so many wonderful things for this community. Mrs. Jordan saw that everything was kept up, with flowers and everything—just beautiful."[14]

Mrs. Smith also commented: "I never heard anybody say anything against Mr. and Mrs. Jordan in the mill. If I had, I would have defended them...Maybe some were jealous because they had money, but money isn't everything. You know, I don't think it went to their heads one bit. They were down-to-earth people. You remember hearing him say, 'You people are my people.' And he never let anybody in Washington or anywhere else forget that he lived at Saxapahaw."[15]

Mattie offered still more praise: "Our son, Colon [also one of Jordan's mill employees], talked to Mr. Jordan about going to college, and Mr. Jordan told him, 'Son, if you want to go to college, I'll see that you go. I know the dean up here at Elon [College], also at Campbell [College]; I'll see that you go to college. You are a benefit to my company.' Now, how many men would do that? Look what he did for the scouts—Eagle Scouts—gave them a chance at college with a scholarship. You don't find people like that everyday."[16]

Everett Jordan's interest in the Boy Scouts went back to his early mill days in Gastonia, where he served for a short time as a troop scoutmaster. Many times, he told the story about his first troop's camping experience. The green young scoutmaster chose to cook oatmeal for breakfast: "I took oatmeal and filled a good-size pot, one big enough, I thought, to feed a dozen or so hungry boys. Then I poured in enough water to cover the oatmeal and put the pot over our campfire. Well, you can imagine what happened. In no time a'tall we had more oatmeal than we knew what to do with. We put oatmeal in every pot and pan in camp and we still had more in the pot. In fact, the stuff expanded and boiled over so fast that I thought it was going to put out our fire! Yeah, everybody had enough oatmeal."[17]

That was not the end of the "tenderfoot" scoutmaster's scouting. In Saxapahaw, he organized Troop Number 65, served as its first committee chairman, and remained on the committee until his death. In addition to underwriting a scholarship program for Troop Number 65's Eagle scouts and financing the cost of materials for the troop's cabin on company-owned land at Saxapahaw Lake, he also personally paid for the new dining hall at the Cherokee Scout Reservation, a facility serving the youth of Alamance, Rockingham, Caswell, and Person counties. For many years, he served on the Cherokee Council's advisory board. In 1966 the council awarded him the Silver Beaver Award, the highest award a council can bestow upon a volunteer for outstanding service. His son John and two of his grandsons, John ["Mac"] McLean Jordan, Jr., and Thomas Carter Jordan, all attained Eagle rank.[18]

Ken Davis, who served as the professional scout executive for the Alamance District in the years 1949 to 1964, said that he always recognized the troop from Saxapahaw by its mode of travel when it came to summer camp. Usually, in those days, the troop came in two vehicles: Pride Overman's well-worn A-Model Ford and Everett Jordan's shiny, black Cadillac. Overman, who worked in the card room for Jordan, also served on the troop's committee and had two sons in the troop. The scouts checked into camp on Sunday afternoons; and the round trip from Saxapahaw to Camp Cherokee, near Wentworth in Rockingham County, took most of an afternoon. Chauffeuring lively scouts on a Sunday afternoon is another indication of Jordan's willingness to lend a helping hand on any level.[19]

When Everett Jordan was an apprentice in Gastonia's Myrtle and Gray mills, time and motion studies, job-load evaluation, and pay-rate structuring had not yet come into vogue. So the mill manager was not versed in so-called "piece rates" and the accompanying paperwork required. Although times were changing, the Saxapahaw mill man was not in the forefront in this area.[20]

When Ben Jordan was interviewed for this volume in 1982, he discussed the differences between him and his father in the way the two ran the mills: "There was a basic difference in that I was not a manufacturer. I had to rely on manufacturing people, and he did not. He could go to the mill and know what was going on. But I had to accept what Joe Neel or Louis Jackson or whoever said. I *had* to trust them. He did *not* trust them, so we started off with a different philosophy...I didn't have any choice—unless I was

Mill Head and Mill Hands

His wife, Katherine, admiringly examines Senator Jordan's Silver Beaver Award, presented to him by the Boy Scouts in 1966. He strongly supported Scouting all his adult life. (Photo by Pat Bailey)

going to stay with it long enough to become a real technician. And there's a lot more to running a cotton spinning mill than knowing what makes a drawing frame work properly."[21]

Ben Jordan explained that his own background, education, training, and environment—era or setting—were different from his father's. Personality-wise, Ben said, there was quite a difference, too:

> I don't think that I was the born politician that daddy was. Good leaders are natural politicians that don't necessarily go into politics. They do things that will attract attention to themselves by being charismatic... I'm not criticizing the politics, but I'm saying that some people are [more natural] at it than others... I'm not a natural politician... That's a big difference between the two of us. There are other differences, all sorts that I couldn't see because he wanted me to be as he was. And that's kind of difficult. I couldn't sell as he did. I couldn't manage as he did, and I think that irritated him because I didn't do it as he said to do it.[22]

Ben contended that his father recognized that his son was dealing with a different era from the one in which he grew up. However, Ben explained:

Board of trustees of Alamance County Hospital, Burlington, N.C. (*left to right*): George Harden, James A. Barnwell, Chairman B. Everett Jordan, R. H. Kale, Sr., Vice-Chairman Reid A. Maynard, Alamance County Commissioner Hale Duncan. (*James W. Maynard*)

[My father] said—and I wouldn't really dispute this—that people are basically the same no matter where they are. That isn't quite true because the era in which he grew up—the educated/uneducated ratio was far, far different. And there was a big difference between management and employee. In the twenties, the number of high school graduates was much fewer than in the fifties and sixties and seventies—college, too. The people we were getting were better informed; mobility was far greater; they didn't have to walk to work. They could drive to Graham in fifteen minutes. The war [World War II] changed things immeasurably. We became a more mobile society, more sophisticated. I was of that generation.[23]

His father, however, according to Ben, seemed to think of people as they had been earlier: "His reference point was the Gray Mill or the Myrtle Mill—'When I was running the Myrtle Mill,' or 'When I was running the Gray Mill.' He was relating to 1925 or 1926, those years and times. Circumstances were somewhat similar, but the people were different."[24]

Concerning overall company policy, Ben doubted if the two had fundamental differences beyond the normal generation gap. But he added, "I think I was a good bit more liberal than he was, particularly in employee relationships. I think his attitude was much more paternalistic than mine... I was more aware of what the people were thinking than he was. He was thinking in the twenties and thirties era." Also, Ben felt that his father was not nearly as progressive in overall management as he was. For example, because the elder Jordan did not think time-study was necessary, it was not fully utilized until after Ben became responsible for day-to-day operations of the plants.[25]

Ben continued: "Daddy thought that the superintendents should be better than they were, and should know all these things that time-study collected data on. He thought the overseers should already know these things, and therefore the superintendent should know everything that was going on in the mill...He thought that to keep records on anything was really a waste of time...He said this paperwork was keeping the superintendents from being the managers that they should have been. Maybe so...Anyway, the kind of superintendent he was looking for was the kind he was himself, and they didn't make many like him."[26]

In Ben's view, a superintendent like his father wanted was one who, like himself, could literally do everything, know everything, and do the managing: "very, very exceptional people." Even if that superintendent existed, Ben allowed, "That's spreading yourself pretty thin."[27]

Another factor that Everett Jordan never seemed to fully appreciate or grasp was that his organization and facilities had grown—tremendously. In 1927 he had begun with a relatively small weaving and spinning mill, Sellers Manufacturing Company, Inc. Its less than 10,000 spindles operated on a one-shift basis. He quickly junked the looms and became a yarn spinner for the knitting and weaving trade. As market changes occurred and his finances—for the most part internally generated—permitted, he engaged in an expansion and modernization program.[28]

In 1939 Sellers Manufacturing Company made its first major acquisition when it acquired the Sapona Cotton Mill in neighboring Randolph County at Cedar Falls, just a few miles up the Deep River above the town of Ramseur, where Jordan had been born while his circuit-riding minister-father served there. The plant was named

The Eli Whitney Volunteer Fire Department serves the Saxapahaw and Eli Whitney communities. In this photo, taken at Saxapahaw, are (*left to right*): D. V. ("Bunn") Andrews, chief second assistant; Amick Lloyd, fire chief; Senator Jordan; and Gordon Marlette, chief first assistant. (Photo by Pat Bailey)

Sellers Manufacturing Company No. 2, and in January 1941 was reorganized as an affiliate and called Jordan Spinning Company. By the time this took place, Sellers Manufacturing Company had filled the industrial space left vacant at Saxapahaw by removal of the looms with additional spinning equipment and had added, first, a silk-throwing department in 1930, and shortly thereafter a mercerizing department. Jordan's simple spinning mill had become much larger and far more complex.[29]

In 1945 Royal Cotton Mill Company, a coarse-yarn spinner at Wake Forest, N.C., was acquired and also National Processing Company, a mercerizer known as Ideal Mercerizing Company, located in Burlington. In 1951 Sellers Dyeing Company, a new package-yarn dyeing facility, was constructed in Saxapahaw on a site adjacent to Sellers Manufacturing Company, which completed the acquisition of production facilities. However, during the 1950s and 1960s, the company installed equipment to enable it to spin a wider range of cotton and synthetic blended yarns.[30]

Aerial view of the center of Saxapahaw in 1970. In the lower left center is the Sellers Manufacturing Company office building; just below it is the residence of the Everett Jordans; in the top center is the Sellers Dyeing Company plant; in the center is the Sellers mill; in the lower right center is the Saxapahaw community building; and in the lower right is the north section of the bridge that was to be replaced in 1990–91. (*Sellers Manufacturing Company, Inc.*)

At peak production, when nearly 1,000 employees were on the payroll, the Sellers Group had approximately 75,000 spindles turning out yarns. Although Everett Jordan had masterminded the whole complex and guided its every step, and, even though times and conditions were vastly different from his initiation days in Gastonia, the mill manager and executive could not completely divorce himself from the 1920s era and the philosophy of management that he knew then. As his elder son said, "His reference point was the Gray Mill or the Myrtle Mill."[31]

When Ben Jordan reflected upon his father's mill policies and concepts, he referred to the fact that "he thought that a card can [a cylinder-like container that receives the rope-like cotton sliver from the carding process] should not be bigger than eighteen or twenty inches [in diameter] because he remembered when card cans were ten or twelve inches. He thought that people that put in thirty-inch cans were going to get into trouble. But they didn't." Ben remembered that his father also thought running cards much faster, producing 90 to 140 pounds per hour compared to 8 pounds in former years, was bad for both machines and yarn quality. Better-quality yarn is produced at much slower speeds, but competition's lower cost at higher speeds dictate industry practice. You either follow suit or get out.[32]

Standardization was another concept that Everett Jordan never accepted or practiced in running his mills. As Ben Jordan said, "We bought machinery [used] from Parkdale [Parkdale Mills, Inc., Gastonia, N.C.] because they were standardizing. Standardization didn't mean much to him. We had all sorts of bobbin sizes...Roberts, Whitin, Saco-Lowell, and various drafting systems within them...he would not modernize. He just hated to spend money on new equipment. He said, 'You don't take care of it.' And he was right. If you came through the thirties era and you didn't have any money, you could take old equipment and make good yarn, but the labor factor was not a big one. Then the Parkdales of this world came along and revolutionized the yarn market."[33]

Ben Jordan was referring to more than just more modern machinery and the standardization by progressive manufacturing plants as exemplified by Parkdale Mills, widely recognized as an industry leader. He explained: "We made more strides in reducing our labor costs and improving our quality after [a job-training program was established]. Time-study wasn't showing [desired] results. Employees just didn't know their job—how to really run the machinery. In the last year or so of his life, daddy agreed...[Before then], we put in some of these programs against his will. But we would not have survived the 1973–74 recession if we had not. [Then] we put in a lot of new machinery [and reduced labor costs dramatically]...But he would never have done these things...I don't think."[34]

During the last few years of Jordan's life, his time and energies were devoted primarily to Senate duties as well as to running for

Sellers Manufacturing Company No. 2, Cedar Falls, N.C., in December 1939. This installation was so known for a brief period until it was re-organized and re-named as the Jordan Spinning Company in 1941. "Sapona Cotton Mill, Inc.," visible on the right, is the former name of this plant, which dates back into the early nineteenth century. (*Sellers Manufacturing Company, Inc.*)

re-election in the 1972 Democratic primary—a contest that resulted in a tiring second primary between himself and Congressman (Fourth District) Nick Galifianakis. Too, his health was failing; he was hospitalized for colon cancer surgery in 1973 prior to his death in March the following year. Consequently, during these final years, the tight-fisted rule of the still-enthroned mill boss was less evident in the day-to-day management efforts, then led by his patient and ever-respectful son Ben. As Ben later said: "He certainly did me a favor by being away, enabling me to learn the business. He hung on, never turned it [control] loose—only to the extent that he had to. You know, he had had some prostate problems, and he had not been real well, off and on, for two or three years prior to that."[35]

Much of Ben Jordan's evaluation of his father's stubbornly held but outdated policies was borne out by another company executive: Alton ("Al") B. Smith, a former vice-president of Royal Cotton Mill Company and son of Senator Willis Smith, whose family bought a half interest in Royal. Alton Smith complained that the company's pay scale and benefits (vacations, pensions, insurance) were below the industry level. He also contended that profits suffered because

South view of the Royal Cotton Mill, one of the Sellers companies, at Wake Forest, N.C., in the 1960s. (*Sellers Manufacturing Company, Inc.*)

of the inefficiency of the used, worn-out machinery of different types that Jordan continually bought and kept repairing as well as re-building—instead of standardizing it so that it would be easy to equip and maintain. This had three ramifications: it made maintenance of the machinery difficult for the relatively uneducated people who were responsible for it; it was a problem to procure replacement parts; and competing with more modernized mills posed a serious problem. Smith made little headway in his arguments on this subject with Jordan.[36]

Royal Cotton Mill Company experienced difficulty in attracting and keeping qualified employees, which Smith attributed mostly to low wages and competition from other industries moving into the area. However, he maintained, "We had a good crew—ultimately— of fine workers who enjoyed working there. We had modernized the mill to the degree that we had air-conditioned it, and we had worked very hard on working conditions and keeping people happy. I think we could have done better if we had paid better wages—I'm sure that we could have." In time, Royal instituted a fairer compensation policy, which Smith helped put in place, that reviewed wage rates and evaluated jobs based on merit.[37]

Eventually, in 1965, the Smith family sold their half interest in Royal to Everett Jordan and his companies. According to Al Smith, this decision was made because "we felt that we had no future as half-owner in a plant that was not modern and had no prospects of becoming a really new mill. We were making money at the time and felt like it was the time to get out when the market was good, and it would be worth more money then than it would ever be, as far as we were concerned."[38]

Al Smith, like many other friends and associates of Jordan, was charmed by his personality. And so was Al's father, U.S. Senator Willis Smith. According to Al: "Dad had great respect for him, both for his ability and his—for lack of a better word—his craftiness or wily nature. He felt like Everett was definitely a deal maker who knew how to compromise a situation; he knew how to accommodate people in a political way. He was not a great intellectual type of political person but extremely intelligent in how he arranged things...My dad felt like Everett Jordan was one of the keenest observers of human nature of anybody he ever knew. He felt he could size up a person better than most people." And Al Smith said he himself benefited from Jordan's understanding of people, particularly mill people, which was passed on to Al when he began as a mill trainee in 1952. Smith felt this was valuable because he was one of the owner's sons and the plant was unionized. It had also just suffered a severe strike that had damaged the mill and heavily strained personnel relationships.[39]

Notwithstanding their differences on mill policies, Smith enjoyed Everett Jordan's company. Smith commented: "[Jordan] used to tell me a whole lot of stories about the old Gray Mill in Gastonia and how he started and some of the labor problems he had. I think he had some walk-outs and one thing and another down there. He had a lot of labor troubles there, too, but he made it through a mighty tough time. One reason for his philosophy in how he operated plants was because he was in the depression and he survived on used, worn-out machinery and innovative methods, really."[40]

J. Harold Smith, prominent Burlington, N.C., business executive and civic leader as well as a friend of Jordan, in a 1987 interview for this volume provided an example of Jordan's "craftiness and wily nature" referred to by Willis Smith. According to J. Harold Smith, Jordan usually outmatched potential customers in the New York-Brooklyn garment district—where people are known to be excellent barterers and thrive through the exercise of their wits—in negotiating price.[41]

There were times, especially in Jordan's earlier years at the helm, when he had been forced to borrow from banks. But his policy was always "Pay as you go." By repute, he early on carried unpaid invoices in his pockets to avoid the possibility of his bookkeeper's paying them and over-drawing the company's bank account. By his very nature, he was the epitome of frugality, but, if he had not kept close watch over every dollar, he could have joined the countless other textile-mill owners who became insolvent during the Terrible Thirties. Therefore, as he saw it, he would rather be a tortoise than a hare and crawl along with patched up, out-of-date equipment instead of following the fast pace with new machinery that he could not pay for—and might cause him to lose everything. That strategy worked well for the mill man for many years, but, as new technology and methods began to dominate the industry, it became increasingly difficult for older plants with make-do machinery to compete. As Everett Jordan, the mill manager, exited, a new era had arrived.[42]

There are many facets in the operation and management of a cotton-yarn manufacturing plant. The managers, therefore, must either assume direct responsibility for each activity or delegate authority and accountability to others. Even if they delegate, they usually control the activity or policy per se. Those under them, in effect, carry out their wishes or instructions implicitly. In the facets of mill life relating to labor relations, unions, and personnel matters, Everett Jordan had strong convictions from which he refused to deviate.[43]

Harry Truman is credited with popularizing the saying "The buck stops here," used in reference to the assumption of final responsibility. In Everett Jordan's case, the buck started and stopped with him. As Ben Jordan said, his father's reference point was the Gray and Myrtle mills.[44] Many of Everett Jordan's ideas and most of his basic policies either originated from his experience in Gastonia's mills or were definitively shaped by the mill environment there. With reference to labor relationships and policies, he was a product of his times. Perhaps his attitude toward labor and labor unions bears this out as much as anything else, reflecting as it did Gastonia's labor conditions and problems during the 1920s and 1930s.[45]

Thomas ("Tom") A. Robinson, a Gastonia native and attorney who practiced law there for a number of years, made this appraisal: "You can ask people now—particularly those that would have been around [Gastonia] in 1929—and, almost without exception, they have a negative idea of labor unions based on the terror of that time."[46]

During the 1929 strike at Gastonia's mammoth Loray Mill, blood was shed on both sides. One of the most notorious criminal trials in North Carolina history ensued. Today, more than half a century later, its impact upon the Southern textile industry endures.[47] Throughout his career, Everett Jordan relentlessly opposed the unionization of labor, and he not only succeeded in eliminating the one union that was organized in one of his plants, but also successfully defeated every attempt that was made to organize any of his other plants.[48]

The Loray Mill strike alone, of course, did not shape Jordan's concept of labor unions, but its influence and the practices of other mill leaders and owners in the Gastonia area help explain why he took his uncompromising stand.[49] What were textile-mill conditions and practices at the time of the Loray strike, just two years after Jordan left his position as superintendent of the Gray Mill, in Gastonia, to head up Sellers Manufacturing Company in Saxapahaw?

A 1927 survey revealed that Gastonia had become the center and symbol of industrial transformation. Some 570 textile plants were operating and nearly 10 million spindles were producing within a radius of 100 miles of its boundaries—more than any other Southern city. By 1939 Gaston County could claim a larger number of textile plants than any other county in the world, and was manufacturing 80 percent of the fine-combed cotton yarn produced in the United States.[50] Because the county had achieved this status and Everett Jordan had developed a working knowledge of the operation of a cotton spinning mill there, it is easy to see why he considered Gastonia to be his "alma mater."

Textile manufacturing first became established in New England but came South for a variety of reasons, mostly economic. Lower labor costs and the absence of unions were the prime considerations. Southerners were quick to recognize the benefits and welcomed the mills with open arms.[51] Because of such a hospitable reception, why did the strike occur in Loray, Gastonia's largest and most prominent spinning plant?

One of the reasons was the nature of the development of the union labor movement at Loray. A local union of the UTW (United Textile Workers of America) had been formed there in 1919, but for many years no major conflicts surfaced between the workers and management. But in March 1929 Fred E. Beal, a seasoned union organizer, working under the auspices of the National Textile Workers Union (NTWU), reportedly a Communist organization, appeared. He quickly set out to organize the employees of Gastonia's largest employer; and, on April 1, 1929, the mill hands at Loray walked out on strike.[52]

Although a list of eight demands was presented to management by the union, in no time the union and its cause were branded as a "Communist movement that was motivated by Communist goals," including the violent overthrow of the government. Employees were evicted from their mill-owned homes, a tent city was erected, picket lines were formed, and both strikers and workers began carrying weapons.[53]

A reign of terror erupted. The National Guard was called out, and Gastonia became the focal point of media attention nationwide. In an encounter between strikers and police, Gastonia's police chief, O. F. Adderholt, was shot; he died the next day. One striker and three other policemen were also wounded. Later, in another incident, Ella May Wiggins, songstress for the strikers, was shot and killed as she rode in a truck with some of her supporters. No one was ever convicted for the murder of Wiggins, but Beal and six others, after a mistrial for first-degree murder, were convicted of second-degree murder of Adderholt and given prison sentences. While released on bond pending appeal of their conviction, the seven fled to Russia.[54]

The convicted person with the shortest term to serve returned shortly; Beal himself returned several years thereafter, was finally apprehended, and taken to North Carolina Central Prison in 1938; in 1942 he was paroled. As writer Tom Robinson stated: "Thus ended the most exciting, dangerous, and bizarre period of Gastonia's history."[55]

Various theories were advanced concerning the true cause of the strike, but the one that blamed "outside agitators" supposedly connected with the Communist party was given greatest emphasis by mill management. Most of the others on the scene, including the press and citizens in general, were disposed to agree. Those in the union, of course, rejected this reasoning because their list obviously consisted of non-Communist demands such as pay, hours of work, and plant conditions.[56]

As author Pope explained: "Employers fought trade unionism and collective bargaining wherever they appeared, but in no other situation did they fight so effectively, and with such complete victory, as at Gastonia. It was easy for employers there to convince the community that the strike represented not simply an effort at modification of the employers' power but a threat to the entire community... Whether or not employers at Gastonia regarded the Communist challenge as serious—and there is considerable evidence that they did—they succeeded in provoking a community reaction more violent in character than that found in any of the other Southern strikes."[57]

By and large the workers were disillusioned. Pope stated: "The outcome of the Loray strike has been one of the chief factors preventing subsequent union activity in the county. It brought complete victory to the employers, confirmed the public in its suspicion of unions and strikes, and most important of all, likewise made many workers skeptical of affiliated unionism of any brand."[58]

During the chaotic aftermath, reports reached Everett Jordan that a "Flying Squadron," an armed mobile group of union organizers whose avowed purpose was to shut down mills, was on its way to Saxapahaw. The mill owner wasted no time in asking the governor for National Guardsmen to come to his mill's defense. Guardsmen with rifles and machine guns positioned themselves about the mill and village, and old-timers still recall vividly this grim scene of the early 1930s. The squadron never appeared, but there was no question about Jordan's stance: he would "fight fire with fire."[59]

The influence of the Loray strike cannot be fully measured even today, but its effect was widespread and long-lasting. And no one

Loray Mill, Gastonia, N.C., in 1986. (Photo by author)

ever had occasion to speculate about Jordan's attitude toward unions or labor-management relationships. He was totally in command, and he never entertained any ideas of abdicating his position and what he considered to be his prerogatives. How much he was affected by the goings-on in Gastonia cannot be pinpointed, but his views were the same as those of the Loray mill superintendent.[60]

For example, Ervin S. ("Blackie") Frazier, a man who worked for Jordan during a period of labor agitation when the employees were being urged to vote for a union, later said: "Mr. Jordan got us all up there in the silk mill one time and just told us, 'Y'all can put it [the union] in, and we'll shut it down!' Thereupon the employees went back to work. As Frazier said, "...he was just a man that would listen to you—sympathize with you—hear your side of the story. Then he would tell you what he could do and what he couldn't do. He was a fine man."[61]

Whether it was in labor relations or other aspects of mill operation, Everett Jordan not only ruled, he also got things done—not always, however, as others might have desired. Unquestionably, his employees would have preferred higher wages—if given a choice—and others in management would have chosen their way instead of his, if given the freedom to do so.

In September 1950 the employees of the Royal Cotton Mill Company voted in favor of the Textile Workers Union of America (TWUA), Congress of Industrial Organizations (CIO). As much as anything else, perhaps, the ensuing battle—and it was literally a battle—tested Everett Jordan's mettle. During the months that followed, union officials accused mill management of refusing to bargain in good faith, and the majority of the employees went out on strike. Although strikers picketed the mill, management kept the plant open, but operated on a curtailed one-shift basis. After a gun battle between the opposing forces, an article in the *Greensboro* (N.C.) *Daily News* dated April 28, 1950, reported that "between 200 and 600 shots were exchanged from pistol, rifles and shotguns." Three persons—a striker, a fourteen-year-old girl, and a newspaper reporter—were injured from gunfire. Some twenty-five highway patrolmen were sent in by Governor Kerr Scott to patrol the mill area and restore peace.[62]

The article quoted Jordan as saying: "We have no objection to workers belonging to a union, but it's not the company's duty to collect union dues." The article stated: "Lewis M. Conn of Greensboro, state director of the T.W.U.A. [Textile Workers Union of America] said the company had failed to reach agreement with the union on anything that would benefit the workers. He added that Jordan had refused to talk with the union since last September when the Royal Cotton Mill workers voted to have the union as their bargaining representative."[63]

The strike dragged on for several months. And at no time did Jordan give any indication that he was willing to accept any of the union's demands. Al Smith started to work at Royal in April 1952, after the bitter strike was over, but events of the preceding year were still fresh in the minds of the participants; and Smith heard many of their stories, including this one: "During the strike, they were having very bitter times. The strikers wanted to meet with Mr. Jordan as a group, so he agreed to come over to Wake Forest. He came over in the big black Cadillac, I was told...that as he drove through the Glen Royal mill village the workers were sort of lining the streets as they were coming to the meeting, and they said, 'Roll, Jordan, roll.'"[64]

Smith continued: "When he got to the old company store building, which had been converted into the mill office, he parked his Cadillac and got up on the porch. He had a conversation with them that I understand was sort of raucous and insulting to him, and they shouted remarks at him that he didn't appreciate. Mr. Jordan got angry, and it was quoted to me that he said, 'I'll tell you one thing—you see that Cadillac over there? I've got another one just like it at home. I won't have to work another day in my life if I don't want to. And, if you don't want to work, that's all right with me, too!' Then he got in his car, and rolled out of there."[65]

The results of this strike and the fate of the union at the Royal Cotton Mill ended very much like that of Gastonia's Loray Mill. Mentally, no doubt, during this prolonged confrontation, Everett Jordan had more than one opportunity to compare notes with his peers and role models in Gaston County. His handling of his labor problems gives ample proof that he could not be pushed around.

During the time of Royal's strike and labor difficulties, the Congress of Industrial Organizations (CIO) also attempted to organize employees at Sellers Manufacturing Company in Saxapahaw. This prompted Jordan to write a six-page letter, dated February 22, 1951, to the employees.[66] Solicitously, he pleaded with them to recognize their existing benefits and reject the union in the forthcoming secret election, which he said they could participate in on company time and without any loss of pay. Stressing the importance of the election to the employees and their families, he said he would present the facts on both sides.

Jordan pointed out that he did not expect the employees to do any favor for the company, but that they should vote purely on the basis of whether or not the union would be in their own best interests. Contending that the CIO organizers were after the employees' money in the form of dues, Jordan claimed that the union could do little to better wages and earnings—which were equal to or above those of competing yarn mills.

During the past year, Jordan said the company had provided two pay raises. He claimed that some mills "not so far away" had the CIO union, but that jobs there were not as regular and steady as at Saxapahaw. Also, at Sellers Manufacturing Company, existing benefits included vacations and vacation pay, holidays, Christmas bonuses, and pension-retirement pay—without the need to pay any union dues. Jordan also listed the steps his company had taken to improve working conditions.

Jordan also claimed that under the union workloads would be higher rather than lower. Unions meant strikes, and the company would not yield to such pressure—which involved "trouble and dissension, strife and misery, lost work and lost pay [plus] cutting and shooting and bloody violence."

Jordan emphasized that those who voted for and joined the union would not receive any preferred treatment over those who did not belong. He also stated that no one needed to join a union in order to hold a job in his company. He stressed the need for everyone to vote because otherwise a minority could control the result.

In conclusion, Jordan made an emotional appeal: "As matters now stand you have a good job at high wages, an up-to-date plant to work in and a good community here to live in. We all hope to make things even better. There is certainly no good reason to bring this outside Union in here, pay dues to it, and at the same time run the risk of tearing apart everything that you now have."

The election was duly held, and the union was defeated. And, like his counterparts in Gastonia, the union never again seriously challenged the Saxapahaw mill man.

Reverend Jesse Bone served as pastor of the Saxapahaw United Methodist Church from 1966 to 1970, during the latter part of Jordan's tenure in the United States Senate. But he knew his distinguished parishioner well. As Bone explained: "To begin with, I think that Mr. Jordan was one who was very committed to his church. He made it a point to be in church any time he was home, so he was actually one of the more regular attenders at Saxapahaw even when the Senate was in session. He was a person who loved young people; he wanted to be around younger people and not people of his age [he was a member and teacher of the young adult class and never moved to the older adult class]. I think he delighted in being in the Sunday school class with younger people where he could discuss issues."[67]

Bone said that, because of Jordan's eminent position in the community, the parishioners were amazed that the minister would talk back to and argue with him in Sunday school—though Jordan seemed to like it. Anyway, Bone stated: "I remember that I was keenly conscious of the fact that I was his pastor and that he was making important decisions."[68]

Bone continued:

> I remember Senator Jordan's attitude on world hunger was that, frankly, many of the people who were hungry deserved it, deserved to be hungry because of ignorance and laziness. My perception was ...he knew that he was accused of having that kind of "Big White Father" attitude, and I think he made a conscious effort to get away from it. There was [however] some paternalism that kept coming out in discussions with him, again and again...I just think it was very obvious that he came into the village when the village was floundering and he made it go, and they followed the pattern of most mill villages [of that era]. They had the company store, and they had the mill owner owning all the property in the village. I think that he was reluctant to move away from that. I think he liked it. I think he liked to have the workers look up to him and him look after their needs.[69]

There is no question that Jordan rescued a defunct mill, ran it through thick and thin, put food on empty plates, and brought renewed life to a mill village gasping for survival. As Sam Rankin observed, Jordan was a "hard bargainer and hard driver" who had to do a lot of "scratching and clawing" in the process. Rankin also made this candid appraisal: "[Jordan] started out and grew up with hard knocks, and I think that anyone that is a self-made man is a little hard to convince there is any way but his way. I think that was typical of Everett Jordan and that might be typical of me or anybody else. Even after he became a senator, his dominance over the business was, I think, typical of the man, and I don't think he would have been any other way."[70]

Reverend Jesse Bone, commenting on Jordan's motivation, said: "I don't think money was that important to him [except] in the [business] sense...And I don't think his motivation was trying to get the limelight...He was...willing to let other people be in the limelight if he got a job done... Even though from some perspectives it might seem that he took advantage of people, in the long run he saw himself as being very benevolent: one who was taking care of people who maybe could not take care of themselves. I guess he had a little bit of a messiah kind of complex."⁷¹

In 1958 Saxapahaw's would-be "messiah" and his steadfast helpmate left for a sojourn in the nation's capital to do "something for the people," as North Carolina's newest United States senator would sum it all up at the end of his tenure.⁷²

10

A Mill Man Goes to Washington

On the evening of May 2, 1958, B. Everett Jordan prepared to board a Southern Railway Pullman car in Burlington en route to Washington as he made the transition from cotton-mill man to lawmaker in the United States Senate. As he and his wife chatted with well-wishers who had come to see them off, the newly appointed senator was the picture of self-confidence; and, to all outward appearances, was fully prepared to assume his new role. To a casual observer, the undaunted textile executive exhibited no outward qualms about his ability to handle one of the most demanding positions in government.[1]

In this respect, in their audacity and ability to adapt to new situations, Everett and Dr. Henry W. Jordan, H. H. Jordan's first and second sons, respectively, were strikingly similar. They shared the mutual trait of supreme self-confidence.[2] As Everett's trusting wife often said, he could do anything. In his Senate assignment, he would be challenged to perform in a position totally strange to him.

In the spring of 1958, Everett Jordan was at the right place, at the right time, with the right people. The tide in the affairs of the Saxapahaw mill man had reached flood stage, and he was riding high. As he surveyed the approving faces in the crowd before him on that balmy May evening, even he himself may not have fully realized that he was on the verge of fulfilling his greatest ambition.

When Everett Jordan arrived in Washington a few days after W. Kerr Scott's death, he found his predecessor's staff essentially intact. For the first time, Everett met William ("Bill") M. Cochrane,

Senator Everett Jordan takes a parting look at his mill in Saxapahaw just prior to leaving for Washington in 1958. (*Jordan family albums*)

who had been Scott's administrative assistant. Cochrane had come to Capitol Hill in 1954 to help the newly elected Scott organize his office. Cochrane was a graduate of the University of North Carolina at Chapel Hill (A.B. 1939 and LL.B. 1941) and also held a master of laws degree (1954) from Yale. After service in World War II, he returned to become assistant director of the fledgling Institute of

View along Jordan Drive in 1990. On the left is the former Jordan home; on the right, the building owned by the Sellers Manufacturing Company that includes its offices. (Photo by author)

A Mill Man Goes to Washington

A view of Saxapahaw in 1989 (*left to right*): Collins Community Center, Sellers Manufacturing Company office building, and the Dixie Yarns, Inc., mill building (barely seen above the bridge that was to be replaced by the Buddy Collins Memorial Bridge in 1990–91). (Photo by author)

Government, in Chapel Hill, and in that capacity had numerous dealings with the state legislature. Albert Coates, the institute's founder, intended it to be an educational center for state and local employees. One of Cochrane's closest colleagues at the institute was Dr. William ("Bill") Friday, who later headed the University of North Carolina system. Cochrane, as Scott's top aide, had intended to stay in Washington only one year, just long enough to organize Scott's staff and ensure its proper functioning. But Scott, finding him valuable, urged him to stay on, and Cochrane was still serving upon the senator's death four years later, in 1958.[3]

Cochrane, at Jordan's request, agreed to stay on as senior administrative assistant, but, as formerly, he intended to return to Chapel Hill just as soon as Senator Jordan had his complete staff in place. But Cochrane never left Jordan. He soon learned that he liked working for the new senator, and the two made a good team. As a matter of fact, Cochrane later stated that "Senator Jordan was like a daddy to me."[4] Conversely, Cochrane understood and directly influenced Jordan during his Senate career as much or more than anyone else whom the senator encountered during his long stay in Washington.[5]

Katherine and newly appointed Senator Everett Jordan say goodbye to friends and well-wishers as they depart for Washington from Burlington via the Southern Railway on May 2, 1958. (*Jordan family scrapbooks*)

Roy Taylor, North Carolina congressman from the town of Black Mountain who served from 1960 to 1977, stated in a 1986 interview: "Bill Cochrane was a brilliant young man, and he had a topnotch staff backing him up and helping him. Few senators or congressmen had a more able staff than Everett Jordan [did]... There weren't any staff members up there better informed than Bill Cochrane was." Evelyn Taylor, the congressman's wife, said, "And Bill worked—he was a tireless worker—when dark came, Bill didn't go home."[6]

Former Congressman Hugh Alexander, of Kannapolis, N.C. (1952–62), who in 1963 became chief counsel for the Senate Rules Committee while Senator Jordan chaired it, also held Cochrane and his staff in high esteem. Alexander, too, described Cochrane as being an extremely capable administrative assistant for Jordan, who not only relied upon him for daily assistance but was also much influenced by his acute perceptions. As Alexander remembers Senator Jordan, "When he made up his mind, he was a stern person and was not easily changed."[7]

Yet, the senator, who was generally considered to be a conservative when he went to Washington, in the opinion of some observers became noticeably more liberal during his stay in office. Congressman Alexander, among many others, thought that Bill Cochrane

A Mill Man Goes to Washington

The newly appointed senator in 1958 with (*left to right*) his wife, Katherine, daughter-in-law Ellen M. Jordan, and daughter, Rose Ann Jordan Gant. (*Jordan family albums*)

played an important part in his evident change of heart—though Alexander indicated that some of Jordan's peers in Washington "thought that Bill was leading the Senator into the liberal camp too much."[8] Back home, some of Everett Jordan's constituents detected a perceptible divergence between the conservative businessman they had known and the more liberal-minded Washington lawmaker he became, complaining that he had forsaken his "class," that is, the mill men and their close associates.[9]

Everett Jordan, early on, recognized Bill Cochrane's talents, and Cochrane had Jordan's ear. On Capitol Hill, the senator merely practiced what Jordan the mill man had found to work so effectively for him on the banks of the Haw River: Keep your ear to the ground; find out what is going on from trusted employees, associates, neighbors, informants, or whomever; and avoid any surprises. Always keep the upper hand by knowing as much or more than the other fellow about what is taking place or about to take place. By doing so, in Saxapahaw he could dictate the outcome there, and in Washington he could influence the results.[10]

Senator Jordan at his Washington office in September 1960. (*Jordan family scrapbooks*)

Jordan, always an attentive listener, was definitely not a reader and did not pore over pamphlets, books, voluminous congressional records, or any other "heavy" written materials. Bill Cochrane, Wes Hayden, and his other staff members could do that through the late hours of the night, but not their boss![11]

Katherine Jordan, throughout her life, had a penchant for the printed page, but her interests were not politically centered, and her husband did not solicit or expect input from her on legislative matters. Too, her reading tastes ran more to current events, religion, cultural trends, and various social happenings. Nevertheless, she did express her views to her senator-husband, and was often a spectator in the Senate galleries. Although a gracious and courteous listener, she was outspoken and frank in her convictions, never inclined to stay quiet and unheard on any issue or matter relevant to her interests and convictions. Therefore, whenever her spouse shared his thoughts with her, he received her firm opinions—solicited or not.[12]

To carry out his duties, Jordan relied heavily upon his experienced staff who, under Cochrane's excellent supervision, functioned effectively. And the lawmaker *could* be influenced in his de-

Senator Jordan with his administrative assistant William ("Bill") M. Cochrane (*left*) and Wesley ("Wes") F. Hayden (*right*), the senator's press and executive secretary. (*Wesley F. Hayden*)

cision-making. But he alone was the senator, and he was not about to let someone else fill his shoes. Except for the very early years when he worked as a sales clerk in his uncle's jewelry store and later on as an apprentice manager in Gastonia's cotton mills, he had always been in charge. That did not change after he took his oath in the Senate.[13]

Nevertheless, in the spring of 1958, Jordan knew the score and understood that he was in a different ball game, playing in a vastly larger arena. The perceptive politician realized that in Saxapahaw he was in an environment that he had largely created and controlled, but that Washington was a totally different situation—one where he would have to learn his way around, find out who really was in charge, and observe how things actually got done.[14]

Cochrane and other staff members realized that probably their most important function was to keep their senator fully informed.[15] In view of the tremendous volume of printed matter relating to proposed legislation that must be scrutinized, the never-ending flow of information concerning major and minor issues requiring analysis, the escalating needs, requests, and demands of constituents, and innumerable telephone communications of every description that must be dealt with, every senator's staff has a burdensome and demanding task. In this respect, every knowledgeable source interviewed for this volume affirmed that Jordan's staff consistently performed in an outstanding manner.

Although Everett Jordan's early years in the Senate could be characterized as a learning experience in the legislative process as he listened to his staff as well as peers and evaluated their opinions and positions before making his own decisions, he never departed from the basic techniques he had practiced back home in local politics and mill management. Outside his closely knit group of business associates and confidants, few realized the scope of his activities and influence.[16]

The North Carolina delegation was a particularly close-knit group and stayed in close contact with each other. When Katherine and Everett Jordan arrived in Washington in the spring of 1958, they rented an apartment in the Calvert-Woodley apartment house, located in the capital's northwest quadrant. During their fourteen-and-one-half-year stay there, about half of the North Carolina lawmakers lived in this same building or nearby.[17]

Included at the Calvert-Woodley were Roy Taylor, who represented the Twelfth Congressional District (1960–76),[18] and his wife, Evelyn; Luther and Martha Hodges, while he served as secretary of commerce in the Kennedy-Johnson administration; Republican Congressman Charlie Jonas; and a number of other Tar Heel Democratic congressmen. This assemblage of the state's congressional representatives enjoyed a close relationship and rapport.[19]

As Roy Taylor explained: "We were neighbors in the daytime, and in the evening-time often we would go as a group to congressional functions where we were all invited to attend. If it were over at the Shoreham Hotel [within two blocks of the Calvert-Woodley apartments], it was just a matter of walking over there, and we'd walk in groups. I felt very close to Senator Jordan [in this association]."[20]

A Mill Man Goes to Washington

Senator Jordan's Washington office staff in December 1972, when he and his wife entertained them at lunch. *Standing, left to right*: Harry Gurkin, "Wes" Hayden, Patty Jordan, Anita Brown, Ellen Jordan (Everett and Katherine's daughter-in-law), Senator and Mrs. Jordan, Patsy Guyer, Anne Buchanan, Nancy Sullivan, "Bill" Cochrane; *seated*: Nancy Bradshaw, Madeline Harvey, Nancy Talley, Nancy Stedman, Rose Ann Jordan Gant, Rachel Spears. (*Jordan family scrapbooks*)

According to Evelyn Taylor: "When you were talking about the North Carolina delegation, people from other states were very attracted to [it] because of the closeness, and the Calvert-Woodley apartment house was often called the 'North Carolina Embassy' because the Jordans, Cooleys, Bonners, Hodgeses, Kitchins, Jonases... lived there. We were all very good friends socially."[21]

The lawmakers also had a close political relationship. Because they kept in close daily contact with each other and discussed proposed legislation, they knew each other pretty well and usually shared the same basic political philosophy, namely, a middle-of-the-road, conservative Southern viewpoint: states' rights, reduced federal taxes, a balanced budget, and a limitation on the growth and power of the federal government.[22]

During that era, the Southern bloc carried great weight in the Congress. As Horace D. Godfrey, a governmental official who worked closely with Jordan on agricultural matters, later explained:

Members of the North Carolina congressional delegation in the sixties (*left to right*): Walter B. Jones (First District), David N. Henderson (Third District), Basil L. Whitener (Tenth District), Horace R. Kornegay (Sixth District), Senator Sam Ervin, Senator Everett Jordan, Roy A. Taylor (Eleventh District), Charles R. Jonas (Ninth District), L. H. Fountain (Second District), Alton Lennon (Seventh District). (Photo by Hugh Morton; *L. H. Fountain*)

"Southern members of Congress were the power structure. They had been there so long—primarily because the South had a one-party system at the time—so they *were* the power structure, and they ran the committees in Congress. At one time in the 1950s, North Carolina had five of the chairmanships in the House of Representatives. That's unbelievable, but we had seniority. We got it by re-electing our members."[23]

During his first few weeks in Washington, while Jordan was trying to get his feet on the ground in the Senate as well as adjusting to a new way of life in the capital city, he relied especially on Cochrane to indoctrinate, advise, and assist him while he faced the challenges of his new assignment.[24]

Cochrane's special skills were quickly required. The same weekend when Jordan was appointed some of Cochrane's colleagues from Senator Scott's "family"—Ben Roney, Roy Wiler, and Terry Sanford—made some critical remarks about Jordan. But, before the year was out, all three men, through Cochrane's efforts, had made their peace with Jordan.[25]

As for the briefly troubled relationship between Jordan and Sanford, whatever differences of opinion or political philosophy that may have existed between the two at the time of Jordan's appointment were soon dissipated. By 1968 Sanford, who was hoping to join Hubert Humphrey on the Democratic ticket as vice-president, had only two elected officials in the entire country who openly supported him: Governor Phil Hoff, of Vermont, and Senator Everett Jordan.[26]

Everett Jordan's ability to adapt to his new situation was quickly tested. Not long after he arrived in Washington, the Senate was debating whether or not to admit Alaska to the Union. At that time, there were ninety-six senators for the forty-eight states, and Senator Jordan was number ninety-six. An informal Senate practice is to have the newest senator, usually from the majority party, preside over the Senate—aided, of course, by the parliamentarian—when the vice-president of the United States is not there or when the president pro tem is absent. Because those two officers are frequently not there, other senators preside most of the time.[27]

Senator Jordan was called to this duty for a considerable part of the six weeks or more debate that occurred concerning the question of admitting Alaska to the Union. According to Bill Cochrane: "He was always very dutiful in respect to any of his responsibilities, so he was over there a good deal. He heard the debate because sitting up there in the chair, responsible for recognizing senators and dealing with points of order and that sort of thing—guided by the parliamentarian—he had to be alert, whoever he [or she] might be... Senator Jordan had the benefit of more of the facts because he was up there presiding and heard and learned more than he would have normally as just a member of the Senate."[28]

As Jordan was also to act later concerning the Vietnam war, this time he also followed his judgment and conscience even though he alienated many of his colleagues and supporters. At the time, the desegregation fight was on. In 1958 the Southerners in the Senate were quite well united against the various civil rights proposals that were made, and they felt that the admission of Alaska would provide two more votes—two more senators who would likely vote with the Northerners on the civil rights question. Ignoring this situation and based on his objective judgment of the reasons why Alaska should be admitted, Jordan voted in the affirmative. Of the fourteen members who were then in the North Carolina delegation, twelve congressmen and two senators, B. Everett Jordan was the only member of that delegation and just about the only Southerner—certainly the only one from the Deep South, leaving Florida and Texas out—who voted to admit Alaska in the Union.[29]

A year later, Jordan followed the same pattern concerning the admission of Hawaii into the Union—even though this involved a new factor: a state that was not even a part of the North American continent. And again Jordan concurred in this action even though two more pro civil rights votes were involved. As Bill Cochrane later said: "I think that in a very real sense Senator Jordan led the way, opened the door. This was what had happened in Alaska. It was well received around the country and in the South, too; and I think he [Jordan] had a lot to do with the fact that those other members of our delegation and some other Southerners voted to let Hawaii in after having turned down Alaska."[30]

Cochrane contended that Senator Jordan never made a wrong vote once he knew all the facts: "I think Alaska ia a good example of that. He had occasion to listen at length to all the facts on both sides of the Alaska issue. It was early in his career—he wasn't quite as crowded as senators become as the years go by with all the things they have to keep up with. But every time he got all sides of the story, as far as I'm concerned personally, I thought he always came out with the right decision. He wasn't a liberal/conservative; it wasn't that kind of pattern. It was what overall seemed to be the best thing to do for the country. That's the way he would come out once he had all the facts."[31]

Cochrane continued: "Never was the senator a patsy for anybody's line if he got a chance to take in what was involved. I had great faith in his good commonsense ability to absorb what was the right thing to do. He really was willing to listen to both sides of any question, and that's the way we operated—looking, searching, and examining the pros and cons [of issues] before we made a decision."³²

Several of Jordan's political supporters and congressional colleagues praised his efforts in the Senate. One of these was "D. J." Walker, a Burlington attorney and local politician-officeholder: "Everett was a good politician—in a good sense...Knowing how to get along with people is the main thing. And he sure did! He knew you everywhere he saw you—came over and shook hands, not just as a gesture, but as a real genuine friendship...He had that all along, but he never had a chance to exhibit it until he got to be chairman of the Democratic party [in North Carolina] and then went to the Senate. He was one of the most gracious people I have ever known. He and his wife together just made a great pair because Mrs. Jordan kind of out-did him. She was a very friendly person."³³

Walker added: "Politics is also knowing how to give and take. When you know all of those things, you know what you can trade—something that doesn't matter for something that does matter to you. I've heard others say this—and I believe it—that Everett Jordan was the greatest trader in the world; and, when he got to the United States Senate, he was in big-time trading."³⁴

According to Walker, any original doubts he had about Jordan's success in the Senate were soon dissipated:

> I wasn't sure of this at first, but after Everett got up there I felt sure he was made for that job. I think that, beginning with the time that Scott appointed him and he really got interested in politics, fate really led him to his place in the Senate... Everett came into his own because he was a born deliberator and trader with people like that. He was up there in "high cotton" where he belonged.
>
> I think he found out after he got there that we had to be more of a world citizen than we had been, and he went along with all that and became sort of an expert on foreign policy with LBJ. He was doing a great job; and—at the same time—he was making folks at

home—of his own class—mad. But they never got mad enough to try to kick him out. He was re-elected twice [two full terms], finally went down running, but he never did quit.[35]

Walker, among others, agreed that Everett Jordan became more liberal after he became a senator, or at least more liberal than North Carolina's Democratic party position. Walker said, "I think that he and his brothers were always men of the people and not 'Lords of the Manor,' and stuff like that. I think his family background gave that to him."[36]

Those who knew Everett Jordan, in business and politics, were invariably impressed with his shrewdness—his skill in the art of compromise. He, himself, referred to it simply as back-scratching: "You scratch my back and I'll scratch yours."[37]

Jordan did a lot of back-scratching on the local scene and then in the larger arena when he later went to the nation's capital. In Washington he felt no need to abandon tried and proven tactics just because he was in a new and more sophisticated environment. As a senator, he freely admitted to "trading votes" with his colleagues in order to obtain the passage of legislation that affected his constituents.[38]

As D. J. Walker later recalled: "So, in any kind of debate, there are always things that you can just throw away. Well, throw them away, but get something for them!... Everett would do all of those things, keeping in mind what he wanted, but whenever he finally decided to make a contract on a deal, he knew he was getting what he wanted; and what he was giving for it wasn't worth that much to him. So he came out on the big end of the deal."[39]

Continuing, Walker said:

> Anyway, the art of compromise and trading what's non-essential for what you really want is most important. I think Everett Jordan had that from the day he was born. Probably did it [as a child] when he was playing marbles with the kids... in the Senate he was on the winning side of the things that he wanted—of the legislation that he wanted. He apparently knew how to get the ear of the president because he and LBJ were great friends and he sponsored a lot of LBJ's legislation, which was a little bit foreign to his quasi-conservative background because LBJ was a great liberal—passed all the civil rights legislation in the sixties... They [North Carolina Democrats and other constituents] were disenchanted with him [Jordan] when

he got to be a champion for American foreign policy and stuff like that. You know they were all conservatives and thought we ought to tell the rest of the world to go to hell, and it doesn't work like that ...

You think of genius as somebody being born that way, but it's really somebody born with an ear that will listen to everything he hears. And that's the way he gets to be a practicing genius, because he doesn't think he knows it all. He listens to everything... Everett Jordan, no matter what or how busy he was, would sit down and listen to you when you wanted to talk to him about something. You end up, and you wouldn't get an answer from him exactly, but you at least felt like you were being heard, and that he was going to give you every possible consideration. And he did hear something every time he listened to somebody that helped him put the whole picture together. I would say that was part of Everett's genius. He never was impolite. You know, people that are impolite never get very far in politics anyway.[40]

D. J. Walker's contention that Everett Jordan knew how to barter and compromise with his political peers is substantiated by Clyde Gordon's account of how the senator maneuvered: "We were in a meeting together up at West Jefferson [N.C.]. There were some tobacco interests there, some coal people, and some from Norfolk and Western Railroad, and they were giving Everett a hard time about subsidies on tobacco. And some were critical of other farm subsidies in other parts of the United States. Everett replied: 'Well, how do you think I'm going to get others to vote for the subsidy on tobacco if I don't vote for the big grain farmers out West? It's a matter of trading it out. You've got to go along with them on their program if you expect them to help you on yours.' "[41]

Gordon continued: "I think that he [Jordan] is, by far, the greatest salesman I ever knew. When he went to Washington, I said, 'He might not make the most flowery speech on the floor, but he's gonna get them in the back room; he's gonna sell them on what he wants.' And after all, that's what counts. You've got to get them on your side, and he certainly was a master at that. What I'm coming around to is, he never let his power go to his head. He was genuine and sincere; he did not want to be like anybody else. He just wanted to be Everett Jordan."[42]

Gordon made another point: "[Jordan] had sense enough not to ask for a lot of things that are not feasible, nor did he come before his colleagues for every little whim." Yet, Gordon contended that, with all the heavy responsibilities which are thrust upon a United States senator, along with the power plays and sophistication of the Washington scene, Jordan never forgot the people—the masses: "Everett never lost his touch with the common people."[43]

Congressman L. H. Fountain (Dem.-N.C. Second District) represented the state for thirty years: 1953 through 1982. Therefore, he preceded Everett Jordan in Congress by five years and was there for ten years after Jordan left. The former was dean of the North Carolina delegation in Washington after the death of Congressman Harold Cooley (Dem.-N.C. Fourth District). Fountain had first met Jordan when he chaired the North Carolina Democratic Executive Committee.[44]

According to Fountain: "Everett was like most of us. When we get into something new, we grow with experience. I noticed that from the time Everett became chairman of the Democratic party when he was not quite as sure of himself—because he was in a new field—as he was later on. But in the Senate he became the one that looked after... the basic legislative problems of the people of my district... Everett was a people-to-people man. He could carry on a conversation with anybody, was pleasant with everybody, and yet Everett could be extremely firm—particularly with some of the agency heads when they would... make what he would consider unreasonable demands."[45]

Fountain contended that Jordan from year to year grew not only in stature and intellect, but also in gaining the favor of the people of North Carolina as well as those in the Senate. For these reasons, Fountain claimed that Jordan was "a vote-getter for the things we wanted... If we could not work something out and agree on it... Everett quite often would suggest a compromise."[46]

Fountain allowed also that if Jordan had a friend who needed some legislative help with a proposed bill but which Everett did not know too much about—but had no specific reason not to go along with it—he would say, "Yeah, I'd be glad to go along with you on your proposition which relates to your state." In so doing, he was establishing credits for the future—the day when his own state would need votes.[47]

From time to time, North Carolina's congressmen and senators—as a group—hold delegation meetings. When he was the senior member of the delegation, Fountain served as its dean. He pointed out: "Quite often we would have people from North Carolina—delegations of farmers, of real estate people, savings and loan, bankers—groups from all over North Carolina would come to Washington, and they would want a delegation meeting... Everett was most cooperative in attending; and, if he could not attend, Bill Cochrane or someone else on his staff was always there. All they had to do was relay the information to him [Jordan] and he went along with what we did."[48]

Fountain commented on Jordan's political leanings:

> ...being in the textile business for a long time, being a part of big business and industry—[Jordan] had, like most who come out of that [background], an image of conservatism automatically, without anybody knowing anything particularly conservative about him. And I think that when he went into politics and started talking to people and realizing there were many, many points of view—and there wasn't any one way, and sometimes a combination of ways, to do things—Everett gave the appearance of compromise, and that compromise appeared to be going from right to left... I would say that Everett was pretty much in the center. When it came to things of North Carolina and things that helped North Carolina—programs that we had—even the spending of money for those programs, I guess you might say that Everett was to the left... But, if you had to make a choice, I would say he was less conservative when he came out than he was when he went in, but I never looked upon Everett as a liberal. I more or less thought of him as a progressive-conservative. Or you could call him a liberal-conservative or conservative-liberal... [In any event] he was a good legislator, and the most important thing to North Carolina about him was that, if we had some legislation that had to go through the Senate, he knew how to get to the individuals and get those votes. That was because of friendship and personality. They had confidence in him, and he knew them all by nickname of some kind, which he had picked up over in the Senate.[49]

Back home in Alamance County, veteran state Senator Ralph Scott, brother of Governor W. Kerr Scott and later a U.S. senator, in a 1981 interview made the following observation, which echoes what many others have said about Everett Jordan working "behind the scenes": "Everett was a good senator; you don't get the whole

Celebrating ten years of Jordan's senatorial service (*left to right*): Congressman L. H. Fountain (N.C. Second District), Senator Jordan, Congressman Roy A. Taylor (N.C. Eleventh District). (*L. H. Fountain*)

story in the paper. Everett might not have his picture in the paper as much as some of them, but he was very effective. People had confidence in him. That was the main thing...He did a superb job up there."[50]

Scott stressed the achievements of Jordan and others on behalf of North Carolina:

> [Jordan] and the manufacturers in Alamance County really ran this county for many years. Now when I say "ran it" I mean they ran it for good. They were progressive people—he and Reid Maynard, Clyde Gordon, Spencer Love, and all those folks...Whatever was good for Alamance County and the state, they were for it. He kept up with the political progress in the county, the state, and the nation more than anybody in this group. They depended a lot on him to

keep them informed and to really keep them on the right track. They were responsible people; none were spendthrift folks, but they were always for the good that helped the county and the state. I admired them greatly.

In fact when he was coming along, all the industry in Alamance County was owned by local people, operated by local people, and they had an interest in this county. Therefore, they had a tremendous influence that included the churches and schools, the total welfare of the people, which couldn't be beat.

Everett is from a great family. As you know, his father was a minister, and I think that being raised in that atmosphere had a lot of influence on Everett and his brothers, too. They were all good people. Progressive people. They did not seem to care too much about material wealth—so many people are judged by that—he had the material wealth, but it didn't affect him in any way. He had a tremendous influence, not only in the county, but statewide. Our state really made progress under the leadership of Everett Jordan and others like him. They dominated this state industrially. You know these large plants now keep transferring people from one place to the next, and they don't get their feet set in any one community for too long at a time before they transfer them to some other place, and I don't think that's good. They don't establish roots in the community and become attached to it and furnish leadership in the schools and in the churches. That is so important to the growth of a community.[51]

Scott also pointed out that he had never seen Jordan cheat in politics: "If he didn't agree with you, he'd beat you fair and square, if he could, and, if he couldn't, he would go on about his business. But he would never compromise to any extent that you could condemn him for it... When he advocated anything, that's what he thought was best for the people. He wasn't a politician to the extent that the Democrat was always right and the Republican always wrong. He'd investigate. You couldn't just tell him anything and get by with it; you had to be able to back it up."[52]

In a 1982 interview, Judge Woodrow Jones, a former congressman and Governor Luther Hodges's choice to replace John Larkins as chairman of the state Democratic party, attributed Jordan's success as a senator to his uncanny understanding of people. Jones extolled his friend and ally Jordan as becoming "a good senator—a statesman at the same time he was a politician and understood politics just about as well as any man I've been acquainted with." According to Judge Jones, the reason he was so effective as a politician was "because of his sincerity and honesty, and his ability to relate to all kinds of people: "[Jordan] could get along with lawyers, farmers, bankers, manufacturers, workers, and everybody else. I never saw him ill-at-ease with anybody or with any group of people. He related to all classes of people, and that's calculated to make a man successful in politics."[53]

Governor Luther Hodges, who insisted that he "never really had any ambition to go to the Senate" and who appointed Jordan, pointed out that he was "very proud" of Jordan's record in the Senate and "happy that I made the appointment, even though some people questioned it at the time."[54]

Dr. Floyd Riddick, who served as Senate parliamentarian during the years Jordan served there, recalled that the latter was "one of the most friendly people I have ever known. He would always come up with his arms wide open to receive you—to talk." Riddick pointed out that, unlike many other new senators, who were not able to enter the mainstream for a couple of years, Jordan was very quickly accepted: "[He] was so friendly and so respected that he didn't need to make speeches, nor did he have to know parliamentary procedures or techniques in order to have some influence."[55]

Jordan's achievements in the Senate were lauded not only by some of his colleagues there, but also by his staff. Bill Cochrane said:

> There's an old saying here [on Capitol Hill]...with respect to members of Congress who come in from their home states. The old saying is that "Some of them come here and grow, and some come in and swell." Senator B. Everett Jordan came and *grew*. He grew in breadth and depth and in understanding and in wisdom. He was very attentive to his duties throughout his time here. He was always anxious to be helpful to people—even just passersby in the hall— and he devoted himself to learning the essence of his legislative re-

sponsibilities. He would study hard; he went to hearings faithfully on the various committees on which he served, including particularly the Senate Committee on Rules and Administration, of which he was chairman. [In that capacity] he was chairman in alternate years of the Joint Committee on the Library of Congress and the Joint Committee on Printing. In many ways, that was his opportunity to be of greatest service to the Senate. But, in the course of all that, along with [serving on] the Public Works Committee, the Post Office and Civil Service committees, and the Agriculture Committee, he grew. He grew and he didn't swell.[56]

Cochrane added: "[Jordan] was very effective in the Senate. He was a 'senator's senator' in many ways. He was probably one of the most beloved people... all the way from the cleaning people to the highest echelons of the Senate. He was friendly; he spoke to people when he passed them in the hall, no matter who they were.[57] He knew how to deal with people. A lot of [his legislative success] was personal; they wanted to go along with B. Everett. They liked him."[58]

Cochrane also stated that Jordan was "loaded with energy. He was able to go-go-go! And he was always cheerful. Very rarely did I see him when he wasn't upbeat. He enjoyed his work as much as anybody I ever knew."[59]

Cochrane continued: "[Jordan] knew the Senate pretty well—he had some little habits that were different and very effective. For example, if he wanted to get something done on the House side, he didn't pick up the phone; he walked over there and talked [personally] to the congressman. Now I want you to know they notice things like that because they are not used to having United States senators come walking over there. And, if he was working on something that involved a staff director or some legislative person on a committee, he would call and say, 'Look, I want to come down and talk to you.' The staffer would say, 'Oh no, I'll come up!' But he would go down and see them himself."[60]

Cochrane then explained how Jordan, when he was chairman of the Coordinating Committee in charge of construction for the Library of Congress's Madison Building, used this "hands-on" technique in a successful defense of the site. Three attempts were made to take that site away. One of these was made by House Speaker Carl Albert. Jordan paid a call on Congressman Clarence Cannon, chairman of the Appropriations Committee, and convinced him to rule against his own Speaker.[61]

As did so many others who were interviewed for this volume, Cochrane stressed that Jordan never sought the limelight, preferring instead to work unobtrusively in the background, where he felt he could be the most effective. In other words, he shunned the news media and concentrated on carrying out his duties in a quiet, responsible, and unassuming manner.[62]

Therefore, Cochrane was angered in 1972 when Washington columnist Jack Anderson dubbed Jordan as one of Congress's "unknown soldiers" and labeled him as "ineffective" and a "softie in the clutch." Cochrane made a quick rebuttal in the *Winston-Salem Journal and Sentinel*:

> I know where the work's been done and where the long hours have been put in. I know where folks come when they have problems. Jack Anderson doesn't know Senator Jordan.
>
> We haven't been out looking for headlines, because it doesn't suit the senator's personality, and it's not the way he likes to work. He likes to help people, but he doesn't go around shouting about it.
>
> The operation of the Senate—which Jordan oversees as chairman of the Rules and Administration Committee—has been improved countless ways since he came here.[63]

Cochrane proudly contended that Jordan always voted correctly when he had studied a situation thoroughly. Once he understood all that was involved, he had the courage to vote his convictions even though this action might cost him the loss of friends and political support.[64] Two instances were his votes to admit Alaska and Hawaii to the Union, discussed earlier in this chapter. Another example was his vote against U.S. participation in the Vietnam war (see chapter 13).

Also, Jordan in 1962, fairly early in his tenure, sided with John F. Kennedy and cast the deciding vote in favor of the administration's Trade Bill, the so-called "Kennedy round" on the tariff questions involved in the General Agreement on Tariffs and Trade (GATT). This is one of the relatively few times that Jordan's impact on legislation attracted widespread public attention. The bill, which eliminated many trade barriers, especially tariffs, by the international community, saved the GATT for the Kennedy administration.

In the process, Jordan split with his colleague Senator Sam Ervin, Jr., who favored a far more protective bill, as did also the textile industry, with which Jordan was prominently identified. Nevertheless, Jordan stated: "If we do not pass a bill or seriously cripple the one we do pass, then the president will not be able to negotiate international agreements or effectively enforce them." In other words, despite the industry's strong opposition, Jordan believed that its long-range interests would be favorably affected by the new legislation.[65]

The textile industry was fearful that a potential increase of cheaper textile imports would inflict even more harm on an industry already hurting; and it was particularly offended because, if Jordan had voted with the protectionist foes, the resulting tie vote would have given them victory. But, over time, they forgave Jordan, who had always been a major supporter of the textile industry.[66]

An editorial in the *Greensboro* (N.C.) *Record* sided with Jordan: "Senator Jordan put what he considered the country's welfare ahead of his own personal interest when he voted against the crippling amendment. He is a textile manufacturer and is closely associated with the industry. Undoubtedly, the senator was under great pressure to vote against a liberalization of the trade policy... It is a source of pride for North Carolinians that Senator Jordan acted as he did in what must be regarded as the best interests of the nation."[67]

Patsy Guyer worked first as a research assistant on the Rules Committee for Jordan when he was chairman and then as a member of his personal staff during the later years of his tenure. Although she was not on the scene during the senator's early years, in the interview for this volume she expressed what she and others experienced as members of his Washington staff: "He was the best employer one could ever hope to have. He was fair; he took a personal interest in everyone on his staff; he was just a joy to work with in every respect. Every morning he would walk through the office... saying 'good morning'—it made your day. He was very concerned about all of us, and it was very easy to work for [him] ... He was *extremely* efficient... he knew how to make things happen. Not only did he understand the legislative process, but he had that personal touch that very few people have. It was very hard to say 'No' to a person like Senator Jordan."[68]

Guyer offered more praise:

> He trusted all of us; he knew we would do our jobs and report back to him...He thanked you profusely for every thing you did...and therefore you were more apt to go the extra mile for him...We all had a very close personal relationship with him...I mean we would not be scared to talk to him about anything...When I think of Senator Jordan, I recall this lovable elderly gentleman with a twinkle in his eyes and the most marvelous smile—just a wonderful human being...I think his performance as a senator was magnificent, but I also think his performance as a human being was just as important ...And as for his wife, I have the same feeling about her. I think she was just absolutely terrific; she was one of my favorite people in the whole wide world. Very easy to work with. Very appreciative. Gracious.[69]

Patsy Guyer was on Jordan's staff when he was defeated in 1972 and left office the following January. In his defeat, she said he was "absolutely magnanimous...a gracious loser" and recounted his efforts to assist his staff: "Well, he was certainly concerned about all of us so far as what was going to happen and what kind of jobs we would find. He went to bat for everybody—peddled our resumes, and I think that is highly unusual. Most senators just don't take the time to make that extra effort for their employees, but he did... Everybody loved Senator Jordan. He was like a father to me."[70]

Wesley ("Wes") Hayden was a key member of Jordan's staff who came on board after the sudden death in 1967 of Bill Whitley, the senator's press and executive secretary. Hayden, like Cochrane, Guyer, and other staff members, verifies Jordan's Pied Piper qualities in attracting and keeping good people to work for him. Hayden came to Washington in 1959 as a reporter for the *Winston-Salem Journal and Sentinel* and nine months later became a "stringer" for out-of-town newspapers, radio, and television stations, feeding Washington news to them. He served in this capacity for eight years before joining Jordan's staff in 1967.[71]

Although Hayden's duties covered a broad range, they more resembled those of an executive secretary than press secretary because Everett Jordan was not an avid publicity seeker. It was only when he had something very specific to announce, a position that needed explaining, or responding to press inquiries on particular issues that Hayden assumed the role of press secretary. As executive secretary, he outlined legislative positions and handled correspondence while working closely with Bill Cochrane.[72]

Hayden described Jordan's working methods: "Senator Jordan was a very practical, a very pragmatic man in many ways. He worked behind the scenes; he developed most of his positions on legislation in private consultation with members of his staff, with other members of the committees on which he served, and with Democratic colleagues. He wasn't a speech-maker by choice. If he had something to say on the Senate floor, he said it very simply and very directly, but primarily he worked behind the scenes."[73]

Whatever satisfaction Jordan gained for his achievements or whatever disillusionment he experienced for his frustrations in the Senate, he enjoyed the sense of power his position bestowed and he used it at his discretion.

His daughter, Rose Ann Jordan Gant, made this assessment in a 1983 interview for this volume:

> Daddy enjoyed the *power* of the office. He didn't abuse it, but he enjoyed it. I don't know that I ever saw him [use his power to] abuse—but he was very human in that respect. It is almost impossible to describe the kowtowing that goes on in Washington. The magic of a license plate; you could park in the middle of the street if you had "SENATE" on there! The policeman would say, "Oh thank you!" for parking in the middle of the street. You can't be subjected to that sort of deferential treatment day in and day out all the time, and it not get to you. To some extent it becomes second nature—you don't pay any attention to it, and yet on the other hand when people came to him and wanted specific things in Washington, he responded.[74]

Rose Ann gave this example:

> The police force within the National Zoo were not under anyone's [authority]; they weren't under the city of Washington; they were somewhat under Congress; they were somewhat under the congressional committee having to do with the city of Washington, but there wasn't anyone specifically that they could go to with anything. So

they went to daddy, and he saw to it that they got a pay raise, which was long overdue...Nothing gave him more pleasure than to do something like that!...It was part of his job, and he enjoyed doing it. But there is also a funny kind of pleasure in the power that allows you to do it, if you understand what I'm saying. He did it because it needed to be done.

You know daddy had a reputation in Washington that he was a "people's senator" and *all* people came to him because they knew he would hear what they had to say and try to address whatever problem they brought him. That was just plain old housekeeping that went on up there that others were just too busy to fool with. He enjoyed doing that sort of thing, and he had the power to do it. That in itself brings tremendous satisfaction.[75]

Not all the people Everett Jordan befriended, however, were police or those simply in need of housekeeping help. In his position as chairman of the Senate Rules Committee, he had the power to help even the president. Unlike many publicity-seeking politicians, he worked quietly and unobtrusively behind the scenes, but his power and influence were felt and recognized by those who knew the score—especially by those on the receiving end, regardless of low, high, or middling status.[76]

On the recurrent theme of back-scratching, Senator Sam Ervin later recalled how he and Jordan clawed as a team: "I know he and I used to have some hard fights up there, when we had some of them like the Kennedys and Senator [John] Williams of Delaware opposing us when we tried to get price supports for tobacco...Oh yes, we were able to get farm programs because we sort of teamed up with the people from the Midwest and North Dakota...You have to work together to get anything."[77]

Ervin continued:

Now Everett was very effective, especially in the fields in which he worked. One thing, principally, was that he realized that legislation is the art of the possible, and the art of the compromise...In other words, if a person helped him on a proposition, he was always willing to return the favor, and consequently he always had a good

A Mill Man Goes to Washington

Senators Jordan and Ervin on the steps of the nation's Capitol. (*Jordan family scrapbooks*)

rapport among the senators. He was also an awful good mixer and on very friendly terms with virtually everybody in the Senate...As a result of his ability to mix with people, and also in the fields where he was knowledgeable—they knew he had made a success in business and manufacturing—people listened to him—just as they will listen to any man who has experience.

Everett's great contribution was his ability to cooperate with other people and, in his quiet way, persuade them about the correctness of his views on the things in which he was particularly interested. Most work in the Senate is done in committee...Everett was very effective in his committee work.[78]

Ervin recalled his common origins with Jordan: "I found that my service in the Senate with Everett was extremely pleasant because we had this association that went back to when we were teenagers and played baseball on the sandlots...[in Morganton]. And, from time to time through the years, we had associations politically... Everett and I were about the same age."[79]

On the other hand, Ervin recognized their differences: "Everett's career and mine were quite different; I'd been in the law, concerned with legal questions. Therefore, I was much concerned with constitutional questions in the Senate [because I served on the Judicial Committee], especially after I became chairman of the Subcommittee on Constitutional Rights. Everett's career, as you know, was in business and manufacturing. He had experience that was quite different from mine, and I had experience in my profession that was quite different from his. So, as a result of that, I think that in the Senate we complemented each other."[80]

In finally characterizing his friend Jordan, Ervin used what he called "Washington terminology derived from the Bible": He summed up Jordan as a pragmatic senator, who was always interested in the "loaves and the fishes."[81]

11

Loaves and Fishes

In a 1982 interview for this volume, Margaret J. Sprinkle, Everett Jordan's younger sister, stated: "Papa said if you try to save a man's soul you ought to also save his body. There was unemployment here, and he started the factory to give work to his parishioners." She was referring to the Reverend H. H. Jordan's part in establishing a chair factory at Mocksville, N.C., around 1900. Everett, then a pre-schooler, was observing and learning from his father's example,[1] and he learned well. Throughout his life, he was keenly aware of his responsibilities as an industrial and political leader to provide "sustenance" to his followers—his employees, constituents, and political supporters.

In 1927 Saxapahaw was the epitome of desolation and economic despair. Its only industry, a run-down and defunct cotton mill, had been idle for four years, and its inhabitants were hangers-on who had nowhere else to go. Everett Jordan, the new mill manager, knew that no one would eat if the mill's spindles did not turn. He determined that they would not stop as long as he was at the helm.[2] Despite personality differences, he and his father had much in common concerning basic values.

Clyde Gordon said that Everett Jordan did not change his perspective or personality when he went from Saxapahaw to Washington in 1958. He was still "the same Everett."[3] Sam Ervin's use of the analogy of Jordan's being a "loaves and fishes" representative seems appropriate.[4] The Reverend H. H. Jordan would have appreciated and approved of that label for his first-born son.

Well before and lasting through Everett Jordan's Senate tenure, the textile industry was predominant in the Southeast, and North Carolina was first in textile employment and production. As a manufacturer himself, Jordan was keenly aware of the industry's status and familiar with the problems of domestic producers.[5]

After World War II, America helped both allies and former enemies to rebuild their economies. This economic aid was especially needed in Japan, conquered and struggling to regain its place in world commerce. Jordan and a number of his congressional peers visited Japan and the Far East during the re-building process, in October–November 1969, to see firsthand that country's transformation from a defeated nation to a formidable competitor in the world market. He was both pleased and perplexed, for he foresaw trouble for textiles in his homeland. American jobs were at stake.[6]

Jordan's major ally in his persistent efforts on behalf of the textile industry was the American Textile Manufacturers Institute (ATMI), whose executive vice-president was Robert C. Jackson (the presidency is a purely honorary position that is occupied by an industry executive). Jackson had assumed this position in 1949, when the two major cotton-textile trade organizations in the country merged to form the ATMI: the American Cotton Manufacturers Association, headquartered in Charlotte, N.C.; and the Cotton Textile Institute, whose executive offices were in New York.[7]

Corporate headquarters were located in Charlotte, but offices were maintained in New York City and Washington, D.C. A small research center originally operated at Clemson University, in Clemson, S.C. Over the succeeding years, the organization was involved in a number of mergers to accommodate changing times and industry needs. Some of the merged organizations were the Association of Cotton Textile Merchants, the National Federation of Textiles, the National Association of Textile Finishers, and the National Association of Wool Manufacturers. The ATMI became the overall central trade organization for the entire textile-manufacturing industry in the United States.

Its major objective was the representation of textile-industry thinking on major issues—statewide, nationwide, worldwide. The Washington staff included attorneys, economists, technical people, and others familiar with government processes. The corporate headquarters in Charlotte, under the direction of another close friend of Everett Jordan's—Secretary-Treasurer F. Sadler Love—handled the statistical operations for a great many years. Industry statistics were collected and disseminated. That program was closely coordinated with agencies in Washington that gathered industry statistics. Also headquartered in Charlotte were six or seven professional public relations people. The New York office basically served the interests of the marketing structure of the industry.

Over the years, reflecting industry activity and attitudes, the ATMI became heavily involved in international trade matters, such as import-export quotas and regulations. As a result, the agency became the focus among textile and fiber interests of the country in efforts to formulate procedures for dealing with imports, then as now a major international trade concern.

Robert Jackson first met Everett Jordan at ATMI meetings before the latter ever went to the Senate, and was on hand when he was sworn into office after his appointment by Governor Hodges. From then on, Jackson had many contacts with the junior North Carolina senator. This was logical not only because Jordan was directly involved in the textile-manufacturing industry, but also because he was a senator from a major textile-producing state. Also, the ATMI was strongly involved in raw-cotton matters concerning farmers, ginners, and warehousemen, as well as textile manufacturers.

During the three decades Jackson worked in Washington, he knew many senators who, term after term, because their personality or method of operations did not fit, were never able to become members of "The Club." This is an informal and unofficial group in the Senate that is a sort of inner circle of senators who relate well with each other, who deal with one another, and who know how to accomplish things. They provide mutual support, and party lines are crossed. "Members" enjoy the support and the understanding of their friends in the Senate; mutual aid is provided where conflicts of interest are not involved.

According to Jackson, Everett Jordan quickly became a member of The Club because of his personality, his sense of humor, his integrity, his honesty, and his ability to get along with people. He was, therefore, able to accomplish things in the Senate just through the power of his personality and his friendships. As Jackson explained: "He didn't get things done by making terrific speeches on the Senate floor. He didn't succeed by becoming the most outstanding expert on any given subject, but he knew enough about all the things for which he was responsible and consequently enjoyed credibility. He was a very effective man in the Senate because of his method of operation." Jackson also lauded Jordan's ability "to influence other senators in a quiet way. His work was done off the floor, not on it, for the most part." As a back-room operator, he made comparatively few appearances on the evening news.

As chairman of the Senate Rules Committee, Jordan was, in effect, in charge of housing, parking, dining-room, and other facilities for his peers, as well as all the "perks" related thereto. His control of office assignments and amenities provided special opportunities for contact and interaction with fellow senators as they came knocking at his door. He, himself, enjoyed certain privileges of his position.

One of these was a private hideaway office in the Capitol. Many senators and virtually all committee chairmen had such quarters. Because these prized offices were assigned by the Rules Committee, of which Everett was chairman, he had one of them.

Jackson explained:

> Frequently, when we had some matter that our organization was interested in and was being considered on the Senate floor, or even being considered by some agency of government, where we were consulting Everett frequently as we went along, and we were developing plans and strategy, he would say, "Well, come to my little hideaway office about 5:30 this afternoon, and we'll talk it over." So, two or three of us would gather there—sometimes there would be people from North Carolina, some of his constituents, with us—some mill men, or part of the time it might be just members of our staff, but we would gather in his office. Frequently, I was there alone with him, and we would evaluate where we were. We would talk it over and think it through, decide what the next move should be, and then he would say, "Well, it's about that time of day, we ought to have a little nip." So, we'd have a little nip and continue our discussion; then he would go his way and we'd go ours.

Jackson pointed out that Jordan was never a member of the board of directors of ATMI, but that his son Ben E. Jordan, Jr., was. Jackson: "Frequently, he [Everett] would be invited to meet with our board of directors. Often, we met in Washington... He was a wonderful source of advice after he became knowledgeable about Senate procedures, and procedures within the... government... He was a constant source of advice and guidance to us, and we valued it very much. He also usually attended our annual meetings, and he spoke at these...on several occasions."

The chairman of the Senate Rules Committee had other responsibilities and powers that helped endear him to those on Capitol Hill. One of these was responsibility for the presidential inauguration ceremonies that occurred there. Particularly because, as soon as one inaugural was over, planning began for the next; the enormous amount of effort taxed Jordan and his staff. On the other hand, distribution of seat tickets proved to be a political advantage.

These powers were valuable aids in gaining support for his legislative goals. A major one of these was elimination of the two-price cotton system. To make American cotton more competitive worldwide, the U.S. government adopted a policy of subsidizing exports of raw cotton—sometimes apparently as much as 25 percent of the value of the cotton. This made it possible for a foreign mill to buy cotton grown in the United States much cheaper than a mill here could purchase it. This gave the Japanese and other importers of homegrown domestic cotton an unfair advantage over American manufacturers. As Robert Jackson explained in a 1988 interview:

> A bale of cotton grown within a mile of a textile mill in Saxapahaw could be bought by a mill in Japan, even after paying all the transportation charges, very substantially cheaper than Everett Jordan could buy it in Saxapahaw. Furthermore, there were few limits on that cotton coming back into this country in the form of manufactured goods to compete with whatever Everett Jordan or other textile mills were producing in this country. It was a terribly unfair situation. Yet the State Department...was all out in favor of it... Through the offices of ATMI, we mounted an all-out campaign to get that situation corrected.

For years, this system was a thorn in the side of domestic cotton manufacturers, but efforts by industry leaders to correct the situation had failed. Everett Jordan, using his contacts and influence, especially as a member of the Senate Agricultural Committee, and working closely with the House Agricultural Committee, the ATMI, other industry groups, and the U.S. Department of Agriculture, led the long and difficult fight in the Senate.

Another major contact of Jordan's on agricultural matters, Horace D. Godfrey, seconded Jackson's opinion on Jordan's major role.

Senator Jordan and Horace D. Godfrey (*right*) at banquet in Washington, D.C., in 1962. (*Horace D. Godfrey*)

Godfrey explained: "Everett was a key player; he was chairman of the Rules Committee, and [this position] can get you some votes from somebody that it doesn't make any difference to—senators that don't care about cotton—they have no cotton you know, no textile mills or the like. Everett was very influential. He and Don Russell [ex-Senator from South Carolina] both were very influential in getting the number of votes that we needed."[8]

Harold Cooley (Dem.-N.C.), who was chairman of the House Agriculture Committee at the time, introduced the original bill, which specified that U.S. mills should be able to purchase American cotton at the same price that it was sold to foreign mills. As Robert Jackson explained: "It took an awful long time and an enormous amount of effort. We had to go into all the cotton-producing states; we initiated scores of meetings with cotton-producer leadership throughout the country because most of them were supporting the two-price system. They thought it was good for cotton producers, and they had to be shown that, in the long run, it was going to react against their best customer, which was, after all, the American textile industry. Finally, we [convinced] all of the cotton-producer leadership in the country [to] support...our position."

Jackson added: "Incidentally, President Johnson had committed, before he came into office, that—if elected—he was going to try to eliminate the two-price cotton system. And he followed through on his word. He went all out; and, because [he and] Everett Jordan ... were close friends, on a good many occasions during that long and difficult fight, Everett was a principal contact with President Johnson. On two or three occasions, we accompanied Everett to see Johnson when he was majority leader of the Senate and also when he was president."

While Johnson was president, and after years of tireless toil, legislation was finally enacted to eliminate the two-price cotton system.

Another key player in agricultural legislation who worked closely with Everett Jordan was a Tar Heel: Horace D. Godfrey. He was then serving as administrator of the Agricultural Stabilization and Conservation Service; and executive vice-president and member of the board of directors (1961–69) of the Commodity Credit Corporation, which handled all the money and funded many agricultural programs. These were presidential appointments requiring approval of the Senate.[9]

Godfrey was cognizant of Jordan's vital role in agricultural affairs. And for good reason: In both the Kennedy and Johnson administrations, Godfrey ran all the farm programs, including, of course, those that related to cotton-acreage allotments and certificates to sell the cotton. Godfrey pointed out: "So, naturally in that job, I got very well acquainted with members of Congress. Half of my time was spent in lobbying for farm legislation." Godfrey, like Bob Jackson, verifies the leading part that Everett Jordan played in farm issues.

Before going to Washington, Godfrey had run the farm programs in North Carolina on a statewide basis. Every county had an office, which went through various name changes, first the AAA (Agricultural Adjustment Administration); then changed in the mid-forties to Production and Marketing Administration; and finally, in the early sixties, to Agricultural Stabilization and Conservation Service (ASCS).

Godfrey's duties while in North Carolina required him to travel over the entire state as he visited each of the 100 county offices and gave speeches so that people would understand and support farm needs. He had a weekly radio program on various stations and a television program on the first TV station in North Carolina at Greensboro. Further, he made it a point to stay in contact with the state's governors.

Godfrey explained: "I met Everett, I think, while he was chairman of the state Democratic party. I was very active in politics, and it didn't take me long to find out that our survival as an agency and farm program depended upon politics."

When Godfrey arrived in Washington in 1961, his junior senator had preceded him there by three years, and by then Everett Jordan knew his way around. When Godfrey appeared before the Senate Agricultural Committee for confirmation, Jordan made a strong statement praising his past work and his qualifications. Because Godfrey was no novice in farm matters or legislation and Everett Jordan was on both the Senate Agriculture Committee and a subcommittee that dealt with tobacco, peanuts, and cotton, the two men worked together closely on behalf of farm interests and programs, an area of prime concern to Jordan's constituents. As Godfrey said: "We had the largest farm program activity of any state in the Union. We were second to Texas in total number of farms. Because we had so many crops that were involved in price supports, acreage allotments, and so on, we had the largest activity of any state."

Some people refer to the Rules Committee as a "housekeeping committee," but Horace Godfrey—and this is confirmed by others—did not belittle its importance. In carrying out the functions of the Senate, other members, in a way, become somewhat indebted to the chairman and his committee. And Everett Jordan was not one to ignore the power possibilities of his position.

As Godfrey said, "I have another good illustration of how important the Rules Committee is. Herman [Talmadge] made the announcement that he was going to leave Congress, go back and run for governor. That really upset us because he was our standby on the Senate Agriculture Committee. We could get things done through Herman because he had the full support of Jordan on something like this, and Everett had his Rules Committee."

Godfrey provided some firsthand insight on Jordan's role as chairman of the Subcommittee on Production and Marketing of the Senate Agriculture Committee: "Everett was a good strong man. We camped out in Everett's private office when legislation was being considered that USDA supported—'we' being some of the industry people like Lou Barringer, Gordon McCabe, and those of us that were lobbying for the government. We were in Everett's office every afternoon."

There were two cotton programs: one for long-staple and one for upland, or regular, cotton. The upland domestic cotton production exceeded domestic needs, and producers were concerned about price, supply, acreage allotment, and exports. They were, therefore, having to cut back on their plantings so they could receive price support and payments. Not so the domestic long-staple cotton producers, whose product was in short supply, and domestic manufacturers had to rely heavily upon imports. According to Godfrey, the long-staple cotton producers opposed this type of program; the United States was actually importing this kind of cotton. The Supima Association in the western part of the United States finally decided to seek a program similar to that for upland cotton. This could not be achieved without help from Jordan, who was chairman of that subcommittee. Working through the Cotton Council, the Supima Association sought to win his approval for their plan. Jordan rejected it because it contained a provision that the USDA could not support, apparently one affecting Peru's right to keep exporting cotton to the United States; and at the same time long-staple cotton production could expand in the United States.

Jordan said, "I'm not going to do anything until they soften up a little." Therefore, they visited Godfrey knowing that he knew Everett real well. Godfrey asked them:

> "Are you willing to make some concessions?" "What kind of concessions?" I told them exactly what they had to do, and they said, "If we make those concessions, can we get a program?" I told them, "Yes." They looked at me like they thought I was crazy and said, "What are you going to do about Senator Jordan?" I said, "You give me your word that you'll make those concessions?" "All right, we'll give you our word." I just reached over, picked up the phone, and called Everett. I said, "Everett, do you mind if I put you on the speaker here for a minute?" He said, "Who you got with you?" And I told him, and he said, "No, I don't mind at all." I turned to them and I said, "This is Senator Jordan here now; you tell him what you'll

do." They told him, and I said, "Now, Senator, this is what you wanted them to do, do they have your support in getting them into the program?" "Yes, sir! They've got it." And those guys never forgot that.

Everett Jordan's first priority was always to take care of the folks back home—his constituents—but he would also work diligently with whomever needed help, so long as their aims and goals did not jeopardize his own. As a senator, he had the ability and power to help enact legislation that affected thousands, and sometimes millions, of people, but much of his endeavors were on behalf of otherwise unrecognized individuals who needed someone to champion their just cause or dire need.

The benefits, of course, did not always accrue in only one way. For example, Godfrey arranged with Jordan for the daughter—Brenda Tie—of a Chinese friend of his from Raleigh to work in Jordan's Washington office. Actually, this turned out to be to Jordan's advantage because he was in the midst of a hard re-election fight; and, because he had no minority persons on his staff, Brenda's assignment was desirable.

Godfrey pointed out that Senator Jordan had another friend at the U.S. Department of Agriculture who was quite influential during the early days of the Kennedy and Johnson administrations. Originally from North Carolina and a graduate of Duke University, he was Charles ("Charlie") Murphy, from Wallace, N.C. He was one of the first two legislative draftsmen in the U.S. Senate—lawyers who drafted legislative proposals for consideration by that body. When Truman became president, he persuaded Charlie (under threat of abolishing his job in the Senate) to become his chief of staff at the White House and he served in that capacity throughout Truman's presidency. He subsequently practiced law until the Kennedy-Johnson campaign. He then worked with Senator Johnson; and, when Kennedy was elected, Charlie requested and received the position of under secretary of agriculture. As Godfrey stated: "Charlie knew more about political Washington than anyone I have ever known. He had tremendous respect for the office of the president and for members of the Senate. He was a great friend of Everett Jordan. [He served] in USDA for three to four years... Charlie Murphy as much as any one individual was the key man in devising strategy for passing agricultural legislation during the early Kennedy and Johnson years."[10]

The longtime growing and manufacture of tobacco—today the massive tobacco industry—both in Everett Jordan's time and since has been one of the major contributors to North Carolina's economy and to that as well of a number of other Southern states. For health reasons, in recent years, this industry has been in disfavor with the medical community and under increasing attack on Capitol Hill.

D. K. Muse, of Mebane, met Everett Jordan in 1948 when the former became chairman of the Democratic party in Alamance County, and the latter was increasingly being involved in political affairs. As politicians, the two men became well acquainted with each other and worked together effectively to elect their party's candidates.[11]

Muse, who was familiar with Senator Jordan's work in Washington on behalf of his home state's tobacco people, explained some of his contributions. For one thing, Dr. Henry Jordan, Everett's brother, consulted a group of tobacco farmers; and then he and Everett devised an acreage/poundage program to switch from acreage to pounds as the primary basis for compensation in the tobacco support program. Legislation was drafted, and Congress eventually approved it.[12]

Everett Jordan was in the front trenches of the battle to sell the tobacco program to his recalcitrant fellow lawmakers. As Muse said: "[Senator Jordan] said, 'I've voted for some legislation that I hated [in order] to save the tobacco program.' And he did. He practically saved the tobacco aid program by himself. Everett said, 'I had to sell my soul to save it!' "[13]

When Horace R. Kornegay was elected to Congress in 1960 to represent North Carolina's Sixth District, Everett Jordan's home district, he had an opportunity to work once again in the political arena with Jordan. Kornegay had also served as chairman of the state's Young Democrats while Jordan was chairman of the senior party organization; and, because the two men traveled over the state many times, they would frequently do so together.[14]

According to Kornegay: "Everett used to flatter me considerably—as a fairly young man in those days—by introducing me or telling people in groups, that I was '*his*' congressman! He always emphasized the *his*. One day I said, 'Senator, I don't know how to take that. I don't know whether you mean I'm representing you, or you mean I'm in your pocket or something like that.' He laughed and he said, 'Oh, no! You're from the Sixth District, and it's the finest in the country. And you and I always work together like two mules.' I said, 'Well, that's what I thought.' As a matter of fact, we did, for the eight years [1960–68] that I was there."

After that, Kornegay joined the Tobacco Institute as vice-president and counsel. Later, he became president, succeeding Earl Clements, former governor and senator from Kentucky, who had headed the institute for many years.

Kornegay described his relations with Jordan: "During all those years in Congress, Everett Jordan and I worked very closely together. Not only on legislative matters that were important to North Carolina, but matters that involved the tobacco industry, the textile industry, the furniture industry—it seems that back in those days there was more to-do about textiles than there was about tobacco, believe it or not, because the biggest and about the only legislative involvement with tobacco in those days was the farm program itself: the [price] support program."

This program, which was initiated in the early 1930s, was inactive for a while, but was reinstated in 1939. In this program, the farmer agreed to limit production of tobacco in exchange for a guaranteed minimum price for it when it was sold on the warehouse floor.

Kornegay's first recollection of this involvement with Jordan on tobacco, other than just general recognition of the importance of it to North Carolina, was in the mid-1960s, when it became clear to many of the industry's people that some changes in the program were needed. Prior to the mid-1960s, the limitation of production was based on acreage: The Department of Agriculture specified to a farmer, based upon the farm's history, the acreage (allotment) he could grow. Because of the advance of agricultural technology, including improved fertilizers, herbicides, MH-30 sucker control, and tobacco-worm control, 2,000 pounds was being produced on an acre of land that ten years before may not have produced but half that amount. In other words, tobacco was being sold by the pound and produced by the acre.

Kornegay, Jordan, and others sought a program whereby, though an acreage allotment would still be involved, production would be limited based on the pounds that a farmer produced, rather than just limit the acreage he had been assigned. As the situation existed then, expensive stocks were being built up in the stabilization program, which was set up under some quasi-government agency. It would buy the tobacco that the commercial buyers did not buy. Too much tobacco was being taken in by the stabilization board; more tobacco was being produced than needed.

Kornegay said, "Everett was one of the leaders to change that; and I remember when he and I would go to farm meetings and meetings of tobacco growers around the state, and particularly in this district, and urge the farmers to recognize what needed to be done. And Everett was very effective in that sort of thing... It was about 1965 that the bill was passed [to correct the problem]... That is, controlling production—authorizing the farmer to sell by the pound instead of selling all he could grow on an acre."

Kornegay paid this further compliment to his co-lawmaker: "He [Jordan] had an understanding of human nature; he had an understanding of business. He had a deep dedication, in my view, to the welfare of the farmers, whether they be tobacco farmers or other farmers. But it seemed like tobacco was always the thing [in this state] because [it was] the number one cash crop."

Everett Jordan stayed abreast of the needs of his home state through knowledgeable friends and contacts with those in positions of leadership and influence. Besides his coordination with agricultural interests, owing to his business career and affiliations before entering the Senate, his communication was good in the industrial arena. But he also had excellent rapport with enlightened educa-

Representative Horace R. Kornegay and Senator Jordan. (*Horace R. Kornegay*)

tional sources throughout North Carolina. His father before him had stressed the value of education—at all levels—to his family, parishioners, and fellow preachers. In this respect, Everett Jordan, in his growing-up years, had seemed impervious to his father's exhortations; or as Everett, himself, might have said, "It was like pouring water on a duck's back." As a mature adult, however, he became a staunch champion of education, both before and after he went to the Senate.

As Bill Cochrane observed: "Once he [Jordan] understood the facts, he had the tendency to be *for* whatever it was, whether it was liberal or conservative. For example... he supported every federal aid to education bill that ever came up in the Senate. Many of the conservative Southerners did not—most of them did not."[15]

It is not surprising, then, that the "loaves and fishes" senator, a Duke trustee and loyalist, worked equally hard for that institution's keenest rival—twelve miles distant—the University of North Carolina at Chapel Hill. The lawmaker was well aware of the funding needs and programs of all his state's institutions of higher learning, as well as those of secondary schools.[16] One of the reasons was that not only do educational systems indirectly provide more and better potential for employers, but they also create jobs at all levels.

Over the years, Jordan and Dr. William ("Bill") C. Friday coordinated their efforts on behalf of the University of North Carolina—in meetings and on the telephone—"always in great spirit...in positiveness" according to Friday, who also praised Jordan as "a very warm and generous man." Fostering this relationship was the friendship of Friday with Bill Cochrane, Jordan's prime aide, with whom Friday had close relations for many years.[17]

Even in minor matters that were only important to the person concerned, such as an immigrant case or a student visa, the senator made certain through Cochrane that the university's needs were met. Concerning federal appropriations for education, Jordan always listened to or helped Friday. On some occasions, Jordan sometimes took the initiative and called Friday's attention to matters or events in which he might be interested.[18]

Friday had known Jordan long before the latter became a senator. Friday's father was a textile-machinery builder, and Bill himself had gone through the textile school at North Carolina State and was in the textile business before World War II. He explained: "I got to know him [Jordan] through the mills at Saxapahaw and other places, but this was sort of a casual kind of 'shake-hands' business. Then, he got involved in politics in the state level as chairman [of the Democratic party]...I would go in frequently, and he was there and we'd stop and talk a while. Then the governor appointed him [to the Senate], which I remember very well...and we were at the Carolina Inn. I was walking out with Governor Hodges, and he took me aside to tell me that he had chosen Mr. Jordan...Hodges wanted me to get together with him [Jordan], and that started a series of visits which ran for the rest of his life."[19]

Friday also praised Jordan's public service career: "There's a general mistrust of the word 'politician.' Everett Jordan was not that kind of politician. He never thought of it that way. He [did not have] a ward dealer-boss mentality. Here was a businessman who had a high sense of public service, and this was his way of expressing that. He gave his life and energy to doing this kind of thing. The tragedy of it is that not enough business people do like he did—are willing to get in there and try to help government instead of complaining about it all the time."[20]

As a further indication of Jordan's interest in education, at the time of his death, he was serving on the boards of trustees of three institutions of higher learning: Elon College, in Elon, N.C.; American University, in Washington, D.C.; and his beloved alma mater, Duke University.[21]

As a legislator, Everett Jordan was consistent and loyal to his basic concepts and concerns. His record in Washington bears ample evidence of his efforts to create and protect jobs for his constituents, be they cotton-mill hands, tobacco-farm hands, or any other hand dependent upon his or her job to put bread on the table. The press labeled Jordan "the service senator" and explained that he "worked to see that his state got its share of federal programs and assistance and that its agricultural and commercial interests were protected"; and, in so doing, comparatively few, other than the recipients of his action, knew what he did.[22]

As Horace R. Kornegay explained: "Everett and I worked on virtually every piece of legislation that was of primary interest here in North Carolina. On projects, he and I did a lot of work. For example, the New Hope Dam down here, which is now Jordan Lake. He and I worked very closely on it.[23]

Harold Cooley, dean of the North Carolina House delegation, as well as some of his constituents were opposed to the dam. He represented Chatham County and Wake County, and Kornegay represented Durham, Orange, Alamance, and Guilford counties. The major part of the lake was not going to be in Kornegay's Sixth District, but it was going to back up into southern Orange County and maybe, to some extent, over in Durham County. He favored it for a number of reasons, but mainly as a flood-control measure on the Cape Fear River because at the junction of the Haw and the Deep were the headwaters of the Cape Fear. Kornegay on the House side, and Jordan on the Senate side, worked hard on this project.[24]

Kornegay lauded the North Carolina Senate representation: "This is one area where we in North Carolina were fortunate in those days with our two senators, Ervin and Jordan. Jordan was a practical, pragmatic type who saw and understood the value of these projects such as the New Hope Dam, better highways, and the like.

Secretary of Agriculture Orville L. Freeman signs a memorandum of understanding in May 1962 to establish cooperation between his department and the newly created Franklin Soil and Water Conservation District, whose headquarters was at Louisburg, N.C. *Standing, left to right*: Administrator D. A. Williams, of the Soil Conservation Service, Senator Sam J. Ervin, Jr., Representative L. H. Fountain, Senator B. Everett Jordan. (Photo by U.S. Department of Agriculture; *L. H. Fountain*)

It's not that Ervin was against them, but Ervin was a scholar and a constitutional lawyer, and he spent his time thinking and working on things of that sort, and the abstract principles. Jordan was the down-to-earth senator. Consequently, at that time, we sort of had the best of both worlds, in that regard, in North Carolina."[25]

Time after time, various interviewees and other sources consulted for this book commented on and oftentimes extolled Everett Jordan's thorough understanding of his home state and its needs. In the realm of soil conservation and flood control, the senator had gotten his feet wet before he ever thought of going to Washington.

Perhaps, it could be better said that he also "got his hands wet" because he labored alongside his mill hands to harness the flood waters of the Haw River and repair the damage done by its ravages from time to time. But that was not his only source of information or direct knowledge of the effects of uncontrolled waters in the Tar Heel state.

One of those sources was Eric W. Rodgers, of Scotland Neck, N.C., who has spent well over four decades in formulating and carrying out a program to dam the Roanoke River to prevent its flooding eastern North Carolina and Virginia. Rodgers, a newspaperman, engineer, and conservationist, served on the state Board of Conservation and Development under Governors Cherry, Umstead, Kerr Scott, Hodges, and Sanford, with occasional breaks during these consecutive administrations. After Jordan went to the Senate, Rodgers's daughter, Suzanne Rodgers [Bush], was a member of Jordan's office staff.[26]

Rodgers praised Jordan's "tireless work" on behalf of soil conservation and flood-control projects. The Roanoke River Basin flood of 1940 had not only inundated thousands of acres of land in eastern North Carolina and tidewater Virginia but also set a record in damages to both crops and property for that area. From Danville, Va., to the Albemarle Sound, the damage was 20 or 30 million dollars—not counting the crops, because the flood came in September when everything was ready to be harvested.[27]

In Roanoke Rapids alone, between 1,000 and 1,500 people were jobless and penniless. Governor Clyde Hoey, because this was before the days of unemployment compensation, persuaded the legislature to provide 5 to 10 million dollars to pay the employees of those mills a supplement or a living wage until they could return to work.[28]

In 1937 a comprehensive survey had been made of the Roanoke River flood basin with an eye toward dam sites, Rodgers recalled, but the Congress had rejected it. After the 1940 flood, the survey was revamped, brought up-to-date, and given congressional approval in 1942, but no appropriations were made until after World War II. Finally, in 1952, money became available, and the first two dams were built. In all, five dams have been built and two more have been approved by Congress for what is now known as the Roanoke River Flood Control Area.[29]

Golda Meir, Israel's minister for foreign affairs, greets Senator Jordan at her office in Jerusalem in December 1965. (*Jordan family scrapbooks*)

Rodgers later reminisced: "On several trips when Everett and I were together, I was attending to my business and he was attending to his. I became very fond of Everett; he and I got along fine... Katherine and my wife got to be very close friends, and we would see them from time to time; we went to the beach together.[30] I met him down there two or three times. During his campaign, or part of it, I drove his car for him whenever he wanted to go out somewhere. I could easily get away from my work down here. And if he had any special objective in riding around I was available at his call."[31]

Because Rodgers's background and interest were centered on water and soil conservation, to him political matters were secondary, so his association and discussions with Jordan primarily concerned flood control and preservation of natural resources. Conceivably, Rodgers's input greatly enhanced Jordan's understanding of these matters when he dealt with them in his role as a United States senator.[32]

Even so, Rodgers's first contacts were purely political. Rodgers worked for William B. Umstead when he was a member of Congress. Later, Rodgers worked for Umstead when he ran for the

United States Senate (in 1948) but was defeated by J. Melville Broughton. When Umstead became governor in 1952, he reinstated Rodgers on the state Board of Conservation and Development (from which Governor W. Kerr Scott had removed him), and he continued to serve during the administrations of Hodges and Sanford.[33]

As a newspaperman and publicity worker on Umstead's behalf and for other Democratic candidates as well, Rodgers was in close contact with Jordan in his work in state politics, especially after he became the party chairman. For a time, the two occupied adjoining offices at the Sir Walter Hotel, in Raleigh. Rodgers explained: "We often had conferences on how to handle this matter and that matter. I was named as director of public relations or something like that [for the Democratic party]; and, when the time came for things to happen for me, it was Everett Jordan that put me on a statewide trip...[Jordan] sent me to a national convention as a [statewide] delegate. Adlai Stevenson was the candidate for president. That was in Chicago [in 1952] when the Southern delegation of New Orleans and Louisiana and places like that walked out and tried to form another party...I had never been to a national convention before."[34]

Rodgers praised Jordan's character: "Everett Jordan was a fine upstanding gentleman; absolutely, he and Bill Umstead were two of the most honorable men in politics that I have ever met. They weren't for any shenanigans or dirty tricks. They were forthright—said what they thought."[35]

After Rodgers's daughter Suzanne started to work in Jordan's Washington office—the Rodgerses had two other daughters also living there—Rodgers later said: "I'd go up to visit them about a week every three months, so I often saw Everett, and we'd go out to dinner together, and Lucy, my wife, before she died and Katherine would have a good time together...I admired him greatly for his strength of character and native honesty of speech. He never attempted to deceive anybody about some plan they wanted to put across of which he did not approve. He came right out with the truth...He never used rough language to say your project was no good or anything like that. He was very polite about it."[36]

Everett Jordan, while sitting on the Senate Public Works Committee, Bill Cochrane revealed, "was a member of, or chairman of

Loaves and Fishes 257

Late in 1969, Senator B. Everett Jordan views North Korean positions across the Demilitarized Zone during a congressional delegation's visit to a front-line Korean army observation post. Standing behind Jordan (*center*) is Representative Robert McClory, and at the right is Senator John J. Sparkman, leader of the delegation. (*United States Army*)

more select, special, joint, and standing committees and commissions than any other member of either House of the Congress; that's something I had the Library of Congress research for me during the last year that he [Jordan] was here. He was into everything!"[37] He worked diligently for various projects—flood control, soil conservation, whatever—especially those that affected his constituents. Eric Rodgers in his area shared his knowledge and expertise with Jordan, who prudently sought out those more knowledgeable than himself on issues that he, first as a businessman and later as a congressman, dealt with.[38]

A number of projects that he worked for in the Senate, including some that were initiated by his predecessors—notably W. Kerr

B. Everett Jordan Dam and Lake, Chatham County, N.C. (Photo by Bud Davis; *U.S. Army*)

Scott—are tangible evidence of his understanding of their validity and his tireless efforts to bring them to fruition. Two outstanding examples are the W. Kerr Scott Dam and Reservoir, on the Yadkin River in Wilkes County; and Jordan Lake, in Chatham County, which is now officially known as "The B. Everett Jordan Dam and Lake."[39]

The much-delayed and maligned Jordan Lake, first known as the "New Hope Dam Project," received so much opposition and adverse publicity that some people thought it would never be completed. Environmentalists and water conservationists contended that the impounded waters of the polluted Haw River and New Hope River would be so contaminated that they could not serve any further useful purpose. After Jordan left office and he was informed that the lake would be named in his honor, he wryly remarked: "I'll be the first man to have a mud hole named for him!"[40]

After the senator's death, in March 1974, the dedication of the B. Everett Jordan Dam and Lake was held. The project was hailed as a major water resource that would make a significant impact on water and soil conservation for the entire Cape Fear River Basin. Bill Cochrane came down from Washington to trace the project's complex history, and Governor James B. Hunt made the keynote address, while dignitaries from throughout the state were on hand to applaud.[41]

Jordan Lake is a living tribute to a man who looked, listened, and committed his knowledge and talents. Two other men might have expressed it somewhat differently. The father, Reverend H. H. Jordan, might have said: "Everett had eyes that saw and ears that heard." And another circuit rider, John Wesley, just as he preached, may have intoned: "Pray as if everything depends upon God, but work as if everything depends upon yourself!"

12

"The Protector"

Lyndon Baines Johnson, later the thirty-sixth president of the United States, preceded B. Everett Jordan in the United States Senate by nine years and four months. Johnson, as a freshman member of the 1948 class, took the oath of office in the following year. By 1953 he had become the Democratic minority leader of the Senate and was firmly established when Everett Jordan arrived to be sworn in as North Carolina's junior senator on May 5, 1958.[1]

Johnson was impressed with Jordan, who, in turn, greatly valued his association with the future president. For many years, a photograph of the two men in a Capitol Hill setting and autographed by Johnson hung in Jordan's Saxapahaw office, along with several others taken at various official functions.[2]

In 1981 Senator Sam Ervin summed up their relationship:

> I guess Everett and Lyndon Johnson were on closer terms than [Johnson was with] any other senator. They were close personal friends. So far as I know, they may have known each other before Everett came to Washington, but not well. Of course, Everett was also chairman of the Rules Committee; he had a lot to do with the inauguration and things like that, so he had a lot of personal contact with Johnson that most of us didn't have. The Rules Committee is a very responsible committee. It's what you might call a "housekeeping committee" for the entire Senate. That's the reason Bobby Baker[3] was under investigation [by the committee], because Baker was an employee, and the committee had charge of all the affairs of the Senate. A very important committee for that reason. Had a lot of power. It considered all the rules for the operation of the Senate.[4]

In an interview for this volume, Dr. Floyd Riddick, Senate parliamentarian during Jordan's entire career on Capitol Hill, also pointed out the close relations between him and Johnson: "Well,

Sam Ervin, Jr. (*left*), and Everett Jordan (*right*) with President Lyndon Johnson. (*Jordan family scrapbooks*)

Everett worked with Lyndon Johnson when he was the majority leader... After [Kennedy's] death, we stayed in session right up to Christmas after Lyndon Johnson took over; and he [was able to get enacted] most of the programs that had been submitted to the Congress by Kennedy... Lyndon Johnson was a power in himself in the Senate and he had Sam Rayburn in the House as Speaker, and between the two they could get most any program enacted that they thought essential—particularly with the good Democratic majority... Senator Johnson, as majority leader, I know, counted heavily on Jordan's support if there was going to be a close vote."[5]

As recounted earlier in this volume, Johnson contended that Everett Jordan "as a freshman senator, adapted to his task quicker than any other senator he knew."[6]

Both Lyndon Johnson and Everett Jordan began their climb to the top by way of a benefactor. Johnson, labeled "Roosevelt's boy," acquired the name and its implications for influence with the help of his friend and fellow Texan, veteran Congressman Sam Rayburn.[7]

In 1935 President Franklin D. Roosevelt established the National Youth Administration (NYA), designed to help young people continue their education at a time when the nation was still in the throes of the Great Depression. Johnson was not quite twenty-seven, but he had more than enough ambition for his years, and he wanted the Texas directorship. With the help of Rayburn, who in turn persuaded Texas Senator Tom Connally to endorse Johnson, Lyndon won this plum. Consequently, after he went to Congress, he became one of Roosevelt's and the New Deal's most faithful supporters. When Johnson encountered situations where FDR was on the opposite side from Rayburn, Johnson would forsake his old friend from home and side with the president, who obviously wielded greater power than Rayburn.[8] Johnson was not one to ignore power, which he always coveted.

During his early career, Everett Jordan was not in a position to receive the blessings of a sitting congressman, senator, or president. He did, however, have his uncle Charlie Sellers. Without Sellers's financial blessing and support when the thirty-one-year-old Jordan was becoming established in textiles, his career, though unpredictable, would certainly have been vastly different. BEJ and LBJ both got a "new deal"—thanks to uncle Charlie Sellers and FDR, respectively.

Both Johnson and Jordan were pragmatists, had an almost uncanny understanding of people, and were men of action and not philosophers or students of international affairs. They were also quick to recognize and use power—political, financial, personal—to accomplish their purposes. This propensity served each man well in his respective setting. Johnson saw to it that his home state received its share—and then some—of federal appropriations for public works. Jordan did likewise for North Carolina. LBJ made sure that his Texas constituents knew that he was in Washington working hard for them—and their votes. And folks in Saxapahaw had no doubts at all about who provided their jobs and signed their paychecks. To succeed, Johnson—like Jordan—had to work closely with and depend upon others he trusted for assistance. To stay informed and keep on top of things, both developed and used their own "intelligence sources."

In Saxapahaw, Everett Jordan, as mill manager and owner, stayed current on what was happening in the mill, village, community, and general area through trusted contacts. These contacts consisted primarily of loyal employees, friends, family, business associates, local storekeepers, and politicians—all of whom he listened to intently and regularly. Nothing escaped his attention; and, if the occasion

Senator Jordan, as chairman of the January 20, 1965, inaugural committee, escorts President Lyndon B. Johnson and his wife to the podium. Vice-President-elect Hubert H. Humphrey and his wife, Muriel, are behind the Johnsons. (*Jordan family scrapbooks*)

required, he would personally check out his source. This quest sometimes meant that he would go, at all hours of the day or night, into the mill as well as out into the village and greater community. No detail was too small or mundane for his attention, whether it be to verify that steps to a village house needed repair or to check on the promptness of an employee's arrival at work.[9]

In Washington, Lyndon Johnson also had his ear to the ground through his chosen contacts. One valuable source, perhaps his favorite and most accommodative when he was in the Senate, was Robert G. ("Bobby") Baker. He had come to Washington as a youthful page boy from Pickens, a small town in upstate South Carolina. He was keen, poor, and ambitious. After becoming chief page, he

Lady Bird (Mrs. Lyndon B.) Johnson and Katherine M. Jordan at the 1965 presidential inauguration. (*Jordan family scrapbooks*)

rose in a surprisingly short time to the administrative position of secretary for the Democratic Senate majority, an employee of the Democratic caucus. Lyndon Johnson, widely known to be Baker's mentor, was given chief credit for his meteoric rise to a position of enormous prestige and influence. Johnson's "fair-haired boy" also became noticeably wealthy in spite of his modest means when he arrived on Capitol Hill.[10] And therein lies another story, one that ultimately sent him to prison.

Before Baker's troubles became generally known, he was wheeling and dealing successfully in the august halls of the Senate, achieving things that few page boys, if any, ever equaled. He made it his business to know what was going on, to ascertain who had influence and what their weaknesses and strengths were, who supported this or that project, how the votes were shaping up, who would come out on top. These gleanings he dutifully reported to the appreciative ears of the Senate majority leader, Lyndon B. Johnson. Baker saw his mentor daily when he was in Washington; and, when the latter was in Texas, he was in regular contact with him."[11]

Earlier, however, in 1952, before Johnson became the majority leader, he had run for leadership of the Democratic Senate minority. This was the first time he held a top position within his party, and it was Bobby Baker who had scurried around to help garner votes for his election.[12]

In much the same manner, if Everett Jordan wanted to know what was going on in Alamance County, he talked to his Rotarian friends, before and after the meetings; if he wanted local political input, he called in the local precinct chairmen, particularly those who worked in his mills; if he wanted mill information, he talked to supervisors; and, more often than not, he conferred directly with mill hands rather than their overseers. Jordan thought highly of the hands and averred many times that "I can get all the bosses I want any day, but it's hard to get hands who can keep the spindles turning and produce good yarn." These seemingly lowly employees stood at the top of his list.[13]

Jordan was known to say to his office personnel: "You are a necessary evil; you don't produce any yarn. My money is made in the mill, not in this office." As company treasurer and chief executive officer, he was quick to convey this opinion to his staff, office manager, and other white-collar workers, especially when they inquired about a salary increase. Even so, he did not turn a deaf ear to any source, including these much-disdained "pencil pushers," though generally this group knew less about what he wanted to know than did those in the mill—the place where he had served his own apprenticeship and learned to rely on those who operated machines.

And all throughout the week he never let up on his intelligence-collecting process, for on Sunday he queried and listened as intently on the church lawn as he did weekdays inside the mill fence and office walls.

No doubt about it, Everett Jordan and Lyndon Johnson knew exactly what was going on within their domains.

When the Saxapahaw industrialist went to Washington after spending thirty-six years in cotton mills, his system was too ingrained to change. Therefore, he was drawn immediately to those who seemed to know the answers to his questions; he was attracted to the "movers"—those who made sure their wants and needs were satisfied and their favored legislation passed.

Mill superintendents had heard Jordan admonish them incessantly to get out of their offices and patrol the aisles between the frames—spinning, carding, winding, twisting—everywhere that there were machines and mill hands. For they alone produced the yarn. In Congress, Jordan himself patrolled the aisles of the Senate—hallways, cloakrooms, dining rooms, social gatherings—wherever senators or anyone with knowledge and influence might be found discussing legislation and legislators. Lyndon Johnson did precisely the same, but he also had Bobby Baker to slip through all the cracks and crevices and report back to him. Both men used the telephone extensively to communicate, verify, exhort, and generally keep up with all the minutiae of current events.

In the late 1950s and early 1960s, Bobby Baker was playing his role to the hilt, earning the title of the "101st Senator" in some quarters. As author Merle Miller explains: "For a while, quite a long while, it looked as if Bobby Baker was invincible. And, if Lyndon had stayed on in the Senate, he might have been; Bobby says in his autobiography that he spent many a sleepless night wondering if his trouble would have happened if Lyndon had not, on the advice of Bobby, among others, accepted the vice-presidential nomination."[14]

Senator Mike Mansfield succeeded Johnson as majority leader on January 3, 1961. His style was soon revealed to be in stark contrast to that of his predecessor. Mansfield was described as an avid reader, who would retreat to a hideaway, smoke his pipe, and devour a book. As author Miller points out: "Bobby could understand and deal with Senators who were hard drinkers, who were, to use a euphemism of the time, 'skirt chasers,' who were anxious for bribes, begged for them even, accepted them almost without exception. But a book reader! Who could deal with a man like that?"[15]

Baker's success had not been confined to the Senate. In 1963 he was part owner of twenty-two corporations, motels, vending-machine companies, housing developments, insurance firms—almost any profitable venture that came his way. According to author Miller: "He could arrange an abortion for a senator's girl friend. He could also provide a girl for the night, the week, or even ten minutes, though he claims to have done the latter infrequently and with pangs of Baptist guilt. It was difficult to find anybody in the Senate of the United States who would speak ill of Bobby, publicly anyway. For one thing, he had the goods on most of them, and no senator doubted in the least that Bobby would use what he knew if he were pressed."[16]

Bobby appeared immune to official reproach, but not quite. John Williams, a soft-spoken senator from Delaware, who had a reputation for *not* looking the other way, decided to check into Bobby's private affairs. The senator asked anyone who could shed light on them to come forth. Bobby, guilt-ridden and apprehensive of embarrassment and exposure, quickly resigned his position on October 7, 1963.[17]

Baker fervently hoped his resignation would end the investigation, but he was dead wrong. Severe misconduct of the sort he was accused of lay within the jurisdiction of the Senate Rules Committee, whose chairman was North Carolina's junior senator, B. Everett Jordan. As such, he guided and controlled both the proceedings and the extent as well as the depth of the probings by the committee.

The Baker investigation went on for many months and the final result was that on January 5, 1966, Baker was indicted by a federal grand jury on nine counts, including income-tax evasion, theft, conspiracy to defraud the federal government, and misappropriating $100,000 in campaign funds. In January 1967 he was convicted on most of the charges; and, after several failed appeals, went to prison on January 12, 1971.[18]

Various members of the press and other observers believed that Lyndon Johnson was closely, even intimately, involved in Baker's misdeeds, but he came through his "fair-haired boy's" investigation virtually unscathed. Many believed that Johnson had been carefully protected. Some people labeled his escape a "whitewash," a polite name for a "cover-up."

As Everett Jordan prepared to run in the 1966 Senate race back in North Carolina, the press, commenting on his prospects for reelection, wondered pointedly about the possible adverse effect of his handling of the Bobby Baker case: "Jordan's handling of that probe undoubtedly won him gratitude at the White House, GOP leaders agree, but they also think that the Baker case can still be used in a campaign against the man who headed the investigating committee, even if it did not hurt Lyndon B. Johnson in 1964. The Baker case is also conceded as the hidden, but perhaps leading, issue in any challenge of Jordan by [aspiring] Democrats."[19]

Even today, unanswered questions remain about Johnson's possible involvement in the Bobby Baker case. On one side are the indignant defenders of Everett Jordan and the Rules Committee; on the other are skeptics who scoff at disclaimers and believe that the president was protected. No one has a definitive answer. But it is well known that Everett Jordan was Johnson's close friend; that Jordan was extremely loyal to his friends; and that he had a history of looking after those within his sphere—from the bottom to the top. So, it is not likely that Everett Jordan would turn a deaf ear to a friend in extreme need.

Beginning in his earliest boyhood days, Everett Jordan had the well-deserved reputation of taking care of his own: family, friends, politicians, anyone for whom he felt responsible.[20] Stories abound among family members that relate to Everett's taking care of his younger brothers when they got into fistfights and needed help to overcome a bigger or stronger opponent. Nearly every new town that their circuit-riding preacher-father moved his family into had a rowdy youthful element who felt the preacher's kids must all be "sissies" and had to be taught a lesson not learnable in the pew or classroom. Everett, the oldest, sturdiest, and most aggressive of his father's four sons, always rose to the challenge and quickly refuted this grossly mistaken impression. His protected siblings were most grateful and, even as adults, felt safe in his care.

Everett Jordan did not always need to resort to strong-arm tactics, however, for he was clever and adept in a number of techniques. For all his surface simplicity, he could be as crafty as any other individual. According to Clyde Gordon, his political confidant, when various candidates in a local election running for the same office came separately to Jordan's Saxapahaw mill office to solicit their party leader's support, he told each one the same thing: "I will take care of you." When questioned later by a perplexed Gordon, Jordan grinned and slyly replied: "But I didn't say how!"[21]

The mill owner strove mightily to run a tight ship cost-wise, convinced that it was better to pay lower wages and keep the mills running than to pay more, lose his competitive edge, and run the risk of losing customers and closing doors. This policy worked so well that he could boast that during the Great Depression he never curtailed production due to lack of orders because he ran short-time only when dry weather and low water in the river caused shortages of the power usually produced by his hydro-turbines. Unquestionably, some employees disagreed with Jordan's philosophy, but he was clearly in control and his way always prevailed.

Many who knew the man admired his ability to take command—to be in charge of a ticklish situation at times, seemingly, when his mere presence sufficed. Certainly this was true in Saxapahaw, but his ability to keep a firm control of quickly changing events was reflected in his career in Washington generally and in the Baker investigation in particular.

Not only did Everett Jordan "take care" of those within his sphere of influence, but—and it cannot be over-emphasized—he was also steadfastly loyal to his friends: they knew they could always count on him. A handshake would serve him just as well as a formal document, a written contract, a letter, or any other tangible evidence of commitment. Once there was an understanding—more clearly spelled out perhaps than that with the local Democratic hopefuls—Jordan would faithfully and steadfastly abide by the terms, and he fully expected those on the other side to do the same. This demonstration of assumed mutual trust was typical of the way he handled business transactions.

Clyde Gordon gave this account: "Rawls Howard, operator of Runneymede Mills in eastern North Carolina, was Everett's customer during the depression days when neither [one] had a lot of money. Howard could not pay his invoices when they became due on their thirty-day terms. So Rawls called Everett and told him he couldn't pay. Everett enquired, 'Rawls, are you worried?' Howard: 'That's why I'm calling you.' Everett: 'Rawls, as long as you are worried, I'm not! How many pounds of yarn do you need?' Howard told him and it was shipped." Gordon said that later, when he visited Howard's office, he saw just two pictures on the wall: one of Howard's father and the other one of Everett Jordan.[22]

This same sense of deep but informal trust carried over into Everett Jordan's relationships with his own employees, and most agreements were carried out with a minimum of paperwork. For example, through his company, loans were made to various employees to buy homes, but he never asked for a mortgage on the property as security.

Inevitably, however, Jordan did not always take care of folks in precisely the ways they felt he should. This variance in perception also included his own family, especially his children who chafed—usually silently—under his iron-clad rule. John, considered by some people to be more like his father than either Ben or Rose Ann, was ever wont to vent strong feelings and express views in conflict with his father's. And, as John grew older and bolder, he increasingly and openly challenged his father. Yet, John admiringly calls him "the greatest man I ever knew" and gives him credit for having more influence upon his own life than anyone else. He is, nevertheless, quite candid about their differences and depicts his father as a relentless authoritarian by saying that he was "the total authority in the family" and "was always right." Reflecting upon his childhood years, John points out that his parents did all the talking and made all the decisions.

John continued: "As I grew older, I think I was more the rebellious child. He was always right and I was always wrong; in our conversations, he indicated I didn't know what I was talking about, or why did I do this or that. Well, I was bull-headed enough to try and show him; I would work harder to prove I was right. This had a tendency to develop a love-hate relationship. You know you love your parents, but, if you are antagonistic or if you have a constant battle on, then it's a hate relationship, too."[23]

According to John, his father was always trying to program him to think of nothing except mills and textiles—to be just like him. He could not understand why John preferred to play ball or pursue his other childhood interests instead of visiting a mill. The father said, "Spend your time thinking about the mill. That's where your bread and butter comes from."[24]

John elaborated: "As I matured, like all men, I did want to make *some* decisions. Everyone wants to make decisions, even little decisions. You always want to progress and grow, and I felt like he was never ready for me to move on. Like if I was in the mill as a fixer for a year I'd say, 'All right, I'm ready to become an overseer.' 'Well, you haven't learned to be a good fixer yet; you just wait.' That's just an example."[25]

Undoubtedly Everett Jordan had a tremendous concern for what he genuinely believed to be his family's best interests. He took care of their wants and needs the only way he knew how: the way his own father had taken care of his family. The two men perceived that it was the inherent—if not divine—right and responsibility of the father to be the absolute head of the house. Consequently, the Reverend Jordan and his eldest son, as family leaders, ruled supreme: To abdicate their position of patriarchal authority would be almost sacrilegious—unthinkable.

One of Everett Jordan's prime concerns—perhaps his major one—was to build financial security for his immediate family. And he accomplished this goal through the success of his mills—success that he worked persistently for and that he unequivocally believed was due to his own judgment and expertise. Not for one moment did he entertain the idea of anyone else usurping his position and rule.

Late in Jordan's life, Ralph Dean, cost accountant for a Greensboro firm, was working one day in Jordan's mill office and politely posed this question to the aging lawmaker-mill man: "Senator, why don't you turn the company over completely to your two sons [Ben and John] and *see* what they can do?" Jordan's quick retort was: "I don't want to see!"[26] Not only was this man the founder of Sellers Manufacturing Company (and its affiliates), but he was also their lifetime protector—in his own mind.

"The Protector" 273

John Jordan, in discussing his father's traits, concluded that the senior Jordan was forever fearful that he, John, would "screw up"—make or commit some embarrassing mistake that would reflect upon his father's reputation, whose main concern was not for the consequences to his son but to himself:

> He didn't want to see me make a mistake, not because of me, but because of him. That permeated from early childhood—I would say almost his entire life and my life. One incident was when I was going to run for the Senate against Ralph Scott and he asked that I not run as long as he was in office. That was motivated he said by the fact that he didn't want to have too many Jordans in public office. At the time there were several Kennedys—John, Bobby, and Teddy—and there was some criticism from the press... And he did not want to give the appearance that the Jordans were trying to take over anything by having too many people in public office at one time. As you know, he discouraged uncle Henry from running at one time for the same reason. He just thought it would look bad. So I felt like his motivation was for himself and not protecting me because, if I screwed up, it would reflect on his name; or if the public perceived that there were too many Jordans in office at the same time that would obviously detract from him.[27]

A story told by daughter Rose Ann is an intimate, poignant, and revealing account of parent-child relationships, and specifically of her father's role as protector of the family name and reputation. It is also the only time when he was known to have encountered a head-on confrontation that he did not win—that is, except for the brief detour occasioned by Robah Steele's .38 pistol when Jordan attempted to enter the Saxapahaw factory's door for the first time.

This incident occurred after Rose Ann Gant had been married for several years, was the mother of two small girls, and lived in Burlington. Like her father, she is not easily "pushed around" by anyone and exhibits exceptional fortitude, determination, and perception. During the early part of her marriage, feeling that she was having trouble in communicating with people, she consulted a psychiatrist.

According to Rose Ann:

> One day Daddy called—it was Friday—and he said, "I would like for you to come down here and spend the night!" And that's the way he approached things—there weren't any pleasantries one way

or another, it was... "I want to talk to you, and I don't want Roger to come." I knew right then and there that somehow or other he had gotten word that I was under a psychiatrist and there was going to be hell to pay! I got so mad... I took two Valium pills and went on down—quaking in my boots!... Daddy said, "I understand you are under a psychiatrist—NO ONE IN OUR FAMILY GOES TO A PSYCHIATRIST!" And I said, "I do." He said, "That's no way to *treat* anything!"... But I told him, "I hate to tell you that somebody in your family is, and it's me!" He said, "I just don't understand it"... Then I said, "Do you realize that for almost all of my life I was *absolutely terrified of you?*"... And I said, "Do you realize that we have had almost *no* communication all of our lives? You were too busy, and I have just never known you except under authority... and I was scared of you!" He said, "I don't understand that." I said, "Be that as it may, I'm telling you that's the way it is!"

And do you know from that moment, from *literally* that moment, all of the feelings of fear left me, and I was left with nothing but love. I could look at him, and I could probably recognize all of his faults better than anyone else—and I knew them well—and the meaning of love came to me in that the faults made no difference in how I felt about him. We all have faults and I could accept him perfectly well, and he did the same for me... From that moment on we could sit in each other's company and not say a word and be perfectly comfortable. If he wanted to talk about the mill, I would sit there and listen and not even understand what he was talking about, but was perfectly happy just to sit and listen. A whole new relationship was born; as I said, I think it was just purely God's grace. It was a spirit of complete love and a lack of criticism.[28]

From that time on, Rose Ann contended that she "felt that no matter what I did, he might not like it, but he would understand. I could have asked him for *anything* in this world... because I fully understood at that point that I was not only the favorite one, but he looked at me with very special eyes. And I looked at *him* with very special eyes."[29]

Thus, Rose Ann had a rapport and relationship with her father that possibly no one else shared except his wife. This provided

Rose Ann with a more intimate knowledge of his personality than most others ever obtained. Once, when she criticized a draft of one of his speeches, he accepted it and she did not ever remember hearing the speech again. As Rose Ann said, "I could say things to him that nobody else could—not even mother."[30]

Once Everett Jordan took a position or pursued a course of action, flawed or wrong it might be, he never confessed his error—not verbally any way. In the above instance, he never once openly admitted that he thought Rose Ann was right, but he stopped using the criticized speech.

On Jordan making amends, Rose Ann elaborated further: "[Daddy] would turn around and do something which makes you know in no uncertain terms that he knew [he was at fault], but he was not going to admit it! That's why I think there were many areas where he was well aware of his shortcomings, and he just wasn't going to admit that he was wrong. He would find some way to get around it in order to get back on the right track because he was not obstinate to the point of doing things that were foolish. He'd find some way to back up and do something else, but he would never admit to you that he had made a mistake."[31]

Rose Ann also stated: "Daddy had a very simple approach to life, and I think that was the key to understanding him. In a lot of ways he was 'black and white'; I mean right or wrong. There was very little 'gray' in his life. If he believed it was right, then you just might as well forget it, because he wasn't going to budge off of that position, which I think he very definitely got from his father and mother." Rose Ann added: "He never complicated his life with tremendous intellect. That was not his thing. He'd say, 'I don't know about that; you can talk about that all you want to, but I just know that it's this way and that's right!' We were discussing the life of a Christian one day in Washington, and his statement was, 'I only know what I believe, and the rest of it doesn't matter.'"[32]

Shedding further light on her father's personality, his decision-making techniques, Rose Ann said: "[He had a way of] reducing big things to a fairly simple concept. He did not like to be bogged down with complex problems. I just can't see him ever trying to read any legal document; he would say 'please get this in three words or less, and hand it to me straight.'" This was true not only of his religious, personal, and family life; this was his practice throughout *every* area of his life. As Rose Ann observed: "I think that's the way he approached Washington—the eloquent and the flamboyant and all the words and so and so forth could be reduced to simple issues. He had to get a handle on it and break it down and say if it's good or not or can we simply not tolerate it. All the words in the world simply would not change it."[33]

Not only did Everett Jordan take care of his family and others—his way—but he also stuck by his friends. Jack Paris is an example. He operates a country store on the outskirts of Saxapahaw that serves as a gathering place for folks in the area, a goodly number of whom are today ex-employees of Everett Jordan's mill. In addition to being a merchant, Jack is also a local politician and has served on the Alamance County board of commissioners. In his late sixties, when interviewed for this volume, he says that ever since he was a small boy he has known Jordan. The walls of his store are covered with pictures of various public figures, including Everett Jordan, who Jack says should have been president. The mill owner-turned-politician found Jack to be a ready and reliable informant about what was going on in his mills as well as in local politics.[34]

In 1972, when Jordan ran in the second primary against Nick Galifianakis, Paris was hospitalized at Alamance Memorial Hospital, in Burlington. Against his doctor's wishes, he procured an ambulance to take him out on the thirty-mile round trip to Saxapahaw so that he could personally cast his vote for Everett Jordan. Later, when the press asked why he lost the election, Jordan's reply was that he "guessed he just didn't have enough people to come out of the hospital to vote for him!" Jordan, for many years before he went to the Senate, was, in return, one of Jack's best customers: He kept a filled gas can in the trunk of his car so he could get back and buy gas from him.[35]

Glenn Pickett, a Burlington textile mill owner, was one of Jack Paris's close friends and a frequent customer. In 1927 Glenn's father had started the Pickett Hosiery Mill in Burlington—the same year that Everett Jordan was re-opening the mill in Saxapahaw. Later,

Pickett and his son, Glenn, operated Glenover Hosiery Mill and Foil Hosiery Mill. Like many new and relatively small enterprises, Pickett's firm did not have a lot of capital and ready cash. Glenn said that Everett Jordan told his father: "If you don't have the money, we'll give you extra credit [terms]. We want you as a customer!" Glenn added: "And my father stayed as a customer for nearly fifty years."[36]

Continuing his recollections, Glenn told about the problems that knitters had in obtaining yarns during World War II because of stringent rationing: "The war came along in '41, and my daddy made a trip down to Saxapahaw to talk to Mr. Jordan because yarn was getting scarce, and the prices were changing [that is, going up]. Mr. Jordan told him: 'Don't worry about it; I'll try to get you every pound that I can, and if you don't have the money right then we'll work out a credit plan for you.'"[37]

When Jordan started operation of his yarn-dyeing plant (Sellers Dyeing Company) in 1952, Glenover bought the first fifteen pounds the plant dyed. According to Glenn Pickett: "They dyed it in a sample fifteen-pound tub and the color was maize." Argyle hosiery had become fashionable, and both yarn producers and knitters prospered. Pickett stated: "Out of the fifteen years that we ran argyles, I don't think I ever missed one day getting the shipment that I was supposed to get. If Sellers didn't have it, they would borrow it from some other account and make it back up with the other account."[38]

Glenn said that his father, who was most appreciative of Everett Jordan's loyalty, admonished him: "Sellers Manufacturing Company has been real nice to me the first years that I went in business at Pickett Hosiery Mill and the first few years I was in business at Glenover Hosiery Mill. Don't you ever forget what Sellers Manufacturing Company and the people that work for Sellers and Everett Jordan have done to help you get along this far. They have been real nice to everybody up here at this mill and you return it to them. If there is any way possible, you buy yarn from them from now on."[39]

In the Bobby Baker scandal, no one ever submitted any factual evidence that directly implicated Lyndon Johnson, nor did anyone reveal the suppression of any evidence by the Senate Rules Committee. However, as already stated, this is not to say that all doubts were dispelled. And, although it was a long, drawn-out investigation, some people were not sure that all the pertinent facts were ever presented and examined.

In retrospect, Senator Sam Ervin summed up the activities of the committee:

> [Jordan] had a very troublesome committee. He had Carl Curtiss, of Nebraska, Republican. I liked Carl and was fond of him personally, but he was so bitterly partisan. The Bobby Baker thing came up several times. The original resolution was introduced by Senator John Williams, of Delaware, to investigate when the charges were made. Well, most everybody in the Senate supported it. Then after the first investigation was completed, there came a charge that Bobby Baker had been instrumental in aiding a Democratic national committeeman from Pennsylvania—I forget his name now—in getting a contract for the Kennedy Stadium in Washington. And so Senator Mike Mansfield introduced the second resolution to reopen the matter and conducted a second investigation. Altogether, the Bobby Baker investigation covered forty-five days. The Republicans introduced a lot of amendments, especially to the Mike Mansfield bill.
>
> I believe the Rules Committee probably had about four Democrats and three Republicans. Anyway, there was just one margin difference. One amendment provided that they had to subpoena and examine any witness that four of them wanted—I mean that three of them wanted. In other words, let a minority of three [that is, the Republicans] run a seven-man committee—that was the effect. Of course, we voted that down. Then Carl Prentiss introduced one that they had to call and examine any witness that any one [on the committee] wanted, and that was voted down.[40]

Ervin went on to say that later the press criticized him, Herman Talmadge, and some other Democratic senators for voting against these amendments, contending that "we had opposed the Bobby Baker thing." Ervin stated: "We did nothing of the kind; like Everett, we were strong for the thing. Everett investigated it thoroughly, except I thought he made one mistake..."[41]

According to Ervin, that mistake was Jordan's failure, in lieu of a subpoena, to write a letter to Walter Jenkins requesting him to testify. Jenkins, who was on the White House staff, had been a longtime employee of Johnson when he was a senator. It was believed he had made some agreements with Bobby Baker under which the latter arranged for someone to furnish insurance for Johnson. Ervin's feeling was that, should Jenkins refuse to testify, the White House, not Jordan, would need to bear the responsibility.[42]

Ervin continued: "That's the only thing I would criticize that Everett did. Otherwise, I think he had a fair, completely honest investigation. Yes, they were trying to link President Johnson with Baker, but my attitude would have been to let the White House protect against that."[43]

Wesley Hayden, Jordan's press secretary and executive secretary, who assumed the position after Bill Whitley's death in the spring of 1967, was well aware of the proceedings, though they had occurred three years earlier. Hayden's surmise was: "He [Jordan] handled that situation as he would have any other issue, on a pragmatic, practical basis, approaching it in the only way that he could have approached it, I think, lacking any legal training or any experience in a judicial or judicatory procedure. In other words, he regarded it as an administrative and fact-finding proceeding which he directed, but [he] let others participate to a very significant degree. He acted as chairman to keep it going but didn't, as I recall, attempt to take the leadership in becoming a prosecutor."[44]

Hayden thought the committee did an "adequate job," but conceded that, try as he might to avoid it, the senator's friendship with the president may have been a factor—but not *the* deciding one in the investigation.[45]

Back home there were also dissenting opinions, and at a later date family members close to the senator did not hesitate to voice them. Margaret Jordan Sprinkle, the senator's only surviving sibling, stated: "[People] think that they [Senate Rules Committee] whitewashed him [Baker] for Lyndon Johnson. [People think that] he [Everett] was protecting Johnson. Everett was sincere in that; he believed in him [Johnson]. Everett was a good friend of Johnson's, and Katherine was a good friend of Lady Bird."[46]

In 1987 Roger Gant, Jr., Everett Jordan's straight-talking son-in-law, commented on the Baker investigation: "Everett saved Lyndon Johnson's skin on that! Again, Everett's ability as a trader and a negotiator kept that matter about as quiet as it could be kept, and Everett certainly pulled the attention away from Lyndon Johnson on the matter and let the heat fall somewhere else. He couldn't keep Lyndon Johnson's name out of it completely, but the heat stopped with the Senate; and, when Lyndon Johnson went to the White House, the heat didn't follow him. Everett maneuvered that."[47]

Gant also made some observations regarding the relationship between the two politicians:

> Everett and Lyndon were very good friends until after the Baker case was settled, and then Lyndon didn't have much more the need of it. Everett did not agree with Lyndon Johnson on very many social programs that Lyndon had adopted. Lyndon changed a great deal. Lyndon was a great politician and certainly controlled the Senate and therefore to a large degree the House also, when he was the majority leader. After he got to the presidency, Lyndon changed his attitude about a lot of things. He looked to the country rather than Texas; his stand changed about a lot of things, and it got farther and farther away from Everett. Therefore, Lyndon couldn't count on having Everett vote the same way he wanted the Senate to vote because Lyndon's requirements changed. So, he no longer had this very close voting ally that he had had before, and he didn't need Everett very much any more. I think he kind of turned away from—turned his back on him [Everett]. Johnson couldn't ever give Everett credit for the Bobby Baker saving—saving his tail on that—he couldn't let that issue rise again.[48]

If Jordan himself sensed that his good friend in the White House had cooled toward him, no one recalls any expression of disappointment on Jordan's part. As Roger Gant pointed out: "I never heard Everett criticize Lyndon Johnson for ignoring him. After Lyndon Johnson got to the White House for the first few months, Everett had his ear, but after that he didn't. I think Everett could still arrange tours through the White House for his Washington guests and that kind of thing, but as far as being a close confidant of Johnson, he no longer was."[49]

Bill Cochrane, who served at Jordan's elbow during the senator's entire fourteen-and-a-half-year tenure, later defended the Senate Rules Committee chairman's conduct of the investigation. Insofar as Cochrane is concerned, his boss handled the affair in an appropriate manner: "Senator Jordan played it right straight—played

Senator Jordan shakes hands with President Johnson at the signing of the Food Stamp Bill (S-953), on September 27, 1967. (*Jordan family scrapbooks*)

straight all the way through. I would say it cost us 50,000 votes in the [1966] primary because of all the critical charges that were made by the other side. The senator didn't pull any punches on that thing; he played it right down the middle."[50]

Not everyone agreed with Cochrane, particularly because of the dramatic circumstances that occurred before the Senate Rules Committee had completed its hearing. On November 22, 1963, the day President John F. Kennedy was assassinated, investigators from the committee were hearing testimony from Don B. Reynolds, head of Don Reynolds Associates, Silver Spring, Md. They learned that Baker was an honorary vice-president of that firm; and, through this association, had procured two $100,000 life-insurance policies on the life of Lyndon Johnson, who a few years earlier had suffered a nearly fatal heart attack. Most orthodox insurance companies would have shunned the risk. But there was more. Reynolds had given Baker a part of the sales commission on the policies; and, acting upon the advice of Walter Jenkins—who had worked for Johnson as a Washington staffer since 1939—he also bought $1,200 worth of television advertising on Johnson's Texas station. Further, before the committee realized that Johnson had become the new president, Reynolds testified that he had sent the Johnsons a $585 Magnavox stereo set chosen by Johnson's wife, Lady Bird, and that he had a receipt as proof.[51]

On that tragic and eventful November day, testimony was becoming extremely interesting and surprisingly close to the vice-president, so much so that the investigating group did not adjourn for lunch and did not, therefore, learn until late afternoon that Jack Kennedy had been assassinated and Lyndon Johnson was the president. This unexpected sequence of events changed the whole complexion of the investigation, for now they were looking into the affairs of the president of the United States and not the relatively ineffectual vice-president—a president who faced trying times and sorely needed help from any and all sources. Under these extraordinary circumstances, the press, aware of the potentially incriminating testimony of Reynolds, tended to tone down their stories.[52]

During the drawn-out Baker proceedings, in the summer of 1964, Everett Jordan, as was his custom from time to time, returned to North Carolina to see family and friends, to check up on the mill business, and to obtain a much-needed respite from the Washington arena. Years earlier, before he went to the Senate, he had acquired a summer home in Montreat, N.C., which served as a refuge from the demanding pace he set as top man of his mills and allowed him to relax and refresh himself in the cool of the western North Carolina mountains.[53]

While there, the Jordans usually attended the Presbyterian church, whose minister was Dr. Calvin Thielman. President Johnson, also, was no stranger to Thielman, who had his early roots in Texas and, as a schoolboy, had worked for Johnson there. According to Thielman: "The president [that is, Johnson] would have me come to Washington and visit him, and then I went on trips for him, and I would stay overnight at the White House many times. This was publicized in the North Carolina papers, and so Senator Jordan knew about my close friendship with the president."[54]

"The Protector" 283

Senator Jordan dusts his hands after the Bobby Baker case is concluded by the Senate Rules Committee, which he chaired. Cartoon by Gib Crockett, *Washington* (D.C.) *Star,* March 5, 1965. (*Ben E. Jordan, Jr.*)

In the summer of 1964, when the press was filled with accounts about Baker and his association with Johnson during his Senate years and when Johnson was running for the presidency, Reverend Thielman visited Senator Jordan's Montreat home. The talk soon turned to the Bobby Baker affair. According to Thielman, Jordan said, "I did not intend to get into this, and I didn't let Johnson get into it because the country is in such a turmoil." Thielman continued: "He [Jordan] said there was just too much unsettledness and disruption in the country. The country was also being threatened at this time by having gone through the Cuban missile crisis just a couple of years before in 1962, then, the year before that, the erection of the Berlin Wall; and the senator, I thought, showed a huge amount of common sense."[55]

Thielman added:

> He [Jordan] knew that Mr. Johnson, regardless of whatever the Rules Committee might—any investigation might have brought out—that the president had great knowledge of the machinery of the government... And... how to make the government work, and we needed a man like that... If you recall, more legislation was actually passed during that 1964 season than probably any other time in the history of the country, with the possible exception of FDR's [Franklin D. Roosevelt's] earliest days...
>
> Then, of course, that summer was the summer that Goldwater ran against Mr. Johnson to see who would get to be president. The country was solidified behind President Johnson because it recognized the need of knowledgeable leadership in the land.
>
> I thought that Senator Jordan used good sense—in the same kind of sense he would have used in running a mill or in any other emergency—in realizing that you can't have a vacuum of leadership; that the first robust, strong force that moved into a vacuum can control it, and he wanted it to be controlled by people who knew the process of government. So, I think he strongly favored President Johnson at that time, even though I'm sure he wouldn't have agreed on a lot of the civil rights stuff.
>
> Senator Jordan said: "Some folks are trying to embarrass the president," but, he said, "I'm in a position on the Rules Committee to keep this from happening. This whole country's been in a mess because of the assassination of President Kennedy, and we've got to have leadership, and I simply am not going to let it come to pass." He was simply not going to let it come up; he wasn't going to see the president embarrassed about it because he needed all the authority that he could muster to run the government.[56]

Unquestionably, Everett Jordan was loyal to his friends. And he took care of them—his way.

13

"Everett, Have You Lost Your Mind?"

Everett Jordan's switch from a "hawk" to a "dove" and his final decision to oppose U.S. participation in the Vietnam war represented a major turning point in his political philosophy. In the first place, it involved a departure from his strong political conservatism; until then, he had supported all the government initiatives to contain communism. Secondly, of equal importance perhaps, this action alienated him from many of his friends, political colleagues, constituents, and supporters—including the other North Carolina senator, Sam Ervin, Jr. Indeed, virtually the entire Southern congressional delegation supported the U.S. role in the war. Moreover, once Everett Jordan took a position, it was extremely difficult for him to change. Even more than he could not say "I'm sorry," he found it unthinkable to admit he was wrong. However, he had come to the conclusion that the administration's policy to pursue the war was untenable; and in the end he decided to stand by his convictions and vote against the U.S. role in the Vietnam conflict.

Like his predecessor, John F. Kennedy, President Lyndon B. Johnson and his administration grappled with the nation's dilemma in Vietnam—how best to end this undeclared war—a conflict that was sapping both the nation's resources and resolve. From the outset, the involvement had seemed justified to many of those both in and out of government, though, as time went on, the protest movement in the nation grew. Meantime, the Vietnamese enigma was a big one and could potentially grow much bigger. China's huge armies were just over the border to the north; and the Soviet Union, it was widely believed, would be willing to exploit any problematic situation—Vietnam, Cuba, Afghanistan—to its own advantage. But no one could foresee the struggle lasting so long and being so costly. North Vietnam, a relatively poor and backward country faced the might—handcuffed though it might be—of the United States, the most powerful nation on earth. Although this country clearly had the means and wherewithal to smash its puny opponent, it dared not do so for a host of political and military reasons.[1]

Based on the Gulf of Tonkin Resolution,[2] America under Lyndon Johnson eased into the affray—that had begun years earlier—on the side of the forces of South Vietnam, which were resisting the steady advance of Ho Chi Minh's Communist troops from the North.

Congress became, through these protracted years of war, paralyzed by two major factions: the "hawks" and the "doves." The administration, supported by the hawks, was determined to bring about a "win situation" by purely military means. The doves, who were in the minority, opposed the policy as being unworkable, contending that the United States should call it quits and bring its fighting men home.

Consistent with past positions, the conservative Democrats from the South mostly fell in the hawk group and stood solidly behind the president and his goal of winning an "honorable victory" and hoping in the process to halt the spread of communism in Southeast Asia. The national press was replete, during this time, with the pros and cons of the great debate as college students, others of draft age, and the public in general took sides over whether to continue on or to withdraw.

America's vast resources were committed, but in the Congress and among the constituents back home there were the uncommitted and increasingly those who were becoming uncommitted. The dissension continued to heighten as American policy and war efforts were ever more carefully scrutinized at home and abroad. While the prolonged controversy raged, the casualties mounted on both sides.

Back in 1961, when another president—John F. Kennedy—had agonized over the Cuban missile crisis, the Burlington, N.C., newspaper quoted Senator Jordan:

There is no doubt in my mind that the people of the United States are ready to take whatever action President Kennedy considers necessary to blow the whistle on Castro and the Communists. Wisely, the President is not making any hasty or impulsive moves, but with firmness he has put the Communist World on notice that we are not going to sit on the sidelines and be just a spectator to what goes on in Cuba.

We have a cancer growing in Cuba. We know it is there, and it is a question of when and how we choose to deal with it. I think the earlier we operate the better for everyone concerned.

... Cuba, I am certain, is only the first stage of a long-range plan of the Communists to take over South America, country by country. Once they are allowed to get their Cuban outpost in operation, they will use it to move to the mainland of South America.

We in the United States have had a long-standing policy of not interfering in the internal affairs of our South American neighbors. By the same token we are obligated not to allow other nations to intervene. In my way of thinking, the Communists have intervened in Cuba and it is up to us to put a stop to that intervention.[3]

Because Everett Jordan had not underestimated the potential Communist threat in this hemisphere in 1961, he was a firm supporter of later presidents who struggled with the confrontation with communism in Southeast Asia that had actually begun during President Dwight D. Eisenhower's administration.

The "solid South" legislative group in Washington strongly backed the president's position as hostilities accelerated between North and South Vietnam in the 1960s, and Jordan was a staunch member of that group.[4] Nor did the Tar Heel senator change his thinking when suddenly his good friend Lyndon Johnson was thrust into the presidency after Kennedy was assassinated on November 22, 1963.

After a hasty swearing-in ceremony at Dallas as the nation's chief executive, on the plane home the new president and commander in chief vowed to pursue his predecessor's goals in international and domestic affairs. In the former realm, the main element was containment of worldwide communism. Dominant in this regard was the Vietnam conflict, where by late 1963 Kennedy had sent approximately 16,000 American troops to South Vietnam to make good the United States pledge to the Southeast Asia Treaty Organization (SEATO), which President Eisenhower had strengthened. Despite this position, Johnson had some misgivings. Congressional and public demands for U.S. withdrawal from Vietnam were becoming more strident and insistent.[5] Johnson believed that consensus—the kind he had achieved in the Senate to obtain needed legislation—was necessary in the conduct of foreign affairs. But what was a virtue in the Capitol proved to be a major liability in the Oval Office.[6]

As noted earlier, during the Cuban missile crisis in Kennedy's administration, Senator Jordan expressed the fear that, if communism took over Cuba, then the South American countries, one by one, would fall victim, too. This same concept was shared by the Johnson administration in relating to events in Southeast Asia. Johnson and most of his closest advisers, including Secretary of State Dean Rusk, subscribed to this "Domino Theory": the belief that, if one nation fell, it would trigger the rapid collapse of surrounding countries.

The Gulf of Tonkin Resolution had given Johnson the leeway to move directly to deal with Ho Chi Minh, his North Vietnamese counterpart and chief adversary. And, in the years that followed, Congress in general went along with Johnson. Saigon's military forces never measured up to the expectations of their American advisers and leaders—either in Washington or South Vietnam—a sore disappointment and one that required ever-increasing assistance from its wealthy foreign allies, particularly the United States. No other nation ever furnished any major help, though New Zealand and Australia did send a few thousand men for combat duty.

As the war escalated and worsened for the South Vietnamese, General William C. Westmoreland, supreme commander of American forces, requested more of everything: materiel and men. President Johnson complied, acting mainly on the advice of a handful of advisers, especially Secretary of Defense Robert McNamara.

Meanwhile, opposition forces within the United States had become more and more visible and vocal. Canada became a refuge for thousands of young Americans of draft age; college students demonstrated noisily and sometimes violently on campuses; the press increasingly voiced the rising opposition of those throughout the land, as more and more people wondered about the ultimate goals and the strategy for their achievement. Defense Department systems analysts took a markedly negative view of the future: "An end to the conflict is not in sight and major unresolved problems remain."[7]

For the United States, this conflict, or undeclared war, was different from those of the past, which historians have seen as reflecting our glorious successes and America's unrestrained sense of pride in its heroes and fighting men. Many of those returning from Vietnam's embattled rice paddies and jungles felt that their sacrifices were not appreciated or understood—that they were treated more like stepchildren than legitimate heroes who deserved to be welcomed with open arms, marching bands, and resounding praise. Had they not fought for their country, too, and had they not striven to help the people of Vietnam to resist their Communist aggressors so that they might have their own choice of government?

In the midst of all this turmoil, Everett Jordan was not one of these detractors of the Vietnam war because he basically supported Johnson's policy, a position largely held by the entire Southern legislative delegation, a group that was essentially conservative and unified in its thinking.[8]

As time went on, however, Jordan changed his position, which was to bring him into direct conflict with the senior North Carolina senator, Sam Ervin, Jr. The two men were similar because they both possessed an inordinate amount of stubbornness in their makeup, but they were miles apart in their personalities and decision-making processes. For that reason, they soon found themselves sharply divided over the great political question of their time: the war in Vietnam. America stood almost alone on a battlefield in Southeast Asia and was, many believed, still fighting to make the world safe for democracy—but this time bogged down in an undeclared and static war. In this conflict, World War I veterans Sam Ervin and Everett Jordan found themselves participants, but on a different battlefield: a political contest waged on the floor of the United States Senate.[9]

Ervin had obtained his seniority over Jordan by preceding him into the Senate by nearly four years; and, like Jordan, had first gotten his seat through appointment, by Governor William B. Umstead following the death of North Carolina's colorful senator Clyde R. Hoey. Hoey had died suddenly on May 12, 1954, while sitting at his desk in the Senate Office Building. At the time of his appointment, Ervin was serving as a state supreme court judge. On June 11, 1954, he was sworn in by Richard M. Nixon, vice-president of the United States.

Everett Jordan was nearly sixty-two years old when he was tapped for the U.S. Senate, and by that time the two men had rubbed shoulders at various political gatherings and conferred with each other on relevant party interests. So when Jordan took his Senate seat he knew he had a trusted friend in Ervin, whom he could turn to as the need might arise.

Because of their contrasting backgrounds and abilities, each senator deferred to the recognized expertise of the other on issues of mutual interest: Ervin the jurist and constitutional authority, Jordan the businessman and "loaves and fishes" proponent. As national lawmakers, they played on the same team. And, as Ervin explained it, they complemented each other in their role of representing the best interests of their constituents.

Although both men had similarities in character and political philosophy, they did not speak or think as one even if they did usually vote together when the "Ayes" and "Nays" were recorded. Physically, both were big men, but Ervin was somewhat taller and heavier. Each in his own way resorted to a good story to win or clinch a point. Ervin's inventory of tales seemed limitless and ran the gamut; Jordan's stories were told with less finesse but with equal gusto as well as good humor and were more confined to the working-world and biblical truisms, which reflected both his upbringing as a preacher's child as well as his work experience. Neither was vulnerable to intimidation, but, intentional or not, both could and did intimidate.

The two politicians, however, had one fundamental difference that cannot be understood without some knowledge of how each arrived at his conclusion or course of action. First, consider Ervin's propensities:

> [Ervin] reached inside himself for the answers, rarely responding to pressures, whether from his colleagues in the Senate, his constituents or the press. He said those constituents who took the trouble to write letters were usually possessed by one extreme or another, while the majority in the middle expected him to make up his own mind and forgave him when he was wrong. He agreed with the judge who once told him, "When I want to know what the people think I go in my office, shut the door, sit down at my desk and communicate with myself'... He listened and studied harder than anyone else. He went to the Senate Library—in fact he was the only member of the Senate to go there regularly—and soaked up the law. Once he made up his mind, almost nothing, certainly not a stampede by others in the Senate or a storm of angry letters, could change his mind...
>
> Once he had decided, there was no use arguing the merits of an issue with Ervin. He had marshalled his arguments and his strategy and would fight in the face of the most persuasive opponents...
>
> In 1972 the "Congressional Quarterly" said that Ervin was the most independent member of the Senate. He frequently swam against the tide, voting 31 percent against bipartisan majorities, both against legislation that passed and for legislation that failed.[10]

Jordan, Ervin's counterpart, was just the opposite in his decision-making process. Not being a student, he probably never went once to the Senate library to read. But his staff certainly did; they engaged in extensive research, and Jordan knew how to listen. However, his decisions were fundamentally his own, and he could be just as obstinate as Ervin in never relinquishing his viewpoint or in changing his position.

Another difference between the two men was that Jordan, a quiet worker behind the scenes, after nearly fifteen years in the Senate—except for the notoriety from the Bobby Baker case—was rarely known outside his home state. Senator Ervin, on the other hand, in his role as defender of the Constitution and from his avuncular conduct of the nationally televised Watergate hearings, became a household name throughout the land.

Caricature of Senator Jordan by Don Barclay, one of the original Walt Disney artists. (*Edward L. Gruber*)

By 1970, after Presidents Kennedy, Johnson, Nixon, and their administrations had waged futile campaigns to bring hostilities to a successful conclusion, many observers believed that the United States was no nearer victory than when the conflict began. The hawks and the doves were committed to their respective positions; and, deeply entrenched, neither side was inclined to hoist a white flag.[11] Among them was Sam Ervin, who remained firm in his conviction that the president ought to have the right and also the support of the government to wage war to a final victory.[12]

From the beginning, Everett Jordan, like Ervin, had been a staunch supporter of those who directed the battle to win Vietnam for democracy. However, he was listening and beginning to have second thoughts. Mail, not only from his back-home constituents, but from all over the country began to pour in. Bill Cochrane and his staff, attuned to the times and prevailing sentiments, dutifully relayed their gleanings and leanings to their senator. Jordan, admittedly mule-headed but ever responsive to those whom he trusted and respected, gave heed and his actions began to reflect what he heard.[13]

In an effort to obtain an unbiased overview on the Southeast Asia conflict, Jordan sent his able and trusted aide Cochrane to the Far East. The latter returned even more convinced of the futility of further U.S. military involvement there. The two men then engaged in extensive discussions, examining the issue from every angle.[14]

From time to time Jordan, assisted by his staff, released statements to the press and general public concerning his stand on various bills and issues. In one on Vietnam dated June 11, 1970, he said: "I have heard from a lot of good, solid people who say we ought to back the President and not pull the rug from under him." Further on in this same release, Senator Jordan also said, "I have talked with a great many people about it—ministers, doctors, lawyers, businessmen, students, fathers, and mothers—who are deeply concerned over the unrest and turmoil which our involvement in Southeast Asia has created."[15]

Then five days later, on June 16, 1970, Jordan cast the most difficult vote of his Senate career. His own "fateful moment" had come. Breaking ranks with the Southern congressional delegation and in opposition to the president and his administration, he voted for the Cooper-Church amendment, a move to curtail military action in Southeast Asia immediately. In the aftermath, the press quoted Jordan as saying that vowing to vote for the resolution was "certainly the hardest decision I have faced in my years in the Senate."[16] It represented not only a basic change in philosophy, but he had also put himself in the unpleasant position of opposing his friends.

Roy Parker, Jr., wrote in the Raleigh *News and Observer*:

> The phone rang at 8:30 a.m. Thursday in Senator Everett Jordan's apartment overlooking Rock Creek Park.
> It was Secretary of State William P. Rogers, trying a breakfast hour bid for votes for the amendment heading off the Senate's bid to limit

U.S. involvement in Southeast Asia. As late as the night before Sen. Jordan had told associates he was undecided.

But Rogers, who made a polite request for Jordan's vote, got a typically polite Jordan reply.

"He said he hoped I could support the Byrd amendment," Jordan recalled. "He didn't twist my arm. I told him I appreciated the call but had decided to vote against it."

Two hours later, Jordan phoned his long time friend, Sen. Robert Byrd, (D-W. Va.) to tell him his decision. "He thanked me... I hated to vote against Robert," said Jordan.

In another two hours, the Senate had completed its historic vote. By 52 to 47, it defeated Byrd's amendment to a resolution putting a time limit on U.S. troops in Cambodia.[17]

The senator's perceptive daughter, Rose Ann, later made these observations:

> During those years I watched daddy grow in scope as one is presented with an enormous picture. We were no longer in North Carolina, no longer in Alamance County, no longer in Saxapahaw; we were on the national scene. Then you begin to push your own horizons out and away and tend to look for the larger picture or even by osmosis—even if you are not looking for it—things get presented in a larger role, and you have to say "I have my duty to see it on a national scale as well as a state scale." I think that over any period of time that was bound to happen to everybody, and it happened to him, too. But I do think that domestic issues were more important to daddy than national or international because he grasped domestic issues more quickly. He could see the effects and ripples that might lead out from legislation [of this type, like dropping] a pebble in [water] and off it would go. It took an entirely different kind of concept and mind to deal with international. I don't mean that he didn't care; it's just that that was not his area... He was not well versed [in foreign affairs] and relied on the men and women whose job it was to be versed.[18]

Rose Ann made these comments concerning her father's about-face on Vietnam: "The move from hawk to dove was... remarkable ... The only explanation I have is that he saw the handwriting on the wall in an inevitable shift in the emotions within the country, and that the young people literally did have to be heard. Now, that in itself is remarkable for him... I do know that it was difficult for him to change his mind! So... there must have been something or a growing awareness that the hard line was simply an untenable one. The other thing: once he had made up his mind, it was very difficult to get him to say, 'I made a mistake; I was wrong,' and that made that shift even more remarkable."[19]

Remarkable, indeed. After Everett Jordan voted for the Cooper-Church resolution, an incredulous Sam Ervin confronted him and blurted out: "Everett, have you lost your mind?"[20]

14

"And I Bequeath..."

"[Everett Jordan] liked to lay claim to a modest beginning—that he swept the mill and what-not," contended his younger sister Margaret Jordan Sprinkle. She reported that Mrs. Connie B. Williams, neighbor and longtime friend of the Jordan family—in both Gastonia and in Saxapahaw—said that "Everett would tell that his mother made his underwear out of flour sacks." Margaret refuted this statement: "But I know that was not so! Mother would go down to Sellars store [in Burlington, N.C.] and buy beautiful cloth." She mostly used the material to make clothes for herself and her two daughters, Margaret and Lucy; and, as part owner of the Burlington dry goods store, the industrious minister's wife saw to it that the rest of her family was well dressed, too. However, Margaret quoted Mrs. Williams as saying, "Well, I *saw* some of that underwear, and it had 'Self Rising' on the pants!" The Williams family has always admired their distinguished neighbor Everett Jordan and takes great delight in relating anecdotes that reveal his exuberant personality.[1]

Although Everett Jordan became a wealthy man, his sister Margaret put into words what many others have observed: "He did not try to build up his image with things that his money could buy." His approving sister said that, even in his final days, "for his funeral—he knew he was dying—he did not want a great show from Washington. He wanted the funeral in his own little church [in Saxapahaw] and with ministers that meant something to him, rather than the chaplain from the Senate. He said he wanted his funeral in his own church, with his own people."[2]

Most of Jordan's friends and colleagues vowed that his personality did not change regardless of place, position, or circumstances. On Capitol Hill and in the Senate chambers, he never made a big

The young adult class, Saxapahaw (now United) Methodist Church, in 1962. Everett Jordan taught this class for many years before going to Washington and continued to attend it when he was at home as long as he lived. *Standing at left*: Rufus ("Buddy") Collins; *sitting, rear row, left to right*: Van Doran Crutchfield, Ben E. Jordan, Jr., his wife, Ellen; *sitting, front row*: Leon Madden, Richard A. Stanford, Jr., T. J. Jones, John Ray Madden, May McLean, Bobby Hardin, Thomas ("Curly") Morton, Albert ("Bosie") Neal, Senator Jordan, Ben Bulla (teacher), Dan Montgomery, Hazel Montgomery, Frances Aycock, unidentified, Darwin Lindley, Nannie Lou McBane, Henry McBane. (*Saxapahaw United Methodist Church*)

splash, even though he associated with men whose names appeared frequently in the headlines and whose faces were known throughout the country.[3]

Besides the considerable wealth he bequeathed to his heirs, Jordan also left behind a legacy of achievement in the textile industry, which was treated earlier in this volume. In his later years, he also established a highly successful record in the United States Senate, which has been traced in the chapters immediately preceding this one. Although Jordan operated quietly behind the scenes, he attained great distinction in the Senate.

Based on President Woodrow Wilson's claim that "Congress in committee is Congress at work," Everett Jordan competed for top honors in that body. The *Congressional Record* reveals that, at the end of his last term, he held more chairmanships of committees, joint committees, and subcommittees than any other member of either chamber of the Congress. He served as chairman of the Senate Rules Committee for ten years—longer than any other chairman in the committee's history. He alternated with the chairman of the House Committee on Administration as chairman and vice-chairman of both the Joint Committee on the Library of Congress and the Joint Committee on Printing. He sat on the Senate Agriculture and Forestry Committee as well as the Public Works Committee. He chaired the latter's Subcommittee on Flood Control and Rivers and Harbors. Other chairmanships included the Joint Congressional Committee on Inaugural Ceremonies, on which he served thrice, which was more than anyone else. And his participation in the Interparliamentary Union took him abroad on numerous trips, particularly in Europe and the Far East, as he became one of the better-informed senators on world hunger and other issues confronting the member nations.[4]

In 1970, near the end of the 91st Congress, Senator Sam Ervin, Jr., assisted by Bill Cochrane, submitted for insertion in the *Congressional Record* a concise statement that summarized Everett Jordan's Senate career. As customary, it was addressed to the president of the Senate.[5]

Ervin pointed out that Jordan had "done as much in a variety of practical ways to serve the interest of North Carolina as any other man representing the state in my memory." Ervin stressed that Jordan's service on the Agriculture and Forestry Committee was especially valuable, representing as he did one of the largest agricultural states in the nation.[6]

After pointing also to Jordan's achievements on the Rules and the Public Works committees, Ervin lauded his "demonstrated courage and his willingness to take an unpopular position when he felt it was necessary." Ervin then proceeded to list the large number of projects that Jordan initiated, took a prominent part in, or strongly supported. Following are the major ones on the list: the acreage-poundage legislation, which was widely credited with saving the

Joint Congressional Committee on Inaugural Ceremonies, which Senator Jordan had chaired for the 1965 inauguration of Johnson, in 1969 (*left to right*): Senator Everett M. Dirksen (R.-Ill.), Senate minority leader; Representative John W. McCormack (Dem.-Mass.), Speaker of the House; Senator Mike Mansfield (Dem.-Mont.), Senate majority leader; Senator Jordan; Representative Carl Albert (Dem.-Okla.), majority leader of the House; Gerald R. Ford (R.-Mich.), minority leader of the House. (*Jordan family scrapbooks*)

tobacco support program; the bill that authorized lease of tobacco acreage allotments—a move hailed by leaf growers; establishment of the one-price cotton system at a time when cotton production was threatened by subsidies; legislation relating to seed quality as well as peanut marketing and amendments tightening the Wholesale Meat Act; completion of the W. Kerr Scott Reservoir, in Wilkes County, N.C.; the New Hope Dam (later officially renamed the B. Everett Jordan Dam and Lake); a start on the Falls of the Neuse Reservoir Project, in Wake County, N.C.; deepening of the harbor of the state port at Morehead City, N.C.; the act authorizing the Cape Lookout National Seashore Park, N.C.; deepening of Wilmington harbor state port and the Cape Fear River Channel; the federal pro-

Senator Jordan surveys preparations for a presidential inauguration at the Capitol. (*Jordan family scrapbooks*)

gram to make available water and sewer treatment plants to thousands of rural communities and small towns throughout the nation; control of air and water pollution, solid waste disposal, and environmental protection; various federal library-aid programs; educational programs at every level from kindergarten to graduate school; and promoting the establishment of U.S. Government Depository Libraries.[7]

A July 31, 1971, news release issued by Senator Jordan gave a further glimpse into his role—one that he relished—of "bringing home the bacon" for his constituents. The release reported that the recently approved Public Works Appropriations Bill provided almost $18.9 million for North Carolina projects, including about $3.7 million in increased allotments specifically requested by Senator Jordan. Nearly $3.8 million was earmarked for construction of the Falls of the Neuse project in Wake County and $10.1 million for continued work on the New Hope Dam; each of these figures

Inauguration scene at the Capitol in 1965. President Johnson (*center*) is followed by Speaker of the House John W. McCormack (*left*) and Senator B. Everett Jordan (*right*), chairman of the inaugural committee. (Photo by U.S. Army; *Jordan family scrapbooks*)

amounted to a $1 million increase over that provided in the House version of the bill. The other major boost was for the Mills River Dam and Reservoir in the Upper French Broad River Basin. The release also listed various other North Carolina construction and planning projects that were included in the bill.[8]

A few weeks before he left his office in Washington, D.C., to return to his home in Saxapahaw for good, Everett Jordan was interviewed by the press about his contributions as a senator. His simple reply was: "I feel I have done something for the people."[9] Specifically, he expressed satisfaction with his work in the Senate and briefly touched upon some of his accomplishments in the area of public works:

> The New Hope Dam [in Chatham County] will be built largely because of me. [As chairman of the Senate Public Works Subcommittee on Flood Control, Rivers, and Harbors, Jordan was instrumental in obtaining money to continue construction of the $55 million project over the protests of environmentalists.]
>
> The Falls of the Neuse Reservoir was bottled up until I got the Secretary of the Army to sign the authorization. Raleigh will be out of water unless they get that dam.

"And I Bequeath..." 303

Lyndon B. Johnson takes the oath of office on January 20, 1965. Looking on at his immediate left is Lady Bird Johnson and Vice-President-elect Hubert H. Humphrey; on Johnson's right is Senator Jordan, who served as chairman of the inaugural committee. (*Jordan family scrapbooks*)

The Kerr Scott Dam [on the Yadkin River near Wilkesboro] was dead as a doornail. I picked it up and saved it. That dam will be the salvation of Winston-Salem's water supply in the future—and a town can't survive without water.

North Carolina has good harbors like Wilmington because I fought to get money to dredge the river. The beach erosion project and the Morehead City harbor dredging were done at my request.

I have worked for projects that were good and were needed. I just hope Helms (Sen.-elect Jesse Helms, the Republican who will succeed Jordan next month) and Ervin (Sen. Sam J. Ervin Jr., North Carolina's Senior Senator) will have the same active interest in trying to push these projects.

According to the press, the one project that Jordan took the greatest pride in was the new Library of Congress building, which was named the James Madison Memorial Library Building.[10] George White, architect for the Capitol, worked closely with Jordan during

Senator and Mrs. Jordan en route to the inauguration of President Richard M. Nixon on January 20, 1969. (*Boy Scouts of America; Jordan family scrapbooks*)

its design and construction, because the latter served as chairman of the Joint Committee on the Library. Other groups and committees were involved also, White said, so a coordinating committee was formed wherein all these groups merged and elected Jordan as chairman on a permanent basis. White: "He [Jordan] was very knowledgeable—he was very pragmatic; he understood the problems whatever they might be, and he understood them very quickly... He cut to the heart of the problem very quickly and would suggest a solution."[11] Jordan never lived to see the building completed because the dedication was held on April 24, 1980. The edifice, built as a memorial to the nation's fourth president, more than doubled the library's available Capitol Hill space.

In Saxapahaw, Everett Jordan, when he was on the scene full time, approved every doorstep that was repaired and every village roof that was replaced. All bills to be paid came across his desk for *his* approval. As for architecture and design, he specified that every company-owned dwelling must have a green asphalt shingle roof, must be painted white with no trimming—for cost reasons—and tobacco brown had to be used for painting all other structures.[12]

White said, "All those decisions for the expenditure of funds and for the design decisions had to be approved by Senator Jordan as

"And I Bequeath..." 305

Pictured here at the Capitol luncheon on January 20, 1969, in honor of newly elected President Nixon given by the Joint Congressional Committee on Inaugural Ceremonies, on which Jordan served, are (*left to right*): Senator Jordan, President Nixon, Mrs. Gerald (Betty) Ford, Katherine Jordan. (*Jordan family scrapbooks*)

chairman of the Coordinating Committee, and all the other senators and members of the House that were involved in that deferred to his judgment. If it happened to be a major policy decision, he would call them all together and have a meeting—from time to time that was done. He was sort of the guiding light for that until he left here."[13] Today, a visit to the magnificent James Madison Memorial Library Building further attests to the fact that the former Saxapahaw mill man could and did change—even in architecture.

Everett Jordan, in "doing something for the people," made his imprint on his peers, the press, and others, who publicly expressed their gratitude to him. Tributes by his Senate colleagues were collected in a special volume. They praised especially his contribu-

James Madison Memorial Library of Congress Building. Senator Jordan served tirelessly as chairman of the coordinating committee that supervised the construction of this building. (*Library of Congress*)

tions to his own state as well as the nation; and to the Democratic party committee work, especially as chairman of the Committee on Rules and Administration and in the Public Works Committee; and cited various major legislation he was associated with.[14]

Former North Carolina Congressman Richardson Preyer, of Greensboro, was considered by many to be one of the most able representatives this state has ever sent to Washington, and as such he earned national press recognition and acclaim for his skills and integrity. In a 1981 interview for this volume, he stated:

> In Washington, Senator Jordan was the kind of senator which I wish we had more of, but they are becoming rarer these days. There's an old saying in the Congress that some members are "workhorses" and some are "show horses." Senator Jordan was definitely a workhorse. Today's public relations techniques that are used so widely on television for elections don't permit us to see the solid kind of senator that Senator Jordan was. There are many kinds of leaders in the world...the charismatic [and] behind the scenes leaders...[The latter live] by influence and example rather than by...charismatic, dramatic leadership...That's the way that Senator Jordan was regarded in Washington. The workhorse-type members get more things done

because they have the respect of other members. They aren't trying to make a name for themselves or are not trying to get publicity for themselves, or insuring a niche in posterity for themselves. They are trying to get the job done. The senator was very good at getting the job done... I think to sum it up, Senator Jordan was a good man—different from the typical political star of today—being loyal to your family, your community, and your country, exercising common sense over ideology and not being dogmatic about your position as always being right. Those qualities are not valued so much today in some circles as being a celebrity, being on the tube [TV].[15]

A member of the press paid this tribute to Jordan:

> History will not record him as one of great oratory or of international statesmanship.
>
> But the people of his state will remember him as a good fellow who never let personal wealth or the U.S. Senate go to his head.
>
> Affected pomposity would have been foreign to his gentle and humble nature.
>
> If he had any transgressions, they were in all probability minor and, for certain, unintentional.
>
> Everett Jordan was a man who would recoil from the idea of saying or doing anything to hurt anyone. It was more the nature of this gentle man to forgive those who transgressed—and this included Bobby Baker, the focal point of the only criticism we ever heard directed against Senator Jordan.[16]

Another member of the press expressed his feelings about Jordan in the following way:

> Some keen observers say that Senator B. Everett Jordan should have a speech-writer. They made the remark after they heard Jordan in a talk before Goldsboro Rotary club and more briefly to a small group at Griffin's... We can't buy the observation. Jordan's strength is his individual sturdiness and unposed self.
>
> Jordan is a poor speech-maker as we have come to regard speeches. But he speaks out of his own convictions. It follows that his words have a ring of sincerity so often missing in the pronouncements of the man running for public office... The man suggesting a speech writer might have had in mind, also, some apparent crudities of Jordan's speech. They are there. But they are the crudities of strength.[17]

And closer to home, the following comments were made by a Saxapahaw-area resident, Jack Paris:

> I suppose everyone is fortunate when there can be a good person to come into our lives and teach us more of the meaning of friendship, honesty and good intent through his actions. Everyone can learn from such people. This is the way I felt about Sen. B. Everett Jordan, and I believe I express the feelings of countless people.
>
> He was important to us in the Saxapahaw area for what he meant to Sellers Manufacturing Co. He also was important to us for what he meant to us as a person and the deep and sincere interests he had in people. This was something that he did every day, not just occasionally.[18]

Pat Bailey, a well-known, local, feature-story writer for the press, paid her respects in this way:

> While he lived, Senator B. Everett Jordan had an understanding that began and ended in Saxapahaw. History teaches us that when we don't like what it is trying to teach us, we can rewrite it. B. Everett Jordan did that for the dying mill village of Saxapahaw...reviving it...giving it new life...and claiming it as home. His house was high on the north bank of the mighty Haw River. He liked to talk about how he repaired the house after he first got the mill on its way to an expanding future.
>
> He had his group...the "Old Timers"...who helped him fight the floods, and high water marks.
>
> He was criticized for being the "big man on the hill."
>
> It was nice to have him around. He was human and humorous.
>
> Even in his role as Senator he had utter dedication to Saxapahaw ...it was home. He enjoyed each return visit with fresh delight... whether it was from the 'bigger Capitol Hill' in Washington or representing the United States in foreign travels.
>
> Sooner or later someone is going to write a book about the Senator from Saxapahaw. I wonder if it will tell the folksy bits...about how he liked to slip into the kitchen when Mrs. Katherine or the cook was away and fix his 'favorite supper,' as he claimed it. He once told a reporter: 'I'd go open a can of tomatoes and with some crackers...it was mighty fine eating!'[19]

In view of this kind of record, Everett Jordan's friends and supporters were shocked when, making a bid for a third full term in the Senate, he was defeated in 1972 in the Democratic primary by Congressman Nick Galifianakis.[20] In prior elections, Jordan had won handily over his opposition; and in the general election for 1960 had achieved the distinction of having the largest plurality of any North Carolina candidate, in which he also set a record by receiving the highest number of votes for his office ever accorded a candidate in North Carolina. He also won again most impressively in 1966. In addition, he had had fourteen years of acknowledged public service and seniority; and in 1972 there were no controversial issues or damaging criticisms of his performance.[21]

Why then did the experienced insider Everett Jordan lose to a relative newcomer: Nick Galifianakis, a Durham attorney and a congressman for just six years, whose name was even a tongue twister and who had no recognized statewide power base?

Senator Sam Ervin later attributed the defeat to a wide variety of factors: Jordan's age, seventy-six, when many of his supporters were dead or unable to help in the campaign and young people as well as numerous others felt he was too old to serve effectively; his loss of contact with his young constituents because his Senate duties made it difficult to campaign back home; his opposition to the Vietnam war, which cost him the votes of many veterans; his recent major surgery for cancer, which many of the public feared might return; and, though he campaigned hard in the second primary, his need to rely for a campaign manager on his brother Frank B. Jordan, a retired Methodist minister who had no experience in politics and who was far less effective than their now-deceased brother, Dr. Henry W. Jordan, a master politician; and Everett's failure to keep in constant contact with his constituents through such devices as radio programs. Of course, Jordan's cause was not helped by Ervin's failure to campaign for him in North Carolina, but Ervin pointed out that the two could not transfer their support from one to another and that it would be unseemly for both North Carolina senators to be absent from Washington at the same time.[22]

Terry Sanford, North Carolina's junior senator, remembered in 1989 that Jordan "was tired, he was old, he was sick" and was competing with a hard-working young man. Sanford particularly la-

Senators Jordan and Ervin during the 1972 electoral campaign. (Photo by Jeff Stark; *Jordan family scrapbooks*)

mented Galifianakis's brashness in running against a dear old friend and taking advantage of his illness and age. According to Sanford, this may have resulted in the voters wanting to get even by voting Galifianakis out of office and switching to Republican Jesse Helms.[23]

The views of Jesse Helms, Jordan's successor in the U.S. Senate, on Galifianakis's victory coincided closely with those of Senator Sanford. Helms, moreover, contended that Jordan received negative publicity from a liberal press; he criticized Galifianakis's tactics saying, "Another thing that bothered me during the campaign was that Galifianakis, everywhere he would go, he would get up and say, 'Now I'm not going to mention the fact that Senator Jordan has cancer or that he's seventy-five or six years old—or whatever he is— I'll take any other questions!' But he planted that seed everywhere he went, which I thought was poor taste and not fair, but apparently it worked."[24]

Helms first came to know Everett Jordan when he was a young administrative assistant to U.S. Senator Willis Smith; Jordan was then serving as chairman of the state Democratic party and was also Smith's close friend and business associate. The two men and their families were majority stockholders and officers in the Royal Cotton Mill Company in Wake Forest, N.C., and so Senator Smith and Everett Jordan saw each other quite frequently. Through this association, Helms said that he developed the "deepest affection for Senator Jordan, of course, he was not senator then."[25]

Incidentally, Helms contended that he only ran for the Republican nomination for the Senate in 1972 because some of his friends were worried that Galifianakis might beat Jordan in the primaries, especially because of Jordan's illness. Helms further stated that, had Jordan won and been his opposition on the Democratic ticket, he never would have pursued his candidacy: "If Galifianakis had not beat him, I would not have run a campaign against a good man [Jordan]. I'm honored to be in the Senate, and I'm honored to have succeeded Everett Jordan, but, if he had won the nomination in 1972, I would have sat on my hands."[26]

Another factor was that, in the first primary, Jordan had not started any serious campaigning until late, contending that his Senate duties required that he spend all his time in Washington—while his young opponent was hard at work politicking back home. And, when Jordan did get started, some observers thought that too many of his supporters considered the election a no-contest and consequently were overly complacent.[27]

The senator's younger son, John—who was elected to three terms in the North Carolina house of representatives and to one term in the senate—felt that his father's defeat was due to poor relations with the press: "Daddy was a conservative and he was scared of the press, which was his downfall. He never used the press because he was scared of bad press. No one likes bad press; the press is like a two-edged sword. If you avoid them, you get no name recognition. Even though he was in the Senate fourteen and a half years, the public did not know Everett Jordan. Never heard of him! He was probably the poorest politician that I knew [publicity-wise]. In politics, the one thing you've got to have is name recognition."[28]

"The Bridge Builder," a poem by Will Allen Dromgoole, best expresses Everett Jordan's life philosophy as affirmed by various members of his family. He, himself, said many times that he tried to pattern his life after the builder in this verse, which reads:

THE BRIDGE BUILDER

An old man, going a lone highway,
Came at the evening, cold and gray,
To a chasm, vast and deep and wide,
Through which was flowing a sullen tide.
The old man crossed in the twilight dim;
The sullen stream had no fears for him;
But he turned when safe on the other side
and built a bridge to span the tide.

"Old man," said a fellow pilgrim near,
"You are wasting strength with building here;
Your journey will end with the ending day;
You never again must pass this way;
You have crossed the chasm, deep and wide—
Why build you the bridge at the eventide?"

The builder lifted his old gray head;
"Good friend, in the path I have come," he said,
"There followeth after me today
A youth whose feet must pass this way,
This chasm that has been naught to me
To that fair-haired youth may a pitfall be.
He, too, must cross in the twilight dim;
Good friend, I am building the bridge for him."[29]

Reverend Henry Harrison Jordan's will, dated May 14, 1930, contains as its fourth stipulation: "I will and bequeath my beloved children (a) a good name, which is more to be desired than silver and gold; (b) an example of high and unselfish endeavor to discharge

Steel girder bridge at Saxapahaw late in 1935. The boy in the foreground is Bruce G. Hackney, playmate of Ben E. Jordan, Jr. (Photo by Walter O. Hackney; *Bruce G. Hackney*)

the obligations which [have] come to me by the Will and goodness of God and the reciprocal responsibilities as a member of society, to the end that I might make my full contribution to the honor and glory of my Heavenly Father and the good of human kind in the hope that they may carry on and be able to make a larger contribution to the world's good than I have been able to do."[30]

On March 15, 1974, after a courageous battle with cancer—having been under the surgeon's scalpel twice in his last three years—when Everett Jordan died at his home in Saxapahaw, the Reverend H. H. Jordan had long pre-deceased his first-born son. We have, therefore, no means to ascertain the minister-father's evaluation of the stewardship of the bequest contained in the fourth stipulation of his will to a son about whom he once entertained dire misgivings. It would be fascinating to know the father's final judgment on

A 1939 photo of the Saxapahaw bridge. In the background are (*left to right*): old gristmill building, the Jordan residence, and the store and office building of Sellers Manufacturing Company. (*Paul E. Morrow, Jr.*)

how well Benjamin Everett made his "full contribution" to the honor and glory of God and the good of mankind.

The night before Everett Jordan's death, various members of the family were gathered in the senator's sickroom, where family and personal topics were discussed. Although everyone realized that the end was near, the conversation—if anything—was upbeat. And an atmosphere of calm composure—so evident throughout Everett Jordan's life—prevailed. Present in the group were Katherine Jordan; her sister May McLean; Margaret Sprinkle, who was soon to be the only survivor of Reverend Henry Harrison and Annie Elizabeth Sellars Jordan's six children; and her husband, Dr. Henry C. Sprinkle.[31]

On Sunday, March 17, 1974, the Reverend Dr. Howard C. Wilkinson, president of Greensboro College, stood before what was, in all likelihood, the largest gathering ever assembled at the white-framed Saxapahaw Methodist Church, perched on the south bank of the Haw River. It was three o'clock in the afternoon. In the over-flowing congregation come to pay final tribute to B. Everett Jordan, Dr. Wilkinson recognized many public leaders, of both local and national stature. He also saw many faces of persons never to be listed in "Who's Who"—they were the mill workers, friends from the

Everett Jordan with his brothers and brothers-in-law (*left to right*): Frank B. Jordan, Charles E. Jordan, Everett Jordan, Henry W. Jordan, Henry C. Sprinkle, husband of Margaret Jordan Sprinkle, and George K. Way, husband of Lucy Jordan (Taylor) Way. (*Ben E. Jordan, Jr.*)

community—just "ordinary folks." But Dr. Wilkinson spoke simply to the hearts and minds of all present with this parable: "A thermometer," he said, "controls nothing. It merely reflects what is happening. Its function is to react, not to act. A thermostat, on the other hand, *controls* the action. It acts to achieve results. Everett Jordan was a thermostat."[32]

The Reverend Mike Jordan, reminiscing recently about his uncle, said, "One thing that happened following uncle Everett's funeral: we had all gone back to Saxapahaw to the Jordan house, and we were standing in the front hall; and other people—not members of the family—were taking their leave and somebody expressed their sympathy to daddy [the Reverend Frank B. Jordan], and he said, 'It's all right; it's all right.' This impressed me as being assured of what we as Christians believe, and that it *was* O.K."[33]

Jordan, the "bridge builder," was not, by any means, a finished craftsman. He lacked the finesse to build skillfully for admirers of the artistic and aesthetic. But he did finish what he set out to do.

Three generations: B. Everett Jordan, his son John, and his grandson John M., Jr. ("Mac"). This was the last photograph ever taken of Jordan. (Photo by Gregg Bulla)

An examination of his handicraft may have revealed a few bent nails and a smattering of unevenly sawn timbers, but it was solid, structurally sound, and, above all, serviceable. A closer scrutiny would show that he utilized non-union labor—labor that was grateful and exceptionally loyal to the builder who gave them something to do—and to eat—when no one else would or could. Nor did he toil altogether for altruistic goals; he kept some for himself.

Once in a press interview, Katherine Jordan mildly protested that someone had written that her husband was a millionaire. The well-informed interviewer agreed: "No, he isn't." But then said: "He's a multi-millionaire!"[34] In 1969 *Parade* magazine listed Jordan as one of the nation's ten richest senators.[35]

The Reverend H. H. Jordan, unswervingly true to Methodist doctrine, surely exhorted his parishioners to strive toward perfection, a goal beyond the reach of mere mortals. As for B. Everett Jordan, possibly—even probably—the minister would have said:

"Well done, my son."

Notes

Chapter 1

1. Jordan was never called by his first name, Benjamin. He used either "B. E." or "B. Everett" for his official signature, and signed all his personal papers simply as "Everett."
2. Harold Makepeace interview, August 6, 1982.
3. Ibid.
4. Ibid.
5. Personal knowledge of the author.
6. "News Desk" column, Burlington (N.C.) *Daily Times-News*, a clipping dated April 1958 in the Everett Jordan family scrapbooks.
7. A colloquial contraction of "at all" that Jordan frequently used in daily speech.
8. Ralph H. Scott interview, March 13, 1981.
9. Ibid.
10. Jordan and Mary White Scott's maternal grandparents were Benjamin A. and Frusannah Kime Sellars.
11. Ralph H. Scott interview.
12. Ibid.
13. Personal knowledge of the author.
14. Ralph H. Scott interview.
15. A. G. Ivey, *Luther H. Hodges, Practical Idealist* (Minneapolis: T. S. Denison & Co., 1968), pp. 121–22. See also Luther H. Hodges, *Businessman in the Statehouse* (Chapel Hill, N.C.: University of North Carolina Press, 1962).
16. Affirmed by many of those interviewed for this volume.
17. Everett Jordan family scrapbooks.
18. Veteran state Senator Ralph H. Scott.
19. Ralph H. Scott interview.
20. John D. Larkins, Jr., *Politics, Bar, and Bench: A Memoir of U.S. District Judge John Davis Larkins, Jr.,* ed. Donald R. Lennon and Fred D. Ragen (New Bern, N.C.: Owen G. Dunn, 1980), p. 73.
21. Ibid.; and see note 15 above.
22. Larkins, *Politics, Bar, and Bench.*
23. Ibid.
24. Ibid., p. 47.
25. Most North Carolina newspapers carried this announcement.
26. Cartoon by Hugh Haynie, in the *Greensboro* (N.C.) *Daily News,* ca. April 20, 1958.
27. *Greensboro Daily News,* April 22, 1958.

28. Clipping from the *High Point* (N.C.) *Enterprise,* dated April 1958, in the Everett Jordan family scrapbooks.

29. Willie C. Mull interview, July 13, 1987.

30. The following account of this association is based on North Carolina Citizens Association, *We, the People of North Carolina* (March 1982 ed., no. 3), p. 28; and Lloyd E. Griffin interview, August 20, 1982.

31. Griffin was educated at Wake Forest College and Harvard Law School. He saw combat duty in France during World War I as a first lieutenant in the 81st Division. Twice elected to the North Carolina senate, he served his first session in 1933; and later held various influential positions in state government, particularly on the state School Commission. Prior to going to Raleigh, he had practiced law in Edenton. Upon his retirement as executive vice-president of the North Carolina Citizens Association in 1968, Governor Dan K. Moore presented him with the organization's Citation for Distinguished Citizenship.

32. Affirmed by many of those interviewed for this volume.

33. Affirmed by many of those interviewed for this volume.

34. Affirmed by many of those interviewed for this volume, especially Clyde W. Gordon.

35. Clyde W. Gordon interview, February 5, 1981.

36. Ibid.; L. P. Best interview, April 11, 1986.

37. Best interview.

38. Ibid.

39. For his skill in wheedling money out of reluctant donors, see, for example, Clyde W. Gordon interview.

40. Elizabeth ("Lib") Johnston interview, June 23, 1982.

41. Daniel Joshua ("D. J.") Walker interview, November 16, 1987.

42. William ("Bill") C. Friday interview, July 21, 1987.

43. Ibid.

44. Affirmed by most of those interviewed for this volume.

45. Beth G. Crabtree, *North Carolina Governors, 1585–1974* (Raleigh: State Division of Archives and History, 1974), pp. 133–34.

46. Ibid., p. 134.

47. Katherine M. Jordan interview, February 14, 1984.

48. Ibid.

49. Ralph H. Scott interview.

50. Aberdeen (N.C.) *Robbins Record,* January 22, 1970. Blue owned this newspaper. In 1932 he had published his first newspaper in the Sandhills, called *The Captain*; moved to Aberdeen in 1936; and was still publisher and editor of the *Sandhill Citizen* newspaper in 1983, when he was interviewed for this volume.

51. Blue, a veteran newspaperman, served nine consecutive terms in the state General Assembly (1947–64), the last two years as Speaker of the house of representatives. He then ran for the office of lieutenant governor and was defeated by a narrow margin in the second primary by Bob Scott, who had

at first promised to support Blue, but then decided to run for the office himself. Clifton ("Cliff") Blue interview, November 14, 1983.

52. Ibid.
53. Terry Sanford interview, February 1, 1989.
54. Ibid.
55. Ibid.
56. Ibid. Beginning in about 1951–52, Gilmore, Hodges, and Jordan were beginning to become involved in owning and operating Howard Johnson restaurants; the last two men were partners, but Gilmore was independent of the two, even though he and Hodges had been good friends for some time. The trio had frequent interactions with each other on a business level that spilled over into political matters. Personal knowledge of the author.
57. Gilmore's resume at the time of his interview in Pinehurst, N.C., for this volume on September 20, 1989, contained the following information: He was born on October 13, 1918, and was a prominent figure in business and political affairs on both the state and national level. He has served as president of the Travel Council of North Carolina, and as a member of the North Carolina Board of Conservation and Development. In 1961 he was appointed as the first director of the U.S. Travel Service (USTS) (later the U.S. Travel and Tourism Administration) by President Kennedy; and served in this capacity in both the Kennedy and Johnson administrations. He directed the opening of USTS offices in nine major foreign cities to promote international travel to the United States. He was mayor of Southern Pines, N.C. (1953–57), a former state senator (1964–68), and has been a candidate for the U.S. Congress. Currently, he is the president of the American Society of Travel Agents as well as owner and president of Four Seasons Travel Service, Inc., Pinehurst, N.C.
58. Voit Gilmore interview, September 20, 1989.
59. Ibid.
60. Ibid.
61. Ibid.
62. Ibid. Hodges inferred that he did not intend to run for Jordan's Senate seat in the 1960 general election.
63. Ibid.
64. Sanford interview.
65. Raleigh *News and Observer,* November 10, 1957, January 9, 1958.
66. Raleigh *News and Observer,* November 10, 1957, January 9, 1958.
67. Raleigh *News and Observer,* November 10, 1957, January 9, 1958.
68. Telephone discussion with Eagles, January 22, 1990; Gilmore interview.
69. Also of interest is the reaction of Jesse Helms, ultimately the successor of Jordan in the U.S. Senate, to Hodges's appointment of Jordan. Helms sent a letter to Hodges thanking and congratulating him for appointing Jordan. Helms also dispatched a telegram to Jordan "because [Helms] felt it was an excellent appointment, and there were some—like Terry Sanford and some of the Scott people—who criticized the appointment. But I didn't feel that way about it. Everett Jordan served well in the Senate, and he was one of the most popular senators up there." Jesse Helms interview, May 25, 1989.

70. Sanford interview.

71. Hodges and Jordan were owners of a number of Howard Johnson restaurants in North Carolina and Virginia. Personal knowledge of the author.

72. Sanford interview.

73. Ibid.

74. Ibid.

75. The three men represented the top political positions in North Carolina at that time: Hodges as governor and Ervin and Jordan as U.S. senators.

76. Sanford interview, February 1, 1989.

77. Ibid.

78. Ibid.

79. Makepeace first met Everett Jordan in 1952 when Jordan and Hodges were setting up and starting to operate a number of Howard Johnson restaurants. At a later date, Makepeace himself became associated with the two men in their restaurant business. Personal knowledge of the author.

80. Makepeace interview.

81. Ibid.

82. Margaret Jordan Sprinkle interview, June 18, 1982.

83. Affirmed by many of those interviewed for this volume.

84. The following description of Jordan's appearance and personality is based on the personal knowledge of the author as affirmed by many of those interviewed for this volume.

85. Rose Ann Jordan Gant interview, September 7, 1983.

86. Rose Ann Jordan Gant interview, May 26, 1987.

87. Various newspaper clippings in the Everett Jordan family scrapbooks.

88. *Winston-Salem Journal and Sentinel,* December 10, 1972.

89. Cartoon by Bill Saunders, in the *Greensboro Daily News,* July 29, 1959.

Chapter 2

1. Octavia Jordan Perry, *These Jordans Were Here* (Provo, Utah: J. Grant Stevenson, 1969). Authored by a High Point, N.C., resident, this book was reviewed in the *High Point* (N.C.) *Enterprise,* October 5, 1969. It deals at length with the ancestral line of Henry Harrison Jordan, the first son of Milas and Lucy Jordan and the father of B. Everett Jordan.

2. Ibid.

3. Steve Mills, "Laid Back," *Winston-Salem Journal and Sentinel,* June 28, 1987.

4. Ibid.

5. Margaret Jordan Sprinkle interview, June 18, 1982; Mary Jordan Hintz interview, August 4, 1986. Mary Jordan Hintz was Everett Jordan's first cousin.

6. Mary Jordan Hintz, of Charlotte, N.C., a granddaughter of Milas, contends that Milas, not Miles, as claimed by some, is his correct name. Hintz interview.

7. The following genealogy of this family was provided to the author by Mary Jordan Hintz:

Milas Chauncey Jordan, Jr. b. 1-7-1837 d. 9-26-1920	M	Lucy Ann Edwards b. 9-30-1840 d. 12-8-1926	

CHILDREN

Henry Harrison Jordan b. 8-14-1862 d. 5-2-1931	M	Annie Elizabeth Sellars	
Margaret Missourri Ann ("Maggie") b. 1-20-1865 d. 7-10-1901		Never married	
Thomas Chauncey b. 4-2-1868 d. 1-18-1939	M	Henrietta Engle Warfield	
William Alvis b. 7-20-1869 d. 12-1-1931	M	Sue Ellen Heffner (Stokes)	
Robert Alexander b. 4-23-1872 d. 10-24-1921	M	Hasseltine Hicks	
Claude Alvin b. 8-12-1874 d. 5-14-1934	M	Mary Alice Blackwelder	
Watt ("Wattie")		Died at age of 12 or 13	
Mary Esther b. 3-15-1880 d. 3-16-1906		Never married	

8. Hintz interview.
9. Ibid.
10. Ibid.
11. See note 31 below.
12. Milas and Lucy Ann are buried there, along with their daughters Margaret Missourri Ann and Mary Esther, as well as other Jordan relatives.
13. Hintz interview.
14. Ibid.
15. Ibid.
16. Ibid. Everett's uncle Bob Jordan, as well as his wife and daughter, also lived with Milas and his family during his later years. Ibid.
17. Ibid.
18. Ibid.
19. Ibid.
20. Ibid.
21. Esther Mae Jordan Arledge to author, October 22, 1986.
22. Ibid. Thomas Carlyle Jordan is buried in the Jordan-Arledge plot in the Oakdale Cemetery at Hendersonville, N.C. Ibid.
23. Ibid. Reverend Thomas ("Tom") Chauncey Jordan is also buried in the Jordan-Arledge plot in the Oakdale Cemetery at Hendersonville, N.C. Ibid.

24. Hintz interview.
25. Ibid.
26. Ibid.
27. See note 31 below.
28. Photocopy of this list is in the possession of the author. It is not in alphabetical order, and whether H. H. Jordan's listing in fourth place has any significance is not known.
29. *Statesville* (N.C.) *Record and Landmark,* April 4, 25, 1889. See note 31 below.
30. See note 31 below.
31. See *Statesville Record and Landmark,* August 7, 1890. See also undated clipping from that newspaper, of twentieth-century vintage, of an article by Homer Keever in a collection of newspaper clippings belonging to the Everett Jordan family. Keever's article embraces all the clippings from the *Statesville Record and Landmark* that appear in this chapter. Sherrill, at the time he joined the Western North Carolina Conference of the Methodist Church, was a Mooresville merchant in the firm of Sherrill and Neal. On Sherrill's career, see clippings dated December 4, 1890, August 14, 1890, April 2, 1891.
32. *Statesville Record and Landmark,* February 28, 1891. See note 31 above.
33. See note 31 above.
34. Certified copy (May 6, 1931) of H. H. Jordan's will, Superior Court, Alamance County, N.C., dated May 14, 1930, in the possession of the author.
35. Hintz interview.
36. Sprinkle interview.
37. Conference journals of the Methodist Episcopal church on file in the Divinity School library, Duke University.
38. Sprinkle interview.
39. Ibid.
40. Ibid.
41. Ibid.
42. Ibid.
43. Hintz interview.
44. Charles Hill Ross interview, June 28, 1982.
45. Sprinkle interview.
46. Ibid.; Hintz interview.
47. Sam J. Ervin, Jr., interview, March 24, 1981.
48. Sprinkle interview; Mike Jordan interview, July 23, 1986.
49. Ross interview.
50. Ibid.
51. Sprinkle interview.
52. Ibid.
53. Ibid.
54. Ibid.
55. Ibid.

Notes to Chapter 2

56. Ibid.
57. Ibid.
58. Ibid.
59. Ibid.
60. Ibid.
61. Ibid.
62. Ibid.
63. Ibid.
64. Ibid.
65. Ibid.
66. Ervin interview.
67. Ibid.
68. Ross interview.
69. Ibid.
70. Roger Gant, Jr., interview, July 17, 1987.
71. Ross interview.
72. Ibid.
73. Ibid.
74. Margaret Jordan and Henry C. Sprinkle interview, April 26, 1985.
75. Related to the author by various members of the Jordan family, including John.
76. Sprinkle interview, June 18, 1982.
77. D. K. Muse interview, July 13, 1987.
78. Personal knowledge of the author.
79. Margaret Jordan and Henry C. Sprinkle interview, March 24, 1981.
80. Chester Davis, "The Jordan Brothers: Remarkable Quartet," *Winston-Salem Journal and Sentinel*, October 29, 1961.
81. Mike Jordan interview, July 23, 1986.
82. Personal knowledge of the author.
83. Personal knowledge of the author.
84. Records of Duke's Alumni Office.
85. Personal knowledge of the author; Henry H. Jordan II interview, September 11, 1986; Thomas A. Jordan interview, August 25, 1987. As the sons of Dr. Henry Jordan, the two men were the nephews of Everett Jordan.
86. Henry H. Jordan II interview.
87. Ibid.
88. Beth G. Crabtree, *North Carolina Governors, 1585–1974* (Raleigh: State Division of Archives and History, 1974), pp. 130, 131.
89. Affirmed by many of those interviewed for this volume.
90. Personal knowledge of the author.
91. Terry Sanford interview, February 1, 1989.
92. Ibid.
93. William ("Bill") M. Cochrane interview, December 8, 1982.
94. Henry H. Jordan II interview.
95. Ibid.

96. Hintz interview.

Chapter 3

1. Reverend Mike Jordan interview, July 23, 1986. Mike was the nephew of Senator B. Everett Jordan. His father, the Reverend Frank B. Jordan (1905–75), was the senator's youngest brother. According to Mike Jordan, beginning with Reverend H. H. Jordan and continuing with the Reverend Frank Jordan down to Mike, himself, his family had been in the western North Carolina Methodist pulpit continuously for a century.

2. Records in the possession of Dorothy Sellars Brawley, B. Everett Jordan's first cousin.

3. Ibid.
4. Ibid.
5. Ibid.
6. Ibid.
7. Ibid.
8. Ibid.
9. Ibid

10. It is interesting to note that one of Rainey's slaves was called Kizzie, an unusual name. In Alex Haley's book *Roots,* he mentions a slave named Kizzie; and Dorothy Sellars Brawley, for one, wonders if this could be the same slave Haley wrote about.

11. Records in the possession of Dorothy Sellars Brawley.

12. The following genealogy of this family was provided to the author by Dorothy Sellars Brawley:

Thomas Sellars, Jr.	M	Nancy Rainey
b. 1782		b. 6-6-1795
d. 10-23-1865		d. 7-22-1881
	CHILDREN	
William	M	Nancy Swift
b. 10-29-1813		
d. 1-3-1857		
Willis Rainey	M	Mary Ellen Ray
b. 4-6-1815		b. 6-5-1823
d. 7-9-1887		d. 9-6-1888
Benjamin Abel	M	Frusannah Elizabeth Kime
b. 11-16-1816		b. 8-3-1833
d. 2-3-1896		d. 10-29-1922
Thomas	M	Adeline Cummins (1)
b. 7-15-1818		Margaret Ann Faucett (2)
d. 1892		
Mary ("Polly")	M	Rev. Geo. Garrison Walker
b. 1-13-1820		b. 10-10-1816
d. 10-30-1883		d. 3-10-1865

Lemuel	M	Sarah D. Huffman
b. 3-20-1821		b. 1824
d. 6-18-1885		d. 1897
Griffin	M	Phoebe Stanford
b. 8-22-1823		b. 12-19-1830
d. 9-23-1888		d. 9-25-1906
Rebecca Jane	M	James V. Moore
b. 7-23-1827		b. 1828
d. 4-12-1905		d. _____
Elizabeth		Died as a small child
b. 10-6-1825		
d. 12-18-1826		
Logan		Never married
b. 9-6-1830		
d. 4-1-1892		
Nancy Elizabeth	M	Dr. John A. Moore
("Bettie")		b. 2-26-1833
b. 10-27-1832		d. 8-8-1882
d. 5-31-1917		

13. The following genealogy of the Benjamin Abel Sellars family, which also consisted of eleven children, was provided to the author by Dorothy Sellars Brawley:

Benjamin Abel Sellars	M	Frusannah Elizabeth Kime
b. 11-16-1816		b. 8-3-1833
d. 2-3-1896		d. 10-29-1922
	CHILDREN	
Mary Augusta	M	Isaac Newton Walker
b. 5-18-1853		b. 4-23-1852
d. 4-1-1945		d. 11-29-1909
Benjamin Rainey	M	Fannie Cheek
b. 3-28-1855		b. 9-18-1874 (or 75)
d. 6-20-1916		d. 2-4-1956
Thomas Leonidas	M	Lila Graves
b. 1-25-1857		b. 6-20-1871
d. 4-5-1940		d. _____
Eliza Ann	M	William Woods White (1)
b. 7-2-1859		b. 1851
d. 5-22-1937		d. 1887
		James Richard White (2)
		b. 7-2-1856
		d. 4-26-1926
Anne Elizabeth	M	Henry H. Jordan
b. 6-6-1862		b. 8-14-1862
d. 5-6-1937		d. 5-2-1931

David Ernest	M Eleanor Juanita ("Nita") Hall
b. 6-12-1863	b. 1874
d. 9-2-1944	d. 6-21-1963
Charles Victor	M Annie Morrow
b. 7-21-1865	b. 2-13-1870
d. 9-20-1941	d. 10-27-1943
Flora Lucina	M Dr. John Brooks
b. 4-25-1867	b. 1865
d. 9-24-1941	d. 1932
Frederick William	M Louisa Planz
b. 4-13-1870	b. 11-1-1872
d. 8-25-1954	d. 5-30-1960
John Earl	Never married
b. 3-24-1872	
d. 8-25-1940	
Walter Raleigh	M Lila Harden Bailey
b. 11-29-1873	b. 10-6-1879
d. 1954	d. _____

14. Alamance County Historical Museum, Inc., comp., *Alamance County: The Legacy of Its People and Places* (Greensboro, N.C.: Legacy Publications, 1984), p. 387; Dorothy Sellars Brawley interview, July 7, 1987.

15. Brawley interview.

16. Ibid.

17. Ibid.

18. The following account of Annie's college days is based on these letters: Annie to her mother and father, October 12, [1880]; to her mother, November 9, 1880, January 20, February 24, March 17, May 15, 1881, October 4, 1882; to her sister Eliza, October 25, 1881. These letters are in the possession of Reverend Dermont Reid, a retired Methodist minister who resides in Burlington, N.C.; the author of this volume possesses photocopies. The letters reveal that Annie, like many people of her era, was a poor speller—a deficiency shared by her son Everett. For example, in an October 18, 1918, letter to his father, he even signed his own name "Everet," omitting the second "t." This letter is also in the possession of Reverend Reid.

19. Annie to her mother, November 9, 1880.

20. Frusannah was noted for being stingy with string and bath water. Brawley interview.

21. Annie to her mother and father, October 12, [1880].

22. Mike Jordan interview.

23. Ibid.

24. Annie to her mother and father, October 12, [1880].

25. Mike Jordan interview.

26. Greensboro College, *The Magazine* (Spring 1986), p. 130.

27. Brawley interview. On the marriage, see *Statesville* (N.C.) *Record and Landmark*, February 28, 1891.

28. Brawley interview.
29. Ibid.
30. "1871 - Sellars Is Celebrating 115 Years - 1986," Burlington (N.C.) *Times-News,* October 1, 1986.
31. Ibid.
32. Personal knowledge of the author.
33. Brawley interview.
34. Ibid.
35. Reid A. Maynard interview, January 23, 1981.

Chapter 4

1. Katherine M. Jordan interview, January 13, 1981.
2. Ibid.
3. Related to the author by various family members.
4. Personal knowledge of the author. Most of these stories were well received. However, ex-Senator Walter Mondale (1964–77)—campaigning for the presidency in 1984 in North Carolina—when introduced to Senator Jordan's younger son, John, at a political gathering said (perhaps tongue-in-cheek): "Your father told the *worst* stories!" (Related to the author by John M. Jordan.) Perhaps the urbanized Mondale may not have fully appreciated his erstwhile fellow senator's rustic humor. Mondale was vice-president in the years 1977–81.
5. Katherine M. Jordan interview, January 13, 1981.
6. Ibid.
7. Margaret Jordan Sprinkle interview, June 18, 1982.
8. Jessie Wiley Voils interview, July 20, 1982.
9. Wellington, Kans., centennial publication, *Trails to Turnpikes, 1871–1971,* copy in the possession of the author.
10. Ibid., p. 7.
11. Dorothy Sellars Brawley interview, July 7, 1987. Most of Everett Jordan's own glasses came from Woolworth's and similar discount stores, where he fitted himself from their counters. Only late in life did he resort to the luxury of an eye doctor to prescribe his glasses. Related to the author by various family members.
12. Voils interview. Eighty-two years old at the time of the interview, Mrs. Voils had returned to Wellington in 1968 following a long career as a broadcaster and reporter in Manhattan. She authored *Summer on the Salt Fork* (New York: Meredith Press, 1969), an account of pioneer life in the Indian Territory (Oklahoma) in 1879.
13. Voils interview.
14. In New York City, his sister Margaret Sprinkle, who lived close to Jessie Wiley Voils, arranged for the three to have dinner when Jordan was in town. When they were saying good-bye, he asked, "Jessie, how did that place on your arm get?" Voils interview.
15. Rose Ann Jordan Gant interview, September 7, 1983.

16. Related to the author by various family members; affirmed by many of those interviewed for this volume.

17. Sprinkle interview.

18. Documentation for Jordan's World War I service consists of only a few letters in the possession of Reverend Dermont Reid, a retired Methodist minister who resides in Burlington, N.C.; photocopies in the possession of the author of this volume: Jordan, from Hempstead, N.Y., to his father (pastor of Main Street Methodist Church, in Gastonia, N.C.), October 18, 1918; from Germany, to his father (in Monroe, N.C.), June 8, 1919; from Hempstead, N.Y., to his older sister Lucy (Mrs. Oscar Taylor) (in Mt. Grogan, S.C.), October 21, 1918, May 24, 1919; from Zinying, Germany, to his mother (in Monroe, N.C.), June 3, 1919. This paragraph, as well as the following three, is based on these letters.

19. Related to the author by various family members.

20. Related to the author by various family members.

21. Personal knowledge of the author.

22. Everett Jordan, from Germany, to his father, June 8, 1919.

23. Related to the author by various family members.

24. The preferred role for women in that era was confined to that of homemaker. Because the ERA (Equal Rights Act) and the radically changing place of women in the workplace would come only generations later, Sellers probably never seriously considered his only child and daughter, Marie, as his possible successor.

25. Related to the author by various family members.

26. Katherine M. Jordan interview, January 13, 1981.

27. Related to the author by various Jordan family members.

28. Robert L. Williams, *Gaston County: A Pictorial History* (Virginia Beach, Va.: Donning, 1981). In 1904 Gray was also one of the incorporators and the first president of Loray Mill, which became Gastonia's first million-dollar company. In 1929 the company gained notoriety for the labor strike there that was one of the biggest strikes in U.S. history and inflamed capitalist-labor relations.

29. Joseph H. Separk, *Gastonia and Gaston County: Past, Present, Future* (Kingsport, Tenn.: Kingsport Press, 1936), pp. 1, 2, 3, 121, 122.

30. Ibid., pp. 121, 122. Everett Jordan said a moonshine still was found under the Gray Mill, presumably operated by some of the employees to enhance their low wages. Related to the author by Robert B. Robinson.

31. Arthur ("Ott") C. Barrett and Ernest Cagle interview, November 18, 1986. At that time, these two men, who were to pass away in 1990, were retired textile employees, who with their families worked first in the "Gastony" mills and later in Jordan's Saxapahaw plant.

32. Personal knowledge of the author.

33. Katherine M. Jordan interview, January 13, 1981.

34. Ibid.; Sprinkle interview.

35. Colossians 3:20.

36. Related to the author by various family members.

37. Margaret Jordan and Henry C. Sprinkle interview, April 26, 1985.

38. Ibid.

39. Margaret Jordan Sprinkle interview, July 7, 1987.

40. Related to the author by Jordan.
41. Personal knowledge of the author.
42. Personal knowledge of the author.
43. Katherine M. Jordan interview, July 30, 1982.
44. Ibid.
45. Ibid.
46. Ibid.
47. Katherine M. Jordan interview, January 13, 1981.
48. Ibid.
49. Ibid.
50. Eulogy delivered by Susan L. Allred, pastor, Saxapahaw United Methodist Church, August 18, 1987, tape in possession of the author.
51. Katherine M. Jordan interview, January 13, 1981.
52. Related to the author by Jim B. Williams, neighbor and friend of the Jordan family.
53. Related to the author by Jim B. Williams.
54. Affirmed by many of those interviewed for this volume.
55. Related to the author by Joseph M. Neel.
56. Excerpts from memorial, prepared by Ben F. Bulla and adopted by the board of directors of Sellers Manufacturing Company on August 25, 1987, a copy of which is in the company files.
57. Richardson Preyer interview, March 16, 1981. In 1989 Senator Jesse Helms paid a similar tribute to Katherine Jordan: "Mrs. Jordan was just a lovely, lovely lady. She was just the epitome of a lady! She was a class act, and she was loved in Washington, D.C., as well." Jesse Helms interview, May 25, 1989.
58. Edward ("Ed") L. Gruber interview, November 13, 1985.
59. Katherine M. Jordan interview, April 7, 1982.
60. Ibid.
61. Ibid.
62. Related to the author by various Jordan family members.
63. Related to the author by various Sellars family members. Charlie's father was a doctor who founded the B. A. Sellars Department Store, in Burlington, on the corner where the First National Bank of Burlington was located when Reid A. Maynard (see following note) was a boy. Reid A. Maynard interview, January 23, 1981.
64. Ibid. Maynard owned the Grace Hosiery Mill, held interests in other hosiery operations, and was one of Everett Jordan's closest business associates and friends. His mills knitted many pounds of yarn produced by Jordan's spinners. Maynard, Jordan, and Spencer Love (founder of Burlington Industries) were all born in September 1896 within a three-week span. Maynard, who died in 1983, pointed out that Everett and Spencer were good friends.
65. Maynard interview; Paul E. Morrow, Jr., interview, April 11, 1983.
66. Morrow interview.
67. Ibid.
68. Brawley interview.

69. At that time, Charlie was president of the Saxapahaw cotton-mill company and Everett Jordan was the secretary-treasurer and general manager.
70. Brawley interview.
71. Morrow interview.
72. Ibid.
73. Charlie also became a dealer for Essex, Hudson, Buick, and Dodge automobiles. George Clapp managed his garage, which was on Front Street across from old City Hall, now gone. All this time his art store was up on Main Street, and he never called his automotive enterprise a dealership, being content with the designation "C. V. Sellers Art Store" for both photographs and Fords. Sellers also sold refrigerators and had the first Westinghouse dealership in the South. Ibid.
74. Mike Jordan interview, July 23, 1986.
75. Sprinkle interview, June 18, 1982.
76. Ibid.
77. Affirmed by many of those interviewed for this volume.
78. Related to the author by various Sellars and Jordan family members.
79. Affirmed by many of those interviewed for this volume.
80. Katherine M. Jordan interview, January 13, 1981.
81. Related to the author by Jim B. Williams.
82. Related to the author by Jim B. Williams.
83. Related to the author by Jim B. Williams.
84. Related to the author by Jim B. Williams.
85. Related to the author by Jim B. Williams.
86. Jordan, from Germany, to his father, June 8, 1919.
87. David F. Swain interview, February 27, 1988.

Chapter 5

1. "Map of Alamance County, North Carolina," prepared by Spoon, Lewis, and Camp, consulting engineers (Greensboro, N.C.: n.p., 1928).
2. Personal knowledge of the author. Saxapahaw is still, perhaps, the most isolated community in Alamance County. Transportation to "town"—that is, Graham, the county seat, or Burlington, the area's shopping center—was for a long time a chronic concern for many employees and village residents. This was especially true in the early years, but became less of a problem after World War II, when automobiles became more plentiful and the economy improved.
3. Ben F. Bulla, "Saxapahaw among Oldest Settlements in Area," Centennial Edition, Burlington (N.C.) *Daily Times-News,* May 1949; Sallie W. Stockard, *History of Alamance* (Raleigh: Capital Printing Co., 1900; reprinted, Burlington, Alamance County Historical Museum, Inc., 1986), pp. 17, 18, 19, 21.
4. See note 3 above.
5. Ernest P. Dixon, "History of the Quaker Settlement of Cane Creek" (unpublished manuscript, 1932), copy in the possession of the author. Dixon, a

southeastern Alamance County educator, was the leading organizer of Eli Whitney High School and served as its first principal.

6. Ibid.
7. Personal knowledge of the author.
8. Sam J. Ervin, Jr., interview, March 24, 1981.
9. Ben E. Jordan, Jr., interview, June 30, 1988; personal knowledge of the author.
10. Bulla, "Saxapahaw among Oldest Settlements."
11. Ibid.
12. Ibid.
13. Ibid.
14. Ibid.
15. Related to the author by Harvey Newlin, Sr., for use in Bulla, "Saxapahaw among Oldest Settlements." Harvey Newlin, Sr., a distant kin of John Newlin, was a student of local history.
16. Bulla, "Saxapahaw among Oldest Settlements."
17. Ibid.
18. Personal knowledge of the author.
19. Bulla, "Saxapahaw among Oldest Settlements."
20. On December 14, 1872, James Newlin had prepared the following description (carbon copy in possession of the author) for submission to Holt for his consideration in purchasing the property:

Description of Factory & Mill Property of Jno. Newlin & Sons

Frame dam across the river. Has been in about 20 years, has had some repairs. Will soon need considerable. Though it is not expensive as it is a low dam.

The dam across the creek is a good stone dam.

The main building of factory 96 × 42 in the clear with basement half the size of the building, two stories with attic.

Lapper House 2 stories, about 8 ft. from main building with frame passway to card room.

Water wheel built in 1863. Overshot 14 ft., 16 ft. buckets. Does not fill the buckets much over half full to run all the machinery in the mill. The large bevel gear and upright shaft have been running since 1848. The pinion & segments on the Water wheel since 1863.

1 Lapper, 6 cards, & 4 spinning frames, drawing & speeder since 1848.

1 Lapper, 10 cards, drawing, speeders, 6 spinning frames & 20 looms since 1854.

The drawing frames have had new fluted rollers put in about a year since. Card clothing all in fair order, some put on within the last 6 months. The most of the spinning frames have had new spindles, 4 of them since the war ended.

No new rollers except to two of the drawing frames.

4 reels spooler beamer & dresser.

Wool carding machine & cotton gin.

12 cards, 2 drawing frames, 2 speeders, 2 flyer frames.

6 ring traveller frames, 20 looms, 1 lapper built by Roger.

1 lapper, 4 cards, 1 drawing frame & speeder, 2 cap frames built by Danforth.

The other improvements on the Factory Lot,

a 2 story brick store house about 36 x 42 with cellars.

A 2 story brick cotton house.

3 Double tenement house, 1 end log the other frame, 1 ½ stories.

8 Frame tenement houses with brick basements, 1 ½ stories above the basement.

On the mill lot there is the same mill house that you saw when here in '46 or '47, with an addition to one end.

The same sawmill.

The old store house with a frame addition to it.

The grist mill has 2 wheels overshot built in 1866.

2 pr. of burrs, 1 pr. corn stone & 1 pr. feed stones with the usual fixtures for bolting & hoisting.

Nearly all of the shafting in the factory is driven by bevel gears from upright shaft. The main lines & most of the cross shafting in the spinning & carding has run since 1848. The line shaft & all the cross shafting in the weaving room & a part of the cross shafting in spinning room since 1854.

Our frames all set across the building.

The main line shaft lengthwise of the building.

The other shafting across the building & driven by bevel gearing. 2 sections of cards & some jack shafts by bolts from other shafts.

There is on the first floor 20 looms, beamers & dressers which does not occupy much over ¼ of the floor.

The wool carding machines are in this room but if necessary can be run under the lapper room.

The card & spinning room will take in two more spinning frames.

The attick is only used as a lumberroom.

21. Bulla, "Saxapahaw among Oldest Settlements."
22. Tubing is a circular knitted fabric. An example of its use is the cuffs on cotton gloves.
23. Bulla, "Saxapahaw among Oldest Settlements."
24. Ibid.
25. Ibid.
26. Broadus Mitchell and George Sinclair Mitchell, *The Industrial Revolution in the South* (New York: AMS Press, 1930), pp. 1, 2, 4, 6, 9, 10.
27. Ibid.
28. Ibid., pp. 52–53.
29. Ibid.
30. Ibid.

31. Ibid.
32. Ibid.
33. Ibid.
34. Ibid., pp. 54–55.
35. In the possession of John Steele. His father, Robah Steele, was the first person hired by Everett Jordan when he came to Saxapahaw in 1927; and John, himself, worked many years for Jordan. Personal knowledge of the author.
36. Mitchell and Mitchell, *The Industrial Revolution in the South*, p. 117.
37. Ibid.
38. Ibid., pp. 166–67.
39. 55.58 hours in the leading Southern states compared to 51.24 hours in the five leading New England states.
40. Mitchell and Mitchell, *The Industrial Revolution in the South*, pp. 167–68.
41. Ibid., p. 168.
42. Ibid.
43. Charlie Scott, president of the National Bank of Alamance, was the receiver and conducted the sale of the mill property. Personal knowledge of the author.
44. John Steele interview, June 29, 1987.
45. Personal knowledge of the author.

Chapter 6

1. Margaret Jordan Sprinkle interview, June 18, 1982.
2. Housing for mill workers was usually furnished—for a fee—by the owners.
3. This paragraph and the following discussion of the funding and early management of the Sellers Manufacturing Company is based on the minute books and stockholder records, which are in the company files.
4. Section 12 of the bylaws of Sellers Manufacturing Company states: "The President shall preside at all meetings of the stockholders and directors, and shall have a general supervision and oversight of the business of the Company." Section 14 of the bylaws states: "The Secretary and Treasurer shall be General Manager and have active charge and management of the business of the Company."
5. Paul E. Morrow, Jr., interview, April 11, 1983.
6. Ibid.; Dorothy Sellars Brawley interview, July 7, 1987.
7. Affirmed by many of those interviewed for this volume.
8. Affirmed by some of those interviewed for this volume.
9. Archie K. Davis interview, November 8, 1982.
10. Ibid.
11. Ibid.
12. Margaret Jordan Sprinkle and Henry C. Sprinkle interview, March 24, 1981.

13. Eugene A. Gordon interview, April 23, 1981.
14. Roger Gant, Jr., interview, July 17, 1987.
15. Ibid.
16. Ibid.
17. Joseph M. Neel interview, January 23, 1981.
18. Ibid.
19. Ibid.
20. Ibid.
21. Affirmed by some of those interviewed for this volume.
22. Robert A. Hunter interview, March 9, 1981. "Jerden" is a colloquial pronunciation of "Jordan."
23. Neel interview.
24. Hunter interview.
25. Ibid.
26. E. Leon Madden interview, April 15, 1987.
27. Ibid.
28. Affirmed by many of those interviewed for this volume.
29. Neel interview.
30. See, for example, ibid.
31. Affirmed by many of those interviewed for this volume.
32. Personal knowledge of the author.
33. Personal knowledge of the author; Sellers Manufacturing Company files.
34. Personal knowledge of the author; Sellers Manufacturing Company files.
35. Affirmed by many of those interviewed for this volume. See especially John Ray Madden interview, July 21, 1987.
36. Robert B. ("Rack") Robinson interview, June 4, 1982; Hazel A. Robinson interview, February 2, 1986. "Rack" was an outdoorsman and, through his association with the Saxapahaw Boy Scout troop, used his skills to train a large number of youths. His influence is felt by many of the Eagle scouts, anglers, hunters, and nature lovers in the community.
37. Ibid.
38. Arthur ("Ott") C. Barrett and Ernest Cagle interview, November 18, 1986.
39. Robert B. Robinson interview.
40. Ibid.
41. Hazel A. Robinson interview.
42. Robert B. Robinson interview.
43. Ibid.
44. Ibid.
45. Ibid.
46. The National Guard was under the jurisdiction of the governor, and Jordan evidently contacted his office for help.
47. Robert B. Robinson interview.
48. Ibid.
49. See, for example, ibid.

50. Kent W. Miller interview, December 15, 1982.
51. Ibid.
52. Kent W. Miller interview, October 23, 1986.
53. Ibid.
54. Affirmed by many of those interviewed for this volume.
55. Neel interview.
56. Ibid.
57. Robert B. Robinson interview.
58. Personal knowledge of the author.
59. Personal knowledge of the author.
60. Personal knowledge of the author.
61. Personal knowledge of the author.
62. Personal knowledge of the author.
63. Ben E. Jordan, Jr., interview, March 16, 1982.
64. Ibid.
65. Rose Ann Jordan Gant interview, September 7, 1983.
66. Ibid.; Ben E. Jordan, Jr., interview.
67. John M. Jordan interview, April 9, 1982.
68. Clyde W. Gordon interview, February 5, 1981.
69. John M. Jordan interview.
70. Sellers Manufacturing Company files.
71. Time-Life Books, *This Fabulous Century: 1930–1940* (New York, 1969), vol. 4, p. 24.
72. Roger Gant, Jr., interview.
73. Affirmed by some of those interviewed for this volume.
74. Roger Gant, Jr., interview.
75. Margaret Jordan and Henry C. Sprinkle interview, March 24, 1981.
76. Sellers Manufacturing Company files.
77. Sellers Manufacturing Company files.
78. Neel interview. About 1932 Sellers Manufacturing Company could not meet its payroll. Everett Jordan asked Neel if he could buy some stock by calling his father in Thomasville, Ga., ask him to loan Joe $5,000, and wire the money to Sellers Manufacturing Company's bank in Burlington, N.C., which Joe did. Ibid.

Chapter 7

1. Willie C. Mull interview, July 13, 1987.
2. Ibid.
3. Ibid.
4. Ibid. The term "silk-throwing" comes from the Anglo-Saxon word *thraw,* which means to twist or spin. Before raw silk can be woven, it must pass through a series of operations that condition it for the loom. The raw silk fiber as it comes from the filature is too fine to withstand the rigors of weaving. It must, therefore, be made into a thicker and more substantial yarn. This involves a series of operations that are known as "throwing." Editors of Amer-

ican Fabrics Magazine, *Encyclopedia of Textiles,* 2d ed. (Englewood Cliffs, N.J.: Prentice-Hall, Inc., 1972), p. 133.

5. Ibid.
6. Personal knowledge of the author.
7. See chapter 12. These letters are in the Papers of Benjamin Everett Jordan, William R. Perkins Library, Special Collections Department, Duke University.
8. Mull interview.
9. W. Franklin ("Frank") Longcrier, Jr., interview, January 22, 1981.
10. Alton B. Smith interview, June 24, 1987.
11. Mull interview.
12. Roger Gant, Jr., interview, July 17, 1987.
13. Affirmed by many of those interviewed for this volume.
14. Registered trademark for stretch yarn made of nylon and cotton.
15. Mull interview.
16. Ibid.
17. Ibid.
18. Ibid.
19. Ibid.
20. Related to the author by John M. Jordan.
21. Kenneth W. Tisdale interview, February 12, 1981.
22. Ibid.
23. Ibid.
24. Ibid.
25. Ibid.
26. Personal knowledge of the author.
27. Affirmed by many of those interviewed for this volume.
28. Katherine M. Jordan interview, April 7, 1982.
29. Staley P. Gordon interview, January 23, 1981. During this period, Staley worked with Joseph Neel, who stayed on at Sellers Manufacturing Company. Gordon's association with Reid Maynard at the Grace and Tower mills, in many respects, paralleled Joe Neel's tenure with Everett Jordan at Sellers Manufacturing Company because both men became highly placed as well as trusted officials and enjoyed a close friendship with their owner-employers. Ibid.
30. Ibid.
31. Ibid.
32. David F. Swain interview, February 27, 1988.
33. Katherine M. Jordan interview, April 7, 1982.
34. Tisdale interview.
35. Mull interview; affirmed by many of those interviewed for this volume.
36. Ibid. The man Jordan hired was John W. Miller, Sr., a mercerization specialist. Miller moved his family to Saxapahaw in 1937, including his teenage son, J. W. ("Jake") Miller, Jr. Jake, like many others who worked for Everett Jordan, stayed with him his entire working life, becoming one of Jordan's most loyal employees. Jake's father also stayed on Jordan's payroll until retirement.

37. Reid A. Maynard interview, January 23, 1981.
38. Longcrier interview.
39. Ibid.
40. Ibid.
41. Ibid.
42. Ibid.
43. Personal knowledge of the author.
44. Maynard interview.
45. Ibid.
46. Sam A. Rankin interview, January 25, 1983; personal knowledge of the author.
47. Longcrier interview.
48. W. Louis Jackson interview, August 26, 1983.
49. Ibid.
50. Ibid.
51. Affirmed by many of those interviewed for this volume.
52. John M. Jordan interview, April 9, 1982.
53. Affirmed by many of those interviewed for this volume.
54. W. Boman Sanders interview, March 16, 1981.
55. Ibid. An example of Jordan's interest in the welfare of Alamance County is his role in the establishment of Alamance County Hospital in Burlington. In the early forties, during and after World War II, when plans were being made and carried out to organize and construct the hospital, which finally opened in 1951, Jordan served as chairman and continued to serve in that position even after he went to the Senate and until his death. He took the major role, especially in obtaining funds, but Clyde W. Gordon, Reid Maynard, and others played important parts, too. Clyde Gordon interview, February 5, 1981.
56. Rankin interview.
57. David F. Swain interview, February 27, 1988.
58. Mull interview.
59. Rankin interview.
60. Personal knowledge of the author. For a long time, Jordan did not own a Cadillac; the reason for the delay provides much insight into his philosophy of life. Long after he became wealthy and could well afford any make of car he desired, he declined to buy a Cadillac simply because he thought it would appear too ostentatious in the eyes of his employees, neighbors, friends, and customers—many of whom owned a Cadillac years before he purchased his first. Robert A. Hunter interview, March 9, 1981; personal knowledge of the author.
61. See chapter 8.
62. Rankin interview.
63. Ibid.
64. Swain interview.
65. Ibid.
66. Ibid.

67. Ibid.
68. Ibid.
69. William ("Bill") C. Friday interview, July 21, 1987.
70. Shoffner and Jordan got along so well in their business dealings that the latter invited the former to serve on the board of directors at Sellers Manufacturing Company. Shoffner was also a Sellers stockholder. Personal knowledge of the author.
71. Clyde W. Gordon interview, February 5, 1981.
72. Edgar A. Cashwell interview, March 11, 1988.

Chapter 8

1. The account in this chapter of the relationship of Everett Jordan with Ira and Edward Gruber is based on Edward ("Ed") L. Gruber interview, November 13, 1985.
2. One valuable way in which Gruber later applied this education was by persuading his father to abandon their outdated system of "hip-pocket" estimates to determine an average cost and to install a cost system that gave accurate costs for individual styles and constructions.
3. Personal knowledge of the author as affirmed by many of those interviewed for this volume.
4. John M. Jordan interview, April 9, 1982.
5. Ibid.
6. Ibid.
7. Ibid.
8. Ibid.
9. An affiliation of yarn mercerizers whose function was to set and maintain standards for the production and sale of yarns produced under the Durene trademark.
10. Pilling is the tendency of fibers to ball or roll up on the surface of a fabric. Editors of American Fabrics Magazine, *Encyclopedia of Textiles,* 2d ed. (Englewood Cliffs, N.J.: Prentice-Hall, Inc., 1972), p. 572.
11. Introduced by DuPont in the 1960s, it is a synthetic fiber that has the drape, hand, scroop, and luster of silk; is wrinkle resistant; and retains pleat. *Encyclopedia of Textiles,* p. 69.
12. Friend or not of whomever, Gruber had the reputation of being a hard taskmaster. Like Everett Jordan, anyone foolhardy enough to tread on him or take unfair advantage of him was in dire jeopardy. Ben Jordan recalls such an episode while on a trip in 1966 or 1967 to Scottsdale, Ariz., with Gruber and several other textile people. See Ben E. Jordan, Jr., interview, June 30, 1988.

Chapter 9

1. Robert A. Hunter interview, March 9, 1981.
2. Ibid.
3. Ibid.

4. Ibid.
5. Ibid.
6. Alice Davis Abernathy interview, December 8, 1983.
7. Ibid.
8. Charlie Page interview, January 23, 1982.
9. Ibid.
10. Ibid.
11. Ben E. Jordan, Jr., interview, March 16, 1982.
12. Ernest Cagle interview, September 11, 1981.
13. Greef and Mattie Smith interview, October 29, 1981.
14. Ibid.
15. Ibid.
16. Ibid.
17. Related to the author by B. Everett Jordan.
18. Personal knowledge of the author.
19. Personal knowledge of the author.
20. Personal knowledge of the author.
21. Ben E. Jordan, Jr., interview.
22. Ibid.
23. Ibid.
24. Ibid.
25. Ibid.
26. Ibid.
27. Ibid.
28. Joseph M. Neel interview, January 23, 1981; Sellers Manufacturing Company files.
29. Neel interview; Sellers Manufacturing Company files.
30. Neel interview; Sellers Manufacturing Company files.
31. Ben E. Jordan, Jr., interview.
32. Ibid.
33. Ibid.
34. Ibid.
35. Ibid.
36. Alton B. Smith interview, June 24, 1987.
37. Ibid.
38. Ibid.
39. Ibid.
40. Ibid.
41. J. Harold Smith interview, November 13, 1987.
42. Related to the author by Joseph M. Neel, Alton B. Smith, Ben E. Jordan, Jr., and other company officials; personal knowledge of the author.
43. Affirmed by many of those interviewed for this volume.
44. Ben E. Jordan, Jr., interview.
45. Affirmed by many of those interviewed for this volume.
46. Thomas ("Tom") A. Robinson interview, June 23, 1987.

47. Ibid.
48. Affirmed by many of those interviewed for this volume.
49. Affirmed by many of those interviewed for this volume.
50. Liston Pope, *Millhands and Preachers: A Study of Gastonia* (New Haven: Yale University Press, 1942), p. viii.
51. Ibid., pp. 24–25.
52. Robinson interview; Pope, *Millhands and Preachers,* p. 240.
53. Robinson interview; Pope, *Millhands and Preachers,* pp. 211, 212, 241, 242, 248, 250, 252, 254, 257, 293, 294, 304, 305.
54. Pope, *Millhands and Preachers,* same pp. as in preceding note.
55. Thomas A. Robinson, "The Economic, Historical, and Social Importance of Gaston County Textile Mills" (Wake Forest University honors program, 1972), p. 21.
56. According to Pope (*Millhands and Preachers,* pp. 241–42), the demands were as follows:

> 1. Elimination of all piecework, hank or cloth systems, and institution of a standard wage scale.
> 2. A minimum standard weekly wage of $20.
> 3. A forty-hour, five-day week.
> 4. Abolition of all speeding and doubling-up of work.
> 5. Equal pay for equal work for women and youth.
> 6. Decent and sanitary working and housing conditions.
>   (a) Immediate installation of baths [inside the houses] without extra charge to workers.
>   (b) Screening of all homes without extra charge to workers.
>   (c) Repair of toilets in mill.
> 7. Reduction by 50 percent of rent and light charges.
> 8. Recognition of the union.

57. Ibid., p. 257.
58. Ibid., p. 313.
59. Related to the author by Robert B. ("Rack") Robinson and Jim B. Williams.
60. Affirmed by many of those interviewed for this volume.
61. Ervin S. ("Blackie") Frazier interview, June 4, 1987.
62. *Greensboro* (N.C.) *Daily News,* April 28, 1950; Sellers Manufacturing Company files.
63. *Greensboro Daily News,* April 28, 1950.
64. Alton B. Smith interview.
65. Ibid.
66. This letter, a copy of which is in the possession of the author, reads as follows:

> February 22, 1951
> To All Employees of
> Sellers Manufacturing Company:

As you undoubtedly have already heard, the CIO Union is claiming that it represents you and is your agent. We have insisted that the question as to whether this is true or not true be put to a vote or an election by secret ballot.

The Labor Board has ruled that this shall be done. So an election has now been set for Thursday, March 8. If the Union does not back out between now and then, you will on that day have the opportunity of voting by secret ballot as to whether you do or do not want this Union to come in here.

The voting place will be in the Testing Laboratory at the Silk Mill. The hours for the voting will be 11:00 A. M. to 12:30 P. M. and 5:00 P. M. to 6:30 P. M. and 11:30 P. M. to 12:30 A. M. You may vote during your working hours and on Company time without any loss of pay for the time which you thus spend in voting.

The question to be decided in this election is important - important to you and to those who are dependent on you - important to your future here and the future of your family. That is the reason I am writing you this letter in order that you may have before you the facts on both sides as you make up your mind about this matter.

I realize that this may look like a rather long letter. Nevertheless, I will appreciate it if you will take your time and sit down in your home or wherever you find it most convenient and give careful thought to the things which I am going to try to bring out. And after I have said what I have in mind to say, you may be sure that I am not going to keep up any continual nagging on the subject, day after day, as the Union organizers seem to do.

I hope you will understand in the first place that I do not expect you, and I do not ask you, to do any favor for the Company on this matter. You should decide whether to vote for this Union, or against it purely on the basis of *whether or not it will be to your own best interest.* If this Union were to come in here, would it benefit you or harm you? Would it be good for you or bad for you? Those are the only questions for you to decide.

For a good many months now the Union organizers have been in and out around here, talking with some of you, putting out circulars, visiting many of you in your homes, etc. Why has the CIO sent these organizers here? Why are they after you? Your common sense tells you the answer. What they are after is - money - YOUR MONEY. They are here for what they hope to get from you in the form of Union dues. They certainly do not expect this Company to pay those dues. But they do expect to collect from you. They hope to get out of you people who work here approximately $11,500 per year in Union dues.

Wherever this Union is voted in, one of the first things it demands is a "check off." This, as you may know, is an arrangement by which the Union takes a slice out of every member's pay check before he or she ever gets it or even sees it. You should be considering whether you would like that or not. *That is definitely what the Union is after.* What they ask is that you *vote for them* and *then start paying them*!

These organizers live right well and spend a good deal of money. Whose money have they been spending? Yours - they hope. They expect to get back from you all that they have spent and then some. The higher officials of this same Union recently admitted in the newspapers that they had spent six million dollars in the last several years and yet had fewer members than they used to have. All of that money - *six million dollars* - they got from the pockets and pay checks of working people, and they spent it all and wound up with fewer members than they had before! Now they want *you* to start paying them so that they can keep on spending.

And what do these organizers claim they can do for you? What do they say they will get for you that you do not already have? As for wages and earnings - your pay is up with, and in many cases above, the mills that are our competitors in the yarn business. And that is where we intend to keep your earnings here - up with the highest level of our competition in this industry. Just this past year you received two wage increases. No Union got those increases for you and you paid no Union dues for them.

To be sure, the organizers might hold up in front of you some special rate for some certain job off yonder somewhere. Almost any mill has some job that carries a rate higher than jobs with the same names in other mills. But are the jobs the same? Are the duties and work-loads on them the same? And how steady does the job run? There are some mills not so far away that have this Union. Yet the jobs there have not run anything like as regularly and steadily as yours. This mill has never yet been shut down for lack of work. All through the hard years of the Depression we ran while others were closed.

Would you rather work in those other mills with the Union or where you are without a Union? And bear in mind that when the people in those plants get through paying dues to the Union, they don't even take home the money which they have earned.

When it comes to such things as vacations and vacation pay, holidays, Christmas bonuses, and the like - you have all these, without paying any Union dues to obtain them. A pension retirement system is something which this Union is just now planning to start asking for in the unionized plants. Yet you already have a pension and retirement plan and have had it for some time.

As for your working conditions, we are, as you know, continually taking steps to modernize this Plant in every way possible and to provide cleanliness, good lighting and up-to-date machinery and equipment throughout the Mill.

It didn't require any Union to get these things for you! It won't require any Union to keep them for you!

I do not mean to claim that everything is just as perfect as it might be at Sellers. I do believe that things have been improved a lot here and we certainly hope to keep on improving them. And I would like to emphasize that if there is anything that you wish to call to our attention at any time, there is no reason why you should not do so and we will sincerely welcome your doing so.

After all, who do you believe is really more interested in your welfare - we who live and work here with you, or these organizers who come from somewhere else looking for Union dues and who will be here just as long as they think they may be able to get some money from you, and no longer. Do you think you would do better to follow us whom you know, who operate the mill, furnish the jobs and meet the payroll, or the Union agents who are here today and gone tomorrow?

The organizers claim that one thing the Union does is to get all job-loads fixed just right. Now what is the truth about that? The fact is that as a rule *Unions mean not lower work-loads but higher work-loads.* If you will look into the job-loads at any of the mills where this Union represents the employees, you will find that they are practically all higher than the job-loads here - and that in most cases they got that way after the Union went in at those plants! Ask the organizers how they explain that.

The truth is that the Union has no magic power to make things go the way it wants them to go. Of course, it can promise anything but carrying out its promises is an entirely different matter. When the organizers tell you that they are going to come in here and make us do this or that or the other, they are seriously misleading you. If the Union were in here there would still be only one way it could try to force us to do anything that we were not willing to do and that would be by pulling you out on strike. And, without intending to seem abrupt, I do hope you will realize and understand in advance that this Company has no intentions of yielding to any such pressure as that.

I am not saying that if the Union were to come in here, this sort of thing would necessarily happen. I certainly hope that it would not and we would certainly do our utmost to prevent it from occurring. I do know, however, that WHERE UNIONS ARE IS WHERE STRIKES GENERALLY OCCUR. Everybody knows that! And everybody knows that strikes mean trouble and dissension, strife and misery, lost work and lost pay. From time to time you have heard and read of the trouble that has come with the Union at other places—trouble that often winds up in cutting and shooting and bloody violence. A Union often costs people more than just the dues it collects from them!

Right now the employees of the woolen mills in the New England States which do not have this Union are working and drawing their pay, while those who do belong to this Union are out on strike *earning nothing.* And just day before yesterday, the President of *this same*

Union, which is now asking you to follow where it leads, announced in the newspapers to all the Union Locals in North Carolina and the South that March 15 "is the deadline. Prepare to strike on that date"!

The leaders of this Union are men whom you do not know - whom you have never seen and probably never will see - yet they ask you to give them the authority to tell you to lay down your jobs and give up your pay on any day they see fit to name. They are now asking you to vote for them on March 8 so that they can order you to strike on March 15!

What benefit, beyond what you already have, have they got for the people at Royal who voted for them last September? The answer is - not one single thing. Yet the people over at Royal will now be included in the arbitrary and wholesale order to give up their pay and go out on strike on March 15 - for how long and through what hardship and struggle and misery nobody knows.

Now if you have been told that those who join and vote for the Union are going to get some advantages over other employees, I want you to know that this is absolutely untrue. Those who join or belong to the Union are never going to receive any preferred treatment over those who do not belong.

And you can bear this in mind also: - *It is not necessary, and it is not ever going to be necessary, for anybody to join this Union, or any other Union, in order to hold a job at Sellers Manufacturing Company. Anybody who tells you anything contrary to this is not telling you the truth.*

If the Union were to come in here, who would be the people who would run it anyhow? A Union often furnishes an easy opportunity to persons who have a hankering for small-time politics. A few such people usually stir around in the Union, pull strings and get themselves set up as shop-stewards and committeemen so that they can handle everybody's affairs and "lord it" over all their fellow employees. Look around you and see who are the people who are active in pushing this Union. Are they persons who you consider to be capable of handling your problems and into whose hands you are ready to trust your business and your affairs?

I hope that you will realize the importance of taking an active interest in this matter. You may have been told, or you may have the idea, that if you don't want the Union then you should just keep hands off and let those who do want the Union vote for it and bring it in here if they wish. Now that is a very misleading and mistaken idea. For if the Union should come in here, then it would represent those who do not want it as well as those who do want it. To illustrate this:

> There are approximately 450 people who are eligible to vote in this election. But if, for example, only 200 actually go and vote on the election day, then a majority of these 200 who vote, that is

101, would control the entire result. Thus, if these 101 voted in favor of the Union, then the Union would represent not only the 101 and not only the 200 who voted, but the entire 450 employees in the Mill.

So when the election is held, you can see the absolute importance of everybody voting. Don't stand aside on the idea that the outcome won't affect you. It will affect you. Take a hand in the matter. Help make it go the way you want it to go. Otherwise, you may find yourself saddled with a Union that you do not want. *By all means vote in this election.*

The voting arrangements will be simple. You merely go to the voting place and there you will be handed a ballot. Then you go into a private booth which will be provided there and mark an "x" on the ballot - either under "Yes," for the Union, or under "No," against the Union. Then you fold the ballot and drop it in the ballot box. You do not sign your name in any way. Nobody is entitled to know and nobody will know how you vote.

And remember that in this election you will be free to vote entirely according to your own conscience and judgment - your own feelings and convictions—on the election day. *You can vote against the Union even though at some time or other you may have signed a Union card.*

I hope you will think carefully about all the things I have tried to bring out in this letter. As matters now stand you have a good job at high wages, an up-to-date Plant to work in and a good community here to live in. We all hope to make things even better. There is certainly no good reason to bring this outside Union in here, pay dues to it, and at the same time run the risk of tearing apart everything that you now have.

In the light of all these considerations, I believe you will surely come to the conclusion - That *you stand to lose if this Union were to come in here and that you stand to gain by keeping it out*!

> Sincerely yours,
> SELLERS MANUFACTURING COMPANY
>
> B. E. Jordan,
> President
> [actually he was secretary-treasurer]

67. Jesse V. Bone interview, June 17, 1988.
68. Ibid.
69. Ibid.
70. Sam A. Rankin interview, January 25, 1983.
71. Bone interview.
72. *Winston-Salem Journal and Sentinel,* December 10, 1972.

Chapter 10

1. Personal knowledge of the author, who was present.

2. For an example of Dr. Henry Jordan's remarkable capacity to adapt—in a World War I band—see Thomas ("Tom") A. Jordan interview, August 25, 1987. Thomas was the son of Dr. Henry Jordan and thus the nephew of Everett.

3. James P. Hughes, "North Carolina's Man on the Hill," *Carolina Alumni Review* (Chapel Hill, N.C.: University of North Carolina, Spring 1984), p. 26; William M. Cochrane interview, December 8, 1982. Before leaving office in January 1973, Senator Jordan appointed Cochrane as the Democratic staff director of the influential Committee on Rules and Administration, which the senator had chaired since 1963. At the time of the 1982 interview, Cochrane was still serving in that position, and was referred to by Capitol Hill old-timers as North Carolina's "third senator."

4. Cochrane interview.

5. Affirmed by many of those interviewed for this volume.

6. Roy A. and Evelyn Taylor interview, January 6, 1986.

7. Hugh Q. Alexander interview, August 11, 1987.

8. Ibid.

9. Daniel Joshua ("D. J.") Walker interview, November 16, 1987.

10. Affirmed by many of those interviewed for this volume.

11. Affirmed by many of those interviewed for this volume.

12. Katherine M. Jordan interviews, January 13, 1981; January 19, 1981; April 7, 1982; July 30, 1982; December 14, 1982; February 14, 1984.

13. Cochrane interview; personal knowledge of the author.

14. Cochrane interview.

15. Ibid.

16. Ibid.

17. Roy A. and Evelyn Taylor interview.

18. After the Twelfth District was enlarged, it became the Eleventh District that Taylor represented. Personal knowledge of the author.

19. Roy A. and Evelyn Taylor interview.

20. Ibid.

21. Ibid.

22. Woodrow Jones interview, June 28, 1982; Roy A. and Evelyn Taylor interview.

23. Horace D. Godfrey interview, February 7, 1989.

24. Cochrane interview.

25. Ibid.

26. Ibid. Many years later, Sanford would also serve in the U.S. Senate.

27. Cochrane interview, November 14, 1985.

28. Ibid.

29. Ibid.

30. Ibid.

31. Ibid.

32. Ibid.

33. Daniel Joshua ("D. J.") Walker interview, November 16, 1987.

34. Ibid.
35. Ibid.
36. Ibid.
37. Ibid.
38. Affirmed by many of those interviewed for this volume.
39. Walker interview.
40. Ibid.
41. Clyde W. Gordon interview, February 5, 1981.
42. Ibid.
43. Ibid.
44. L. H. Fountain interview, February 8, 1989.
45. Ibid.
46. Ibid.
47. Ibid.
48. Ibid.
49. Ibid. Re Jordan's political philosophy, Congressman Roy Taylor expressed similar views to those of Fountain. Roy A. and Evelyn Taylor interview.
50. Ralph H. Scott interview, March 13, 1981.
51. Ibid.
52. Ibid.
53. Jones interview. At the time of the interview, Jones was district judge of the Western North Carolina District.
54. Column by Charles Osolin, Washington Bureau, *Winston-Salem Journal and Sentinel*, December 10, 1972.
55. Floyd M. Riddick interview, January 8, 1983.
56. Cochrane interview, November 14, 1985.
57. In an interview for this volume, Mrs. Jordan remarked that her husband's overt friendliness—speaking in a familiar manner to total strangers in elevators, on sidewalks, or wherever—gave her some cause for concern because she thought that the public might not understand his outgoing personality and might misinterpret his good intentions. Katherine M. Jordan interview, April 7, 1982.
58. Cochrane interview, January 8, 1983.
59. Ibid.
60. Ibid.
61. Ibid.
62. Ibid.
63. Column by Charles Osolin, Washington Bureau, *Winston-Salem Journal and Sentinel*, December 10, 1972.
64. Cochrane interview, January 31, 1989.
65. Ibid.; Raleigh *News and Observer*, September 19, 1962.
66. Cochrane interview, January 31, 1989. According to him, after Jordan died, Washington columnist Jack Anderson wrote a book in which he referred to Jordan as a "textile baron" from North Carolina who pursued the interests of the textile industry against those of the United States. The irritated Coch-

rane called Anderson's attention to Jordan's key role in the passage of the 1962 Trade Bill. Ibid.

67. Editorial entitled "Commendation," *Greensboro* (N.C.) *Record,* September 22, 1962.
68. Patsy J. Guyer interview, December 8, 1982.
69. Ibid.
70. Ibid.
71. Wesley ("Wes") F. Hayden interview, December 10, 1982.
72. Ibid.
73. Ibid.
74. Rose Ann Jordan Gant interview, September 7, 1983.
75. Ibid.
76. Affirmed by many of those interviewed for this volume.
77. Sam J. Ervin, Jr., interview, March 24, 1981. At the time of this interview, Ervin had retired from the Senate to his hometown of Morganton, N.C. He had earlier gained special prominence on the national scene for his role as chairman of the Senate's Watergate investigation, a long and painful process that resulted in the resignation of President Richard Nixon. Ervin's craggy face, homey personality, and vast legal expertise in interpreting and defending the Constitution were projected on television screens across the nation, making him, in the eyes of many, their hero.
78. Ibid.
79. Ibid.
80. Ibid.
81. Ibid. On the "loaves and fishes," see King James version of the Bible, Matthew 14: 14–20.

Chapter 11

1. Margaret Jordan Sprinkle interview, June 18, 1982.
2. Affirmed by many of those interviewed for this volume.
3. Clyde W. Gordon interview, February 5, 1981.
4. Sam J. Ervin, Jr., interview, March 24, 1981.
5. Affirmed by many of those interviewed for this volume.
6. Senator Jordan's address on the trip presented at the Saxapahaw United Methodist Church; the author was present.
7. The following account of Jordan's relationship with Jackson and the ATMI is based on Robert C. Jackson interview, February 28, 1988. When Jackson retired in 1976, he had served as executive vice-president of the American Textile Manufacturers Institute (ATMI) for twenty-seven years and had spent the last thirty years of his working career continuously in Washington. Earlier, in 1938, he had served as Mississippi field director for the National Cotton Council of America; shortly thereafter, he moved to the Memphis headquarters, where he supervised the five Mississippi Valley states. From 1946 to 1949, he directed the National Cotton Council's Washington office.
8. Horace D. Godfrey interview, February 7, 1989.

Notes to Chapter 11   349

9. The following account of Jordan's relationship with Godfrey is based on ibid. After leaving his position in the federal government, Godfrey was named as one of the one hundred most powerful men in private life in Washington. "Power Elite," *Regardie's* (Washington, D.C., January 1989 edition), p. 81.

10. After his service in the USDA, seeking to broaden his experience, Murphy asked for a different assignment; and Johnson appointed him as chairman of the Civil Aeronautics Board. Later, at Johnson's request, he returned to the White House to manage the staff during Johnson's last year there.

11. D. K. Muse interview, July 13, 1987.

12. Ibid.

13. Ibid.

14. The following account of Jordan's relationship with Kornegay is based on Horace R. Kornegay interview, January 11, 1989.

15. William M. Cochrane interview, January 31, 1989.

16. Affirmed by many of those interviewed for this volume.

17. William ("Bill") C. Friday interview, July 21, 1987. By the time of this interview, Friday had retired as head of the sixteen-member University of North Carolina system and was serving as president of the William R. Kenan Trust and the William Kenan Fund. He also hosted the WUNC-produced television program "North Carolina People," and worked as a volunteer with the North Carolina literacy project and anti-poverty movement. Ibid.

18. Ibid.

19. Ibid.

20. Ibid.

21. Affirmed by many of those interviewed for this volume.

22. Burlington (N.C.) *Daily Times-News,* March 16, 1974. For an illustration of one of these unsung actions, on behalf of North Carolina Memorial Hospital re Hill-Burton funding for the Ambulatory Patient Care Facility, see University of North Carolina, *Carolina Alumni Review* (Chapel Hill, N.C., Spring 1984), p. 28.

23. Kornegay interview.

24. Ibid.

25. Ibid.

26. Eric W. Rodgers interview, February 7, 1989.

27. Ibid.

28. Ibid.

29. Ibid. The largest dam in the system is the one at Kerr Lake near Clarksville, Va., which controls the flow of the Roanoke River; the other dams are below Kerr Lake. Gaston Lake, in the system, has been set aside solely for use by fishermen and sportsmen.

30. It should be noted that Jordan much preferred the mountains of North Carolina, specifically his summer home at Montreat, and was not a frequent beach-goer. However, in 1955, Sellers Manufacturing Company made an investment in some real estate that at one time had been a hotel on Bogue Sound at Morehead City, where the mill man and politician spent some quiet

time with family and friends. This is the "place at the beach" where Rodgers and his wife usually visited with the Jordans. After a few years of relatively limited use, Jordan's company interest in this property was sold. Personal knowledge of the author.

31. Rodgers interview.
32. Ibid.
33. Ibid.
34. Ibid.
35. Ibid.
36. Ibid.
37. Cochrane interview.
38. Affirmed by many of those interviewed for this volume.
39. Affirmed by many of those interviewed for this volume.
40. Personal knowledge of the author.
41. Personal knowledge of the author.

Chapter 12

1. Merle Miller, *Lyndon* (New York: G. P. Putnam's Sons, 1980), pp. 141–54, 155, 156.
2. Personal knowledge of the author.
3. Robert G. Baker, secretary for the Democratic Senate majority.
4. Sam J. Ervin, Jr., interview, March 24, 1981.
5. Floyd M. Riddick interview, January 8, 1983. On Jordan's relations with Johnson, see also Daniel Joshua ("D. J.") Walker interview, November 16, 1987.
6. *Winston-Salem Journal and Sentinel,* December 10, 1972.
7. Miller, *Lyndon*, pp. 53–54, 71–78.
8. Ibid., pp. 35, 67–71.
9. Personal knowledge of the author as affirmed by many of those interviewed for this volume.
10. Rowland Evans and Robert Novak, *Lyndon B. Johnson: The Exercise of Power* (New York: New American Library, 1966), pp. 68-69.
11. Miller, *Lyndon,* pp. 142, 295, 299.
12. Ibid., p. 154.
13. This and the following five paragraphs are based on the personal knowledge of the author as affirmed by many of those interviewed for this volume.
14. Miller, *Lyndon*, p. 295.
15. Ibid.
16. Ibid.
17. Ibid., p. 296.
18. Ibid., p. 299
19. Raleigh *News and Observer,* July 18, 1965.
20. This section is based on the collective interviews that were conducted for this volume.
21. Clyde W. Gordon interview, February 5, 1981.
22. Ibid.

Notes to Chapter 13

23. John M. Jordan interview, April 9, 1982.
24. Ibid.
25. Ibid.
26. Related to the author by Ralph M. Dean.
27. John M. Jordan interview, March 15, 1990.
28. Rose Ann Jordan Gant interview, September 7, 1983.
29. Ibid.
30. Ibid.
31. Ibid.
32. Ibid.
33. Ibid.
34. Jack Paris interview, January 24, 1983.
35. Ibid.
36. Glenn Pickett, Jr., interview, February 6, 1987.
37. Ibid.
38. Ibid.
39. Ibid.
40. Ervin interview.
41. Ibid.
42. Ibid.
43. Ibid.
44. Wesley ("Wes") F. Hayden interview, December 10, 1982.
45. Ibid.
46. Margaret Jordan Sprinkle interview, June 18, 1982.
47. Roger Gant, Jr., interview, July 17, 1987.
48. Ibid.
49. Ibid.
50. William M. Cochrane interview, January 31, 1989.
51. Miller, *Lyndon*, p. 297.
52. Ibid., pp. 298–99.
53. Personal knowledge of the author.
54. Calvin Thielman interview, January 6, 1986.
55. Ibid.
56. Ibid.

Chapter 13

1. Because the Vietnam war is of peripheral interest in this book, only a brief account is provided in this chapter. It is based on Clark Dougan, Stephen Weiss, and the Editors of the Boston Publishing Co., *The Vietnam Experience: Nineteen Sixty-Eight* (Boston: Boston Publishing Co., 1983), passim; Edward Doyle, Samuel Lipsman, and the Editors of the Boston Publishing Co., *The Vietnam Experience: America Takes Over, 1965–67* (Boston, Boston Publishing Co., 1982), passim; Samuel Lipsman, Stephen Weiss, and the Editors of the Boston Publishing Co., *The Vietnam Experience: The False Peace, 1972–74* (Boston: Boston Publishing Co., 1985), passim; Lyndon Baines Johnson, *The*

Vantage Point (New York: Holt, Rinehart, and Winston, 1971), pp. 537–42, 548-52; and Merle Miller, *Lyndon* (New York: G. P. Putnam's Sons, 1980), pp. 494–514, 517–27.

2. A resolution passed in 1964 by the U.S. Congress that was later used by President Lyndon B. Johnson as constitutional authorization for the official entry of U.S. armed forces into the Vietnam conflict. As the war escalated, disagreement rooted in an ongoing rivalry between the president and Congress concerning the source of the authority to wage war resulted in the Senate's finally repealing the resolution in 1970, a move that went unopposed by President Richard Nixon, who claimed he was not relying on the authority of the resolution for his conduct of the war in Vietnam, but upon his power as commander in chief. *The Americana Annual, 1985,* yearbook of the *Encyclopedia Americana* (Grolier Enterprises, Danbury, Ct.), p. 839.

3. Burlington (N.C.) *Daily Times-News,* April 25, 1961.

4. Affirmed by many of those interviewed for this volume.

5. Johnson, *The Vantage Point,* pp. 42–44.

6. Many political analysts contend that the major reason, if not the reason, Johnson did not seek re-election for a second full term was because of his administration's failure to resolve the Vietnam conflict, a problem that plagued him throughout his tenure in the White House.

7. Doyle, Lipsman, and the Editors, *The Vietnam Experience: America Takes Over, 1965–67,* p. 178

8. Affirmed by many of those interviewed for this volume.

9. The following comparison of the personalities and political orientation of Jordan and Ervin is based on the latter's biography by Paul R. Clancy, *Just a Country Lawyer* (Bloomington, Ind.: Indiana University Press, 1974); Sam J. Ervin, Jr., interview, March 24, 1981; and various other interviews conducted for this volume.

10. Clancy, *Country Lawyer,* pp. 234–36.

11. See note 1 above.

12. Ervin interview.

13. William ("Bill") M. Cochrane interview, November 14, 1985; personal knowledge of the author.

14. Cochrane interview; personal knowledge of the author.

15. Senator Jordan news release, June 11, 1970, in the Papers of Benjamin Everett Jordan, William R. Perkins Library, Special Collections Department, Duke University, photocopy in the possession of the author.

16. Raleigh *News and Observer,* June 16, 1970.

17. Ibid.

18. Rose Ann Jordan Gant interview, May 26, 1987.

19. Ibid.

20. William McWhorter Cochrane, "A Third of a Century in Senate Cloakrooms" (Chapel Hill, N.C.; North Caroliniana Society, Inc., 1988), p. 15.

Chapter 14

1. Margaret Jordan and Henry C. Sprinkle interview, March 24, 1981.

Notes to Chapter 14

2. Ibid.
3. Affirmed by many of those interviewed for this volume.
4. *Congressional Record,* 93d Cong., 1st sess., March 22, 1974, vol. 120, pt. 6, p. S 4326.
5. Ibid., 91st Cong., 2d sess., December 19, 1970, vol. 116, no. 205, pp. 42792–42793.
6. Ibid.
7. Ibid.
8. Following is the complete text of the news release, which is on file in the Papers of Benjamin Everett Jordan, William R. Perkins Library, Special Collections Department, Duke University:

WASHINGTON...A total of almost $18.9 million for North Carolina projects—including about $3.7 million in increased allotments specifically requested by Senator B. Everett Jordan—is provided in the Public Works Appropriations Bill for this fiscal year as approved by the Senate Saturday.

The measure earmarks nearly $3.8 million for construction of the Falls of the Neuse project in Wake County and $10.1 million for continued work on the New Hope Dam, with the figure in each case amounting to a $1 million increase over that provided in the House version of the appropriations bill.

The other major boost was in the allotment for the Mills River Dam and Reservoir in the Upper French Broad River Basin.

The Senate version calls for a new appropriation of $1.7 million in addition to the $2.3 million available in budgetary reserve from prior years. The House bill made no provision for that addition.

In each case, the increases were in line with requests which Jordan had presented earlier this year to the Senate Appropriations Committee to bring allotments in line with the Army Corps of Engineers capability for the projects in question.

"I am extremely pleased by the action of the committee and the Senate on this bill," Jordan said after the vote. "I very much hope the House will agree to these additional appropriations in conference so that work on these projects, already too long delayed by past funding cutbacks, can be pushed toward completion as rapidly as possible."

Other North Carolina construction and planning projects included in the bill are:

Howards Mill Lake	$ 92,000
Ocracoke Island	80,000
Randleman Lake	364,000
Reddies River Lake	100,000
Morehead City Harbor	60,000

Funds for the Morehead City Harbor were not included in the House-passed version, but Jordan said he is hopeful that the conferees will agree to retain the $60,000 allocated by the Senate.

The measure also provided funds for numerous general investigations designed to lay the groundwork for additional North Carolina public works projects. These are:

Intercoastal Waterway Bridges (N.C. and Virginia)	$ 15,000
Bogue Banks	20,000
Cape Fear River	56,000
Carolina Beach Inlet	7,000
Eastern N.C. above Cape Lookout	35,000
Hatteras Inlet	10,000
Neuse River	50,000
Roanoke River (South Boston and vicinity, N.C. and Va.)	40,000

These studies are designed to find the best means of improving navigation, and controlling floods and beach erosion, and provide a total of $233,000 for North Carolina.

9. Charles Osolin, "Jordan: I Feel I've Done Something for the People," *Winston-Salem Journal and Sentinel,* December 10, 1972.

10. Ibid.

11. George M. White interview, November 15, 1985.

12. Personal knowledge of the author.

13. White interview.

14. *Tributes to the Honorable B. Everett Jordan of North Carolina in the United States Congress* (Washington, D.C.: U.S. Government Printing Office, 1972).

15. L. Richardson Preyer interview, March 16, 1981.

16. *Goldsboro* (N.C.) *News-Argus,* March 18, 1974.

17. *Goldsboro News-Argus,* October 3, 1959.

18. Open Forum, Burlington (N.C.) *Daily Times-News,* March 21, 1974.

19. Graham (N.C.) *Alamance News,* March 21, 1974.

20. Jordan also ran in the 1958 general election—but not primary—and was elected to serve the two years of Kerr Scott's unexpired term. Personal knowledge of the author.

21. "Achievements in Two Careers," Burlington (N.C.) *Daily Times-News,* February 6, 1961.

22. Sam J. Ervin, Jr., interview, March 24, 1981.

23. Terry Sanford interview, February 1, 1989.

24. Jesse Helms interview, May 25, 1989.

25. Ibid.

26. Ibid.

27. Affirmed by many of those interviewed for this volume.

28. John M. Jordan interview, April 9, 1982.

29. From a reprint in the Everett Jordan family scrapbooks.

30. Certified copy (May 6, 1931) of H. H. Jordan's will, Superior Court, Alamance County, N.C., dated May 14, 1930, in the possession of the author.

31. Margaret Jordan and Henry C. Sprinkle interview, March 24, 1981.
32. Personal knowledge of the author, who was present.
33. Mike Jordan interview, July 23, 1986.
34. Personal knowledge of the author.
35. Jack Anderson, "Memo to the Senate—Open Those 100 Sealed Envelopes," *Parade,* May 11, 1969.

Bibliography

Interviews

All the interviews conducted for this volume, which are listed below alphabetically, have been transcribed and are in the possession of the author. Scholars who are interested in using these transcripts should contact Ben F. Bulla, P.O. Box 35, Saxapahaw, N.C. 27340.

Abernathy, Alice D. Graham, N.C., December 8, 1983.
Alexander, Hugh Q. Kannapolis, N.C., August 11, 1987.
Barrett, Arthur ("Ott") C., and Ernest Cagle. Gastonia, N.C., November 18, 1986.
Best, L. P. Mebane, N.C., April 11, 1986.
Blair, William ("Bill") F. Woodstock, Va., September 3, 1986.
Blue, Clifton ("Cliff"). Aberdeen, N.C., November 14, 1983.
Bone, Jesse V. Fayetteville, N.C., June 17, 1988.
Bradshaw, Nancy L. Washington, D.C., January 8, 1983.
Brawley, Dorothy Sellars. Burlington, N.C., July 7, 1987.
Brown, Anita R. Washington, D.C., January 8, 1983.
Brown, James C. P. and Charlotte. Graham, N.C., March 13, 1981.
Cagle, Ernest. Saxapahaw, N.C., September 11, 1981.
Cannon, Howard W. Washington, D.C., December 9, 1982.
Cashwell, Edgar A. Saxapahaw, N.C., March 11, 1988.
Cochrane, William ("Bill") M. Washington, D.C., December 8, 1982, January 8, 1983, November 14, 1985, January 31, 1989.
Crutchfield, Mabel T. Isle of Palms, S.C., July 1, 1989.
Daley, Mary G. Washington, D.C., January 8, 1983.
Davis, Archie K. Winston-Salem, N.C., November 8, 1982.
Ellington, Thomas R. ("Doc"). Saxapahaw, N.C., October 10, 1983.
Ellis, Viola C. Saxapahaw, N.C., June 7, 1983.
Ervin, Sam J., Jr. Morganton, N.C., March 24, 1981.
Frazier, Ervin S. ("Blackie"). Saxapahaw, N.C., June 4, 1987.
Fountain, L. H. Tarboro, N.C., February 8, 1989.
Friday, William ("Bill") C. Chapel Hill, N.C., July 21, 1987.
Gant, Roger, Jr. Glen Raven, N.C., July 17, 1987.
Gant, Rose Ann Jordan. Saxapahaw, N.C., September 7, November 22, 1983, May 26, 1987.
Gilmore, Voit. Pinehurst, N.C., September 20, 1989.
Godfrey, Horace D. Littleton, N.C., February 7, 1989.
Goley, Willard C. Graham, N.C., April 20, 1983.
Gordon, Clyde W. Burlington, N.C., February 5, 1981, February 5, 1984.

Gordon, Eugene A. Greensboro, N.C., April 23, 1981.
Gordon, Staley P. Burlington, N.C., January 23, 1981.
Griffin, Lloyd E. Edenton, N.C., August 20, 1982.
Gruber, Edward ("Ed") L. Pottstown, Pa., November 13, 1985.
Guyer, Patsy J. Washington, D.C., December 8, 1982.
Hayden, Wesley ("Wes") F. Washington, D.C., December 10, 1982, November 15, 1985.
Helms, Jesse. Raleigh, N.C., May 25, 1989.
Hewlett, Addison. Wilmington, N.C., December 1, 1983.
Hintz, Mary Jordan. Charlotte, N.C., August 4, 1986.
Hodges, Luther H., Jr. Washington, D.C., December 8, 1982.
Hunter, Robert A. Saxapahaw, N.C., March 9, 1981.
Jackson, Robert ("Bob") C. Naples, Fla., February 28, 1988.
Jackson, W. Louis. Saxapahaw, N.C., August 26, 1983.
Jobe, W. Adrian. Saxapahaw, N.C., June 19, 1987.
Johnston, Elizabeth ("Lib"). Black Mountain, N.C., June 23, 1982.
Jones, Walter B. Washington, D.C., January 31, 1989.
Jones, Woodrow. Rutherfordton, N.C., June 28, 1982.
Jordan, Ben E., Jr. Saxapahaw, N.C., March 16, 1982, June 30, 1988.
Jordan, Henry H., II. Winston-Salem, N.C., September 11, 1986.
Jordan, John M. Saxapahaw, N.C., April 9, 1982, August 8, 1988, March 15, 1990.
Jordan, Katherine M. Burlington, N.C., January 13, 19, 1981, April 7, July 30, December 14, 1982, February 14, 1984.
Jordan, Mike. Gibsonville, N.C., July 23, 1986.
Jordan, Thomas ("Tom") A. Liberty, N.C., August 25, 1987.
Kornegay, Horace R. Greensboro, N.C., January 11, 1989.
Larkins, John D., Jr. Hillsborough, N.C., August 7, 1982.
Lingerfelt, Charles. Saxapahaw, N.C., July 15, 1987.
Long, Claude V. Burlington, N.C., December 30, 1982.
Long, George A. Graham, N.C., July 9, 1987.
Longcrier, W. Franklin ("Frank"), Jr. Burlington, N.C., January 22, 1981.
Lupton, Floyd. Washington, D.C., February 1, 1989.
McLean, Margaret Alice. Saxapahaw, N.C., June 1, 1982.
McLean, May. Burlington, N.C., March 18, 1981.
Madden, E. Leon. Saxapahaw, N.C., April 15, 27, 1987.
Madden, John Ray. Saxapahaw, N.C., July 21, 1987.
Makepeace, Harold. Sanford, N.C., August 6, 1982.
Mason, Betty M. Washington, D.C., January 8, 1983.
Maynard, Reid A. Burlington, N.C., January 23, 1981.
Miller, Kent W. Saxapahaw, N.C., December 15, 1982, October 23, 1986.
Moore, Dan K. Raleigh, N.C., February 19, 1982.
Morrow, Paul E., Jr. Graham, N.C., April 11, 1983.
Mull, Willie C. Burlington, N.C., July 13, 1987.
Muse, D. K. Mebane, N.C., July 13 1987.

Nance, Alex. Cedar Falls, N.C., January 25, 1983.
Neal, Doyle. Saxapahaw, N.C., August 1, 1986.
Neel, Joseph ("Joe") M. Burlington, N.C., January 23, 1981, April 13, 30, 1982, November 18, 1983, May 17, 1985.
Page, Charlie. Saxapahaw, N.C., January 23, 1982.
Paris, Duke. Graham, N.C., June 23, 1987.
Paris, Jack. Graham, N.C., January 24, 1983, June 22, 1987.
Parrish, Peggy L. Washington, D.C., January 8, 1983.
Pickett, Glenn, Jr. Graham, N.C., February 6, 1987.
Preyer, L. Richardson. Chapel Hill, N.C., March 16, 1981.
Purvis, John C. Saxapahaw, N.C., June 5, 1987.
Rankin, Sam A. Ramseur, N.C., January 25, 1983.
Riddick, Floyd M. Washington, D.C., January 8, 1983.
Robinson, Hazel A. Graham, N.C., February 2, 1986.
Robinson, Robert B. ("Rack"). Saxapahaw, N.C., June 4, 1982.
Robinson, Thomas ("Tom") A. Saxapahaw, N.C., June 23, 1987.
Rodgers, Eric W. Scotland Neck, N.C., February 7, 1989.
Ross, Charles H. Morganton, N.C., June 28, 1982.
Sanders, W. Boman. Burlington, N.C., March 16, 1981.
Sanford, Terry. Washington, D.C., February 1, 1989.
Saunders, William ("Bill") P. Raeford, N.C., November 14, 1983.
Scott, A. H. ("Jim"). Haw River, N.C., July 16, 1987.
Scott, Ralph H. Burlington, N.C., March 13, 1981; Haw River, N.C., February 10, 1986.
Sloan, James ("Jim"), Jr. Montreat, N.C., January 6, 1986.
Sloan, Mr. and Mrs. James. Gastonia, N.C., February 2, 1986.
Smith, Alton B. Raleigh, N.C., June 24, 1987.
Smith, Greef and Mattie. Saxapahaw, N.C., October 29, 1981.
Smith, J. Harold. Gibsonville, N.C., November 13 1987.
Spears, Rachel W. Washington, D.C., January 8, 1983.
Sprinkle, Margaret Jordan. Mocksville, N.C., June 18, July 28, 1982, July 7, 1987.
Sprinkle, Margaret Jordan and Henry C. Mocksville, N.C., March 24, 1981, April 26, 1985.
Staton, Bill. Sanford, N.C., March 19, 1983.
Steele, John. Saxapahaw, N.C., June 29, 1987.
Swain, David F. Naples, Fla., February 27, 1988.
Taylor, Roy A. and Evelyn. Black Mountain, N.C., January 6, 1986.
Thrift, Margaret. Graham, N.C., June 22, 1987.
Thurmond, J. Strom. Washington, D.C., November 14, 1985.
Thielman, Calvin. Montreat, N.C., January 6, 1986, May 20, 1987.
Tisdale, Kenneth W. Saxapahaw, N.C., February 12, 1981.
Tulloch, James R. Saxapahaw, N.C., June 22, 1987.
Vaughn, Silas ("Si") M. Montreat, N.C., January 6, 1986.
Voils, Jessie Wiley. Wellington, Kans., July 20, 1982.

Walker, Daniel Joshua ("D. J."). Burlington, N.C., November 16, 1987.
White, George M. Washington, D.C., November 15, 1985.
Wilkes, Eddie C. Saxapahaw, N.C., July 1, 1987.
Williams, Connie Baber. Saxapahaw, N.C., January 30, 1981.
Williams, Jim B. Saxapahaw, N.C., November 2, 1981.
Williams, Jim B. and Ann G. Saxapahaw, N.C., January 15, 1981.

Archival and Manuscript Collections

PAPERS OF BENJAMIN EVERETT JORDAN. *William R. Perkins Library, Special Collections Department, Duke University, Durham, N.C. 27706.*

In 1973, the year before he died, Senator B. Everett Jordan donated his papers to his alma mater, Duke University. They were finally processed in 1988, partially supported by a gift from his family; and a complete inventory was prepared the following year. The collection now occupies 110 linear feet of shelf space, and consists of approximately 104,000 items.

The papers span the years 1936 to 1974, but the bulk of them cover Jordan's years of senatorial service (1958–72). The few pre-1958 items in the collection include background information on several topics and a few files of Jordan's predecessor, Senator W. Kerr Scott.

The collection consists strictly of files from the senator's Washington office; there are no personal or business papers or materials documenting his political campaigns, the activities of his Senate offices in North Carolina, or political activities prior to 1958. For all these reasons, the collection reveals little about his personal life and thoughts and is of only limited value for a biography, though it was researched for this volume.

The papers are made up largely of correspondence, especially with constituents; memoranda; legislative documents; writings as well as speeches; and background materials. The legislative files contain a nearly complete record of bills that the senator sponsored or co-sponsored or on which he participated in debates.

Files documenting topics of greatest concern to Jordan—the state of North Carolina, the South, agriculture, public works including water projects (particularly the New Hope Dam and Reservoir Project in the Cape Fear River Basin, which in 1973 was renamed Jordan Lake in honor of the senator), and foreign relations (especially the Vietnam war and Southeast Asia during the late 1960s and early 1970s)—have been retained virtually intact.

The newspaper and magazine clippings that were retained were photocopied to preserve a chronological outline of Jordan's Senate career, including his electoral campaigns of 1960, 1966, and 1972, which are not documented elsewhere in the collection.

The correspondence throughout the collection includes scattered letters from many prominent North Carolina and national politicians as well as agricultural and business leaders, but these have not been indexed. The Jordan Papers are complemented by those of Senator Sam J. Ervin, Jr., which are located in the Wilson Library, Manuscript Department, University of North Carolina, Chapel Hill. Because Ervin's years of service in the Senate from 1954 to 1974 closely paralleled those of Jordan, the two collections together extensively document on a national and regional level a large number of the political, economic, and social concerns of the era.

SELLERS MANUFACTURING COMPANY, INC., FILES.
Saxapahaw, N.C. 27340

The corporate records of Sellers Manufacturing Company, which were used extensively by the author of this volume, provide much information on Jordan's role as a prime organizer as well as the head of several closely held textile companies and reveal much about the nature of the textile industry. Particularly useful are the minute books of the meetings of the board of directors and stockholders. The files, which date back to the inception of the Sellers Manufacturing Company, the parent company of those that followed, cover the years from 1927 to Jordan's death in 1974 as well as later ones.

The Sellers Manufacturing Company files are not open to the public, but specific scholarship requests for access would be considered. Address: President Ben E. Jordan, Jr., at the above address.

PRIVATE COLLECTION OF CERTAIN SELLARS AND JORDAN FAMILY LETTERS.
Held by Reverend J. Dermont Reid, 603 E. Davis Street, Burlington, N.C. 27215. Photocopies of the letters in this collection are in the possession of the author of this volume.

These letters, which are listed below, shed considerable light on B. Everett Jordan's personality and also those of his parents and maternal grandparents, especially his mother, Annie Sellars Jordan:

I. Annie Sellars's (Jordan) College Letters to Her Family
   October 12, 1880, to her mother and father, Dr. and Mrs. B. A. Sellars.
   November 9, 1880, to her mother, Frusannah Kime Sellars.
   January 20, 1881, to her mother.
   February 24, 1881, to her mother.
   March 17, 1881, to her mother.
   May 15, 1881, to her mother.
   October 25, 1881, to her sister Eliza Sellars.
   October 4, 1882, to her mother.
II. B. Everett Jordan's World War I Letters
   October 18, 1918, to his father, Reverend H. H. Jordan.
   October 21, 1918, to his sister Lucy Jordan Taylor.
   May 24, 1919, to his sister Lucy Jordan Taylor.
   June 3, 1919, to his mother, Annie Sellars Jordan (Mrs. H. H.).
   June 8, 1919, to his father.

III. Other Sellers and Jordan Family Letters
  September 16, 1909, Reverend H. H. Jordan to James McGuire.
  January 29, 1916, Frusannah Sellars to her daughter Annie Sellars (Jordan).
  July 28, 1917, Frank Jordan to his sister Lucy Jordan.
  May 28, 1918, Reverend H. H. Jordan to his daughter Lucy Jordan.
  July 30, 1919, Annie Sellars Jordan to her daughter Lucy Jordan Taylor.

Books and Articles

Alamance County Historical Museum, Inc., comp. *Alamance County: The Legacy of Its People and Places.* Greensboro, N.C.: Legacy Publications, 1984.

Clancy, Paul R. *Just a Country Lawyer.* Bloomington, Ind.: Indiana University Press, 1974.

Crabtree, Beth G. *North Carolina Governors, 1585–1974.* Raleigh: State Division of Archives and History, 1974.

Dixon, Ernest P. "History of the Quaker Settlement of Cane Creek." Unpublished manuscript, 1932. Copy in the possession of the author of this volume.

Dougan, Clark, Stephen Weiss, and the Editors of the Boston Publishing Co. *The Vietnam Experience: Nineteen Sixty-Eight.* Boston: Boston Publishing Co., 1983.

Doyle, Edward, Samuel Lipsman, and the Editors of the Boston Publishing Co. *The Vietnam Experience: America Takes Over, 1965–67.* Boston: Boston Publishing Co., 1982.

Editors of American Fabrics Magazine. *Encyclopedia of Textiles.* 2d ed. Englewood Cliffs, N.J.: Prentice-Hall, Inc., 1972.

Evans, Rowland, and Robert Novak. *Lyndon B. Johnson: The Exercise of Power.* New York: New American Library, 1966.

Hodges, Luther H. *Businessman in the Statehouse.* Chapel Hill, N.C.: University of North Carolina Press, 1962.

Ivey, A. G. *Luther H. Hodges, Practical Idealist.* Minneapolis: T. S. Denison & Co., 1968.

Johnson, Lyndon Baines. *The Vantage Point.* New York: Holt, Rinehart, and Winston, 1971.

Larkins, John D., Jr. *Politics, Bar, and Bench: A Memoir of U.S. District Judge John Davis Larkins, Jr.* Edited by Donald R. Lennon and Fred D. Ragen. New Bern, N.C.: Owen G. Dunn, 1980.

Lipsman, Samuel, Stephen Weiss, and the Editors of the Boston Publishing Co. *The Vietnam Experience: The False Peace, 1972–74.* Boston: Boston Publishing Co., 1985.

Miller, Merle. *Lyndon.* New York: G. P. Putnam's Sons, 1980.

Mitchell, Broadus, and George Sinclair Mitchell. *The Industrial Revolution in the South.* New York: AMS Press, 1930.

Perry, Octavia Jordan. *These Jordans Were Here.* Provo, Utah: J. Grant Stevenson, 1969.
Pope, Liston. *Millhands and Preachers: A Study of Gastonia.* New Haven: Yale University Press, 1942.
Robinson, Thomas A. "The Economic, Historical, and Social Importance of Gaston County Textile Mills." Wake Forest University honors program, 1972.
Separk, Joseph H. *Gastonia and Gaston County: Past, Present, Future.* Kingsport Tenn.: Kingsport Press, 1936.
Stockard, Sallie W. *History of Alamance.* Raleigh: Capital Prtg. Co., 1900; reprinted, Burlington: Alamance County Historical Museum, Inc., 1986.
Time-Life Books. *This Fabulous Century: 1930–1940.* Vol. 4. in series published by decades. New York, 1969.
Tributes to the Honorable B. Everett Jordan of North Carolina in the United States Congress. Washington, D.C.: U.S. Government Printing Office, 1972.
Williams, Robert L. *Gaston County: A Pictorial History.* Virginia Beach, Va.: Donning, 1981.

Newspapers (North Carolina)

Aberdeen: *Robbins Record.*
Burlington: *Daily Times-News* and *Times-News.*
Goldsboro: *Goldsboro News-Argus.*
Graham: *The Alamance News.*
Greensboro: *Greensboro Daily News* and *Greensboro Record.*
High Point: *High Point Enterprise.*
Raleigh: *News and Observer.*
Statesville: *Statesville Record and Landmark.*
Winston-Salem: *Winston-Salem Journal and Sentinel.*

Index

AAA, 243
Aberdeen, N.C., 318
Abernathy, Alice Davis, 182, 184
Abilene, Kans., 83
Adams, Chuck, 93, 94
Adderholt, O. F., 200
A.E.F., 87
Afghanistan, 285
Africa, 13
Agricultural Adjustment Administration (AAA), 243
Agricultural Stabilization and Conservation Service (ASCS), 243
Air pollution. *See* Environmental protection
Alabama, 122
Alamance (N.C.), Battle of, 70
Alamance (village), N.C., 116, 149, 151, 164
Alamance County, N.C.: and B. Everett Jordan, 16, 133, 157, 160, 266, 294, 337; and Orange County, 69, 77, 118; and Scott, 5; bodies of water in, 137; Boy Scouts in, 17, 187–88, 189, 334; business and civic leaders in, 16, 79, 102, 157, 226–27; commissioners of, 17, 190, 276; county seat of, 77, 111, 330; Democratic party in, 16; explored and emigration to, 111, 112; farms and farming in, 5, 6, 15, 70; founded and settled, 70, 71, 111, 112; hospitals in, 4, 190, 276, 337; industry in, 15, 106, 112, 113, 147, 226–27 (*and see* Sellers Manufacturing Co., Inc.); isolated sections of, 107, 330; land in, 70, 71, 111; landmark in, 78; politics, politicians, and elections in, 16, 18, 22, 59, 186, 225, 247, 276;

residents of, 70, 71; roads in, 111, 113–14; Rotary Club in, 266; rural nature of, 107; sheriffs of, 17; stores in, 78; U.S. congressional representative of, 252; vegetation and trees in, 111, 167, 171, 177, 179–80. *See also specific cities and topics*
Alamance (N.C.) County Hospital, 190, 337
Alamance (N.C.) District (Boy Scouts), 188
Alamance (N.C.) General Hospital, 4
Alamance (N.C.) Hotel, 16
Alamance (N.C.) Memorial Hospital, 276
Alaska, 219–20, 230
Albemarle Sound, 254
Albert, Carl, 229, 300
Alcohol and alcohol consumption, 31, 57, 58, 61, 74, 81–82, 134, 139–40, 267. *See also* Bootlegging; Temperance movement
Alexander, Hugh, 212–13
Allen, Hugh, 178
Altamahaw, N.C., 113
American Cotton Manufacturers Association, 238
American Expeditionary Force (A.E.F.), 87
American Society of Travel Agents, 319
American Textile Manufacturers Institute (ATMI), 238–39, 240–41, 348
American University, 59, 252
Amity and Amity Hill (N.C.), 44
Anderson, Jack, 230, 347, 348
Andrews, D. V. ("Bunn"), 192
Andrews, N.C., 43
Architects and architecture, 303

Index

Arizona, 176, 338
Arkansas, 145
Arledge, Esther Mae Jordan (cousin of B. Everett Jordan), 43
ASCS, 243
Asheville, N.C., 3, 14, 43, 46, 48
Asia, 286, 278, 288, 289, 293
Association of Cotton Textile Merchants, 238
Athletes and athletics, 53, 61, 102, 121, 136, 154, 176, 235, 272
ATMI, 238–39, 240–41, 348
Attorneys. See Courts, lawyers, and legal-judicial system
Aultman, Wilson, 143
Australia, 288
Automobiles, 5, 89, 99, 105–6, 107, 111, 113, 123, 141, 144, 161, 188, 203, 204, 255, 330, 337
Aycock, Frances, 298

Baber, Connie. See Williams, Connie Baber
Baber, J. R. ("Dad"), 108, 109, 178
Bailey, Lila Harden. See Sellars, Mrs. Walter Raleigh
Bailey, Pat, 308
Baker (Robert G. "Bobby") case, 150, 261, 264–66, 267–69, 270, 278–84, 291, 307
Banks and banking, 13, 14, 124, 130, 147, 176, 198, 225, 228, 329, 333, 335. See also Savings and loan associations
Baptists and Baptist church, 37, 39–40, 42, 47–48, 56, 112, 143, 268
Barclay, Don, 292
Barnwell, James A., 190
Barrett, Aretta, 184
Barrett, Arthur ("Ott"), 139, 328
Barringer, Lou, 245
Battle of Alamance (N.C.), 70
Beal, Fred T., 200
Belk, Thomas M., 14
Bellewood farm (Pa.), 171
Belmont, N.C., 14, 63, 132, 140

Berks County, Pa., 167
Berlin Wall, 284
Best, L. P., 16–17
Bethel Church, 116
Bibles, 44, 70, 89, 90, 91, 98, 290. See also Christians and Christianity
Bingham, Harvey, 44
Bingham and Caldwell (firm), 45
Black, J. T., 128
Black Mountain (city), N.C., 145, 212
Black people, 39, 45, 76, 134, 135, 141–42, 177–78, 181, 183. See also Civil rights movement; Minorities; Slaves and slavery
Blackwelder, Mary Alice ("Mayce"). See Jordan, Mrs. Claude Alvin
Bliss Fabyan Co., 163
Bloxsom, William H., Sr., 178
Blue, Clifton ("Cliff"), 17, 22, 318–19
Boarding houses, 118
Bogue Banks, 354
Bogue Sound, 349
Bone, Jesse, 205–7
Bonner family, 217
Booth, John Wilkes, 77
Bootlegging, 58, 90, 91, 328. See also Alcohol and alcohol consumption
Boston, Mass., 161
Boy Scouts, 17, 187–88, 189, 316, 334
Bracey, James, 128
Bradshaw, Nancy, 217
Brawley, Dorothy Sellars (cousin of B. Everett Jordan), 78, 83, 104, 324, 325
"Bridge Builder" (The) (poem), 312
Bridges, 113–14, 115, 138, 141, 179, 193, 211, 313, 314
Brooklyn, N.Y., 197
Brooks, John H., 127, 128, 326
Brooks, Mrs. John (Flora Lucina Sellars), 73, 75, 326

Broughton, Joseph Melville, 4, 18, 30, 256
Broughton Hospital, 55
Brown, Anita, 217
Brown Mountain, 48
Buchanan, Anne, 217
Budget: of N.C., 13, 25; of U.S., 13, 217
Bulla, Ben F., 298
Burke, Mrs. W. R., 128
Burke County, N.C., 40
Burlington (Company Shops), N.C.: and B. Everett Jordan, 16, 150; and Rose Ann Jordan, 103; and Saxapahaw, 167; attorneys in, 18, 221; autos in, 105; banks in, 329, 335; business and industry in, 16, 55, 78, 90, 102–7, 154, 157, 164, 192, 276, 329, 330; City Hall of, 330; community in, 70, 71; hospitals in, 4, 190, 276, 337; marriage at, 46, 76; mayor of, 16; named, 76; newspaper in, 4, 160, 286; prominent individuals in, 16, 48, 79, 102, 136, 157, 160, 164, 197, 221; railroad in, 209, 212; residents of, 76, 129, 273, 326; Rotary Club in, 16, 129; schools in, 71; streets in, 71, 77, 78, 105, 106, 330
Burlington (N.C.) *Daily Times-News*, 4, 160, 286
Burlington Industries, 90, 329
Burlington Mills, 90
Bush, Suzanne Rodgers, 254, 256
Business and businessmen. *See* Commerce, trade, and industry
Byrd, Robert, 294

Cabarrus County, N.C., 45
Cagle, Ernest, 185, 186, 328
Caldwell County, N.C., 40, 46
California, 28, 43, 176
Calvert-Woodley Apartments, 216, 217
Cambodia, 294

Campbell College, 187
Camp Cherokee (N.C.), 188
Canada, 171, 288–89
Cane Creek, 112, 116
Cannon, Clarence, 229–30
Cannon Mills, 172
Cape Fear River, 252, 300, 354
Cape Fear River Basin, 259
Cape Lookout National Seashore Park, N.C., 300, 354
Capitol, U.S., 235, 240, 288, 301, 302, 303, 305
Capitol Hill (D.C.), 213, 228, 241, 247, 261, 265, 297, 304, 308
Captain (The) (newspaper), 318
Carolina Beach Inlet, 354
Carolina Inn, 251
Carr, Leo, 16
Cars. *See* Automobiles
Carter, Margaret. *See* Jordan, Mrs. John M.
Cartoons, political, 9–10, 11, 12, 34–35, 283
Cashwell, Edgar, 165
Castro, Fidel, 287
Caswell County, N.C., 188
Catawba County, N.C., 45
Cates, Clarabel L., 178
Cates, Glenn H., 178
Cattle. *See* Farms and farming; Planters and plantations
Cedar Falls (village), N.C., 54, 63, 65, 153, 159, 182, 191, 195
Census reports, 37
Century Hosiery Corp., 151, 165
Century Hosiery Mill, 151
Chapel Hill, N.C., 20, 24, 210, 211, 250
Charleston, S.C., 70
Charlotte, N.C., 14, 131, 151, 161, 238, 239
Chatham County, N.C., 111, 252, 258, 302
Chattanooga, Tenn., 131, 156, 161, 183

Cheek, Elwood, 119
Cheek, Fannie. *See* Sellars, Mrs. Benjamin Rainey
Cheek, James, 119
Cheek, Mattie, 119
Cherokee Council (Boy Scouts), 188
Cherokee Scout Reservation (N.C.), 188
Cherry, R. Gregg, 18, 29, 63, 254
Chicago, Ill., 23, 83, 161, 163, 256
Child labor, 121, 122, 340
China and Chinese, 246, 285
Chisholm Trail, 83
Christians and Christianity, 112, 113, 121, 143, 227, 275, 315. *See also* Religion; *specific churches, denominations, and sects*
Churches. *See* Christians and Christianity
CIO, 203, 204
Civil Aeronautics Board, 349
Civil rights movement, 220, 222, 284. *See also* Black people
Civil Service, 229
Civil War, 38, 39, 44, 77, 116, 117, 120
Clapp, George, 330
Clark, Sam N., 14
Clarksville, Va., 349
Clements, Earl, 248
Clemson, S.C., 238
Clemson University, 238
Cline family, 136
Cline, Carl, 161
Cline (J. A.) and Son (firm), 161
Clover, S.C., 159
Cluett, Peabody, and Co., Inc., 175, 177
Coal industry, 223
Coates, Albert, 211
Coble, J. M., 128
Cochrane, William ("Bill") M.: and Anderson, 230, 347–48; and Baker case, 280–81; and Ervin, 299; and William Friday, 211, 251; and Hayden, 233; and B. Everett Jordan, 26, 27, 28, 209–16, 219–21, 225, 228–30, 250, 251, 259, 280–81, 299, 346; and Henry Jordan, 64–65; and 1960 national Democratic convention, 28; and N.C., 346; and Sanford, 28; and Vietnam war, 293; career of, 209–11; photos of, 27, 215, 217; present assignment of, 346; wins award, 27
Coddle Creek Township, N.C., 45–46
Colleges and universities. *See* Educators and educational system
Collins, Robert ("Rob"), 9
Collins, Rufus ("Buddy"), 298
Collins Community Center, 211
Collins (Buddy) Memorial Bridge, 211
Colonial period, 69
Colored people. *See* Black people
Commerce, trade, and industry, 5, 10–26 passim, 31, 40, 46, 53, 55, 65, 77–78, 79, 81–86 passim, 95, 101, 107, 108, 109, 111, 113, 114, 120, 121, 132, 141, 147, 168, 173–74, 175, 176, 179, 186, 204, 227, 230, 231, 239, 241, 249, 252, 263, 268, 276, 293, 297, 319, 322, 327, 329, 330, 338. *See also* Banks and banking; Depressions; Economy and economic trends; Recessions; Savings and loan associations; Textile industry; *particular businesses, businessmen, industries, and industrialists*
Commodity Credit Corp., 243
Communists and communism, 200, 201, 285, 286–87
Company Shops, N.C. *See* Burlington, N.C.
Company stores, 108, 109, 113, 114, 121, 141, 179, 204

Index 369

Confederates and Confederacy, 13, 39, 117, 206
Congregationalists and Congregational church, 82, 84
Congress, U.S. *See* United States Congress
Congressional Quarterly, 291
Congressional Record, 299
Congress of Industrial Organizations (CIO), 203, 204
Conn, Lewis M., 203
Conservation of natural resources. *See* Environmental protection
Cooley family, 217
Cooley, Harold, 224, 242, 252
Cooper-Church amendment, 293, 295
Cornwell, C. C., 128
Cotton. *See* Farms and farming; Planters and plantations; Textile industry
Cotton Council, 245
Cotton Textile Institute, 238
Council, Bill, 168
Courts, lawyers, and legal-judicial system, 7, 8, 25, 37, 39, 44, 45–46, 50, 58, 106, 121, 131, 140, 146, 149, 151, 199, 200, 212, 227, 228, 236, 238, 246, 248, 268, 275, 293, 309, 318, 348. *See also particular judges and lawyers*
Cowan, J. C., Jr., 14
Crime, criminals, law enforcement, and penal system, 17, 37, 39, 40, 70, 156, 199, 200, 233, 265, 268
Crisson, Grover, 178
Crockett, Gib, 283
Crops. *See* Farms and farming; Planters and plantations
Crutchfield, Jim, 178
Crutchfield, Molly, 119
Crutchfield, R. C., 178
Crutchfield, Van Doran, 298
Crutchfield, "Vonie" Johnson, 119
Cuba and Cuban missile crisis, 283, 285, 286–87, 288

Culbreath, Homer, 93
Cummins, Adeline. *See* Sellars, Mrs. Thomas, III
Curtiss, Carl, 278

Dallas, N.C., 140
Dallas, Tex., 287
Dams, 114, 115, 136–37, 148, 182, 252, 254, 258–59, 300, 301–2, 303, 349. *See also* Floods and flood control
Dancing, 53
Danville, Va., 254
Davidson College, 43
Davis, Alson T. ("A. T."), 124, 133, 134, 156, 178, 181, 182–83, 184
Davis, Archie K., 130, 176
Davis, Chester, 62, 63
Davis, Ken, 188
Dean, Ralph, 272
Deep River, 191, 252
Delaware, 268, 278
Democrats and Democratic party: and Baker case, 265; and Hodges, 3–35 passim; and Larkins, 7–8; and Rodgers, 256; and Vietnam war, 286; conservatives among, 286, 289, 293; in N.C., activities and officials of, 5–35 passim, 45, 63, 64, 66, 195, 221, 222–23, 224, 227, 233, 244, 247–48, 251, 256, 266, 268, 270, 276, 281, 309, 311, 327; on national level, 262, 265, 266, 268, 278, 286, 300, 306, 327, 346; national conventions of, 8, 23, 24, 256, 278; presidential races of, 65, 66; Young Democrats branch of, 23, 247. *See also* Elections and voting; *specific Democrats*
Departments of U.S. government. *See under* United States
Depository Libraries, U.S., 301
Depressions, economic, 114, 125, 136–37, 147, 162, 168, 198, 262,

270. *See also* Economy and economic trends
Dickson, R. S., 14
Dirksen, Everett M., 300
Disease. *See* Sickness, disease, and medical care
Disney, Walt, 292
District of Columbia (D.C.). *See* Washington, D.C.
Dixie Mercerizing Co., 165
Dixie Yarns, Inc., 134, 151, 211
Dixon, Ernest P., 330–31
Doctors. *See* Sickness, disease, and medical care; *specific doctors*
Dodson, Leona, 119
Dodson, Sallie, 119
"Domino Theory," 288
Doughton, Robert L., 13
Douglas, Jim, 9
Drinking. *See* Alcohol and alcohol consumption
Dromgoole, Will Allen, 312
Duke of Windsor, 43
Duke University (Trinity College): and B. Everett Jordan and his family, 50, 55, 59, 61–62, 74, 82, 136, 168, 250, 252; and Charles Jordan, 55, 61, 63; and Frank Jordan, 55; and H. H. Jordan, 54, 55; and Margaret Jordan, 55; and Murphy, 246; and Sanford, 22; athletics at, 61; divinity school of, 54; officials of, 61; photo of chapel at, 62
Duncan, Hale, 190
DuPont Co., 173, 174, 338
Durene Association of America, 172, 174
Durham, Carl, 20
Durham, N.C., 14, 59, 309
Durham County, N.C., 252
Dutch people, 112

Eagles, Joseph C., Jr., 25–26
Eagle scouts. *See* Boy Scouts
East (world), 13, 99, 238, 293, 299

Eastern North Carolina [Judicial] District, 7
Eastern United States, 13, 91, 121, 150
Economy and economic trends, 13, 15, 39, 116, 238, 247. *See also* Commerce, trade, and industry
Eden, N.C. *See* Leaksville, N.C.
Edenton, N.C., 318
Educators and educational system, 13, 18, 23–24, 40, 42, 43, 44, 45, 50, 54, 55, 58, 71, 72–74, 90, 93, 109, 121, 168, 187, 190, 196, 211, 227, 250–52, 262–63, 301, 318, 331, 349. *See also specific educators and educational institutions*
Edward VIII (King), 43
Edwards, Lucy Ann. *See* Jordan, Mrs. Milas Chauncey, Jr.
Edwards, Richard ("Dick"), 39
Egypt, 98, 174
Eisenhower, Dwight D., 287, 288
Elasticot yarn, 151–52. *See also* Textile industry
Elections and voting, 10, 16, 17, 34, 45, 276, 309, 310, 311, 354
Electricians, 124, 181
Elias, Don S., 14
Ellington, Johnnie, 178
Elon (city), N.C., 252
Elon College, 59, 187, 252
Emory University, 132
Engineers, 146, 254
England. *See* Great Britain
Environmental protection, 254, 255, 258, 259, 301, 302, 303
Equal Rights Act (ERA), 328
ERA, 328
Erosion, 39, 303, 354. *See also* Environmental protection
Ervin, Sam, Jr.: and Alaska, 220; and Cochrane, 299; and international trade, 231; and Johnson, 28, 261, 279; and B. Everett Jordan, 7, 28,

51–52, 56, 57, 113, 149, 231, 234–36, 237, 261, 285, 289, 290–91, 295, 299, 309; and H. H. Jordan, 56–57; and Larkins, 7; and Sanford, 28; and Vietnam war, 285, 289–90, 292–93, 295; and Watergate affair, 291, 348; appearance of, 290; as judge, 290; as storyteller, 290; as U.S. senator, 149, 234, 236, 253, 290, 303, 320; childhood friends of, 56, 57, 149; father of, 149; hometown of, 348; on Bobby Baker case, 278–79; personality of, 289, 291; photos of, 218, 235, 262, 310; political activities of, 28; retires, 348; supports farm programs, 234; supports tobacco industry, 234; well known, 291; youth of, 235
Europe, 6, 13, 88, 299
Ewing-Thomas, 172
Eyeglasses, 17, 81, 82, 83, 84, 327

Fairview Academy, 44
Falls of the Neuse Reservoir Project, 300, 301–2, 353
Far East, 13, 99, 238, 293, 299
Farms and farming, 5, 6, 15, 26, 37, 38–39, 40, 48, 70, 77, 78, 83, 87, 90, 91, 107, 112, 114, 120, 121, 122, 146, 167, 171, 172, 217, 223, 225, 228, 229, 234, 239, 241, 242, 243–47, 252, 254, 299, 300, 301. *See also* Planters and plantations; Soils and soil conservation
Faucett, Margaret Ann. *See* Sellars, Mrs. Thomas, III (2)
Fawcett, Bill, 161
Ficklin, J. S., 14
Fieldcrest Mills, 6
Fighting, 139, 269
Fires and fire departments, 153, 192
First National Bank of Burlington, 329

Fishing. *See* Recreation
Floods and flood control, 114, 136–37, 138, 139, 168, 252, 253–54, 257, 299, 302, 308, 354. *See also* Dams
Florida, 106, 171, 220
"Flying Squadrons," 141, 201
Fogleman, C. E., 128
Foil Hosiery Mill, 277
Food Stamp Bill, 281
Ford, Gerald R., 300
Ford, Mrs. Gerald R. (Betty), 305
Ford, Henry, 105
Foster Shoe Store, 103
Fountain, L. H., 218, 224–25, 226, 253
Four Seasons Travel Service, Inc., 319
Foust, ——— (woman), 116
Foust, Allene T., 184
Fowler, George H., 128
Fox hunting, 176
France, 6, 86, 87, 318
Franklin Soil and Water Conservation District, 253
Frazier, Ervin S. ("Blackie"), 202
Freeman, Orville L., 253
French (Upper) Broad River Basin, 302, 353
Friday, William C.: and Cochrane, 211, 251; and B. Everett Jordan, 18–19, 163–64, 251; and politics, 18; as educator, 18; retirement and present activities of, 349; television show of, 349
"Friends" (Quakers), 112, 114, 116, 143
Furniture industry, 14, 16, 54, 55, 237, 248

Galifianakis, Nick, 195, 276, 309
Gant family, 16
Gant, Roger, Jr. (son-in-law of B. Everett Jordan): and B. Everett Jordan, 33, 57, 131, 146–47, 151, 274, 279–80; as straight talker,

279; as textile executive, 132, 146; photo of, 103
Gant, Mrs. Roger, Jr. (Rose Ann Jordan) (daughter of B. Everett Jordan): and her father, 33, 85, 145, 233–34, 271, 273–76, 294–95; childhood of, 102–3; children of, 273; educated, 61; marries, 273; personality and character of, 273–76, 294; photos of, 101, 106, 213, 217; residence of, 273
Gardner, James C., 29
Garret, Alice, 74
Garrou family, 136
Garrou, Al, 161
Gaston County, N.C., 90, 91, 92, 140, 142, 199, 204
Gastonia, N.C., 14, 53, 55, 56, 81, 86, 90, 91, 92, 93, 94, 95, 99, 107, 108, 109, 111, 112, 114, 129, 131, 132, 139, 140, 147, 161, 187, 193, 198, 199, 200, 201, 202, 204, 205, 215, 328
Gastonia Cotton Manufacturing Co., 90
Gaston Lake (N.C.), 349
GATT, 230–31
General Agreement on Tariffs and Trade (GATT), 230–31
General Assembly (N.C.). *See* Legislature
George, Ann. *See* Williams, Mrs. Jim Baber
Georgia, 37, 122, 131, 132, 335
Germans and Germany, 78, 87–89, 96, 112
Gilmore, Voit, 23–25, 26, 319
Glasses, eye, 17, 81, 82, 83, 84, 327
Glenover Hosiery Mill, 277
Glen Raven Mills, 16, 131, 132, 146
Glynn, ———, 163
Godfrey, Horace D., 217–18, 241–42, 243–47, 349
Goldsboro, N.C., 307
Goldwater, Barry, 284

Goley, Willard, 16
Gordon family, 136
Gordon, Clyde W., 16, 146, 150–51, 154, 157, 164–65, 223–24, 226, 237, 270–71, 318, 337
Gordon, Eugene, 131, 140
Gordon, Staley P., 154, 336
Governments: of N.C., 18 (*and see* Legislature); of U.S., *see entries under United States*
Governors, of N.C., 4, 14, 17, 18, 19–20, 21, 22, 25, 26, 28, 29, 30, 33, 62, 63, 64, 65, 116, 201, 244, 254, 256, 259, 290, 318
Grace Hosiery Mill, 157, 329, 336
Graham, Frank Porter, 30
Graham, N.C., 77, 103, 106, 107, 111, 116, 124, 190, 330
Graves, Lila. *See* Sellars, Mrs. Thomas Leonidas
Gray, George A., 90, 91, 328
Gray, J. Lander, 91
Gray, May. *See* Separk, Mrs. Joseph
Gray Manufacturing Co., 91, 92
Gray Mill, 92, 93, 112, 129, 137, 139, 140, 188, 190, 193, 197, 198, 199, 328
Gray-Separk Mills, 91, 93
Great Britain, 43, 69, 79, 111, 171
Great Depression. *See* Depressions
Great Wagon Road, 112
Greensboro (Greensborough), N.C., 10, 11, 12, 14, 34, 71, 74, 76, 131, 136, 203, 231, 244, 272, 306, 314
Greensboro (N.C.) College, 71, 76, 231, 314
Greensboro (N.C.) *Daily News*, 11, 12, 34, 203
Greensboro (N.C.) *Record*, 231
Greensborough (N.C.) Female College, 71–74
Greenville, N.C., 14
Greenville, S.C., 131, 156, 158
Griffin, Lloyd E., 15, 318
Griffith, Robert H., 161

Gristmills, 115, 117, 118, 314
Gruber, Edward: and his father, 167, 168–69, 171, 175–76; and B. Everett Jordan, 98, 161, 167–80 passim, 338; and Ben E. Jordan, Jr., 338; career of, 167–80 passim; educated, 168, 171; on Katherine Jordan, 98–99; relations of, with mill hands, 168; reputation of, 338
Gruber, Ira, 167–69, 171, 172, 175–76, 180
Guilford County, N.C., 252
Gulf of Tonkin Resolution, 286, 288, 352
Guns, 52, 102, 105, 124, 141, 154, 200, 201, 203, 273
Gurkin, Harry, 217
Guthrie, George, 117
Guthrie, Sallie Dodson, 119
Guyer, Patsy, 217, 231

Hackney, Bruce G., 313
Hairfield, ———, 50
Haithcock, Randa D., 178
Haley, Alex, 324
Hall, Aretta, 178
Hall, Eleanor Juanita ("Nita"). *See* Sellers, Mrs. David Ernest
Hall, R. Dave, 14
Hanes, Jake, 54
Harden, George, 190
Harden, John, 70
Harden, Mrs. John (Eliza Sellars) (great-great-aunt of B. Everett Jordan), 70
Hardin, Bobby, 298
Hardin, Nell, 178
Hardin, Roosevelt ("Rosie"), 178
Harriman, W. Averill, 65
Harris, Shearon, 14
Harvard University, 318
Harvey, Leo, 14
Harvey, Madeline, 217
Hatteras Inlet, 354
Hawaii, 220, 230

Hawfields (N.C.), 5, 6, 112
Haw River (river): and B. Everett Jordan, 213; and Jordan Dam and Lake, 258; and Cape Fear River, 252; and Saxapahaw, 15, 111, 113; bridges over, 113, 114, 115, 138, 141, 179, 193, 211, 313, 314; church along, 314; dams along, 114, 115, 136–37, 148, 182; floods, 114, 136–37, 138, 139, 168, 254, 308; fords along, 115; Indians along, 111–12; industrial and other development along, 70, 71 (*and see particular companies*); land along, 70, 71; level of, 270; polluted, 258; provides power, 111, 136; residence along, 308; soil along, 115; terrain along, 115
Haw River (town), N.C., 16
Hayden, Carl, 33
Hayden, Wesley ("Wes") F., 214, 215, 217, 232–33, 279
Haynie, Hugh, 11, 12
Heffner, Sue Ellen (Stokes), 40
Helms, Jesse: and Galifianakis, 310, 311; and Hodges, 319; and B. Everett Jordan, 303, 310–11, 319; and Mrs. B. Everett Jordan, 329; and N.C. projects, 303; and Sanford, 310; and Senate seat, 311; and Smith, 311
Henderson, David N., 218
Hendersonville, N.C., 321
Hickory, N.C., 43, 53, 136
Hicks, Hasseltine. *See* Jordan, Mrs. Robert Alexander
High Point, N.C., 10, 14
High Point (N.C.) *Enterprise*, 10
High schools. *See* Educators and educational system
Highway patrol (N.C.), 4, 203
Highways. *See* Roads and highways
Hildebran, N.C., 161
Hill-Burton bill, 349
Hillsborough, N.C., 77

Hinderlite, J. H., 96
Hinshaw, Melvin, 42
Hinshaw, Mrs. Melvin, 42
Hintz, Mary Jordan (cousin of B. Everett Jordan): and B. Everett Jordan, 40, 50; and Henry H. Jordan, 47; and Milas Jordan, 47; parents of, 40, 41; lives with grandparents, 40, 42, 43–44, 47; photo of, 47
History and historians, 30, 111, 140, 289
Ho Chi Minh, 286, 288
Hodges, Luther H.: and Democratic party, 3–35 passim; and Eagles, 25–26; and William Friday, 251; and Gilmore, 23–25, 26, 319; and Helms, 319; and Johnson, 28, 33; and Jones, 227; and B. Everett Jordan, 3–35 passim, 64, 65, 99, 160, 219, 228, 239, 251, 319, 320; and Kennedy, 28; and Larkins, 7–8, 20, 227; and Makepeace, 3–4, 30; and Rodgers, 254; and Sanford, 26–29, 64; and Scott, 5, 27; and Senate seat, 3–35 passim, 228; and Stevenson, 28; and Trotter, 3–4; as businessman and textile industrialist, 5–6, 7, 8, 19, 29, 65; as governor of N.C., 3–35 passim, 64, 254, 256, 320; as lieutenant governor of N.C., 5, 6, 18, 19, 29; as politician, 3–35 passim; as state legislator, 19; as U.S. secretary of commerce, 216, 217; cartoons about, 9–10, 11, 12, 34–35; national political potential of, 20, 25; photos of, 6, 7, 9
Hodges, Martha. See Hodges, Mrs. Luther H.
Hodges, Mrs. Luther H. (Martha), 216, 217
Hoey, Clyde R., 4, 20, 254, 290
Hoff, Phil, 219
Holderness, H. Dail, 14

Holderness, Howard, 14
Hollies, 167, 171, 177, 179–80
Holman's Mill, 116
Holt, Edwin M., 116, 117–18, 120, 331
Holt, John, 111
Holt, Nellie. See Sellars, Mrs. Thomas S., Sr.
Holt, Ralph, Sr., 16
Holt, White, and Williamson (firm), 118
Hopedale community (N.C.) 70, 71
Horner, Earl, 16
Horses, 71, 78, 111, 112, 115, 120
Hospitals. See Sickness, disease, and medical care
Hot Springs, Ark., 145
House of Representatives. See United States House of Representatives
Howard, Rawls, 270–71
Howard County, Va., 43
Howards Mill Lake, 353
Huffman, Sarah D. See Sellars, Mrs. Lemuel
Humphrey, Hubert H., 264, 303
Humphrey, Mrs. Hubert H. (Muriel), 264
Hunger, in world, 206, 299
Hunnewell, Kans., 84
Hunt, James B., 259
Hunter, Charlie, 178
Hunter, Robert A., 134, 135, 181–82, 183

Ideal Mercerizing Co., 192
Illinois, 83, 161, 163, 256, 300
Income taxes. See Taxes and taxation
Indians, 111–12
Indian Territory. See Oklahoma
Industrial revolution, 118
Industry. See Commerce, trade, and industry
Institute of Government, 23, 210–11
Insurance industry, 14, 78, 195, 268, 279, 281

Index 375

International trade. *See* Commerce, trade, and industry
Interparliamentary Union, 299
Interstate highways. *See* Roads and highways
Intracoastal waterway, 354
Iredell County, N.C., 37, 38, 39, 44, 45, 77
Irish people. *See* Scotch-Irish people
Israel, 255
Italy, 74

Jackson, Robert C., 238, 239, 241, 242–43, 348
Jackson, W. Louis, 159, 170, 188
Jails. *See* Crime, criminals, law enforcement, and penal system
Jamestown colony (Va.), 37
Japan and Japanese, 99, 156, 238, 241
J. C. Penney stores, 173–74, 175, 176
Jenkins, Walter, 278–79, 281
Jerden. *See Jordan entries*
Jerusalem (Israel), 255
Jewelry, 81, 82, 83, 94, 154, 215
Jobe, W. Adrian, 178, 184
Johnson, Jessie, 178
Johnson, Lady Bird. *See* Johnson, Mrs. Lyndon B.
Johnson, Lyndon B. (LBJ): and Bobby Baker case, *see* Baker case; and Connally, 263; and conservative Democrats, 286; and Ervin, 28; and Goldwater, 284; and Hodges, 28; and Jenkins, 278–79, 281; and B. Everett Jordan, 28, 33–35, 221, 222, 243, 261–69, 279–80, 281, 284; and Kennedy, 262; and Mansfield, 267; and Murphy, 349; and Rayburn, 262, 263; and Roosevelt, 262, 263, 284; and Texas, 262, 263, 266, 280, 282, 287; and Thielman, 282–84; and two-price cotton system, 242–43; and Vietnam war, 285, 286, 287–89, 292; as U.S. president, 216, 222, 242–43, 246, 247, 261–69 passim, 280, 283, 285–86, 287–89, 292, 300, 302, 319, 352; as U.S. senator, 33, 243, 246, 261–69 passim, 279, 284, 288; as U.S. vice-president, 267, 282; covets power, 263; health of, 281; insured, 281; personality of, 263; photos of, 262, 264, 281, 302, 303; television station of, 281–82
Johnson, Mrs. Lyndon B. (Lady Bird), 98, 264, 265, 282, 303
Johnson, Peter, 119
Johnson, "Vonie," 119
Johnson (Howard) restaurants, 5, 6, 29, 65, 319, 320
Johnston, Mrs. W. T. (Elizabeth "Lib"), 17
Johnston House, 45, 46
Jonas, Charles ("Charlie") R., 216, 217, 218
Jonas, Mrs. Charles R., 217
Jones, Dr. ———, 74
Jones, Mrs. (Dr.) ———, 74
Jones, Halbert M., 14
Jones, T. J., 298
Jones, Walter B., 218
Jones, Woodrow, 8, 227
Jordan family, 10, 37–67, 69, 83, 110, 130, 160, 227, 269, 273. *See also specific family members*
Jordan, B. Everett, family, 10, 21, 129, 139, 145, 276, 297, 312, 322. *See also particular family members*
Jordan name, 37
Jordan, A. A., 83
Jordan, Benjamin Everett, Sr. *See* Jordan, B. Everett, Sr.
Jordan, Benjamin Everett, Jr. *See* Jordan, Ben E., Jr.
Jordan, B. Everett, Sr.: achievements of, 285–316 passim; age and

birthdays of, 9, 32, 57, 91, 123, 149, 153, 235, 290, 309, 310, 329; ancestors and relatives of, 37–80; and alcohol, 31, 58, 61, 134, 139–40, 240; and architecture, 304–5; and ATMI, 238–39, 240–41, 348; and Bobby Baker case, *see* Baker case; and black people, 76, 134, 135, 141–42, 177–78, 181, 183; and Boy Scouts, 187–88, 189; and civil rights, 220; and Cuban missile crisis, 283, 286–87, 288; and Duke University, 50, 55, 59, 61–62, 74, 82, 136, 168, 250, 252; and education, 40, 50, 55, 58–59, 61, 74, 82, 168, 250–52; and his father, 32, 37, 44, 48, 51, 54, 55, 57, 60, 66, 77, 79, 81, 82, 83–84, 86–87, 88, 89–91, 96, 101, 110, 154, 163, 237, 250, 259, 275, 290, 313–14, 316; and food, 31, 75–76, 87, 308; and his mother, 77; and N.C. Citizens Association, 14–15; and N.C. governorship, 29; and office staff, 143–45, 209–16, 217, 246, 254, 256, 266; and reading, 54, 60, 82, 214, 291; and Saxapahaw, *see* Saxapahaw: and B. Everett Jordan; and Sellers Manufacturing Co., *see* Sellers Manufacturing Co., Inc.; and smoking, 108; and University of North Carolina, 163–64; and U.S. presidency, 276; and world hunger, 206; appearance of, 31–32, 84, 232, 290; as "Pied Piper," 93, 108, 127–48 passim; as salesman, 31, 32, 108, 129, 130, 146, 150, 154, 155, 159, 160, 161, 168, 189, 215, 223; as storyteller, 61, 63, 81–82, 84, 87, 113, 150, 290, 327; as businessman, entrepreneur, textile executive, and mill owner, 3, 5, 6, 9, 12, 15, 19, 29, 31–33, 54, 55, 57, 61, 63, 65, 73, 79, 80, 81–207 passim, 209, 213, 215, 216, 225, 231, 235, 236, 237, 249, 251, 257, 263, 266, 267, 270, 272, 274, 276, 277, 282, 290, 297, 298, 305, 311, 347; automobiles of, 161, 203, 204, 255, 337; birthplace of, 191; cares for family, followers, friends, employees, and constituents, 58, 124, 141–43, 157, 177–78, 179, 185, 186, 216, 224, 237, 240, 246, 249, 252, 253–59, 269–71, 273, 276–77, 299–303, 353; caricature of, 292; cartoons about, 9–10, 11, 12, 34–35, 283; charisma of, 141, 189; courts and weds, 32, 89, 93–96, 97, 108, 150; covets power, 233–34, 244, 263; dam and lake named after, *see* Jordan Dam and Lake; demise, death, funeral, and estate of, 125, 146, 154, 156, 158, 187, 195, 259, 297, 313–15, 337, 347; dress of, 31–32, 297; educates his children, 61; ethics of, 32; favorite poem of, 312; friends of, 16, 22, 25, 30, 61, 79, 81, 93, 96, 109, 110, 130, 131, 141, 146, 150, 156, 157, 161, 164, 167–80 passim, 197, 221, 227, 238, 246, 249, 261, 263, 269, 270, 276–77, 282, 284, 285, 293, 297, 310, 314, 329, 337, 350; frugality of, 144–45, 153, 154, 155, 158–59, 194, 198; grammar of, 152; health of, 32, 145, 182, 195, 309, 310, 311; hobbies and recreation of, 136, 153, 176; income and wealth of, 99, 127, 129, 146, 147–48, 154, 159, 160, 176, 177, 184, 185, 187, 206, 227, 263, 266, 272, 297, 298, 307, 316, 337; "intelligence" sources of, 143, 185, 186, 213, 215, 263–64, 266, 267, 276; lives in Kans., 81–86, 88, 91, 93, 99, 215; not well known, 12, 15–16,

19, 226, 291, 297–98, 311; on architectural design, 303; opposes communism, 285, 286–87, 288; opposes unions, 316, 340–45; opposes U.S. participation in Vietnam conflict, 219, 230, 285–95, 309; owns farm, 146; papers of, 360–61; philanthropy of, 10, 15, 17, 59, 76, 142–43, 175, 187–88, 337; photos of, *see passim*; political interests, activities, associates, and stance of, 3–35 passim, 15, 22, 30, 58, 63, 64, 96, 137, 146, 150, 151, 157, 159, 160, 164, 189, 197, 212–13, 217–18, 220, 221, 222, 223, 224, 225, 227, 228, 230, 237, 241, 247, 250, 251, 255, 256, 263, 266, 269, 270, 276, 285, 290, 311, 319; public relations of, 33, 152, 226, 230, 232–33, 234, 240, 279, 293, 297–98, 301, 311; relations of, with his brothers and sisters, 62–65, 157, 209, 269, 315; relations of, with his children, 145–46, 157, 168, 169, 171, 189–91, 271–76; relations of, with his employees, 76, 93, 99, 100, 131–32, 143, 168, 187, 266; relations of, with various individuals, *see specific individuals*; religious life of, 32, 82, 131, 143, 157, 179, 205, 266, 276, 298; reputation of, 234, 273; residences of, 52, 61, 109, 114, 149, 193, 210, 293, 308, 314, 315; serves in U.S. Army, 84, 86–89, 96, 290; size of, 31; social life of, 136, 154, 157, 217, 267; speech habits and public speaking of, 100, 131, 233, 239–40, 241, 256, 307, 317; spelling of, 326; supports admission of Alaska and Hawaii to Union, 219–20, 230; supports agriculture, 217, 229, 234, 241, 243–47, 299, 300; supports textile industry, 231, 238–43, 248; supports tobacco industry, 223, 234, 247–49; talents, personality, interests, philosophy of life, and motivations of, xvii, 15, 16–19, 23, 31–35, 40, 48, 55, 57, 63, 66, 79, 82, 84, 85–86, 87, 89, 91, 93–94, 96, 99–100, 105, 106, 107, 110, 125, 130, 131, 134, 135, 136, 137, 140, 141, 146, 150, 151, 152–53, 154, 156, 157, 159–60, 163–64, 165, 168, 171–72, 175, 177–79, 184, 185, 188, 197, 202, 205–7, 209, 212, 220–21, 223–24, 227, 228, 229, 230, 231–32, 234–35, 237, 239–40, 249, 252, 256, 263, 264, 270, 271, 273–76, 284, 285, 289, 291, 293, 294–95, 297–98, 307, 308, 312, 315–16, 347; travels and vacations of, 98, 99, 106, 145, 153, 238, 255, 257, 282, 283, 299, 308, 349; uses alteration of his name, 317; U.S. Senate career of, 3–35 passim, 62, 64, 97, 98, 99, 113, 129, 130, 144, 145, 150, 151, 152, 160, 170, 194, 205, 206, 207, 209–311 passim, 320, 337; voice of, 32; wears glasses, 17; weight of, 31; wife supports and influences, *see* Jordan, Mrs. B. Everett, Sr.: and B. Everett Jordan; wins honorary degree, 62; youth and upbringing of, 48–53, 57, 76, 81–86, 105, 149, 157, 222, 227, 235, 237, 250. *See also* Sellers Manufacturing Co., Inc.; *specific topics*

Jordan, Mrs. B. Everett, Sr. (Katherine Augusta McLean) (wife of B. Everett Jordan): admired and praised, 98–99, 184, 186, 187, 221, 232, 255, 329; and her children, 271; and her daughter, 103; and her husband, 10, 21, 29, 32, 54,

60, 66, 81, 85, 94–95, 96–98, 99, 100, 101, 107, 145, 154, 157, 164, 189, 209, 212, 214, 217, 256, 274, 275, 308, 314, 316, 347; and Lady Bird Johnson, 98, 279; and the Rodgerses, 255, 256, 350; and Sanford, 29; dies, 94–95, 96–97; friends of, 96, 97, 109, 255, 256, 297, 350; owns stock, 128, 129; personality of, 98–99, 214; photos of, *see passim*; residences of, 61, 109, 114, 193, 210, 293, 308, 314, 315; travels of, 98, 99, 106, 255; wooed and wed, 32, 89, 93, 96, 97, 108, 150

Jordan, Ben E., Jr. (son of B. Everett Jordan): and his father, 33, 145, 185, 188–91, 193–94, 198, 271, 272; and Gruber, 338; as ATMI director, 240; as textile executive, 33, 170, 171, 188, 191, 193–94, 195, 240; birth of, 99; childhood playmate of, 313; educated, 61, 109, 189; photos of, 100, 106, 298

Jordan, Mrs. Ben E., Jr. (Ellen McMasters), 104, 145, 213, 217, 298

Jordan, Charles E. (brother of B. Everett Jordan), 49, 53, 55, 61, 62, 63, 75, 149, 315

Jordan, Mrs. Charles E. (sister-in-law of B. Everett Jordan), 53

Jordan, Claude Alvin (uncle of B. Everett Jordan), 38, 43, 321

Jordan, Mrs. Claude Alvin (Mary Alice "Mayce" Blackwelder) (aunt of B. Everett Jordan), 43, 321

Jordan (later Arledge), Esther Mae (cousin of B. Everett Jordan), 43

Jordan, Frank B. (brother of B. Everett Jordan), 49, 55, 62, 63, 75–76, 309, 315, 324

Jordan, Henry H., II (nephew of B. Everett Jordan), 63, 66, 69

Jordan, Henry Harrison (father of B. Everett Jordan): ancestors of, 37; and A. A. Jordan, 83; and B. Everett Jordan, 32, 37, 44, 48, 51, 54, 55, 57, 60, 66, 77, 79, 81, 82, 83–84, 86–87, 88, 89–91, 96, 101, 110, 154, 163, 237, 250, 259, 275, 290, 313–14, 316; and Mary Jordan (Hintz), 43, 47–48; and his parents, 43, 44, 47, 48; and Separk, 90, 91; and Trinity College, 54; appearance and dress of, 44, 49; as businessman, 53, 54, 157, 237; as lawyer, 44, 45–46, 58, 76; as minister, 37, 39, 40, 41, 44, 46–48, 49–50, 51–52, 54–57, 58, 66, 77, 149, 191, 227, 237, 250, 269, 313–14, 316, 324; as politician, 45–46; as teacher and educator, 42, 44; birth of, 37, 321; cares for family, 44, 58, 272; daughters of, 44, 48, 49, 55, 58, 314; death and estate of, 54, 61, 64, 312–13; educated, 44; educates his children, 58, 71, 168, 250; friends of, 40; invests in stocks, 55; marries, 46, 54, 76, 321, 325; opposes alcohol, 58; personality of, 15, 32, 44, 46–47, 50, 55, 56–57, 63, 79, 87, 91; philanthropy of, 61; photos of, 41, 42; salary of, 48, 54–55; scholarly interests of, 54, 57, 82; sons of, 32, 44, 58, 62–66, 314; struggles of, 77

Jordan, Mrs. Henry Harrison (Anne "Annie" E. Sellars) (mother of B. Everett Jordan): and her daughters, 48, 49, 55, 74, 297; and her husband, 54, 75, 77; and B. Everett Jordan, 275; and Rose Ann Jordan, 103; educated, 71–72, 74; marries, 46, 76, 77, 321, 325; part owner of store, 297; personality of, 15, 55, 79; photos of, 49, 73; sons of, 32, 49, 62–66, 74; wealth of family of, 54, 55

Jordan, Henry W. (brother of B. Everett Jordan), 15, 40, 48, 49, 54, 62–66, 75–76, 127, 128, 209, 247, 273, 309, 315, 346
Jordan, Mrs. Henry W. (sister-in-law of B. Everett Jordan), 66
Jordan, John McLean (son of B. Everett Jordan): and his father, 33, 58, 60, 145, 159, 169–71, 271–73, 311; and Mondale, 327; as Boy Scout, 188, 316; as politician, 146, 273; as textile executive, 170, 171; educated, 61; interests of, 146; photos of, 102, 316
Jordan, Mrs. John M. (Margaret Carter), 104
Jordan, John McLean, Jr. ("Mac") (grandson of B. Everett Jordan), 188, 316
Jordan, Lucy (sister of B. Everett Jordan). See Taylor, Mrs. Oscar, Sr.; Way, Mrs. George K.
Jordan, Margaret (sister of B. Everett Jordan). See Sprinkle, Mrs. Henry C.
Jordan, Margaret ("Maggie") Missourri Ann (aunt of B. Everett Jordan), 38, 41, 321
Jordan, Mary. See Hintz, Mary Jordan
Jordan, Mary Esther (aunt of B. Everett Jordan), 38, 41, 321
Jordan, Mike (nephew of B. Everett Jordan), 69, 74, 75, 105, 315, 324
Jordan, Milas Chauncey, Sr. (great-grandfather of B. Everett Jordan), 37
Jordan, Milas (Miles) Chauncey, Jr. (grandfather of B. Everett Jordan), 37, 38, 39–42, 43, 44, 47, 48–49, 56, 58, 66, 321
Jordan, Mrs. Milas Chauncey, Jr. (Lucy Ann Edwards) (grandmother of B. Everett Jordan), 37, 38, 39–42, 43, 44, 47, 48, 49, 321

Jordan, Patty, 217
Jordan, Robert Alexander (uncle of B. Everett Jordan), 38, 39, 41, 43, 321
Jordan, Mrs. Robert Alexander (Hasseltine Hicks) (aunt of B. Everett Jordan), 321
Jordan, Rose Ann. See Gant, Mrs. Roger, Jr.
Jordan, Samuel, 37
Jordan, Thomas A. (nephew of B. Everett Jordan), 346
Jordan, Thomas Carlyle (cousin of B. Everett Jordan), 43, 321
Jordan, Thomas Carter (grandson of B. Everett Jordan), 188
Jordan, Thomas Chauncey (uncle of B. Everett Jordan), 38, 39, 40, 41, 43, 321
Jordan, Mrs. Thomas Chauncey (Henrietta Engle Warfield) (aunt of B. Everett Jordan), 43, 321
Jordan, Watt ("Wattie") (uncle of B. Everett Jordan), 38, 321
Jordan, William Alvis (uncle of B. Everett Jordan), 38, 40, 41, 43, 321
Jordan, Mrs. William Alvis (Sue Ellen Heffner Stokes) (aunt of B. Everett Jordan), 40
Jordan (B. Everett) Dam and Lake (New Hope Dam Project), 252, 258–59, 300, 301–2, 353
Jordan Drive (street), 210
Jordan (H. H.) Lending Library, 54
Jordan (Annie Sellars) Parlor Theatre, 76
Jordan Spinning Co. (Sellers Manufacturing Co. No. 2), 63, 192, 195
Jorden name, 37
Jordon name, 37
Jourdain name, 37
Jourdon name, 37
Journalism. See Newspapers

Judges. *See* Courts, lawyers, and legal-judicial system
Judicial system. *See* Courts, lawyers, and legal-judicial system
Jurdan name, 37
Juries. *See* Courts, lawyers, and legal-judicial system

Kale, R. H., Sr., 190
Kannapolis, N.C., 212
Kansas, 81–86, 88, 91, 93, 99
Kayser-Roth Co., 151
Keever, Homer, 322
Kenan (William) Fund, 349
Kenan (William R.) Trust, 349
Kennedy, John F. (JFK), 28, 66, 216, 230, 231, 234, 243, 246, 247, 262, 273, 281, 282, 284, 285, 286, 287–88, 292, 319
Kennedy, Robert, 234, 273
Kennedy, Theodore ("Ted"), 234, 273
Kennedy Stadium (D.C.), 278
Kentucky, 248
Kerr Lake, 349
Kime, Frusannah Elizabeth. *See* Sellars, Mrs. Benjamin Abel
Kimesville, N.C., 71
King Edward VIII, 43
Kinston, N.C., 14
Kitchin family, 217
Kizzie (slave), 324
Klumpp, Joseph, 161, 163
Knighten, Cephus, 178
Knighten, Troy, 178
Korean War, 257
Kornegay, Horace R., 218, 247–49, 250, 252

Labor, labor unions, and strikes, 121, 140–41, 159, 176, 194, 197, 198–205, 328, 340
Land acquisition and distribution, 70, 111, 127
Larkins, John D., Jr., 7–8, 20
Lashley, Leona Dodson, 119
Laurinburg, N.C., 14
Law enforcement. *See* Crime, criminals, law enforcement, and penal system
Laws. *See particular laws and lawmaking bodies*
Lawson, John, 111–12
Lawyers. *See* Courts, lawyers, and legal-judicial system
Leaksville (Eden), N.C., 3, 5
Leazar, A., 46
Legal matters. *See* Courts, lawyers, and legal-judicial system
Legislature, of N.C., 8, 13, 14, 19, 20, 21, 25, 30, 64, 146, 211, 254, 318, 319
Lennon, Alton, 4, 22, 218
Lenoir, N.C., 14, 39, 40, 46, 48, 54
Liberty, N.C., 71
Libraries, 301 (*and see following entry*)
Library of Congress, 229–30, 257, 299, 303–5, 306
Lieutenant governors, of N.C., 5, 6, 18, 19, 29, 318–19
Lilesville, N.C., 43
Lincoln, Abraham, 77
Lincolnton, N.C., 14
Lindley, Darwin, 298
Liquor. *See* Alcohol and alcohol consumption
Literacy, 349
Livestock. *See* Farms and farming; Planters and plantations
Lloyd, Amick, 192
Local government and politics, in N.C., 13, 15, 16, 30, 45, 211, 216, 221, 222, 266, 270, 314, 331
Long, Dolph, 16
Longcrier, W. Franklin ("Frank"), Jr., 150, 156–57, 158, 159, 170
Loray Mill and Loray Mill strike, 90, 140–41, 199–202, 204, 328
Los Angeles, Calif., 28
Louisburg, N.C., 253

Index 381

Louisiana, 256
Love, Cornelia S., 90
Love, F. Sadler, 238
Love, James Lee, 90
Love, J. Spencer, 90, 226, 329
Loy, Martin (great-great-uncle of B. Everett Jordan), 70
Loy, Mrs. Martin (Polly Sellars) (great-great-aunt of B. Everett Jordan), 70
Loyalists, 70
Lumber industry, 24, 43, 91

McAdams, Thelma ("Red"), 178
McBane, Henry, 298
McBane, Nannie Lou, 298
McCabe, Gordon, 245
McClory, Robert, 257
McCormack, John W., 300, 302
McEwen family, 16
McGuire, William B., 14
McLean family, 95
McLean, J. F., 45
McLean, Katherine Augusta. See Jordan, Mrs. B. Everett, Sr.
McLean, Margaret Alice (sister-in-law of B. Everett Jordan), 183
McLean, Mary, 93
McLean, May (sister-in-law of B. Everett Jordan), 298, 314
McLean, Robert (father of Mrs. B. Everett Jordan), 93, 95
McLean, Mrs. Robert (Rose May) (mother of Mrs. B. Everett Jordan), 93, 94, 95
McMasters, Ellen. See Jordan, Mrs. Ben E., Jr.
McNamara, Robert, 288
McPherson, Holt, 10, 14
McPherson, R. G., 128
McVey, Ella, 119
Madden, E. Leon, 134, 135, 298
Madden, John J., 178
Madden, John Ray, 298

Madison (James) Memorial Library of Congress Building, 229–30, 303–5, 306
Magistrates. See Courts, lawyers, and legal-judicial system
Mail. See Post offices
Makepeace, Harold, 3–4, 24, 29, 30, 320
Mallory, Lina, 74
Manassas, Va., 43
Mann, Clarence, 178
Mansfield, Mike, 267, 278, 300
Manufacturers. See Commerce, trade, and industry
Marion, N.C., 50
Marlette, Gordon, 192
Marshall Field Co., 19
Maryland, 281
Mason-Dixon line, 77, 116
Massachusetts, 122, 161, 300
May, Ben, 16
May, Will H., 16, 128
Maynard family, 136
Maynard, Reid A., 16, 79, 102, 156, 157–59, 164, 190, 226, 329, 336, 337
Mebane, N.C., 16, 247
Mechanics, 124, 181
Mecklenburg County, N.C., 45
Media. See News media
Medicines and medical care. See Sickness, disease, and medical care
Meir, Golda, 255
Memphis, Tenn., 348
Mercersburg, Pa., 168
Merchants. See Commerce, trade, and industry
Methodist Academy, 37
Methodists and Methodist Episcopal church, 37, 39–40, 42, 43, 45, 46–49, 52, 54, 57, 61, 63, 67, 71, 74, 76–77, 81, 90, 91, 112, 139, 142–43, 149, 157, 177, 178, 205, 297, 298, 309, 314, 322, 324, 326

Index

Michigan, 300
Middle Ages, 37
Middle District of North Carolina (judicial), 131
Midwestern United States, 82, 162, 163, 234
Miller, John W., Sr., 156, 336
Miller, John W. ("Jake"), Jr., 156, 161, 183, 336
Miller, Kent W., 135, 141, 178
Miller, Merle, 267, 268
Miller, Oscar L., 128, 132
Miller, Mrs. Oscar L. (Rose), 132
Mills. See Gristmills; Textile industry
Mills River Dam and Reservoir (N.C.), 302, 353
Minges, Harold, 4–5, 6, 7
Minorities, 246. See also Black people
Mississippi, 348
Mississippi Valley, 348
Mitchell, Broadus, 122
Mitchell, George, 122
Mocksville, N.C., 49, 51, 52, 54, 237
Mondale, Walter, 327
Monroe, N.C., 89
Montana, 300
Montgomery, Dan, 298
Montgomery, Hazel, 298
Montreat, N.C., 18, 79, 145, 282, 283, 349
"Moonshine." See Bootlegging
Moore, Dan K., 318
Moore, James V., 325
Moore, Mrs. James V. (Rebecca Jane Sellars), 325
Moore, John A., 325
Moore, Mrs. John A. (Nancy Elizabeth "Bettie" Sellars), 325
Mooresville, N.C., 40, 45, 46, 322
Morehead City, N.C., 300, 303, 349, 353
Morganton, N.C., 50, 51, 52, 55, 57, 149, 235, 348
Morrow, Annie M. See Sellers, Mrs. Charles V.
Morrow, Molly Crutchfield, 119
Morrow, Paul, Jr., 103–4, 105, 129
Morrow and Bason (store), 104
Morton, Thomas ("Curly"), 298
Motes Creek, 115
Mull family, 149
Mull, Willie, 10–11, 149, 150–52, 155, 161, 164–65
Murphy, Charles ("Charlie"), 246–47
Muse, D. K., 59, 247
Myrick, G. Harold, 14
Myrtle Mill, Inc., 91, 92, 93, 188, 190, 193, 198

National Association of Hosiery Manufacturers, 157
National Association of Textile Finishers, 238
National Association of Wool Manufacturers, 238
National Bank of Alamance, 333
National Cotton Council of America, 348
National Federation of Textiles, 238
National Guard (N.C.), 141, 200, 201, 334
National Processing Co., 192
National Textile Workers Union (NTWU), 200
National Youth Administration (NYA), 262–63
National Zoo, 233
Naval Air Transport Service, 24
Neal, Albert ("Bosie"), 298
Neal, Bettie, 178
Neal, W. Grover, 178
Nebraska, 278
Neel, Joseph M., 96, 128, 132, 133, 134, 135, 143, 151, 153, 155, 156, 170, 178, 185, 188, 336
Negroes. See Black people
Neuse River, 112, 300, 301–2, 354
New Deal, 13
New England, 118, 120, 121
New Hope Dam Project. See Jordan Dam and Lake

Index 383

New Hope River, 258
"New Institute" (N.C.), 37
Newlin, Harvey, Sr., 331
Newlin, James, 114, 116, 117, 120, 331–32
Newlin, John, 114–17
Newlin, Jonathan, 114, 116, 117
Newlin, Oliver, 116
New Orleans, La., 256
News and Observer (Raleigh), 293–94
News media, 230. *See also* Newspapers; Radio; Television
Newspapers, 4, 9, 10, 11, 12, 13, 14, 19, 21, 23, 25, 33, 34–35, 39, 62, 105, 160, 201, 203, 215, 230, 231, 254, 256, 268, 273, 278, 282, 283, 286, 291, 293–94, 302, 303, 305, 306, 307, 308, 310, 316, 318, 322. *See also* News media
New York (city and state), 55, 83, 118, 160, 161, 163, 197, 238, 327
New Zealand, 288
Nixon, Richard M., 290, 292, 304, 305, 348, 352
Norfolk and Western Railroad, 223
Norman, Frank, 139
North American continent, 220
North Carolina: as "Dixie Dynamo," 20; "third senator" of, 346. *See also entries immediately following; particular counties, cities, and villages; and specific topics and individuals*
North Carolina A & M, 50
North Carolina Advisory Budget Commission, 25
North Carolina Board of Conservation and Development, 254, 256, 319
North Carolina Central Prison, 200
North Carolina Citizens Association (North Carolina Citizens for Business and Industry; "The Voice of Business"), 10, 13–15, 318

North Carolina Highway Commission, 63
North Carolina Highway Department, 113
North Carolina Memorial Hospital, 349
"North Carolina People" (television show), 349
North Carolina School Commission, 318
North Carolina State Hospital for the Insane, 55
North Carolina State University, 50, 61, 251
North Carolina Supreme Court, 45
North Carolina Tax Study Commission, 25
North Dakota, 234
Northeastern United States, 121
Northern United States, 13, 77, 120, 121, 122
North Hollywood, Calif., 43
North Korea, 257
North Vietnam. *See* Vietnam and Vietnam war
NTWU, 200
NYA, 262–63
"Nylile," 175

Oakdale Cemetery, 321
Ocracoke Island, 353
Ohio, 116
Oklahoma, 83, 300, 327
Old-Timers Club. *See* Sellers Manufacturing Co., Inc.: retirees and Old-Timers Club of
Olin, N.C., 37
Orange County, N.C., 69, 70, 77, 118, 252
Ossippee, N.C., 113
Overman, Pride C., 178, 188

Page, Charlie, 184–85
Parade (magazine), 316
Paris, Jack, 186, 276, 307–8
Paris, Lawrence, 9

Paris (France), 6
Parkdale Mills, Inc., 139, 194
Parker, Roy, Jr., 293
Park House (Kans.), 84, 86
Pate, Edwin, 14
Patents, 151
Penal system. *See* Crime, criminals, law enforcement, and penal system
Penney (J. C.) stores, 173–74, 175, 176
Pennsylvania, 69, 112, 118, 161, 167–80 passim, 278
Pennsylvania Dutch, 112
Person County, N.C., 188
Peru, 245
Petty, Floyd, 178
Phi Beta Kappa, 25
Philadelphia, Pa., 118, 161, 176
Philanthropy, 10, 15, 17, 59, 61, 76, 142–43, 175, 187–88, 337
Phillips, George G., 178, 184
Phillips, Ola Smith, 178
Physicians. *See* Sickness, disease, and medical care
Pickard, Ella McVey, 119
Pickens, S.C., 264
Pickett, Glenn, Sr., 276–77
Pickett, Glenn, Jr., 276–77
Pickett Hosiery Mill, 276
Piedmont, 70, 90, 147
Pima cotton, 173. *See also* Textile industry
Pinehurst, N.C., 319
Planters and plantations, 70, 120. *See also* Farms and farming; Slaves and slavery
Planz, Louisa. *See* Sellers, Mrs. Frederick William
Poetry, 312
Police. *See* Crime, criminals, law enforcement, and penal system
Political science, 23
Politics and politicians. *See particular politicians and political topics*

Pollard's Insurance Co., 78
Pollution. *See* Environmental protection
Poor people. *See* Poverty
Pope, Liston, 201
Pope, R. L., 13, 14
Post offices, 144, 229
Pottstown, Pa., 167, 171
Poverty, 121, 349
Power companies. *See* Public utilities
Prentiss, Carl, 278
Presbyterians and Presbyterian church, 5, 45, 95, 96, 112, 282
Press. *See* News media
Preyer, L. Richardson, 98, 306
Printing and publishing, 14, 299
Prisons. *See* Crime, criminals, law enforcement, and penal system
Production and Marketing Administration, 243
Psychiatry, 273–74
Public relations, 35, 152, 226, 230, 232–33, 234, 239, 240, 256, 279, 293, 297–98, 301, 311
Public utilities, 14, 18
Public works, 229, 256, 263, 299, 301, 302, 306
Public Works Appropriations Bill, 301, 353
Publishing. *See* Printing and publishing
Pullen (A. M.) and Co., 136

Quakenbush, Ceton, 124
Quakenbush, Grady, 178
Quakers ("Friends"), 112, 114, 116, 143

Radio, 244, 309. *See also* News media
Railroads, 10, 54, 91, 145, 146, 209, 223
Rainey, Benjamin, 70
Rainey, Mrs. Benjamin (Nancy Sullinger), 70

Index

Rainey, Nancy. *See* Sellars, Mrs. Thomas, Jr.
Raleigh, N.C., 5, 13, 14, 17, 61, 66, 74, 153, 246, 256, 293–94, 302, 318
Raleigh *News and Observer*, 293–94
Ramseur, N.C., 160, 191
Ramseur Interlock Knitting Co., 160
Randleman Lake (N.C.), 353
Randolph County, N.C., 64, 71, 191
Rankin, Mary Ruth. *See* Jordan, Mrs. Henry W.
Rankin, R. Grady, 14
Rankin, Sam, 160, 161, 162, 206
Rankin, S. C., 45
Ray, Mary Ellen. *See* Sellars, Mrs. Willis Rainey
Rayburn, Sam, 262, 263
Real estate industry, 225
Recessions, 194. *See also* Economy and economic trends
Reconstruction Era, 38–39, 44, 77, 117, 120
Recreation, 81, 82, 84, 102, 121, 136, 154, 349. *See also* Athletes and athletics
Reddies River Lake, 353
"Regulators," 70
Reid, J. Dermont, 326, 328, 361–62
Reidsville, N.C., 43
Religion, 214. *See also* Christians and Christianity; *specific denominations and sects*
Republican party, 18, 216, 227, 269, 278, 300, 303, 310
Research Triangle Park, N.C., 20
Restaurants, 5, 6, 29, 65, 129, 319, 320
Revolutionary War, 70
Reynolds, Don B., 281–82
Reynolds (Don) Associates, 281
Rhine River, 87
Richmond, Va., 43
Ricks, R., 46
Riddick, Floyd M., 228, 261–62

Right-to-work laws, 176
Roads and highways, 4, 37, 63–64, 71, 111, 113–14, 115, 142, 203, 252
Roanoke Rapids (city), N.C., 254
Roanoke River, 254, 349, 354
Roanoke River Basin, 254
Roanoke River Flood Control Area, 254
Robbins Record (newspaper), 318
Roberson, Lillie, 178
Robinson, Hazel A. *See* Robinson, Mrs. Robert B.
Robinson, Robert B. ("Rack"), 137–39, 140, 141, 142, 143, 178, 334
Robinson, Mrs. Robert B. (Hazel A.), 137–39, 140, 142, 178
Robinson, Thomas A., 199, 200–201
Rock Creek Park (D.C.), 293
Rockingham County, N.C., 5, 188
Rodgers, Eric W., 254–57, 350
Rodgers, Mrs. Eric W. (Lucy), 350
Rodgers, Suzanne, 254, 256
Rogers, William P., 293–94
Roney, Ben, 26, 219
Roosevelt, Franklin Delano (FDR), 13, 262, 263, 284
Roots (book), 324
Ross, Charles H., 50, 53, 57, 58, 59
Rotary Club and Rotary International, 5, 6, 16, 29, 129, 266, 307
Roth, Chester H., 151, 152, 164–65
Rowan County, N.C., 45
Royal Cotton Mill Co., 153, 155, 156, 159, 174, 192, 195, 196, 203–4, 311
"Royal Egyptian" cotton, 174–75. *See also* Textile industry
Ruffin, William H., 14
Runnymede Mills, 270
Rural life. *See* Farms and farming; Planters and plantations
Rusk, Dean, 288
Russell, Don, 242
Russia. *See* Soviet Union

Rutherford College (college), 40, 42, 50
Rutherford College (village), N.C., 40, 43, 48, 49
Rutherfordton, N.C., 43

Salisbury, N.C., 46
Sanders, W. Boman, 16, 160
Sandhill Citizen (newspaper), 318
Sandhills (N.C.), 318
Sanford, Terry: and Cochrane, 26, 28; and Democratic national convention, 23, 28; and Eagles, 25; and Ervin, 28; and Galifianakis, 310; and Gilmore, 23; and Helms, 310; and Hodges, 22, 25–26, 28, 64; and B. Everett Jordan, 22, 23, 26–29, 64, 219, 310, 319; and Henry Jordan, 64; and Kennedy, 28; and Rodgers, 256; and W. Kerr Scott, 22, 23, 26–27, 64, 219; and Whitley, 26; as candidate for vice-presidency, 22, 219; as governor of N.C., 22, 26, 28, 29, 254, 256; as university president, 22; as U.S. senator, 22, 23, 26–27, 309; well known in N.C., 23, 27, 64
Sanford, N.C., 3
Sapona Cotton Mill, 191, 195
Saunders, Bill, 34
Saunders, Calvin C., 178
Savings and loan associations, 225. See also Banks and banking
Sawmills. See Lumber industry
Saxapahaw, N.C.: aerial view of, 193; and Haw River, see Haw River; and Hodges, 5, 6, 7; and B. Everett Jordan, 3, 5, 7, 9, 15, 16, 29, 33, 61, 81, 92, 93, 102, 109, 110, 113, 125, 129, 131, 132, 137, 140, 141, 149, 150, 154, 156, 161, 170, 174, 179, 184, 187, 188, 199, 201, 205, 206, 207, 209, 210, 213, 215, 237, 241, 251, 261, 263, 266, 270–73, 276, 277, 294, 302, 305, 308, 313, 315; and Katherine Jordan, 98; and Rose Ann Jordan, 103; and Neel, 132; and Jack Paris, 276; Boy Scouts in, 17, 187–88, 189, 316, 334; black people in, 39, 45, 76, 134, 135, 141–42, 177, 181, 183; bridges at, 113–14, 115, 138, 141, 179, 193, 211, 313, 314; church in, 139, 142–43, 178, 205, 297, 298, 314; community building in, 193, 211; condition of, in *1927*, 123; dams at, 114, 115, 136–37, 148, 182; declines, 107, 110, 114, 139, 140, 147, 206, 237, 308; description and nature of, 113–14; farm near, 5, 6; fire department serves, 192; floods at, 137, 138, 139, 168, 254, 308; founded and settled, 112; gristmills in, 115, 117, 118, 314; growth of, 111, 125, 308; industry in, 6, 15, 49–150 passim (*and see particular companies*); isolated, 107, 113, 330; lake at, 188; location of, 5, 111, 113; photos of, *see specific subjects*; postmaster of, 165; religious denominations in and near, 112; residents of, 108, 132, 140, 141, 184, 237, 307, 336; restaurants in, 136; roads in and near, 5, 6, 111; stores near, 111, 276; streets in, 210; tenements in, 127
Saxapahaw Indians, 111–12
Saxapahaw Lake (N.C.), 188
Saxapahaw Methodist Church and Saxapahaw United Methodist Church, 139, 142–43, 178, 205, 297, 298, 314
Schools. See Educators and educational system
Scotch-Irish people, 112
Scotland Neck, N.C., 254
Scott, Charlie, 124, 333
Scott, Mary. See Scott, Mrs. W. Kerr
Scott, Ralph H., 7, 16, 21–22, 225–27, 273

Scott, Red, 158–59
Scott, Robert, 318–19
Scott, W. Kerr: and Graham, 30; and B. Everett Jordan, 23, 26, 27, 28, 30; and Rodgers, 256; and Sanford, 22, 27, 28, 64; as a liberal, 22; as governor of N.C., 5, 10, 18, 21–22, 23, 30, 63–64, 203, 254, 256; as local politician, 16; as N.C. official, 23; as U.S. senator, 3, 7, 9, 21, 25, 26, 27, 28, 64, 210, 211, 219, 257–58, 319, 354; dam and reservoir named after, 258, 300, 303; death and burial of, 4, 5, 9, 25, 26, 209, 211, 319, 354; home of, 5, 6
Scott, Mrs. W. Kerr (Mary White) (cousin of B. Everett Jordan), 5, 66, 71, 128, 317
Scott (W. Kerr) Dam and Reservoir (N.C.), 258, 300, 303
Scottsdale, Ariz., 176, 338
Sears, Roebuck & Co., 173, 174, 175, 176
SEATO, 288
Sellars/Sellers family, 55, 69–80, 102, 106, 107, 110, 127, 130
Sellars, Anne ("Annie") Elizabeth. *See* Jordan, Mrs. Henry Harrison
Sellars, Benjamin Abel (grandfather of B. Everett Jordan), 46, 48, 54, 55, 71, 72, 76, 77–78, 79, 101, 105, 324, 325
Sellars, Mrs. Benjamin Abel (Frusannah Elizabeth Kime) (grandmother of B. Everett Jordan), 46, 48, 55, 69, 71, 72, 73, 74, 75, 77, 78, 79, 80, 101, 324, 325, 326
Sellars, Benjamin Rainey, 73, 78, 325
Sellars, Mrs. Benjamin Rainey (Fannie Cheek), 325
Sellars, Dorothy. *See* Brawley, Dorothy Sellars

Sellars, Eliza. *See* Harden, Mrs. John
Sellars, Eliza Ann. *See* White, Mrs. William Woods; White, Mrs. James Richard
Sellars, Elizabeth, 325
Sellars, Flora Lucina. *See* Brooks, Mrs. John
Sellars, Griffin, 325
Sellars, Mrs. Griffin (Phoebe Stanford), 325
Sellars, John Earl, 73, 326
Sellars, Lemuel, 325
Sellars, Mrs. Lemuel (Sarah D. Huffman), 325
Sellars, Logan, 325
Sellars, Mary ("Polly"). *See* Walker, Mrs. George G.
Sellars, Mary Augusta. *See* Walker, Mrs. Isaac Newton
Sellars, Nancy Elizabeth ("Bettie"). *See* Moore, Mrs. John A.
Sellars, Polly. *See* Loy, Mrs. Martin
Sellars, Rebecca Jane. *See* Moore, Mrs. James V.
Sellars, Thomas S., Sr. (great-great-grandfather of B. Everett Jordan), 69–70
Sellars, Mrs. Thomas S., Sr. (Nellie Holt) (great-great-grandmother of B. Everett Jordan), 70
Sellars, Thomas, Jr. (great-grandfather of B. Everett Jordan), 70–71, 324
Sellars, Mrs. Thomas, Jr. (Nancy Rainey) (great-grandmother of B. Everett Jordan), 70–71, 324
Sellars, Thomas, III, 71
Sellars, Mrs. Thomas, III (Adeline Cummins), 324
Sellars, Mrs. Thomas, III (Margaret Ann Faucett), 324
Sellars, Thomas Leonidas, 73, 78, 127, 128, 325
Sellars, Mrs. Thomas Leonidas (Lila Graves), 325
Sellars, Walter Raleigh, 73, 78, 79, 104, 127, 128, 326

Sellars, Mrs. Walter Raleigh (Lila Harden Bailey), 326
Sellars, William, 324
Sellars, Mrs. William (Nancy Swift), 324
Sellars, Willis (brother of Thomas S. Sellars, Sr.), 69
Sellars, Willis (great-great-uncle of B. Everett Jordan), 70
Sellars, Willis Rainey, 324
Sellars, Mrs. Willis Rainey (Mary Ellen Ray), 324
Sellars (B. A.) and Sons (firm), 78
Sellars Department Store, 55, 105, 297, 329
Sellers, Bessie Lea, 128
Sellers, Charles ("Charlie") Victor ("C. V.") (uncle of B. Everett Jordan): and B. Everett Jordan, 32, 101, 102, 105–7, 127, 129, 160, 263; and Rose Ann Jordan, 103; and Morrow, 105, 129; and Sellers Manufacturing Co., see Sellers Manufacturing Co., Inc.; as entrepreneur, 101–4, 105, 106, 107, 127, 128, 129, 132, 330; changes name from Sellars, 78, 104; described, 103–4; dies, 129, 130; frugality of, 102–4, 106, 129; honesty of, 79; marries, 78, 104, 326; personality of, 102, 103–4, 105, 107; photos of, 73, 106; travels, 79, 106; wealth of, 102, 103
Sellers, Mrs. Charles Victor (Annie M. Morrow) (aunt of B. Everett Jordan), 78–79, 104, 105, 106, 127, 129, 326
Sellers, David Ernest (uncle of B. Everett Jordan), 73, 78, 79, 104, 127, 128, 326
Sellers, Mrs. David Ernest (Eleanor Juanita "Nita" Hall), 326
Sellers, Fannie C., 128
Sellers, Frederick ("Fred") William (uncle of B. Everett Jordan), 73, 78, 81–86, 88, 89, 94, 99, 106, 128, 215, 326
Sellers, Mrs. Frederick William (Louisa "Lula" Planz) (aunt of B. Everett Jordan), 81, 82, 84, 128, 326
Sellers, J. E., 128
Sellers, Marie (cousin of B. Everett Jordan), 82, 84, 128, 328
Sellers, R. O., 127, 128
Sellers, W. W., 127, 128
Sellers (C. V.) Art Store, 101–2, 105, 330
Sellers Dyeing Co., 192, 193, 277
Sellers Manufacturing Co., Inc.: affiliates, branches, and assets of, 63, 127, 153, 155, 156, 159, 162, 174, 191–93, 195, 196, 203–4, 277, 311; and Bliss Fabyan Co., 163; and Century Hosiery Corp., 165; and death of Katherine Jordan, 96–97; and Durene yarn, 173–74; and Elasticot yarn, 151–52; and Henry Jordan, 63; and Neel, 335; and Pickett family, 277; and Roth, 151–52; and Shannonhouse and Wetzell, 162; and Spring City Knitting Co., 172–80 passim; and Standard Hosiery Mill, 155; audited, 136; employees of, 156, 183, 186, 187, 188, 193, 314, 330, 333, 336; establishment, ownership, management, and officials of, 10, 32, 33, 63, 96, 97, 104–5, 107, 127–30, 132, 156, 158, 170, 199, 266, 272, 273, 336, 338; files of, 361; growth of, 147–48, 156, 191–93; location of mill of, 107; manufacturing problems of, 150, 155–56, 159, 160, 168; offices and buildings of, 123, 138, 179, 182, 193, 210, 211, 237, 314; original condition of, 161–62, 206; owns real estate, 349; pay and benefits provided by, 204–5, 335;

production of, 150; retirees and Old-Timers Club of, 123, 132, 135, 158, 162, 178, 179–80, 184, 185, 205, 276, 308, 328, 336; successor company of, 134; unionization of, attempted, 203–4
Sellers Manufacturing Co. No. 2. *See* Jordan Spinning Co.
Selloz (spelling of Sellars/Sellers name), 78
Senate: of N.C., *see* Legislature; of U.S., *see* United States Senate
Separk, Joseph H., 56, 90, 91, 92, 96, 107, 108
Separk, Mrs. Joseph (May Gray), 90
Sewage treatment, 301
Shannonhouse, Frank M., Jr., 161, 162
Shannonhouse and Wetzell (firm), 162
Sharpesburg, N.C., 39
Shaw, John, 178
Sheriffs. *See* Crime, criminals, law enforcement, and penal system
Sherrill, W. L., 40, 46, 322
Sherrill and Neal (firm), 322
Shiloh Township, N.C., 44
Shoffner, John, 16, 128, 149, 164, 338
Shoreham Hotel (D.C.), 216
Sickness, disease, and medical care, 4, 19, 32, 38, 39, 40, 45, 55, 63, 64, 71, 72, 73, 77, 78, 85, 94, 98, 128, 132, 141, 146, 171, 182, 186, 190, 195, 247, 276, 281, 293, 309, 313, 337, 349
Silver Beaver Award, 188, 189
Silver Spring, Md., 281
Simpson, Wallis Warfield, 43
Sims, Allen H., 14
Sir Walter Hotel, 13, 256
Sissipahaw Indians, 111–12
Slaves and slavery, 70, 115–16, 120, 121. *See also* Black people
Smith family, 196
Smith, Alton ("Al") B., 150, 195–97, 203

Smith, Colon, 187
Smith, Greef, 186
Smith, J. Harold, 197
Smith, John H., 135
Smith, Julius C., 14
Smith, M. B., 16
Smith, Mattie, 186, 187
Smith, Robert Neal, 178
Smith, Willis, 4, 30, 195, 197, 311
Snow Camp community (N.C.), 112, 116
Social life, 112, 121, 136, 154, 157, 214, 217, 267, 276
Social Security system, 153
Soils and soil conservation, 115, 253, 254, 255, 257, 259. *See also* Farms and farming
South America, 118, 287, 288
South Boston vicinity, N.C. and Va., 354
South Carolina, 37, 70, 121, 122, 131, 140, 156, 158, 159, 242, 264
Southeast Asia, 286, 287, 288, 289, 293
Southeast Asia Treaty Organization (SEATO), 288
Southeastern United States, 91
Southern Franklin Processing Co., 156
Southern Pines (city), N.C., 24, 319
Southern Railway, 209
Southern United States, 38–39, 70, 77, 91, 118, 119–22, 140, 150, 173, 217–18, 220, 247, 250, 256, 285, 287, 289, 293, 333. *See also specific places and topics*
South Vietnam. *See* Vietnam and Vietnam war
Soviet Union, 200, 285
Sparkman, John J., 257
Spartanburg, S.C., 140
Spears, Rachel, 217
Spelling, 326
Sports. *See* Athletes and athletics; Recreation

Spray, N.C., 43
Spring City, Pa., 161, 167–80 passim
Spring City Knitting Co., 161, 167–80 passim
Sprinkle, Henry C. (brother-in-law of B. Everett Jordan), 130, 314, 315
Sprinkle, Mrs. Henry C. (Margaret Jordan) (sister of B. Everett Jordan): and Bobby Baker case, 279; and her brothers, 53, 54; and her father, 48, 50, 54, 56, 58, 60, 237; and her husband, 315; and B. Everett Jordan, 30, 48, 49–50, 52, 59, 60, 105, 106, 127, 147, 279, 297, 314; and her mother, 55, 75–76, 297; and Sellars family, 106; and Voils, 327; educated, 55; on Charlie Sellers, 105–6; photo of, 60
Standard Hosiery Mills, 149, 151, 155, 164
Stanford, Phoebe. See Sellars, Mrs. Griffin
Stanford, Richard A., Jr., 298
States' rights, 217
Statesville, N.C., 37, 39, 44, 45, 46, 322
Statesville (N.C.) *Record and Landmark*, 39, 44, 45, 46, 322
Stedman, Nancy, 217
Steel, Judie, 74
Steele, John, 121, 123, 333
Steele, Robah, 123–25, 273, 333
Stelter, Harry, 160, 161
Stevens, William E., Jr., 14
Stevenson, Adlai, 28, 65, 256
Stockton, Richard G., 13, 14
Stokes, Sue Ellen Heffner. See Jordan, Mrs. William Alvis
Stores. See Commerce, trade, and industry
Storrs, Thomas I., 14
Storytelling, 48, 61, 63, 81, 87, 104, 113, 150, 290, 327
Strikes, labor. See Labor, labor unions, and strikes

Sullinger, Nancy. See Rainey, Mrs. Benjamin
Sullivan, Nancy, 217
Summer on the Salt Fork (book), 327
Summerville, N.C., 43
Sumner City, Kans., 83
Supima Association, 245
Swain, David F., 110, 154, 161, 162–63
Sweet Home (N.C.), 39
Swepsonville, N.C., 113
Swift, Nancy. See Sellars, Mrs. William

Talley, Nancy, 217
Talmadge, Herman, 244
Tanks, military, 87, 89
Tanneries, 118
Tarboro, N.C., 14
Taxes and taxation, 13, 25–26, 64, 70, 144, 153, 176, 217, 268
Taylor, Elizabeth, 51
Taylor, Lucy Jordan. See Taylor, Mrs. Oscar, Sr.
Taylor, Mrs. Oscar, Sr. (Lucy Jordan) (sister of B. Everett Jordan), 49, 51, 55, 75–76, 297, 315
Taylor, Oscar, Jr., 51
Taylor, Roy A., 212, 216, 218, 226, 347
Taylor, Mrs. Roy A. (Evelyn), 212, 216, 217
Teachers. See Educators and educational system
Television, 244, 348, 349. See also News media
Temperance movement, 82. See also Alcohol and alcohol consumption
Tennessee, 37, 70, 131, 156, 161, 183, 348
Terrain. See Topography
Tew, Cameron, 16
Texas, 220, 244, 262, 263, 266, 280, 282, 287

Textile industry: and Hodges, 5–6; and international trade bill, 231; and B. Everett Jordan, see Jordan, B. Everett; and World War II, 277; booms, 147, 199; center of, 55; child labor in, 121, 122, 340; company stores in, 108, 109, 113, 114, 121, 141, 179, 204; costs in, 122, 144, 159, 194, 338; different eras in, 116, 121; domestic, 238, 241, 242, 245; education concerning, 61, 194, 251; foreign, 231, 238, 241, 242, 245; history of, 118–22, 237–43; hosiery manufacturing in, 147, 149, 150, 151, 154, 155, 157, 161, 164, 276–77, 329, 336; in Alamance County, 147; in Burlington, 90; in Dallas, N.C., 140; in Gastonia, 90–91, 92, 93, 99, 140, 199; in N.C., 270; in New England, 199; in Saxapahaw, 15, 81–207 passim, 241; in South, 116, 140, 150, 173, 199, 200, 201; in Southeast, 91, 237; influence of, on government, 18; location of mills in, 91; machinery in, 100, 114, 115, 116, 118, 120, 127, 132, 133, 134, 143, 144, 146–47, 154, 155, 159, 162, 167, 170, 185, 191, 192, 193, 194, 196, 197, 198, 199, 251, 267; management in, 92; marketing by, 114, 120, 239; mercerizing in, 151, 154, 155–56, 157–58, 161, 163, 164, 165, 172, 173, 174, 192, 336, 338; operations in, 63, 81–207 passim; parlance and terms in, 79; professional organizations representing, 238–39, 240–41, 348; public relations of, 239; silk-throwing in, 149–50, 151, 156, 192, 335; standardization in, 194, 196; statistics on, 238–39; two-price cotton system in, 241–43; unions and strikes in, see Labor, labor unions, and strikes; uses various types of textiles, 156, 161, 172, 173, 174, 175; wages and income in, 90, 92, 120, 121, 122, 131, 133, 144, 146, 159, 181, 188, 195, 196, 201, 202, 204, 254, 270, 328, 340. *See also particular companies as well as textile executives and personnel*
Textile Workers Union of America (TWUA), 203
Thacker, Arthur, 178
Theatres, 76
Thielman, Calvin, 282–84
Thomas, Joe, 178
Thomasville, Ga., 131, 132, 335
Thomasville, N.C., 13, 14
Thompson family, 115
Thompson, George D., 142, 183
Thompson, L. K., 128
Tie, Brenda, 246
Tisdale, Kenneth W., 152–53, 154, 155
Tobacco industry, 14, 26, 223, 234, 247–49, 252, 300
Tobacco Institute, 248
Tomlinson, R. H., 46
Topography, 39, 115
Tower Hosiery Mill, 157, 336
Trade. *See* Commerce, trade, and industry
Travel industry, 24, 319
Travel Council of North Carolina, 319
Trinity College. *See* Duke University
Tronbull Creek (Tenn.), 70
Troop Number 65 (Boy Scouts), 187
Trotter, Ben, 3–4
Truman, Harry, 65, 198, 246
Tryon, William, 69–70
TWUA, 203

Ulster (Northern Ireland), 112
Umstead, William B., 4, 18, 19, 29, 254, 255–56, 290

Unemployment, 54, 237, 254
Unions. *See* Labor, labor unions, and strikes
Union School, 71
United States Army and armed forces, 86–89, 285–95 passim, 302, 352, 353
United States Capitol, 235, 240, 288, 301, 302, 303, 305
United States Commodity Credit Corp., 243
United States Congress: and business, 13; and Godfrey, 243; and Johnson, 268; and B. Everett Jordan, 299; and Kennedy, 262; and National Zoo police, 233–34; and N.C., 14; and Roanoke River flood plan, 254; and tobacco legislation, 247; and Vietnam war, 286, 288, 352; districts for, in N.C., 195, 216, 218, 224, 226, 247, 248, 252, 346; functions of, 216; joint committees of, 218, 257, 299, 300, 302, 304, 305, 306; legislation passed by, 284; library for, 229–30, 257, 299, 303–5, 306; members of, from N.C., 98, 216, 217, 218, 220, 224–25, 247 (*and see specific individuals*); members of, visit foreign countries, 257; pay of members of, 146; records of, 214; Southern bloc in, 217. *See also* United States House of Representatives; United States Senate
United States Constitution, 236, 290, 291, 348, 352
United States Department of Agriculture (USDA), 241, 245, 246, 248, 253, 349
United States Department of Commerce, 216
United States Department of Defense, 288, 289
United States District Court of the Western District of North Carolina, 8

United States government, 13, 122, 217, 252, 263, 268, 284. *See also specific branches, agencies, and departments*
United States Government Depository Libraries, 301
United States House of Representatives: committees of, 13, 218, 230, 241; majority leader of, 300; members of, from N.C., 13, 20, 212, 216, 218, 227, 252, 255; minority leader of, 300; Speakers of, 229, 262, 300, 302; staffs in, 212
United States Library of Congress, 229–30, 257, 299, 303–5, 306
United States Navy, 24
United States presidents: and Congress, 352; and Ervin, 292; and B. Everett Jordan, 17, 234, 287, 293; and Murphy, 246; and Vietnam war, 352; appointments of, 243; inaugurations of, 241, 264, 265, 299, 300, 301, 302, 303, 304, 305. *See also specific presidents*
United States Senate: amenities for members of, 233, 240; and Bobby Baker case, *see* Baker case; and Murphy, 246; and presidential appointments, 243; and Vietnam war, 294–95, 352; building of, 290; chaplain of, 297; committees and subcommittees of, 212, 229, 230, 231, 234, 235, 236, 240, 241, 242, 244, 245, 256–57, 261, 264, 268, 269, 278, 279, 280, 281, 283, 284, 299, 302, 303, 304, 306, 346; drafting of legislation in, 246; independent members of, 291; library of, 291 (*and see* United States Library of Congress); majority leader of, 243, 262, 266, 267, 280, 300; members of, from N.C., 4, 20, 3–

35, 51, 59, 62, 64, 76, 81, 93, 195, 197, 225, 256, 290; minority leader of, 261, 266, 300; 101st member of, 267; parliamentarian of, 219, 228, 261; passes legislation favoring N.C., 353; presidents of, 33, 219, 299; richest members of, 316; staffs in, 212; The Club in, 239. *See also particular senators*
United States State Department, 241, 288, 293
United States Travel and Tourism Administration, 319
United States Travel Service (USTS), 319
United States vice-presidents, 219
United Textile Workers of America (UTW), 200
Universities. *See* Educators and educational system
University of North Carolina, 23–24, 25, 30, 163, 210, 211, 250, 251, 349
University of Pennsylvania, 71
Urbanization, 121, 132
USTS, 319
UTW, 200

Valdese, N.C., 161
Vance, Zebulon B., 116
Vegetation and trees, 111, 114, 167, 171, 177, 179–80
Vermont, 219
Vietnam and Vietnam war, 219, 230, 285–95, 309, 352
Virginia, 5, 37, 43, 117, 132, 254, 320, 349, 354
"Voice of Business" (The). *See* North Carolina Citizens Association
Voils, Jessie Wiley, 84–85, 327
Voting. *See* Elections and voting

Wachovia Bank & Trust Co., 130, 176
Wade, H. M., 14

Wake County, N.C., 252, 300, 301–2, 353
Wake Forest, N.C., 153, 155, 156, 159, 182, 192, 196, 203, 311
Wake Forest College, 318
Waldensian Hosiery Mills, 161
Walker, A. M., 45
Walker, Daniel Joshua ("D. J"), 18, 221–23
Walker, Edith, 128
Walker, George Garrison, 324
Walker, Mrs. George Garrison (Mary "Polly" Sellars), 324
Walker, Isaac Newton, 325
Walker, Mrs. Isaac Newton (Mary Augusta Sellars), 325
Walker, Mary A., 128
Walker, Mary Sellars, 73
Walkertown, N.C., 54
Wallace, N.C., 246
Warfield, Henrietta Engle. *See* Jordan, Mrs. Thomas Chauncey
Washington, D.C., 4, 10, 17, 21, 24, 25, 43, 81, 98, 113, 145, 151, 152, 155, 160, 187, 207, 209, 210, 212, 213, 215, 216, 217, 218, 219, 222, 223, 224, 225, 230, 233, 234, 237, 238, 246, 252, 259, 261, 263, 264, 266, 270, 275, 276, 278, 281, 282, 287, 288, 297, 298, 302, 306, 308, 309, 311, 348, 349
Washington (D.C.) *Star*, 283
Waste disposal, 301
Watergate affair, 291, 348
Water conservation and pollution. *See* Environmental protection
Waterpower, 111, 114, 115, 117, 118, 120, 124, 136–37, 148, 168, 270. *See also* Dams
Watlington, John F., Jr., 14
Way, George K. (brother-in-law of B. Everett Jordan), 315
Way, Mrs. George K. (Lucy Jordan Taylor) (sister of B. Everett Jordan), 49, 51, 55, 75–76, 297, 315

Wealthy people, 17, 55, 56, 70, 121, 176, 177, 184, 185, 187, 227, 263, 265, 297, 298, 307, 316, 337
Weathers, Bahnson, 94, 95
Weatherspoon, W. Herbert, 14
Wellington, Kans., 81–86, 89–90
Wentworth, N.C., 188
Wesley, John, 67, 259
Western North Carolina Conference. *See* Methodists and Methodist Episcopal church
Western North Carolina Judicial District, 8
Western United States, 81, 82, 106, 158, 176, 223, 245
West Indies, 118
West Jefferson, N.C., 223
Westmoreland, William C., 288
Wetzell, W. L. ("Bill"), 161, 162
Wharton School of Business, 168
Wheat Belt, 83
Whiskey. *See* Alcohol and alcohol consumption
Whitaker, Jim, 156
White, Mrs. E. A., 128
White, Eliza Ann Sellars. *See* White, Mrs. James Richard; White, Mrs. William Woods
White, George, 303–5
White, Howard, 4, 160
White, James Richard, 325
White, Mrs. James Richard (Eliza Ann Sellars) (aunt of B. Everett Jordan), 71, 72, 73, 325
White, James W., 118
White, Mrs. James, 118
White, M. W., 46
White, Mary. *See* Scott, Mrs. W. Kerr
White, Osborne, 128
White, William Woods, 325
White, Mrs. William Woods (Eliza Ann Sellars) (aunt of B. Everett Jordan), 71, 72, 73, 325
Whitehead, R. H., 127, 128
White House (D.C.), 18, 246, 269, 279, 280, 282, 349

Whitener, Basil L., 218
White-Williamson Co., 106, 114, 118, 119, 121, 123, 127, 131, 132
Whitley, William, 26, 27, 279
Whitney (Eli) community (N.C.), 192, 331
Whitney (Eli) Volunteer Fire Department, 192
Wholesale Meat Act, 300
Wichita, Kans., 83
Wiggins, Ella May, 200
Wiler, Roy, 219
Wiley, Jessie. *See* Voils, Jessie Wiley
Wilkesboro, N.C., 303
Wilkes County, N.C., 258, 300
Wilkinson, Howard C., 314
Williams family, 96, 109, 297. *See also following entries*
Williams, Connie Baber, 96, 108, 109, 297
Williams, D. A., 253
Williams, Jim Baber, 96, 107–8, 109
Williams, Mrs. Jim Baber (Ann George), 109
Williams, John, 234, 268, 278
Williams, Walter M., 128
Williamson, Banks, 118
Williamson, Ben, 118
Williamson, Bonner, 118
Williamson, Doc, 133
Williamson, Edwin, 118
Williamson, Ethel, 118
Williamson, Finley, 118
Williamson, George, 118
Williamson, Mrs. George, 118
Williamson, John L., 118
Williamson, Mrs. John L., 118
Williamson, Lawrence, 118
Williamson, Walter, 118
Wilmington, N.C., 300, 303
Wilson, Woodrow, 299
Wilson, N.C., 25
Wilson (Rufus) building, 151
Windsor, Duke of, 43
Winston-Salem, N.C., 13, 14, 62, 63, 69, 130, 176, 230, 303

Winston-Salem Journal and Sentinel, 62, 230
Women, role of, 74, 89, 112, 121, 122, 272, 328, 340
Wood, F. H., 46
Woods, Sam, 45
World War I, 84, 86–89, 114, 290, 318, 346

World War II, 13, 14, 15, 24, 63, 156, 190, 210, 238, 254, 277, 330, 337
Wright, John, 143, 178
Wright, Lannie Petty, 178

Yadkin River, 258, 303
Yale University, 210
YMCA, 52